*Animal Life
in Nature, Myth and Dreams*

Elizabeth Caspari

ANIMAL
LIFE
in
NATURE,
MYTH
and DREAMS

---

with Ken Robbins

Introduction by
Ann Belford Ulanov

Chiron Publications
Wilmette, Illinois

On the frontispiece:
Imprisoned Power (Tier im Berg)
Oil Painting by Peter Birkhauser, ca. 1958
Photograph by Dave Rossi
Courtesy of Iris Drey, M.D.

Book and cover design:
Susan Kress Hamilton / Phineas
Portsmouth, New Hampshire

Printing:
Penmor Lithographers, Lewiston, Maine

Library of Congress Cataloging-in-Publication Data

Caspari, Elizabeth, 1926-
  Animal life in nature, myth and dreams / Elizabeth Caspari, with Ken Robbins ; introduction by Ann Belford Ulanov.
      p. cm.
Includes bibliographical references.
  ISBN 1-888602-22-8 (alk. paper)
 1. Symbolism (Psychology)--Encyclopedias. 2. Animals--Psychological aspects--Encyclopedias. 3. Animals--Symbolic aspects--Encyclopedias. 4. Animals--Mythology--Encyclopedias. 5. Animals--Folklore--Encyclopedias. I. Robbins, Ken, 1945- II. Title.
  BF458.C37 2003
  156'.03--dc22
                            2003014444

CONTENTS

INTRODUCTION

Many people at the turn of the twenty-first century feel a double dissociation, from the animal root-impulse in their own psyches and from the spiritual connection to reality. The animal root-impulse is the base we grow from; all our inherited potential flows from there, and must be engaged if we are to unfold into the real world as a real person. Root-impulse is the animal in us. It is the spine where Kundalini energy mounts through successive body zones to bloom into the transcendent. It is the stem from which we flower or wither, for spirit inhabits a body and must find roots in the body to thrive. The psyche needs a body, and the spirit needs a psyche-body to incarnate. Animal root-impulse is not elusive; it defines us, connects body and spirit. We experience it as aliveness, readiness to be. From this instinctive source new life emerges, relaxed moments of mutuality, intense perceptions of what is there and what is not there in reality around us. We see afresh and surprise ourselves. We need to find our way back to our animal root-impulse.

Wild animals, for Jung, are the original appearances of the gods. Jung says, "A wild animal is a pious, law-abiding being who fulfills the will of God in the most perfect way." (Jung 1984, 37). These "doctor-animals" are central to a lively spiritual life, for the animal is the only devout creature that lives its own patterns to reach self-fulfillment (see Jung 1988, 1, 529). Indeed, Jung goes so far as to say, "When animals are no longer included in the religious symbol or creed, it is the beginning of the dissociation between religion and nature. Then there is no mana in it. As long as the animals are there, there is life in the symbol…" (Jung 1976, 284).

The animal follows God's will because instinct guides and contains its life. It has no choice; it does what it is supposed to do. As human animals, we too have a way that is specific to each of us, that is our right path. But such a path does not unfold automatically, with the clicking into place of instinct. We experience a hiatus, a gap, a pause that demands conscious reflection and free response to instinct, a choice. We cannot directly approach the mystery at the heart of life and of ourselves. We need symbolic discourse to convey this mystery. We must create our way to find it, call it into our view. Our response makes us see what awaits us. But when it finds us, we know that we did not invent it. It is like looking into the eyes of a wild animal.

Drawing on a rich combination of factual and symbolic knowledge of animals, Elizabeth Caspari offers the reader avenues to this animal root-impulse embodied in wild animals, and in animals as images who prowl our nightly dreams, as well as in animals as symbols of human potentiality. This information helps bridge the gap between ourselves and what Jung calls "the instinctual behavior of animals [which] are individual and creative" (Jung 1950, para 1492). We feel a connection to the rhinoceros as an actual beast, with its hairless tough hide, who is quite timid unless trapped and then turns ferocious, and to the dream beast who symbolized for the Buddhists one of the enlightened ones. We find the enormous and lethal size of the tiger (six hundred pounds) compelling, as is its astonishing beauty, and the challenge of the symbolic image of ourselves riding a tiger connecting us with the possibility of madness and ecstatic transformation. What a surprise to read in Caspari's text that on a symbolic level a childlike attitude of spontaneity and innocence toward the dangerous tiger-power breeds respect for the intense affects of ruthless aggression associated with the animal. Such openness allows us not to be dissolved by such violent affects and creates a path for them to be transformed into strong protection of deepest values.

The author has made it her task to give much information about the animals presented here, along with marvelous photographs by various artists. We learn of the animals' habitats, habits of eating, mating, socializing and rearing of the young. We read descriptions of their size and appearance, their intelligence and keen senses, as well as about their symbolic contexts in different cultures. The jaguar, for example, who kills with one bound, is also shy and solitary. It is central in Mexican Olmec culture's myth as the embodiment of life and death, and in the Aztec civilization as bespeaking fertility and the hidden secrets in the depths of the earth. A familiar of the shaman, the jaguar bodies forth the creative mystery of the unconscious, a source of vitality and courage, all of which turn destructive in the extreme if unused and unchanneled. To look at the magnificent beast in the splendid photograph brings home to us the tension of the opposites not only in this animal, but also between its life and our own. For to dream of the jaguar is to be confronted with deep psychic processes rooted in instinct that confront our human mental state symbolized in the dream by ourselves. Caspari's material reinforces the experience of learning from such dreams the patterns of energy symbolized by the animal root impulse in ourselves. Immediate experience of jaguar-energy asks of us what are we going to do with it and what is it going to do with us.

Such questions introduce that pause, that hiatus, that space in the human that allows us response to instinct instead of determination by instinct. Thus accumulates in the reader the moving sense that we may relate to the animal, not become the animal nor shun it, but become its neighbor on this planet and align with the energy it symbolizes in our psyche. Across the differences between us, there also stretches a bond of animal root-impulse. The difference is that the animal elegantly embodies the root-impulse of life, and we embody the mysterious capacity of consciousness. We can grow to consider the animal root-impulse; we can hesitate and make a space between it and us, learn to contemplate, communicate and then act.

Out of that space of contemplation and accumulating choice grows the individuation process where we learn to confer in individual and creative ways with what the unconscious presents us. Caspari helps us in this task by making these animals accessible to us. The reader will have the fun of looking up their own dream beasts in her large selection.

Ann Belford Ulanov

References

Jung, C.G. 1950/1976. "Foreword to Allenby: 'A Psychological Study of the Origins of Monotheism.'" *The Symbolic Life CW* 18 Princeton: Princeton University Press.
_____. 1976. *The Visions Seminars.* 2 books. Zürich: Spring Publications.
_____. 1984. *Dream Analysis.* Princeton: Princeton University Press.
_____. 1988. *Nietzsche's Zarathustra.* 2 vols. Ed. James L. Jarrett. Princeton: Princeton University Press.

ACKNOWLEDGMENTS

I would like to sincerely thank Ken Robbins for his invaluable contributions towards organizing and formulating my research material, and especially for his editorial and writing abilities. This book has been greatly enhanced by his considerable photographic skills, as well as his research in the selection of the photographs. My deepest gratitude to Nathan Schwartz-Salant, who has so caringly accompanied me on my own inner journey, for his invaluable input to this book, especially on matters of psychology and dream interpretation. Without his participation and constant encouragement this book would not have come to fruition. Roger Riendeau brought an order and cohesiveness to this manuscript, and I greatly appreciate his patient support. To Jane LeCompte a special thanks for her painstaking editing and for urging me to find answers to some obscure questions. My appreciation to Sarah J. Gallogly for her meticulous edit, and for leaving no stone (error) unturned. My gratitude to Susan Kress Hamilton for her creative design and imaginative production of this book. My thanks to the librarians at the Kristine Mann Library, the Archive for Research and Archetypal Symbolism (ARAS), and the American Museum of Natural History, all of whom never seemed to tire of my many queries. I am also grateful for the excellent secretarial/research services of Martine McManus, Darien Schanske, Brig Boonswang, Chris Randolph, Michelle Krazmien, Carol Hall, and other students from Columbia University, who have assisted me so ably in this project. A special thanks to Dr. Iris Drey for giving me permission to use the painting by Peter Birkhäuser entitled *Imprisoned Creative Power.*   E.C.

Photography Credits:

Sandy Butwin: *vulture.* Ron Caspari: *dog.* Elizabeth Caspari: *lion, zebra.* "City Bugs"/UC Berkeley: *ant, wasp.* Phillip Colla: *dolphin, fish, seal, squid, whale.* Howie Garber/Wanderlust Images: *ape, bear, butterfly, deer, fox, goat, leopard, monkey, parrot, pelican, puma, wolf.* Steven Holt: *falcon, opossum, squirrel, turkey.* Index Stock Imagery: *alligator/crocodile, ass/donkey, bat, beaver, bee, beetle, boar, bull, camel, chicken/hen, coyote, crab, crow, duck, eagle, eel, elephant, fly, giraffe, grasshopper, hare/rabbit, hawk, hippopotamus, horse, hyena, jackal, jaguar, lynx, moth, octopus, otter, pig, piranha, porcupine, raccoon, ram, rhinoceros, salamander, salmon, shark, snake, tiger, turtle.* Wernher Krutein/PhotoVault: *bird, cat, cockroach, cow, frog, goose, lizard, peacock, rooster, sheep, toad, worm.* Al Larson: *spider, stork.* McDonald Wildlife Photography: *badger, rat.* Erwin Bud Nielsen/Index Stock: *kangaroo.* John Noble/Corbis: *swan.* Tony Palliser: *albatross.* Photo Vault/Noriko Carroll: *dove.* Eric van Poppel: *cheetah.* Ken Robbins: *buffalo/bison.* Gregory K. Scott: *mouse.* Simpson's Nature/Rob & Ann Simpson: *insect, ostrich, swallow, weasel.* Sandy Stockwell/Scot Stockwell: *scorpion.* John Warden/Index Stock: *wolverine.* Harold Wilion Photography: *caterpillar, owl.*

PREFACE

The connection between animals and human beings is a strong one — diverse, enduring, extensive, and formative — going back for half a million years to *Homo erectus*. This book is a study of animals — their natural history, mythology, folklore, and symbolic significance around the world, from the Inuits of the Arctic to the Aborigines of Australia, as well as their role in our lives, dreams, and everyday language. Animals are also prevalent in religious thought and ritual. Many animals either have been considered sacred to a god or goddess or were actually venerated as gods or goddesses themselves. I have used many of these disciplines to give the reader a deeper awareness of the link between the world of animals and our own world.

In the mid-nineteenth century, Charles Darwin developed the theory of evolution — that all living matter, plants, animals, and humans, stem from one single cell or root. An article in the *New York Times* (10/2/2001, page F3, John Noble Wilford) tells of new fossil discoveries by paleontologists that show whales, porpoises and dolphins, all cetaceans, as related to mammals such as cows, camels, pigs and hippopotami. It is thus entirely believable that we humans carry a part of the animals in our bodies, minds, and psyches, so that our connection to all the animals, as well as plant life, is lasting and deeply rooted in us all. Accordingly, it behooves us to appreciate the wonder and majesty of the animals as the first marvelous presence on this earth, to consider the uses we make of them in our lives through imagination, myths, symbols, and even our projections, and to begin to realize how they function within and outside us.

Natural history has been explored from Aristotle and Pliny, who wrote extensively on the subject, to the recent studies of Dr. Jane Goodall, whose work with chimpanzees and other primates is well known, and many other ethologists and zoologists who study the behavior and physiology of animals. The importance of how the animal looks, communicates, adapts, and evolves in its surroundings, and socializes and interacts with its conspecifics, is reflected not only by our human observations but also by our fantasies. One of the tasks of mythology is to relate thoughts, actions, and beliefs to the great mystery that is the basis of the living experience. Myths change with the life and times of people as well as their geography. Animals play a great role and have a very special importance in both mythology and symbolism.

Dreams are here to stay. Everyone has them; some are remembered, some forgotten, but they are considered the language of the unconscious. They speak of things not known, consciously realized, or consciously experienced. They contain parts of the human being that are often hidden, repressed, and unfathomable. Their purpose is to respond and balance, adjust and supplement a conscious orientation and/or a one-sided conscious attitude. Dreams let the psyche bring to awareness contents with which consciousness needs to deal. Animals are a big part of our being, and when they visit us in our dreams, their emergence tells us something important about ourselves. This is what happened to me:

I grew up in a very rigid European culture that extolled tradition and valued discipline. There was little room in my early life for the spontaneous expression of emotions, either anger or joy. Later — much later — at a time in my life when the responsibilities of work, marriage, and motherhood were occupying much less of my life, one night I dreamed of two monkeys — one a pet, house-broken, domesticated, and well-behaved — the other a newborn, naked, untrained, and crying.

The dream was a mystery to me at the time, but I later learned that in many cultures, the spontaneous expression of emotions is associated symbolically with the monkey. On reflection the young monkey clearly seemed to be a new, emerging aspect of myself. I actively imagined a conversation with the older monkey, who took on the aspect of a mentor, inviting me to join it in a topsy-turvy, but beautiful and liberated world. It became stunningly clear to me that I needed to learn the ways of the monkey, so different from the inflexible ways I had known and experienced, and that possibly, in some sense, I had to turn my careful, safe world upside down.

This entire experience — the dream itself, as well as the research and intro-spection that followed — was a turning point of sorts for me. My lifelong interest in animals came to be focused on the symbolic impact they have on our collective culture, and particularly on our own personal and interior lives. Even as I have tried to become more knowledgeable about animal behavior and symbolism, I have been fascinated to discover the incredible variety of species and the intricate and amazing adaptations, both physical and behavioral, that have evolved in response to the environment.

Conceivably our collective interest stems from the fact that animals are so often perceived as free, existing in nature without restraint, unburdened by the self-consciousness that is the curse and defining characteristic of humans. Perhaps we envy this. Small matter that it is a fallacy. For in fact, every animal must carve out an ecological niche on this planet in order to better find sustenance, shelter from the elements, safety from predation, and the opportunity to repro-duce. Moreover, many species are in a strict hierarchy wherein individual impulses are inhibited by the collective will.

But when dream images are expressed in the form of an animal or animals, it usually means that the dreamer's mental or physical behavior must become more deeply rooted in instinct. The challenge to a person hoping for under-standing is to make these inner animal images more conscious without losing the connection to their deep instinctual roots. In some cases, the powerful psy-chological qualities that animals come to represent may reflect their actual size, behavior, and habitat. Bulls are massive, powerful, aggressive, and fecund; birds enjoy the freedom of flight; whales occupy the unfathomable depths of the sea.

In other cases symbolic associations may be more oblique, even accidental. The fish is a conventional symbol of Christ, yet it also symbolized many gods of different cultures. The fish lives deeply in the unseen aspect of the human psyche symbolized by the waters of the unconscious.

Discovering an animal image in a dream is a gift, an opportunity, a window through which, with careful consideration, we can glimpse the inner workings of our unconscious selves. Like poets and writers who use metaphor to get at hidden truths, we can use animal symbolism to unlock the conundrum of a thought, a feeling, an impulse, or a deep-seated unconscious fear; that is, to bridge our conscious and unconscious lives and move us closer to the instinctive core of our beings.

Obviously, animal dream symbols may carry a multitude of meanings and of shadings — always dependent on the situation of the dreamer and the context in which the dream occurred. The image of an animal may convey a message or warning, appearing in a compensatory way, to reflect an attitude or position that is ill adapted or inappropriate to one's life. Animals may also make us aware of our shadow side — those dark, secret, hurt, or angry parts of ourselves that we so readily disavow. When animal symbolism is encountered and properly recognized, I have come to believe, considerable healing may occur.

One of the major ways to understand dreams is through the process of amplification that C.G Jung developed in which an image is related to a previous historical, mythological, religious, and ethnological contexts. This book provides a chapter for each of 101 animals, explaining how to understand the meaning of each animal in a dream. But what is especially intended is that anyone using this book could amplify the image of an animal with the material given from mythology and natural history. In actual practice, one would want to call forth this material explicitly for the dreamer, taking into account the dreamer's unique life situation.

Each animal has distinctive and evocative qualities that stimulate our imagination. When we see a monkey, and reflect on the experience, we can see a part of ourselves. We can see that its playfulness could be our own, as well as its thievery and mischievousness.

In a wolf we may see ferocity, an insatiable hunger that is our own, and be aware of how the longing for satiety can overcome us. We may fear the wolf, as our superstitious ancestors did, or we may identify with it, as many Native Americans did (and do). At the same time, however, we may respect the wolf's genius for hunting and tracking, its strength, speed, and endurance, and its cunning intelligence.

It is certainly true that the actual physical and behavioral characteristics of an animal may be at odds with culturally conceived notions about it — especially notions of primitive societies rooted in magical or mythical consciousness. And both may differ strongly from the way the animal appears in dreams. It is remarkable, though, that certain shared and essential qualities begin to emerge when these conflicting views are reflected and meditated upon.

Alien cultures — those distant from us in time or space — naturally have perceptions about animals that are very different from our own; and yet these views are a legitimate, even crucial, element of the vast global body of lore and mythology. What may seem foreign and even irrelevant to us in our conscious lives may nonetheless touch us in our dream lives. Upon waking we tend to lose that awareness, but reflecting on what other cultures say about animals can help to revive it.

This book is intended for anyone interested in the actual behavior and nature of animals, and the world we live in. A good deal of ethological and mythological material is also presented here. But the book is meant to be more than a mere compilation of facts. My aim (admittedly an ambitious one) has been to arouse the imagination of the reader in his or her personal journey of discovery, connecting the world of real, living animals with the symbolic world of animal images in human thought, both conscious and unconscious. I also want to stimulate readers to go all out to save those wonderful species of animals (and plants) that are dying off every day and becoming extinct. Each one we lose lessens our opportunity to understand a part of our multifaceted selves.

We live in a time of growing interest in a holistic approach to the world; we are beginning to see how, on this planet, in this universe, everything — animal, vegetable, or mineral — is linked. Everything that advances or retreats, acts or reacts, moves or holds still, grows or shrinks, eats or is eaten, lives or dies — all are connected. The harmony or disharmony of these things will be our children's heritage, and it is my hope that by contemplating the significance of our fellow creatures we may approach a more holistic and healing world view.

Elizabeth Caspari

Albatross

An ungainly creature on land, the albatross is almost laughably awkward as it takes flight, thus earning its common name, the gooneybird. Once aloft and dynamically suspended in the wind's embrace, with a giant wingspan of up to fourteen feet and a light, streamlined body, the albatross is a commanding master of graceful, gliding, long-distance flight. It is a solitary wanderer of the open sea with uncanny skill in exploiting the thermal updrafts produced by ocean currents.

Like other seabirds, albatross drink seawater, eliminating much of the salt through their nasal glands. The salt solution dripping from the bird's beak has often been mistaken for stomach-oil — a gastric secretion that young albatross spit up indiscriminately (other birds of similar species use it as a mechanism of defense).[1] The albatross' main food is squid, but they also prey on fish, crabs, and penguin chicks, and may even scavenge on the carcasses of dead seals. Their scavenging instinct apparently motivates their habit of trailing ships. They are normally silent at sea unless they are fighting for food; on breeding grounds, they are capable of a wide range of sounds, such as beak clattering, low-pitched calls, high-pitched whistles, and various groanings and croakings.[2] Most albatross nest in colonies, sometimes numbering thousands of pairs closely packed. A few species nest alone on cliff ledges, and in general, nest sizes vary among species. They are physiologically capable of breeding at three or four years of age, but most wait longer, some as long as fifteen years. Barring a succession of breeding failures, once mating has occurred, the pair usually remains devoted to each other until one dies. At the beginning of the breeding season, the male arrives at the colony first, and mating occurs when the female appears. Depending on the species, both parents incubate a single egg in alternate shifts of several days. After assiduously brooding, guarding, and feeding the newly hatched chick, the parents depart on their separate and solitary ways, leaving the chicks to fledge on their own some ten months after hatching.[3]

Primarily ranging the tropics and southern hemisphere, albatross populations were effectively protected by the isolation of breeding grounds on islands with no natural predators until human discovery of their habitat brought in egg collecting and the killing of adults not only for their flesh but even more for their feathers.[4] The albatross is an exotic bird for Europeans and North Americans. For people with no direct experience of the albatross in nature, its mention often brings to mind Samuel Coleridge's "The Rime of the Ancient Mariner" (1798), in which an albatross is thoughtlessly killed, bringing disaster to the mariner and his ship:

> God save thee, ancient mariner!
> From the fiends that plague thee thus! —
> Why look'st thou so? — "With my cross-bow
> I shot the albatross."[5]

From a sailor's point of view the albatross can cut an eerie figure, pursuing ships at sea (as is its habit) with seemingly effortless, even relentless, persistence, night and day for hundreds of miles — as dogged, it might seem, as the Fates themselves. Albatross have been likened (with some poetic justice) to restless, transmigrating souls; credulous seamen have imagined them to be the reincarnated spirits of dead sailors, searching for their friends.[6]

Dreams of an albatross could represent the potential for acknowledgement of the presence of destiny, not just a momentary glimpse but rather an ongoing experience that accompanies life. The common phrase "an albatross around one's neck" reflects another symbolic meaning of this bird. A person's burdens — nagging conflicts in relationships, financial problems, despairing losses, illnesses, and the like — often feel like an "albatross," but on deeper reflection and acceptance prove to be a living connection to one's fate. Coleridge's poem of the mariner — his arbitrary killing of the albatross, the resulting guilt and consequent burden that weigh heavily on the mariner's life — reflect the deep guilt that accompanies rejection of fate or individuation. This particular poem also reflects Coleridge's personal guilt and agony about misusing his special talents and the resulting life of loneliness and suffering, as reflected in his letters.[7]

Notes
[1] Grzimek 1984, 7: 142.
[2] Grzimek 1984, 7: 142-43.
[3] Perrins and Middleton 1989, 44-45.
[4] Perrins and Middleton 1989, 45-46.
[5] Coleridge 1989, 119-46.
[6] Ackerman 1995, 67-68.
[7] Boulger 1969, 84-85.

ALBATROSS
Family: Diomedeidae.
Size: Royal and Wandering Albatross have bill-tail length of 68-93 centimeters (27-37 inches).
Wingspan: 200-320 centimeters (79-126 inches).
Weight: 7-8 kilograms (15-18 pounds).
Longevity: Approximately 30 years.
Incubation: 65-79 days.
Distribution: Sub-Antarctic, South America, the Galapagos Islands, South Africa, Southern Australia and New Zealand, the Pacific Ocean, and Japan.
Habitat: Islands are used for breeding and as bases.

Ant

With their diminutive size and myriad numbers, ants, although ancient in form, have evolved some of the most complex and rigorous social structures in the animal kingdom. Their tireless laboring is legend, and many colloquialisms refer to busy or restless humans as ants. Their extraordinary geographic range and omnipresence make their overall environmental impact very significant. In most places, they are the primary predators of other insects and small invertebrates, and they turn more soil than earthworms.

Ants are quintessentially community-dwelling insects, and a fully developed colony can vary in number from as few as a dozen to over a million. Their highly developed social systems may involve a level of cooperation and coordination that is nothing short of staggering to humans, who are often surprised to discover that they share many of their own supposedly unique traits with ants. Ants are capable not only of organized warfare against other colonies or species, but also acts of altruism and self sacrifice in the defense of their colonies, particularly of the immature ants called nymphs. Some types engage in highly sophisticated forms of agriculture — growing and nurturing fungi to be harvested at a later date — and some even keep livestock in the form of aphids, which they feed and herd in order to gather a syrupy substance they secrete called honeydew.[1]

Not only sexually dimorphic, ants have developed at least three distinct body types. The queens (of which a colony may have just one, or in some cases a few) are large and have wings. Their sole function is to mate and lay eggs. The males, smaller and also winged, have even less to do, and less time in which to do it. They attempt to mate with the queen during a nuptial flight (many are called, only one succeeds), and then all must promptly die. After insemination, the queen bees discard their wings, lay their eggs, and may even re-absorb the nutrients in their now useless flight muscles.[2]

The vast majority of eggs will eventually become workers. Female, but infertile and wingless, they forage for food, build, defend, and repair the nests, which can be quite elaborate, and care for the young. In the case of the honeypot ant of Australia, the workers have an additional task. With a specialized, fourth body type, highly mutated workers called "repletes" basically cling to the roof of an underground chamber — rank after rank, tier after tier of them — in a state of grotesque engorgement; each becomes a kind of "ant-like" food jar — a repository of nectar and honeydew fed to them by foraging workers to be disgorged (one might almost say "dispensed") in times of need.

Workers are preyed upon by spiders and robber flies and can in some instances live for as little as six days, but in the space of that time each may gather up to twenty times her own body weight in provender. Individual lives are very much subsumed into the welfare of the colony.[3]

Foraging ants must be able to find their way back to their nests and, in order to exploit food sources efficiently and cooperatively, must be able to communicate locations or directions. In this regard, the sense of smell is of paramount importance. Successful foragers create an olfactory trail with smelly secretions, which they and their nest-mates can follow back to the food source.[4] Ants rely on several means of orientation. They have excellent vision, a great sensitivity to degrees of incline and the force of gravity (geotoxic sense), and an ability to detect the direction of polarization in indirect light. The latter ability apparently allows them to navigate by the position of the sun in any weather.[5]

The ant plays an important role in the symbolism of many cultures. In Africa, the anthill often appears in cosmogenic myth and is sometimes associated with female fertility.[6] In China, the ant represents all the values of good citizenship: neatness, patriotism, virtue, and obedience.[7] In Greek mythology, the Myrmidons, fierce followers of Achilles, sprang, with the help of Zeus, from ants in Thessaly, where indeed ants were worshipped.[8] In Native American culture, the ant is considered a model of patience. In Central America, the god Quetzlcoatl, in the guise of an ant, steals maize to give to humans.[9] In a number of myths, the ant, like the Egyptian scarab, is instrumental in the resurrection of the sun each morning. Since the sun is a potent symbol of consciousness, this underscores the role of the ant as a kind of pre-conscious urge toward order, structure, and reason — things normally associated with consciousness itself.[10]

The ant is frequently used to symbolize positive qualities, such as diligence, forethought, and prudence, which are often contrasted (as they are in Aesop's tales) with the voracious self-indulgence of the grasshopper, which stores nothing but eats until all food is gone.[11] But the sheer numbers of ants, and their tireless diligence, can seem more like a kind of random, seething energy, especially viewed from some distance. And that in turn can be disturbing. In India, this kind of restless scurrying symbolizes the futility of all human — indeed, all earthly — effort.[12] Some ants and termites are capable of exquisitely complex architectural feats of nest building. These require an extraordinary degree of coordination, yet the specific mechanisms and precise nature of these "behaviors," and the ways in which the insects communicate and transmit information to each other, remain quite mysterious.[13]

Culture is a difficult balancing act between the needs of the individual and the needs of the collective, whether the latter is family, state, race, or species. The ant is first and foremost an archetype of the subordinated social self. As such, it is the antithesis of the individual so revered in Western culture. Alienation plays no part that we know of in the social lives of ants.

Symbolically, the ant represents industriousness guided by the deepest, most instinctive, organizing patterns of the unconscious. These patterns are the non-rational underpinnings of social structure, and being linked to this realm of order is so important that in "primitive" cultures people submit to the painful bites of ants in puberty rites, to recover from disease, and to initiate new stages of life. As the power of the psyche, often hidden (or better yet, camouflaged) in chaos, can manifest itself like the ant, it can also create a miraculous form of order.

On the one hand, swarms of ants in dreams can often signal a process of disintegration. Flying ants in particular may be associated with a dangerous sort of dissociation, in which a person becomes disoriented and confused, and loses a sense of unity and orientation. An example of this psychological state can be seen in the story of Nero, the fifth Roman emperor, who was said to have had dreams in which he was pursued by a swarm of flying ants, both before and after he had gone mad and killed his mother.[14] On the other hand, ants appearing in dreams also represent the positive and creative qualities of the dreamer's inner growth, which can be achieved through purposeful collaboration, patience, diligence, perseverance, and a selfless surrender to what is felt to be life's purpose or greater cause. An example of this is shown in the myth of Psyche and Eros, where the ant performs a helpful and conscientious task. In its loyalty to the community, careful, steady adherence to deeply ingrained behavior, and settled place within its social structure, the ant can represent our own beliefs, our loyalty toward ourselves, and our deepest values and truths.

Notes
[1] Grzimek 1984, 2: 441.
[2] Grzimek 1984, 2: 442.
[3] Hölldobler and Wilson 1990, 179.
[4] Grzimek 1984, 2: 443.
[5] Grzimek 1984, 2: 442.
[6] Becker 1994, 19.
[7] Cooper 1992, 14.
[8] Jobes 1962, 1: 101.
[9] Cooper 1992, 15.
[10] von Franz 1980c, 88-89.
[11] de Vries 1976, 16.
[12] Becker 1994, 19.
[13] von Franz 1980a, 93.
[14] von Franz 1980a, 122.

ANT

Family: Formicidae.

Size: Length can range from less than 1 millimeter (0.04 inches) to 4 centimeters (1.57 inches).

Weight: *Formica japonica* worker ants weigh 0.004 grams. They can walk while holding an object weighing 5 times their body weight in their mouth and can even drag a 25-times heavier object.

Longevity: In laboratory nests, the queen ant in the United States can live from 4.6 to 13 years, while the worker ant can live over 3 years. In Australia, the queen can live up to 21 years, and the worker up to 2 years. In the wild, the queen termite has a maximum longevity of 25 years.

Distribution: Various members of the approximately 8,800 known species are found from the Arctic Circle to the southernmost reaches of Tasmania, Tierra del Fuego, and southern Africa. Some species can even survive underwater.

Habitat: Ants can adapt to a great variety of situations. Outdoors, nests are usually located in moist soil, next to or under buildings, along sidewalks, or beneath boards. Indoors, they can be found in dwellings in and around food and service areas.

Ape

The great apes, particularly the magnificent lowland gorillas, with their immense size and superhuman strength, have spawned numerous literary and pop-cultural fantasies of the great, chest-thumping, tree-shaking, hairy, beast-like "King Kong" or "Mighty Joe Young," which humans try to master at their peril. However, apes are our nearest neighbors on the evolutionary ladder; they include three genera: chimpanzees, orangutans, and gorillas. All three are large, tailless primates, generally hairy but nearly barefaced, with opposable thumbs and prehensile toes. They can walk erect and do so for short periods of time. Their long front limbs are clearly recognizable as arms rather than legs, but they do walk on "all fours" much of the time. Their arms are longer than their legs, and to a greater or lesser degree are used for swinging from branch to branch — a method of locomotion called brachiation. The ability to manipulate objects varies from species to species. Males are usually larger than females.[1] In the vernacular, "ape" is a derogatory term for clumsiness and ugliness, and "to ape" is often used to describe mimicry or mirroring.

Physiologically, the great apes are remarkably similar to humans, not only in general shape, but also in the structure and function of the internal organs, the basic capacities of the nervous system, and the composition of the blood. Apes' mental capacities are the second-highest in the animal kingdom. They have substantial ability to reason and learn from experience, and while they lack a spoken language, experimenters have had well-publicized successes teaching chimpanzees to use sign language. Apes use simple tools and are intensely curious; the tendency to explore and investigate is one of the signposts of what we call intelligence. Average brain size among the apes, however, remains substantially below human norms. A six hundred-pound gorilla may have a brain less than half the volume of a two hundred-pound human.[2] The eating habits of the great apes vary greatly, because they are less governed by innate behavioral patterns and, like early humans, better able to adapt to local conditions and variations in the supply of available food.[3]

Gorillas are the giant apes of the African forest, depicted by Hollywood as enormous and terrifying. They are, however, placid vegetarians. Some males live a solitary existence. In hierarchical family groups, the females outrank the young, the males outrank the females, and the highest-ranking silver-backed males lord over all of them. Gorilla groups are very tightly organized and cohesive. Observed in the wild, they are peaceful and tolerant, feeding, unlike most animals, always with their hands, on bamboo and blue pygeum berries, leaves, shoots, and the hearts of stalks.[4]

Orangutans, huge red-haired apes of Borneo and Sumatra whose name means "man of the forest," are largely arboreal in habit, using their highly developed arms and grasping feet to move about in the forest canopy. They have a great capacity for learning, although certain fairly complicated behaviors, like nest building, are innate and do not have to be learned. Males develop a semicircular jowl that gives them a distinctive moon-faced aspect.[5]

The common chimpanzees have a predominantly black coat, which may turn gray on the back after twenty years. Both sexes have a short white beard, and baldness is common among adults. Although the skin on their hands and feet is black, facial skin may be any shade of pink, brown, or black, generally darkening with age.[6] Another species, the pygmy chimpanzee, or bonobo, is found only in Zaïre between the Zaïre and Kasai rivers. Despite their name, the pygmy chimpanzees are not markedly smaller than the common chimpanzees, although their body is slighter of build. They have a narrower chest, longer limbs, smaller teeth, a black face, and hair on their heads that projects sideways.[7]

Male chimpanzees are larger and stronger than the females, and their bigger canine teeth can inflict serious, even fatal, wounds in fights among themselves. Females show prominent swellings in the genital region when they come into heat, and they copulate promiscuously as often as six times a day. The males have, for their size, unusually large testicles. Contrary to the usual practice in other animal societies, the males remain with their birth community, while the females usually strike out and join new communities at adolescence.[8]

Chimpanzees make good use of tools, more so than any other non-human. They are known, for instance, to break off, strip, and clean a thin, straight branch (two feet or more in length) that they then dip into a driver ant nest, withdrawing it when the ants have crawled onto it, and then swallowing them before they can sting. They also use stones to break open hard-shelled fruit and make fly-whisks for themselves.[9]

As with many animals, mythic and cultural traditions concerning apes tend to follow perceived affinities and associations more than actual, taxonomic divisions. Their symbolic significance may be colored or influenced by that more properly attached to monkeys: for instance, macaques or baboons. The names "monkey" and "ape" are popularly, albeit imprecisely, interchangeable.

The Egyptians revered several kinds of ape, the most sacred being the dog-headed ape, or baboon, which was companion to Toth, the Moon god. This baboon sits on the standard of the Great Scales of Judgment and reports to Toth what the pointer registers, whether the soul has sided with good or evil in its lifetime. Sacred apes were also kept in many temples dedicated to lunar gods, such as the temple of Khensu at Thebes. The ancient Egyptians thought that certain spirits singing praises at dawn turned into apes when the sun rose. In the pre-dynastic period, dead apes were embalmed with great care and buried.[10]

In the Hindu tradition, the ape (as well as the monkey) is associated with Hanuman, the ape god and powerful assistant of Rama, who was the embodiment of chivalry and virtue, a tribal hero of ancient India, and an emissary in the *Ramayana,* an epic poem of India. The ape represents benevolence and gentleness, as well as strength, loyalty, and self-sacrifice.[11] In China, the ape was held in high esteem. Stories are told of the ape named Sun Wu-k'ung, famous for acts of bravery as well as many pranks it is said to have played in the company of Hsüan-tsang, a Buddhist pilgrim who journeyed to India.[12] In the Far East, the ape is often a symbol of wisdom.[13] In ancient Mexican civilizations, the ape is a calendar symbol: its name, Ozomatli in Aztec and Ba'tz in Mayan, denotes the eleventh day of the month in both cultures. The ape was also a god of dance. In an ancient Mexican myth, at the end of one of several millennial ages, great tornadoes caused vast devastation, and humans were transformed into apes.[14]

In contrast to these civilizations, Christianity, with its devaluation of the body and instinctual life, has seen the ape as representing every kind of evil, from the devil, paganism, and heresy to lust, vice, malice, and cunning slavish imitation. In art and literature, both the ape and the monkey are used to caricature and satirize humans.[15]

The ape has been associated with the Greek god Dionysos, who was linked to the fruit of the vine and to madness. This god's emotional, bodily, and instinctive psychic awareness contrasted to the clarity, pristine consciousness, and rationality of the sun god Apollo in the Greek Pantheon. Being turned into an ape as a punishment for displeasing a god is an ancient Middle Eastern tradition. In rabbinical tales, some of the builders of the Tower of Babel were turned into apes, as were the Jews of Elath, who fished in the Red Sea on the Sabbath in a Muslim story.[16] Aesop tells a fable in which a mother ape fondled her young so much that they were crushed to death, and the notion of foolish or excessive simian love is echoed by the Roman authors Pliny (c. 23–79) and Aelian (c. 170–235).[17]

Symbolically, the ape image can often have a trickster quality that, like the king's jester, can be both devilish and destructive; or it can manifest the wisdom of the body and of instinctual processes, changing an overly rigid attitude into a more flexible one. More than three quarters of a century after the famous Scopes "monkey" trial (in which Tennessee school teacher John Scopes defended his right to teach evolutionary theory within a state educational system that required him to teach creationism), we are still loath to acknowledge our kinship, uncomfortable with such closeness.

As with every dream image, exactly what the ape might represent must be influenced by the context in which it appears in the dreamer's conscious life. On the one hand, the ape might symbolize "aping," moving away from genuineness and authenticity. On the other hand, the ape could represent the life of the body that the dreamer might be neglecting; and he or she might need to learn how to connect to the body's deeper wisdom. Generally, the ape is a powerful, vibrant (creative or demonic) symbol that can call the dreamer to contact a great deal of vitality and energy.

Notes

[1] Grzimek 1984, 10: 488.
[2] Grzimek 1984, 10: 390-91.
[3] Grzimek 1984, 10: 489.
[4] Grzimek 1984, 10: 533-35.
[5] Grzimek 1984, 10: 504, 516, 517.
[6] Macdonald 1987, 422.
[7] Ibid.
[8] Macdonald 1987, 422-26.
[9] Grzimek 1984, 10: 488-548; Macdonald 1987, 412-39.
[10] Budge 1969, 2: 364-65.
[11] Biedermann 1994, 15.
[12] Ibid.
[13] *The Herder Symbol Dictionary* 1986, 9.
[14] Biedermann 1994, 15.
[15] Cooper 1992, 18.
[16] *Funk & Wagnalls Standard Dictionary* 1972, 741.
[17] Cooper 1992, 17.

APE
Family: Pongidae (Chimpanzee).
Size: Female has a head-body length of 70-85 centimeters (28-33 inches). Male has a head-body length of 77-92 centimeters (30–36 inches).
Weight: Female weighs 30 kilograms (66 pounds); male weighs 40 kilograms (88 pounds).
Gestation: 230-240 days.
Longevity: 40-45 years.
Distribution: West and Central Africa, north of River Zaire, from Senegal to Tanzania.
Habitat: Humid forest, deciduous woodland, or mixed savanna; presence in open areas depends on access to evergreen, fruit-producing forest; sea level to 2,000 meters (6,560 feet).

APE
Family: Pongidae (Gorilla).
Size: Female height is up to 150 centimeters (5 feet); male height is up to 170 centimeters (5.6 feet).
Weight: Female weighs 90 kilograms (200 pounds). Male weighs 140-180 kilograms (310-400 pounds).
Gestation: 250-270 days.
Longevity: 35 years in the wild.
Distribution: Central Africa.
Habitat: Tropical secondary forest.

APE
Family: Pongidae (Orangutan).
Size: Female head-body length is 78 centimeters (31 inches); male head-body length is 97 centimeters (38 inches). Female height is 115 centimeters (45 inches); male height is 137 centimeters (54 inches).
Weight: Female weighs 40-50 kilograms (88-110 pounds); male weighs 60-90 kilograms (130-200 pounds).
Gestation: 260-270 days.
Longevity: Up to about 35 years in the wild.
Distribution: North Sumatra and most of lowland Borneo.
Habitat: Lowland and hilly tropical rain forest.

Ass/Donkey/Mule

A humble mount, the quintessential beast of burden, the embodiment of the phrase "patience of an ass," the first donkeys (also called burros by the Spanish) were generated from the domesticated wild ass. The ass depicted in ancient Egyptian and Assyrian carvings is probably the Onager, a much larger, more horse-like cousin of the wild ass.[1] Tamed long before the horse, the domesticated ass was bred and cross-bred from three species of African wild asses and reached Europe around 2000 BCE, during the Bronze Age — probably brought there by the Etruscans.[2] Asses can be induced to breed with horses to form generally sterile hybrids. The mule is the offspring of a female horse (mare) and male donkey (jackass), while the hinny is a cross of a female donkey (called a jenny) and a male horse (stallion). Both mules and hinnies have been bred for thousands of years.[3] The donkey is generally smaller than the horse or the mule.

Usually led by an older, cautious mare, wild asses live in herds of ten to fifteen animals. They are skittish and retiring when alerted or suspicious, and, being excellent and sure-footed climbers, they will often elude pursuers in steep or difficult terrain. They can thrive in desert conditions on little more than mimosa, thorny bushes, and sparse, hard grass; asses, like camels, are capable of surviving for long periods of time without water.[4] Because it requires relatively little water and food and is capable of traveling great distances with heavy loads, the donkey (or ass) was once widely used as a work animal. The ancient Egyptians and Assyrians, for example, used the Onager to draw heavy chariots and military baggage trains.[5] Mules, being almost always larger than asses, are often used as mounts, draft animals, and beasts of burden. They are famously unafraid of fire, and as a result were used for years by firefighters and in military campaigns.[6] David painted Napoleon most romantically on a fiery, white Arabian stallion, but Napoleon crossed the Alps on a less glamorous but decidedly more sure-footed mule.[7]

Indeed, the donkey is the very model of the beast of burden, lowly but faithful. Smaller and less powerful than a horse, the ass was the humble steed of Jesus and Sancho Panza (of *Don Quixote* fame). Yet the ass is also regarded as foolish and ignorant as well as lazy and stubborn.[8] We use the terms "ass" and "donkey" to denote stupidity (for example, the "donkey hat" of a school child who did not know the answer to a question) and as the epitome of foolishness and insults. But, contrary to popular belief, donkeys can be quite clever. They are exceedingly docile, yet they have retained some of the aggressiveness of their wild ancestors. When beset by enemies, a group of donkeys will form a circle for mutual protection, fending off even the largest predators with their hooves.[9]

Perhaps because of its supposedly lascivious nature, the ass was the mount of ancient Greece. Circe, wishing to enslave Odysseus sexually, attempts to give him an ass head by means of a magic unguent.[10] The *Physiologus* asserts that the wild ass bites off the genitals of its male foals to make eunuchs of them, so that they will live celibate and spiritual lives of self-mastery.[11] The Romans thought it to be an emblem of Priapus, the male god of procreation and fertility, and also included it in the retinue of Ceres, his female equivalent. A medieval legal custom obliged those convicted of adultery to ride through the streets on a donkey.[12]

In Buddhist tradition, the ass, with its minimal needs, is seen as a symbol of asceticism. In the Orient, it is admired for its strength, courage, and intelligence. In the Middle East, according to Plutarch, Jews revered it because it found water in the desert during the Exodus.[13] In Genesis 49:14, the ass was a symbol of the Hebrew tribe of Issachar.[14] The Old Testament (Numbers 22-24) contains the story of Balaam's ass, which reproves its master for beating it and understands God's will before his master does. According to Zechariah 9:9, Jesus rode into Jerusalem on an ass.[15]

The notion of a donkey/human hybrid is a persistent one — either a human with donkey head or ears (or genitals), or else a donkey with some human attributes or powers. These conceits can be satiric — like Bottom in Shakespeare's *A Midsummer Night's Dream* or the common image of a donkey musician, which juxtaposes the beastly coarseness of the ass with the refinement of music.[16] Along with the satiric, however, one should see in these symbols a union of contradictory opposites.

In the Indian *Rig-Veda*, the earliest record of Indian culture, the ass is both a divine and demonic figure. In ancient Egypt, the murderous and evil god Set was often represented in hieroglyphs with a long-eared animal head, and as a consequence the ass has been associated with him.[17] An ass represented the god of the Old Testament, while an ox represented the god of the New Testament, both witnessing Christ's birth in the manger. By virtue of its patience, the ass was used symbolically by medieval Christians to represent the cryptic ways in which the Old Testament supposedly prefigured the Christian faith. Quarrelsome Christians and Jews have in the past accused each other of worshipping the ass.[18]

Symbolically, the ass often receives the human projection of unbridled lust, in which case it is seen as demonic. As an animal that can be mastered and ridden, it may signify crude instincts that can be tamed. It can also be viewed as a balky creature that reveals its "stupid" animal nature at some awkward, inopportune moment, acting foolishly or destructively on lustful impulses, and ending up humiliated,[19] thus giving rise to the phrase "making an ass of yourself."

In a dream of someone who is especially impatient and deals poorly with frustration, the appearance of an ass, donkey, or mule could represent a compensatory image; it means that the dreamer may need to become more patient, absorb burdens, not be overly reactive, and thereby raise prospects to heal that impatience. Or, because of the alleged lasciviousness of the animal, the dream may symbolize overwhelming sexual fantasies. The dreamer may be either indulging in such fantasies or may be far too arid and intellectual and in need of feeling more of his or her sexual life. It should be emphasized that often the experience of the image alone, rather than an interpretation of what the image means, can influence the conscious attitude of a person. Both approaches, experiential and interpretive, are usually significant.

Notes

[1] Cooper 1992, 19-20.
[2] Grzimek 1984, 12: 550.
[3] Drimmer 1954, 1: 661.
[4] Grzimek 1984, 12: 548-49.
[5] Cooper 1992, 19-20.
[6] Grzimek 1984, 12: 555.
[7] Ibid.
[8] Biedermann 1994, 100.
[9] Grzimek 1984, 12: 550.
[10] De Gubernatis 1968, 1: 366.
[11] Curley 1979, 15.
[12] Biedermann 1994, 100.
[13] Cooper 1992, 19-20.
[14] Jobes 1962, 1: 462.
[15] Biedermann 1994, 100.
[16] Charbonneau-Lassay 1991, 109.
[17] De Gubernatis 1968: 1: 364-65.
[18] von Franz 1980b, 39.
[19] von Franz 1980a, 46-47.

ASS/DONKEY/MULE

Family: Equidae.

Size: The African wild ass has a head-body length of 200 centimeters (79 inches) and a tail length of 42 centimeters (16 inches). The Asiatic ass has a head-body length of 210 centimeters (82 inches) and a tail length of 49 centimeters (19 inches).

Weight: The African wild ass weighs 275 kilograms (606 pounds); the Asiatic ass weighs 290 kilograms (640 pounds).

Gestation: Approximately 360 days.

Longevity: 10-12 years in the wild; up to 24 years in captivity.

Distribution: African wild ass is found in Sudan, Ethiopia, and Somalia; Asiatic ass is found in Syria, Iran, Northern India, and Tibet.

Habitat: African wild ass is found in rocky desert terrain; Asiatic ass is found in highland and lowland deserts.

Badger

Sturdy, compact, powerful, and feisty, the badger is a strong-clawed digger of dens and a robust night-hunter, capable of extreme aggression. Being a mustelid, it is descended from the earliest terrestrial carnivores — difficult, at that stage of development, to distinguish from raccoons. There are six badger genera with a total of eight species.

Mainly a woods dweller, the European badger thrives in overgrown ravines, hedges, and parks. It digs an underground den that may be thirty meters wide, complete with multiple exits, entrances, and air holes. These abodes, often lined with moss or grass, are passed from one generation to the next; some dens can be in continuous use for centuries. Although badgers are not particularly social animals, they generally maintain amicable relations with neighboring badgers.[1]

Primarily nocturnal, with poor eyesight and hearing, badgers do have an extraordinary sense of smell, a fact that might be guessed from the constant snuffling sounds they make as they forage with noses to the ground. Most species are characterized by powerful jaws and cranial teeth adapted for crushing.[2] Relying so much on smell, badgers use their dung for scent marking, staking out the boundaries of their territories.[3]

The European badger will eat any dead animal that it encounters, as well as any living ones that it can subdue, but it is especially fond of earthworms, insects, snails, and small vertebrates that it may find in the ground. It also consumes fruit, seeds, mushrooms, and roots. It is a potentially destructive pest in corn and beet fields, in vineyards, and in berry plantings. The American badger has a similar diet, although with distinctly less emphasis on vegetable matter.[4]

Badgers are largely inactive in extremely cold weather, which may extend their hibernation period by several months in colder climates. Badger pairs mate for life. Mating generally occurs in midsummer, resulting in a March or April litter of one to five young, which the mother will suckle for six weeks.[5] Although fertilization occurs immediately after copulation, implantation of the blastula may be delayed significantly.[6] Apparently, European badgers in heat, as well as mortally wounded badgers, give a heart-rending, piercing scream that may seem uncannily human.[7] Lynx sometimes prey on them, and cubs may be taken by large raptors. Humans prize badger fur, using it for shaving brushes.[8] While badgers raised in captivity can become quite docile, captured adult animals cannot be tamed.[9] Badgers are very clean and are known to spend hours on assiduous grooming.[10]

Although generally quite playful,[11] the badger in Native American mythology is considered bold, ferocious, and vicious — the very model of sudden, angry aggression put to use in fierce digging below the surface of things.[12] A powerful and persistent digger and creature of the earth, the badger is imagined in many myths to have special knowledge of natural elements in the ground, particularly minerals and roots associated with medicine and healing — both physical and psychological.[13] As the keeper of the medicine root, the badger is considered to be a deep source of healing in nature, and thus the familiar of the medicine women.[14]

In Hopi legend, the ancestors of the people, before coming to earth through a hole in the sky,[15] first sent Badger, and the Badger Clan (divided into Gray, Brown, and Black) is one of their most important.[16] The Micmac people[17] considered the badger a trickster figure (one which can change form), and the Zuni thought it stout-hearted but weak-willed. The remarkable symbolic attributes of the badger extend beyond Native American mythology. In China, the badger is a trickster and shape-shifter, a mischievous,[18] lunar, *yin* creature. In Japan, Tanuki, the badger, possesses great magical powers and extraordinary cunning — bringing luck but also deceiving unwary travelers.[19] The badger is not much mentioned in Middle Eastern or European lore, save in Christian art, where it is considered the steed of avarice personified.[20]

If a badger appears in a dream, its significance could be to make the dreamer aware of his or her tendency to "badger" others or to feel "badgered," but especially that he or she possesses a powerful, inner potential to overcome hindrances and to pursue goals fiercely in the service of healing.

Notes

[1] Grzimek 1984, 12: 68.
[2] Macdonald 1987, 130.
[3] Attenborough 1990, 192.
[4] Grzimek 1984, 12: 68-71.
[5] Ibid.
[6] Neal 1986, 175.
[7] Grzimek 1984, 12: 69-70.
[8] Pfeffer 1989, 35.
[9] Grzimek 1984, 12: 69-70.
[10] Neal 1986, 154.
[11] Neal 1986, 152.
[12] Reichard 1974, 382.

[13] Andrews 1993, 247.
[14] Sams and Carson 1988, 153.
[15] *Funk & Wagnalls Standard Dictionary* 1972, 102.
[16] Cooper 1992, 22.
[17] *Funk & Wagnalls Standard Dictionary* 1972, 102.
[18] Jobes 1962, 1: 171.
[19] Cooper 1992, 22.
[20] *The Herder Symbol Dictionary* (1986), 17.

BADGER
Family: Mustelidae.
Size: 50 centimeters to 1 meter (20-39 inches) according to species.
Weight: 2-12 kilograms (4.4-26 pounds) according to species.
Gestation: 3.5-12 months including period of delayed implantation.
Longevity: Up to 25 years in captivity (not known in wild).
Distribution: Widespread in Africa, Eurasia, and North America.
Habitat: Chiefly woodlands and forests, also urban parks and gardens; some species. in mountains, steppe, or Savanna.

Bat

Spooky, fluttering, night-flying mammals, bats are creatures of both the earth and the air. Bats look strange, hanging upside down, enshrouded in their own folded wings, and often gathered in large colonies in caves or trees.[1] They are the only true flying mammals; their leathery wings evolved from the front limbs of ancient, rodent-like quadrupeds. The two suborders of bats, the fruit bats and the insectivorous bats, together comprise over 950 species.

All bats are active primarily at night, although many species can be seen in the late afternoon or early evening as well. Both suborders of bats navigate by echolocation, emitting high-pitched sounds (well above the range of human hearing) from their mouths or noses. Receiving the echo of these sounds with their large, sensitive, and finely-tuned ears, they create a sound picture, like a sonar image, that allows them to navigate with little or no light. Not surprisingly, this talent is more exquisitely developed in the insectivorous bats, which take a moth on the wing in total darkness. Their ears are said to be so sensitive that they can hear the sound of an insect walking. Insectivorous bats are a kind of self-sustaining pest control; a large, foraging colony of bats may consume as much as a half a million pounds of insects every night.[2] They are, however, virtually blind; hence the colloquial phrase "blind as a bat."

Fruit bats have an excellent sense of smell and large eyes; they are partially dependent on at least some light to find their way.[3] Because fruit bats eat flowers as well as fruit, they are responsible for pollinating or dispersing the seeds of hundreds of trees and shrubs.[4] Economically significant crops like bananas, avocados, vanilla beans, dates, peaches, figs, and cashews benefit immensely from the bat's attentions.

Male bats have, for their size, rather large penises (sometimes decked out with spines), which in many societies is sufficient to make them potent symbols of fertility. Most mate promiscuously and do not "pair up" for the rearing of young. Nor do the females nest, *per se.* They give birth wherever they may be; the newborn bat immediately and instinctively clings to the mother's fur with its hind feet. Pregnancies usually result in just one birth, but, as if in compensation, survival rates are high.[5]

The so-called vampire bats of South America are parasitic on domestic fowl and mammals — including people. Victims are bitten, often while they are sleeping, and an enzyme in the bat's saliva keeps the wound bleeding freely while the bat laps up the flow. The quantity of blood taken is rarely significant, but the victim is often exposed to a number of diseases in the process.[6] For this reason, the bat is feared as carrier of rabies.

In Greek lore, the bat is often depicted as timid, though shrewd. In the *Odyssey,* Homer describes the souls of the dead in the underworld as if they were bats. In Babylon, bats were thought to incarnate the souls of the deceased.[7] In Christian symbolism, the bat is intimately associated with Satan, who is often depicted with bat-like wings.[8] The ancient Egyptians worshiped the bat as a mother goddess, later assimilated into the figure of the love goddess, Hathor. For them, bats also symbolized darkness, black magic, madness, and greed.[9] In South America, bats are thought to be connected with the underworld, bloody sacrifice, and more positively, with rain and fertility.[10] In the Mayan culture, the bat is a chthonic divinity,[11] considered destructive, a master of fire, and a devourer of light. To reach the land of the dead, one must cross the bat's subterranean realm. The bat is also associated with death in Mexican folklore, where it is connected symbolically with the principal northern compass point. Thus, the bat is subject to many negative projections.

As is always the case, a sinister symbol may have a positive and renewing effect when confronted without fear, as it does in Native American lore. For example, since the caves from which bats emerge at night are easily seen as symbols of the earth-womb, it is not surprising that in some Native American rituals the bat represented rebirth.[12] The bat is always a positive symbol in China, emblematic of the five traditional blessings: wealth, health, love of virtue, old age, and a natural death.[13]

Since the bat is an animal of the darkness, it has often been construed as an image of the dark, gloomy, or forbidding Stygian underworld. In modern psychology, the bat has become a symbol of the largely unseen unconscious aspect of a person. Able to navigate in the dark, the bat is also believed to possess uncanny powers, which operate for good or ill, although in popular culture the emphasis is often on the negative. Because people tend to dwell on the very small number of species that suck blood, bats can symbolize "shadowy" vampiric forces of the human psyche, which, like Dracula, drain our energy, vitality, or spirit. The bat's swift but jagged flight is the very model of disturbing impulses that flit and flutter at the edges of awareness.

People dreaming of a bat, and perhaps feeling depleted in life, might consider what environmental circumstances are exhausting their energy. Possibly projections onto other people or various kinds of destructive communications are "draining energy away" in a vampire-like process. This feeling is common to people whose dominant mode of operation is withdrawal from reality rather than confrontation with outer or inner conflicts. If the dreamer can learn to tolerate dark, chaotic, even mad and disordering states — epitomized by the colloquial expression "bats in the belfry" — and feel anxiety without judgment, old ways and habits of functioning can break down. Then a new attitude, which engages the unconscious and its creative "irrational fluttering" at the edge of conscious awareness, may emerge.

Notes
[1] Grzimek 1984, 11: 67-68.
[2] Brody 1991, C1.
[3] Grzimek 1984, 11: 71-81.
[4] Grzimek 1984, 11: 94-95.
[5] Fenton 1984, 106.
[6] Grzimek 1984, 11: 116.
[7] Biedermann 1994, 29-30.
[8] Cooper 1992, 26.
[9] Jobes 1962, 1: 185.
[10] Peterson 1992, 104-05.
[11] Cooper 1992, 26.
[12] Cooper 1992, 26.
[13] Fenton 1984, 179.

BAT

Order: Chiroptera (19 families).

Size: The head-rump length of the fruit bat is 60-400 millimeters (2-15 inches). The insectivorous bat measures 3-6 centimeters (1.15-2.5 inches) from head to rump.

Weight: The fruit bat weighs 15-900 grams (0.05-2 pounds). The insectivorous bat weighs 5-20 grams (0.01-0.05 pounds).

Wingspan: The fruit bat's wings span 24-140 centimeters (9.5-55 inches), while the insectivorous bat's wings span 18-70 centimeters (7-30 inches).

Gestation: Variable, and with delayed implantation can range 3-10 months in a single species.

Longevity: Lifespan averages 4-5 years but can reach a maximum of 30 years.

Distribution: Worldwide except Arctic, Antarctic, and the highest mountains.

Habitat: Highly diverse.

Bear

For people of the northern hemisphere, the bear is the quintessential wild beast. Its name may derive from the Latin *ferus*, meaning "wild." These huge, shaggy, plantigrade (walking on the soles of their feet, as humans do) creatures are among the largest terrestrial carnivores.[1] However, the apparently ferocious bear has also been depicted as an object of human affection. A clumsy, affectionate embrace is commonly referred to as a "bear hug," while the furry "teddy bear" is one of the most beloved toys of childhood. This huge animal represents the human need to transpose fear by transforming a wild, vicious quality in nature into a magical form of play.

Common species include the Kodiak bear of Alaska, the polar bear, the brown or grizzly bear, the black bear, and the relatively small Malayan sun bear. The grizzly bear *(Ursus horribilis)*, named not for its grisly or gruesome inclinations but for its grizzled or gray-tipped fur, is no doubt the most fearsome and aggressive as well as the largest of the bears living today. Like most bears, it will generally flee when people approach. The grizzly bear will rear up into its awesome defensive posture (up to ten feet tall) or simply charge when surprised, especially with cubs to defend or if disturbed while hibernating. Some bears may lose their fear of humans and become dangerous. They then may have to be relocated or destroyed.[2]

Though capable of surprising speed given their substantial bulk — up to fifty-five kilometers (thirty-five miles) per hour[3] — all bears rely on their acute sense of smell to locate food. Bears' teeth are partially adapted for grinding plant matter, and most bears are, to a certain degree, herbivorous.[4] Polar bears are partial to ringed seal, but they will also eat reindeer, caribou, musk oxen, fish, and even rodents. In summer, they will eat seaweed, lichens, mosses, and berries. Grizzlies use their claws to scratch up insects, roots, and small rodents. They also feed on nuts, berries, carrion, and, primarily in the spring, on larger, wild or domestic animals.[5] With their great size and prodigious strength, they can bring down prey of any size with a single swipe of a paw.[6]

In autumn, bears typically increase their food intake, putting on fat to sustain them through the winter, which they will spend "denned up" in a protected space, mostly sleeping. This sleep is not strictly hibernation, since bears can be aroused and will leave their dens if they feel threatened.[7] Polar bears generally remain active all winter, although they may take shelter for extended periods in hollows they create in snowdrifts, usually near the coast.[8]

Because of their size and strength, bears have no natural enemies in the wild; however, as with so many wild animals, advancing "civilization" has forced them into ever-diminishing areas of wilderness habitat. Considered "big game," they are generally killed by sportsmen; in particular, the gall bladder of the black bear is sought as a remedy in traditional Chinese medicine.[9]

The fierceness of the female bear's defense of her cubs[10] and her emergence with them from an earthen den or cave in the spring make a strong impression — one sufficient to make the bear a common symbol of the Great Mother.[11] The "big sleep" of the bear is death-like, suggesting a resurrection of sorts. Its awesome strength and its supremacy in the wilderness make the bear seem the incarnation of nature.

As a natural wonder, the bear has served as a sacred symbol to many ancient cultures. Bear cults are evident in the earliest reaches of history; Neanderthals constructed shrines or altars to the Master Bear and buried bear skulls and bones alongside their own. Ancient shamans in North America, Iceland, Finland, Siberia, and Japan carved, engraved, painted, or otherwise depicted the bear as a sacred animal. The Inuit people worshiped a Great Spirit in the form of the polar bear, and many Native American tribes (not to mention the Cub Scouts) recognize the bear as a totemic figure.[12] The bear has both solar and lunar aspects in Scandinavian and Teutonic traditions, being sacred to the masculine sky god Thor, master of thunder and lightning, as well as to the lunar goddesses of the waters.[13] In Greek mythology, the great huntress Artemis (Diana in Rome) had a bear for her emblem, as if the most fearsome creature of nature was her subject.[14]

Symbolically, the bear can represent not only great majesty and forcefulness, but also the devouring aspect of instinct and unconscious forces. An attacking bear is a creature of overwhelming size, imbued with strength and rage, and one is advised that to survive an attack one must not resist, but simply curl up and be still. Psychologically, the bear can thus symbolize the irrepressible rage of the unconscious that can totally overpower a person. When such an animal appears in a fantasy or dream, the person needs to submit imaginally but consciously to this image and to feel his or her own smallness and weakness relative to the strength represented by the bear.

Given its power, the bear's capacity to tear and shred is often a symbol of madness. The word "berserk," which etymologically means "bear shirt," originally referred to the reckless, almost unchecked battle fury of certain Norse warriors. Now, to go "berserk" denotes madness, conjuring up the image of a raging bear. However, when such force is tamed through awareness and experienced without succumbing to the fragmentation and chaos brought by the bear image, it becomes extremely protective, lending its strength to the conscious aspect of the personality. Viewed in this light, the bear becomes a clever creature, prudent and cautious in some ways, agile and dexterous, purposeful and methodical. Rearing up and even walking on its hind legs, the bear has an eerily human shape — a fact not lost on circus trainers, who dress up bears and teach them to do any number of "human" tricks. Many cultures give the bear familiar or affectionate names like "grandfather" or "grandmother," or create characters like "Winnie the Pooh," underscoring our unusual sense of connection with this wild creature.[15]

The appearance of a bear in dreams can signify the emergence of positive maternal capacities. But more often it represents psychic forces that can devour consciousness and even lead to madness. The dreamer may be called upon to flee from this bear image or to meet its force, adopt an attitude of cognizant submission to a greater power, or, in some instances, even actively confront it. In these cases, while danger is clear, transformation, indeed a rebirth of consciousness, is a strong possibility.

Notes
[1] Nowak 1991, 2: 1083.
[2] Grzimek 1984, 12: 119-20.
[3] http://www.state.ak.us/local/akpages/FISH.GAME/wildlife/geninfo/game/bearfax.htm
[4] Pfeffer 1989, 64.

[5] Pfeffer 1989, 64.
[6] Grzimek 1984, 12: 126.
[7] Nowak 1991, 2: 1083.
[8] Grzimek 1984, 12: 128.
[9] Pfeffer 1989, 63-65.
[10] Grzimek 1984: 12, 120.
[11] von Franz 1980a, 119.
[12] Cooper 1992, 26.
[13] Cooper 1992, 28.
[14] Kerényi 1980, 44.
[15] Johnson 1988, 338.

BEAR

Family: Ursidae.
Size: Sun bears measure 1.1-1.4 meters (3.6-4.6 feet) in overall length while polar bears measure 2-3 meters (6.6-9.8 feet).
Weight: Sun bears weigh 27-65 kilograms (60-143 pounds), while polar bears weigh 150-650 kilograms (220-430 pounds); fat-laden males can reach 800 kilograms (1,760 pounds) or more.
Gestation: 210-255 days.
Longevity: Approximately 25 years.
Distribution: Arctic, North America, Europe, Asia, and South America.
Habitat: Arctic coasts to tropical jungle, chiefly forests.

Beaver

The beaver, like the ant, is a paragon of social industry; like humans, it is a bold manipulator of its physical environment. The fervor of its activity inspired the expression "eager beaver" to designate someone who may be power hungry, desirous of recognition, or exceedingly enthusiastic in carrying out a task. The beaver's evolutionary roots date back some thirty-five to forty million years, and it is one of the largest extant members of the rodent family. During the Ice Age, giant beavers as large as small bears roamed the wilderness.[1] The first Europeans to penetrate the wilds of the American West were trappers looking for the beaver pelts from which felt hats were (and still are) made.

Although it is somewhat awkward on land, with its webbed hind feet and broad, flat tail, the beaver is a graceful and powerful swimmer, capable (because of its large lung capacity) of diving and remaining submerged for up to fifteen minutes. Sexually mature after three to four years, beavers mate between January and March, the male swimming on his back under the female to accomplish his procreative mission. The beaver is one of the few mammals that mates for life.[2] Young beavers, predictably enough, learn to swim very quickly. Typically, three generations will occupy one den, though parents will drive off the oldest offspring to make room for a new litter.[3]

Beavers' eyes and ears are noticeably small, reflecting poor development of the corresponding senses. They are strict vegetarians, browsing in summer on tender shrubs, bulrushes, the buds from softwood trees, and the roots of water lilies. In winter, they are able to derive sufficient nourishment from the bark of shrubs and trees that they have cut down and stored.[4] Although they do not hibernate, beavers become less active during the winter, remaining in their dens for as much as a week at a time and living off their stored supply of branches.[5]

The musky scent of the beaver is used to mark its territory. Beavers also slap their tails against the water's surface, making a loud, booming sound that serves as a danger signal.[6] Today, the disappearance of their habitat is the beaver's primary enemy, although bears, wolves, martens, otters and lynx prey on them.

The beaver's chief asset, and most notable physical feature, is its twenty rootless teeth, including the two protruding front incisors with which it fells trees and cuts branches for dens and dams. With these incisors the beaver can exert a chewing force of 80 kilograms (177 pounds). By comparison, humans exert a force of only 40 kilograms (88 pounds).[7] The teeth grow continuously, and only constant use and wear keep them from growing too large to allow the consumption of food.[8]

Accordingly, beavers are the builders, architects, and engineers *par excellence* of the animal world. In the process of creating their dens, dams, and canals, they affect and reshape their environment on a grand scale. They can cut through a small willow tree, eight centimeters (three inches) in diameter, in just five minutes; larger trees may take several days, or even months. They work on big trees cooperatively, generally taking turns.[9]

Dam building for beavers is a means to an end, not an end in itself. If conditions suit them, they will merely build themselves a lodge by the side of a river, with entrances and exits below the waterline, and get on with their lives. Only when water levels drop, exposing the accesses to their lodges, do beavers look for ways to dam up the water and raise its level. Their interest is in security and convenience. When needed, they place tree trunks and branches upright and perpendicular to the riverbed, anchoring them with stones, mud, and grasses, to build dams. The den or lodge is then built within the structure of the dam. A beaver dam on the Jefferson River, near Three Forks, Montana, is approximately seven hundred meters long — surely built, maintained, and expanded by many generations of beavers.[10] How they organize and coordinate the complex and highly cooperative tasks involved in dam building is still largely unknown.

The effects of beaver activity on the landscape can be beneficial. The clearing of trees facilitates the growth of brush, which, in turn, provides fodder for deer and moose. In the long run, dam building creates arable land for humans. When a beaver pond silts up the beaver will abandon it; eventually, the dam will break, and the water will drain off, leaving a flat patch or field of unusually rich soil.[11]

In many Native American cultures, the beaver was seen as a creator god and totemic figure — "creative" in the sense that its dam building creates new landscapes, new worlds. In the Cherokee creation myth, the earth was covered with water until the Great Spirit sent the beavers to dredge up mud from the bottom and form the land. Others see a close connection between humans and the beaver, finding in the latter's industriousness a mirror of their own values. Various tribes trace their ancestry back to the beaver. In Europe, too, the beaver is noted primarily for its diligence.[12]

In ancient times, the male's testicles were believed to produce castoreum, a substance precious for its supposed healing powers and for which the poor creature was hunted mercilessly. No scientific documentation exists for the notion that the male beaver, when pursued, bites off his testicles to evade capture. However, this belief once had great currency, having been repeated by the Egyptian priest Horapollo, as well as Apollonius, Pliny, and Juvenal in the *Physiologus*.[13] In modern times, the word "castoreum" or "castor" is used for musky oil produced by glands in the beaver's groin (not the testicles) and used in perfumery and for medicinal purposes.[14]

Symbolically, the main attribute of the beaver is its social cooperation. Thus, in a dream, the beaver could signify a necessity for cooperative work within the context of the community or group, rather than alone. The other major characteristic of the beaver is its great capacity to work against the normal, natural flow of life. This movement is *contra naturam,* and is a leitmotif of the process of individuation, in which the individual personality must move against the chronic tendency of inertia. Human beings have managed to move against this energy-reducing flow and create higher, more spiritual structures. The beaver beautifully represents the movement of energy from a lower to a more spiritual level. Consequently, if someone were to dream of a beaver, it could highlight these questions: In what areas of his or her life does this person need to be more industrious? Where does he or she need to move against lethargy or automatic behavior, raising energies, perhaps with some additional or new behavior or meditative / creative technique?

Notes
[1] Grzimek 1984, 11: 286.
[2] Masson 1999, 178.

[3] Grzimek 1984, 11: 281.
[4] Grzimek 1984, 11: 276.
[5] Grzimek 1984, 11: 280.
[6] Macdonald 1987, 608.
[7] Grzimek 1984, 11: 280.
[8] Andrews 1993, 253.
[9] Grzimek 1984, 11: 279–80.
[10] Grzimek 1984, 11: 277-78.
[11] Andrews 1993, 253.
[12] Rue III 1964, 131.
[13] Curley 1979, 15.
[14] Cooper 1992, 30.

BEAVER
Family: Castoridae.
Size: Head-body length is 80–120 centimeters (32-47 inches); tail length is 25-50 centimeters (10-20 inches); shoulder height is 30-60 centimeters (12-23 inches).
Weight: 11–30 kilograms (24-66 pounds).
Gestation: Approximately 105 days.
Longevity: 10-15 years.
Distribution: North America, Scandinavia, Europe, Central Asia, and Northwest China.
Habitat: Semi-aquatic wetlands associated with ponds, lakes, rivers, and streams.

Bee

Busy, buzzing paradigms of industry and social devotion, bees are responsible for most of the pollination of flowering plants in the world; thus, they are truly central players in the interwoven drama of biological life on earth. Kept domestically by humans since antiquity for their honey, their crucial role in the planet's ecology has only recently been clearly understood. Grouped in the order

Hymenoptera, along with wasps and ants, bees are so socially bound, so strictly regimented, that one can easily imagine the hive itself to be the living organism and the individual bees to be its cellular components.

Bees in general (members of the superfamily Apoidea, which comprises over twenty thousand species)[1] evolved from wasps, whose sting is primarily an instrument of predation. Although bees are exclusively vegetarian, in most cases they have retained their stings for defensive purposes. The habits and even the physiology of the superfamily are so diverse and varied — some species so exotic, and valid generalizations about them so few — that the following discussion is limited to the more familiar honeybee.

Bees have three basic ranks or castes: the queen, whose life is to mate once and lay eggs (up to fifteen hundred a day); the workers, the female laboring class of the hive, and the males or drones. The male bee's sole function is to become the single hero to assay a nuptial flight, providing the queen with enough outside genetic material to engender a multitude of subsequent generations. Males are produced parthenogenetically from unfertilized eggs. Lacking two sets of chromosomes, they are, in effect, drones.[2] The worker bees are the ones we are likely to see buzzing about our gardens, collecting nectar from the flowers and pollinating them in the process. They also feed and care for the queen and her retinue of indolent drone suitors, and build, maintain, and defend the hive. Maintenance includes a fascinating method of regulating air quality and temperature within the hive. When carbon dioxide levels are elevated, or temperatures fluctuate beyond acceptable levels (approximately thirty-five degrees Celsius or ninety-five degrees Fahrenheit), large groups of workers begin to fan their wings to circulate air throughout the hive. If it is too warm, they station themselves at the entrance to blow in cool, fresh air. And if the outside air is not cool enough, other workers will fetch water to add evaporative cooling to the process.[3] With wax secreted from their abdomens, the workers also build combs — the ranks of hexagonal chambers that contain the larvae or stores of honey and pollen.

The drones or male bees, although larger than the females, are not physically equipped for work, nor do they. The workers feed them, even pamper them, one might say, until early summer, when the young queen, or queens, takes flight. A brief frenzy ensues to mate with any appropriate-smelling female. In late summer, the drones are driven out of the hive; helpless as they are, they starve to death.[4] As for the old queen, faced with a new generation of potentially fertile competitors, she may choose to abandon the hive in a royal huff, flying off — with approximately half of the old hive's population swarming in attendance — to found a new hive.

The exceedingly complex social interactions of bees have made them a fascination for scientists, and, thanks to the world-famous studies by Carl Von Frisch, we know that a successfully foraging honeybee shows her hive-mates the location of her find by performing a series of dances (the now-famous circle dance and waggle dance). These dances indicate, by varying orientation, figure, and speed, both the distance to the food supply and its direction relative to the position of the sun. This dance "language" is also used to help pinpoint the location of a new hive site. Other factors, including scent marking and electromagnetic fields, play a part in apian navigation as well. Recent observations suggest that they also appear to rely on their visual sense to maintain direction during flight, keeping fleeting ground images in line with the angle of the sun.[5]

The symbol of bee and honey is widely linked with erotic life. For example, Tantric tradition says that the hum of love-struck bees comes from the sleeping Shakti, paramount goddess and/or consort of a male deity, generally Shiva, who as a dancer dissolves into a swarm of bees. Kama, the god of erotic love, had a bowstring of bees.[6] In many mythologies, the craving for sweetness (until recently honey was the only unrefined sweetener readily available in the world) and sexual craving are considered analogous. Bees are thought to ravish the flowers that they visit in search of food; indeed, from the flower's point of view, it is a quintessentially sexual event.[7] The pantheon of the Warao Indians of South America includes the "Mother of Honey," who frees men simultaneously from the bonds of hunger and sex.[8] Symbolically, honey is linked to the sweetness of life, to a passion and desire that can overcome depression, and part of that passionate uplifting force is sexuality.

Like birds (and all creatures of the air), bees are seen as winged messengers between the mortal world and heaven. Ancient authors Pliny and Aristotle both comment on the divinity of bees and the notion that they are reincarnations of dead souls. Indeed, the bee is sometimes used to represent the soul itself.[9] In Western culture, one can encounter folkloric notions that dreaming of a bee means death is near and, conversely, that if a bee flies into the mouth of a corpse, the corpse will return to life. To "tell the bees" is to send news to the souls of the dead.[10] In numerous cultures, the various social behaviors of the bees have been used to illustrate bravery, chastity, loyalty to authority, and, of course, industriousness. Honey has been considered to have medicinal properties, and bee stings have been considered therapeutic throughout the ages for rheumatism, arthritis, and neuritis.[11]

Bees demonstrate incredible interaction and cooperation, especially the worker bees. "Busy as bees," they constantly maintain the welfare of the hive. Thus, bees can symbolize a very joyful state, what M.L. von Franz called "instinctual oneness with one's task and surroundings"[12] — a spontaneous collaboration of all parts of one's being. Psychologically speaking, bees can thus represent a powerful innate capacity to overcome dissociation in favor of cooperation, thus allowing all the parts of the human being — body, mind, soul, and spirit — to work together. To dream of a bee could signify the need to be open to this organizing potential and also to a sense of delight — a milk-and-honey apprehension of the providence of the world, as well as an instinctive sexuality that includes an aggressive (stinging) component. Additionally, it could represent a link to the larger organizing self, which mysteriously connects both conscious and unconscious aspects and is the source of a sense of purpose and/or meaning of life.

Notes
[1] Grzimek 1984, 2: 454.
[2] Dale-Green 1959, 30-48.
[3] Attenborough 1990, 150-51.
[4] Dale-Green 1959, 36.
[5] O'Toole 1984, 122.
[6] Jung 1975, 9i: 312 note.
[7] Jung 1976, 14: 698, 704.
[8] Burton and Burton 1975, 165-66.
[9] Cooper 1992, 30-33.
[10] Biedermann 1994, 35.
[11] *Funk & Wagnalls Standard Dictionary* 1972, 130.
[12] von Franz 1974, 46.

BEE
Superfamily: Apoidea (a variety of families and more than 20,000 species).
Size: 2 millimeters (0.08 inches) to 4 centimeters (1.5 inches) in body length.
Weight: Worker bees weigh 81-151 milligrams (0.003-0.005 ounces); drones weigh 196-225 milligrams (0.007-0.008 ounces); queen bees weigh 178-292 milligrams (0.006-0.010 ounces).
Incubation: 16 days for queens; 24 days for drones.
Longevity: Queen bee lives 4-5 years. The drone dies after copulation.
Distribution: All continents, except Antarctica.
Habitat: They are most abundant and diverse in regions such as deserts of southwestern North America and in the Mediterranean basin.

Beetle

Streamlined and armored like tiny, gothically inspired battle tanks, beetles comprise 290,000 species — more than forty percent of the named insects in the world. Although they exhibit a staggering variety of shapes, sizes, and habits, beetles have in common an exoskeleton made up of a hard, horny substance called chitin and a pair of wings that are radically modified to form hardened wing covers. In some species these wing covers, called elytra, fold back to allow another, fully functional pair of wings to operate freely. In other species, the wing covers are fused, and the insect is flightless.[1]

Beetles have chewing mouthparts, with mandibles generally modified into strong pincers. Among carnivore beetles, the pincers are not used for cutting or tearing, but rather to seize and hold a victim while it is dissolved by digestive enzymes vomited up by the beetle, which then slurps its victim down like custard.[2] Many insects included in the order Coleoptera, such as the Sexton beetle, feed on dead animals, performing a valuable service by removing corpses, small and large, from field and forest. Dung beetles, drawn to freshly laid dung, roll and pat a ball of it — often many times their own size — to bury in an underground chamber as food for their emerging young. Collectively, they clean up millions of tons of fecal matter each day, sanitizing the ground's surface as they add nitrogen to the subsurface.[3]

Females generally lay fertilized eggs, often following a specialized form of courtship behavior and copulation. Indeed, some wooing involves rather complicated rituals. Hopeful male fireflies (they are, despite their name, beetles, not flies) flash their lights in coded patterns, which are answered in matching code only by receptive females of the correct species. Most species undergo a metamorphosis from egg, larva, and pupa to adult.[4]

Beetles employ a wide variety of defensive strategies. Some, like skunks, secrete or squirt substances that are obnoxious to smell or taste. Others merely mimic the coloration of their foul cousins.[5] Some species have worked out a symbiosis with ants, among which they are permitted to live in return for light house-keeping (cleaning up the bodies of sick or dead ants) and certain secretions that the ants seem to find irresistible. In extreme cases, the ants even feed their beetle guests.[6]

The scarab, or sacred dung beetle of Egypt, was thought to push the disk of the sun over the edge of the horizon, launching it on its daily journey across the sky. Thus, the beetle becomes the symbol of resurrection and the unending daily re-creation of the (sun) god as he comes into existence at dawn.[7] In the mythology of the Chaco Indians in South America, the beetle is responsible for the creation of the world, as well as of man and woman. The Toba people even today consider black beetles to be supernatural spirits.[8] The Zia Indians of North America tell how Utset, the Mother of Indians, gave a pouch of stars to Beetle and bid him carry them from underground all the way to the heavens. Beetle allowed them to escape into the sky, and for this error the Mother of Indians made him blind. In many parts of the world, people believe that beetles are both deaf and blind (although most are not), and so they have come to be widely considered symbols of stupidity.[9]

Within the context of Egyptian myths of solar resurrection the beetle or scarab symbolizes the emergence of life and consciousness from a deadened state, such as despair or depression. Thus, an emerging consciousness is closely linked with these dark states of despondency. Depending on the context — stories, mythologies, or the life of the person dreaming of it — the beetle can take on a remarkable array of qualities, from a powerful impulse to create to a wish to be dead and dull.

A dream of a beetle can signal a remarkable renewing process — far from awareness, but nonetheless real. Or a person may be suffering dark states with little courage and a secret death wish. Dreaming of a beetle in this condition can signify the danger of such a passive attitude; yet even here the beetle could be seen as a possible renewal of consciousness.[10]

Notes
[1] Wootton 1988, 207; Grzimek 1984, 2: 231.
[2] Grzimek 1984, 2: 237-38.
[3] Angier 1991b, C1.
[4] Grzimek 1984, 2: 244.
[5] Grzimek 1984, 2: 238-42.
[6] Grzimek 1984, 2: 259-60.
[7] von Franz 1980c, 88-89.
[8] *Funk & Wagnalls Standard Dictionary* 1972, 131.
[9] Ibid.
[10] Jung 1977, 12: 530-31.

BEETLE
Order: Coleoptera (includes about 290,000 species in about 135 known families, of which 120 live in the western hemisphere).
Size: 0.25 millimeters (0.01 inches) to 16 centimeters (7 inches) in length. The South American *Dynastes herculeanus*, at 7 inches, is probably the longest beetle in the world.
Weight: 0.4 milligrams (0.00001 ounces) to 30 grams (1.05 ounces).
Wingspan: Not all beetles have wings.
Incubation: In some beetles, such as "foreign grain," "dried fruit," and "sawtoothed grain" beetles, the eggs can take from 1 to 5 days to hatch.
Longevity: The maximum age of beetles fluctuates widely from one species to another. The "boring" beetle lives just 1 week, while the "pales weevil" beetle can live as long as 3 years.
Distribution: Almost everywhere except in the sea.
Habitat: Varied.

Bird

Creatures of the sky, birds routinely slip the bonds of earth and defy gravity; by taking flight, they provoke the envy and stoke the fantasies of humanity. Distributed widely over the seven continents and seas, the class of birds, Avis, are warm-blooded, egg-laying vertebrates that share these further qualities: a coat of feathers, forelimbs modified into wings, scaly legs, and a beak. Beyond that, the degree of variation is astounding; roughly 8,700 species range from the drab little sparrow to the garish bird of paradise, from the tiny hummingbird to the giant condor, and from powerful, globe-circling flyers like the white stork to flightless birds like the emu or penguin. The smallest living bird is generally acknowledged to be the bee hummingbird of Cuba, which is 6.3 centimeters (2.5 inches) long and weighs less than 3 grams (about 0.1 ounce). The largest living bird is the ostrich, which may stand 2.5 meters (8 feet) tall and weigh 135 kilograms (300 pounds).[1] Birds comprise twenty percent of all vertebrates, or up to two percent of all animal species.

"Free as a bird," we say, and indeed, the power of flight gives birds unmatched mobility as well as their hold on the human imagination. Some species have seasonal migrations involving 3,500-4,000 kilometers (2,000-2,500 miles), as in the case of the arctic tern.[2] Until recently human navigation lagged behind its avian equivalent in accuracy and dependability. So the ability of migrating birds to return unerringly to nesting sites and other seasonal habitats, often thousands of miles away, aroused great scientific interest, not to mention wonder. Young birds of some species may be guided by their flocking instinct to follow the lead of more experienced, older birds, but the individuals of many species migrate alone, often in weather that would preclude any celestial observation. The answer to this mystery seems to be that certain species are sensitive to the earth's magnetic field, having developed what amounts to an internal biological compass.[3]

Almost all birds are visual animals (except the nearly blind kiwi). Larger birds are well known for their exceptional sight. Eagles are said to be able to see details that a human would require a six-power telescope to discern. Birds also tend to have excellent hearing, but their relatively underdeveloped olfactory organs indicate lesser sensitivities to taste and smell.[4]

Birds are social animals, and their ritual courtship behavior is sometimes quite elaborate. Some oviparous animals simply deposit their eggs and crawl, swim, hop, or slither away. However, almost all birds' eggs need incubation, and that requirement dictates and shapes a great deal of the cooperative or social aspects of bird behavior.[5] Birds are notoriously territorial in the breeding season, and mated pairs often remain together until the young are self-sufficient. Nest building and food gathering are often cooperative efforts between male and female. While birds practice various forms of polygamy, monogamy is by far their most common form of mating.[6]

Birds, whether in pairs or flocks, communicate extensively and subtly by means of vocalizations, often unique to a species or even to local subspecies and sometimes so musical that humans call them songs. Postures or ritualized actions can take on the function of language, stimulating predictable responses from those birds that recognize them. Parrots and mynahs, famously, can be taught to emulate human speech. And despite the common epithet "birdbrain," many birds, like crows, show signs of high intelligence.[7]

Creatures of the sky, as elusive and ephemeral as dreams, birds are frequently seen as messengers of the unconscious, representing flights of thought, fantasies, and intuitive ideas.[8] In Christian iconography, the Holy Spirit is represented as a dove, and winged creatures are widely associated with spirit. Angels are depicted with wings, as are the souls of the dead in many cultures. For ages, birds have been considered the messengers of gods of the sky. The Romans examined the behavior of birds for "auspicious" (from the Latin word for bird, *avis*, and look, *specio*) signs of divine intentions. Often thought to predict the future, birds were associated in Roman mythology with Apollo, founder of the Delphic Oracle, and in German mythology with Wotan, god of war and magic.[9]

Because they are far-ranging, sharp-eyed, and sometimes inconspicuous, we have a sense that birds may have an uncanny knowledge of our affairs. "A little bird told me" is a common expression, and throughout time and across cultures birds have been regarded as prophetic or oracular agents of supernatural aid. In the legend of Romulus and Remus, the supposed founders of Rome, a woodpecker put food into the children's mouths. A helpful bird appears on the tree that grows from of the grave of Cinderella's mother.[10] An ancient European tradition depicts goddess figures with three-fingered "hands" that are actually bird's claws, and many folktales have witches and fairies with bird's feet. The Russian Baba Yaga, an ogress who steals, cooks, and eats her victims — usually children — and is also a guardian of the fountains of the water of life, lives in a hut that stands on chicken legs. In Lithuania, the Laumas, infertile, fairy-like creatures who yearn for children and thus often kidnap babies to raise as their own, have chicken legs.[11]

Symbolically and factually, birds are creatures of the air and prescience, and thus may symbolize the ability of the unconscious to point us to the intuitive, the less literal. When a bird appears in a dream, it might lead us toward a more spiritual and perceptive capacity, in opposition to the factual; it might be a call for the dreamer to become more familiar with this innate potential of human life. One must look more deeply into the particular kind of bird involved in the dream to make sense of its symbolic meaning in one's specific life situation.

More can be learned about unique physical characteristics and symbolic significance by referring to individual birds (see albatross, chicken/hen, crow/raven, dove, duck, eagle, falcon, goose, hawk, ostrich, owl, parrot, peacock, pelican, rooster/cock, stork, swallow, swan, turkey, vulture).

Notes
[1] "Ostrich." *Encyclopedia Britannica*, 1997.
[2] Grzimek 1984, 7: 29.
[3] Slater 1987, 52.
[4] Grzimek 1984, 7: 58-59.
[5] Grzimek 1984, 7: 67-68.
[6] Grzimek 1984, 7: 69-70.
[7] Grzimek 1984, 7: 56.
[8] von Franz 1980b, 54; Jung 1976, 5: 538.
[9] von Franz 1974, 43.
[10] Jung 1976, 5: 547 note.
[11] Gimbutas 1989, 244.

Boar

With its wickedly sharp tusks, wiry strength, and aggressive ways, the wild boar stands in sharp contrast to its docile, domestic porcine cousins. The term "boar" is used to distinguish the male swine from the sow, and to distinguish wild swine, whether male or female, from domestic breeds. A creature of forests, steppes, savannas, and swamps, the boar can survive in a wide variety of habitats so long as some form of fresh water is available — mud baths being critical for cooling off and keeping down parasites. Females and their young live in herds led by an old sow, while adult males live more or less solitary lives, joining the herd only during the rutting season for fighting and copulation. Gestation takes three to four months, producing a first litter of three or four and subsequently a dozen or more.[1]

The omnivorous boar subsists primarily on acorns, chestnuts, fruit, insects, earthworms, reptiles, mice, and birds and their eggs.[2] Because it is also a scavenger of carrion, the boar has become symbolically associated with death.[3] The boar can also represent aggressive qualities that are sometimes admired, such as strength, fearlessness, tenacity, and battle-lust. Highly compact of body, big-headed, short-necked, and most often short-legged as well, the boar can barrel through dense thickets that discourage predators. Its upward-curving tusks can do substantial damage to enemies, and although competitions between boars are rarely fatal, they are nevertheless bloody affairs — especially when males are evenly matched.[4]

In the story of the Caledonian boar from Homer's epic poem *The Iliad,* the beast personifies wilderness; as the gods send a monstrous boar to ravage the vineyards, trampling spaces that epitomize human civilization and social order.[5] Ambivalence is reflected in Nordic myth. The golden-bristled boar Gullinbursti is a solar animal, the mount of the sun god Frey, and is sacrificed to him at

Yuletide. But the white boar that dwells in swamps is associated with the moon, with the watery element, and represents regressive forces.[6] In Egyptian mythology, the boar was considered an attribute of the devil Set, the personification of wild and untamed emotions and enemy of Osiris, god of death and resurrection, and of the hero Horus. For the Hebrews, as well as for the followers of Islam, the boar is an unclean animal, and in Psalm 80:13 a destroyer of vineyards (an echo of the Caledonian boar story).[7]

In Christian symbolism, the boar is associated with brutality, "swinish" sexuality, and the Antichrist. Illustrations of the "terrible mother goddess," the archetypal feminine in her negative form, often give her boar tusks or a boar for a mount. The boar is generally associated with her destructive qualities toward her son-lover, whose task is eventually to own this boar aggression for himself if he is to develop his own personality. Such characteristics can represent the power and might in the symbol of the boar.[8]

In Celtic culture, the boar was considered a magical creature, associated with warfare but also with the hunt, and by extension with hospitality and protection. The boar's head in particular symbolized health and preservation from danger, thought to contain the mana, the absorbable life force of the animal. As a result it was the traditional center of Yuletide feasts in many countries.[9]

This creative aspect of the boar is evident in other cultures. In the Hindu tradition, for example, the serpent and boar are complementary, antagonistic, and mutually limiting aspects of the creator god Vishnu. As the cold-blooded serpent, Vishnu represents entropic, regressive forces that push the world back into formlessness and unconsciousness. But as the creator and maintainer of the world, Vishnu is also represented as the warm-blooded boar that opposes the serpent.[10] In China, the boar personifies the wealth of the forests, and a white boar is associated with the moon in a very positive way. In Japan, the moon is called the "white boar," and it symbolizes courage in battle.[11]

As mount of the sun god, the boar can represent light and consciousness; yet, given its association with the moon, it can also represent darkness and waning strength. The boar often stands for sexuality and aggressiveness, as well as magic and courage. In a psychological mode, the boar can sometimes symbolize the dark, shadow side of a person, laden with intense rage, strength, belligerence, or ruthlessness — barely, or not at all, under conscious control. These potentially destructive states can drain energy and lead to depression, withdrawal, fear, or terror, or can turn outward in wrathful displays of power and cruelty. Yet when these energies are effectively subdued (as symbolized by the many mythic stories of the hero in combat with the boar) and consciously deployed, this dangerous aggression can liberate the conscious personality from passivity and unhealthy states of dependency.

If one were to dream of a boar, one would need to face dynamic energies that could be unleashed in a ferocious display of temper. The appearance of a boar in a dream could be an attempt by the unconscious to tell the dreamer of powerful but dormant aggressions that have not been integrated and controlled by the conscious personality, but that may be ready to spring forward — for example, in reaction to deep-seated feelings of inferiority and weakness. The boar could represent deep aggressive power and energy for protection, a vital tool against the intrusiveness of others. A dream of a boar may compensate for a tendency to withdraw from aggression, and it might urge one to own the power and aggressiveness of one's actions.

Notes
[1] Burton 1981, 589-90.
[2] Ibid.
[3] Gimbutas 1989, 195.
[4] Grzimek 1984, 13: 77-82; Burton 1981, 589.
[5] Bonnefoy 1992, 129-30.
[6] Cooper 1992, 39.
[7] Cooper 1992, 40.
[8] Ibid.
[9] Cooper 1992, 39.
[10] Zimmer 1974, 78-79.
[11] Cooper 1992, 40.

BOAR
Family: Suidae.
Size: Head-body length measures 90-180 centimeters (35-70 inches); tail length measures 30-40 centimeters (12-15 inches).
Weight: 50-200 kilograms (110-440 pounds).
Gestation: Approximately 115 days.
Longevity: 15-20 years.
Distribution: Europe, North Africa, Asia (notably Sumatra, Japan, and Taiwan); introduced into North America.
Habitat: Broad-leaved woodlands and steppe.

Buffalo/Bison

The American buffalo, also called bison, once roamed the North American plains in thunderous herds so large that they took days to pass a single spot. During the eighteenth century, an estimated sixty million of these great, noble, shaggy beasts roamed in more or less continuous herds from Alaska to the Rocky Mountains to Northeast Mexico and almost to the Atlantic Ocean. Neither hunting by the Native Americans nor the severe winters, droughts, fires, and natural catastrophes diminished these huge herds. But in the 1830s, as the railroads were being built, the methodical destruction of this animal began, and within half a century the largest concentration of game animals on earth had been almost completely destroyed. Thus, their prior behavior and habits can only be inferred from recent observations of the vastly diminished herds that survive.[1]

Misnamed by early European visitors to the New World, this largest land animal in the Western hemisphere is, in fact, not a buffalo at all; its closest living relative is the wisent or European bison. The American buffalo consists of two kinds, which are more or less distinct geographically, if not morphologically, and whose status as separate species is widely disputed. The plains bison usually feeds on grass and herbs, while the wood bison feeds on leaves, shoots, and the bark of trees and bushes. In spite of its bulk, the bison is agile and fast. Unpredictable, it can sometimes be approached closely and at other times will stampede at the least provocation.[2] Possessing great stamina and periodically migratory, the bison herds reportedly could run at a canter for a day at a time.[3]

The bison has a convex forehead, a distinct shoulder hump, and a dark brown coat that is distinctly longer and shaggier on its head, neck, and shoulders, which are held low. Both sexes have heavy, curved horns, although the cow's are smaller.[4] In winter, all bison can use their massive heads as a kind of snowplow to uncover lichen, moss, and dry grasses. During the mating season, the bulls utter a throaty, rumbling roar that can be heard over more than five kilometers. At that time, males and females form large herds. Fights proliferate, and victorious bulls gain the right to mate with the cows, which usually give birth to a single calf after about nine months' gestation.

To the Native Americans, the bison may well have seemed a miraculous source of life and abundance, a reservoir of food and spiritual power — the key in many ways to their survival. Every piece of the bison's anatomy was used to provide food, clothing, shelter; its hides were used as robes and tents, and its horns, bones, and innards became everyday utensils as well as ceremonial and ritual objects.[5] Tribes like the Fox, Pueblo, Mandan, and Sioux held imitative tribal dances to call to the spirit of the buffalo in hope of a successful hunt. The Lakota Sioux revered the legendary "White Buffalo Woman," who taught the people how to use the pipe in their prayers and perform proper rituals. Indeed, the albino or white buffalo became for many Native Americans the most sacred of living creatures, with great spiritual and medicinal power. The Blackfoot tribes believed that the white buffalo belonged to the sun god. A white robe was made from the buffalo's skin to be worn on special occasions and zealously protected from harm.[6]

The North American buffalo died off because of a loss of habitat, the fencing of the once seemingly limitless frontier. Yet we persist in associating it with the grandeur of vast, open spaces, unlimited opportunity, and the absence of boundaries. When we think about the origins of the United States, the powerful, majestic image of the bison immediately comes to mind. This animal symbolizes the heart and soul of the U.S. as it was in pioneer times. The bison further provides vast and varied forms of physical and especially spiritual nourishment, which can be likened to the soul of each human being. This uniquely U.S. symbol, celebrated in songs like "Home on the Range" and commemorated on the Buffalo Nickel, can represent the organizing center of the psyche, the self, which provides vast and varied forms of spiritual nourishment.

From the depths of dreams, the image of the buffalo can call up great unconscious sources of nurture and the possibility of a new spiritual awareness, validating the potency of the unconscious. Recognizing the potential of this image can help one achieve vast creative purposes and spiritual development. To those aware of the way great herds of buffalo were decimated, dreaming of the buffalo might represent not only the nourishing and life-giving self but also the way that deep psychic structure can be repressed and decimated by one's own and other people's power drives.

Notes
[1] Grzimek 1984, 13: 388-89.
[2] "Bison." *Encyclopedia Britannica.* 1997.
[3] Grzimek 1984, 13: 393.
[4] "Bison." *Encyclopedia Britannica.* 1997.
[5] Brown 1992, 121-22.
[6] Pickering 1997, 16-27.

BUFFALO/BISON
Family: Bovidae.
Size: Male's head–rump length is up to 300 centimeters (118 inches); body height is 190 centimeters (75 inches). Females are smaller by one-quarter or one-third.
Weight: Males weigh over 1,000 kilograms (2,200 pounds or 1.1 tons). Females are lighter by one-quarter or one-third.
Gestation: 270–300 days.
Longevity: 20–25 years.
Distribution: Plains bison in Central United States, the wood bison in northern United States; some bison may be found in Canada.
Habitat: Prairies, grassland, aspen parkland, and forests.

Bull

A massive, horned ungulate, and an ancient and permanent model of virility and power, the bull or wild ox evolved from the more ancient auroch, which became extinct in 1627. The wild ox thrived in peak numbers during the Glacial Period and was domesticated nearly eight thousand years ago, giving rise to the many breeds of cattle raised today for meat, milk, leather, and other by-products. The use of oxen as plow and draft animals revolutionized agriculture and may well have effected a more profound change in human history than any other single factor. Wild oxen were hunted to extinction in the western hemisphere and Europe, although untamed species, including Asiatic buffaloes (water buffalo), African buffaloes (Cape buffalo), true cattle (koupreys, gaurs, and yaks), and bison still roam free in Asia.[1]

Bovine species occupy dense forests, open grass steppes, and mountainous habitats up to six thousand meters (twenty thousand feet) in elevation. All seek water not only to drink, but also for bathing and wallowing; all are ruminants — that is, true herbivores. They rely heavily on their keen sense of smell; their hearing is good, but their vision is not particularly sharp, especially when objects are stationary.[2] Lacking the musculature for facial expression, cattle communicate through posture: as an assertion of rank within the herd generally, and when facing an antagonist in particular. The carriage of the head and horns is extremely significant, indicating aggression and/or appeasement.[3]

With the onset of the mating season, herds gather more closely together, and the bulls are vigilant for signs of estrus in any cow. The moment a cow shows signs of heat, all the bulls crowd around, with the highest-ranking bull claiming his place — closest to the cow in question. Within days, the female will become receptive, and copulation occurs.[4] As twin symbols of fertility, the bull and the cow have an ancient connection with religious impulses. The beauty, even majesty, of the bulls in the famous cave paintings at Lascaux, traced by firelight in charcoal and umber, persuade us that these creatures have inspired numinous feelings in the people of ancient cultures, just as they do today.[5]

The bull represents procreative power and fertility in many myths and ancient ritual practices. For example, one of the oldest animal cults in Egypt was that of the bull Hapi, widely worshiped as a personification of strength and virility. The creator god Osiris brought the Nile into being, making the dry sands fertile, but it was the bull, the ox, whose strength plowed the land, preparing it for crops.[6] In Greek myth, Europa was raped by Zeus in the form of a bull, and Pasiphae, impregnated by a bull, gave birth to the Minotaur, which Theseus, the hero of Athens, had to slay.[7] In Scandinavian myth, the bull was an attribute of Thor and sacred as well to Freyja.[8] Celtic warriors aspired to the qualities of the bull, which, like horses, stags, and swans, was associated with the sun.[9]

The ancient religious and secular histories of many important cultures include the bull as a dominant figure. In the epic of the Mesopotamian hero Gilgamesh, Ishtar, goddess of war and sexual love, begs her father Anu, the sky god, to create the bull of heaven and thereby destroy Gilgamesh, who had rejected her.[10] The bull cult also appears in Sumero-Semitic religions, wherein the bull is worshiped as a sacred, fertilizing power. Canaanites, as well as the Syrian and Phoenician cultures, worshiped Baal as a bull. The Canaanite god Moloch, to whom human sacrifice was made, was bull-headed, and human-headed bulls guarded the palaces of the Assyrian kings.[11] Although Moses inveighed against the worship of the golden calf, the bull was sometimes revered as representing the god who had freed the Israelites from Egypt.[12]

In Christian iconography, the ox (along with the ass) is the invariable mute witness to the birth of Christ. This has been seen as an allegory in which the ass represents the God of the Old Testament and the ox stands for the God of the New Testament. Initiates at Mithraic mystery rites were baptized in the blood of a bull, and bull fighting, as still practiced in Spain and Mexico, is a remnant of the ritual slaughter of bulls that was a central part of Mithraic ritual. The bull was an attribute of Jupiter, the Roman sky god, who is sometimes depicted as having bulls under his feet. Perhaps because the horns of the bull suggest the shape of the crescent moon, the bull was also lunar and associated with goddesses like Venus and Diana.[13] In Hindu traditions, the bull is an attribute of Agni, "the Mighty Bull," and is one of the forms taken by Indra, chief of the Vedic gods. It is also the mount of Siva, Guardian of the West. In the *Vedas,* the holy texts of Hinduism, the sacred drink Soma was associated with the moon god, and the powers it conveyed were often equated with those of the bull.[14]

Its physical strength, dangerous, penetrating horns, imposing size, and powerful procreative capacity make the bull a symbol of power, whether in the form of sexuality, aggression, or simply an overwhelming force.[15] Some cultures have also noted that the skull of the bull bears more than a passing (if entirely coincidental) resemblance to the shape of the human womb with its uterine "horns." That association may certainly have bolstered the bull's regenerative symbolism.[16]

By its nature, the power of the bull is not controlled or well focused. On the contrary, although we put the ox in harness, we speak of the "raging bull" as a paragon of mindless, undirected power, or the proverbial "bull in a china shop" as clumsiness personified. Passion is only controlled as the toreador controls the bull — through skill, courage, and patience. The killing of the bull (ritually or otherwise) becomes a symbolic expression of the civilizing impulse — the triumph of human will and strength over the seemingly ungovernable instincts of wild nature. Yet the bull is a natural force that is not necessarily destructive; one of the primary challenges of spiritual maturity is to retain what is positive and necessary about instinct in an increasingly civilized world that discourages this influence.[17] The power of the bull's symbolism appears to be continually rediscovered, for example, in the rising and forward thrust known as a "bull market."

To dream of a bull suggests being called to face strong levels of internal aggression and sexual passion. Depending on the life context, it may also refer to one's "bullheadedness." Another possible meaning of a bull image in a dream could be "taking the bull by the horns," suggesting the need for the dreamer to direct and control his or her aggressions and passions more consciously. Various forms of sexuality and power usually dominate the symbolism of the bull, yet this animal image can also represent instinctual life. For example, the herd instinct, that inbred desire to adapt to collective norms, is as strong in cattle as it is in humans.[18] Consequently, in addition to power and passion, understanding the dream image of a bull may require a person to reflect on how he or she is ignoring the normative pressures of society. Dreaming of being chased by a bull might represent such a warning: flout these pressures, and they can trample you.[19]

Notes

[1] Grzimek 1984, 13: 331-32; Nowak 1991, 2: 1426.
[2] Grzimek 1984, 13: 332.
[3] Grzimek 1984, 13: 333.
[4] Grzimek 1984, 13: 334.
[5] Andrews 1993, 257.
[6] Budge 1969, 350-51.
[7] Johnson 1988, 296-97.
[8] Cooper 1992, 44.
[9] Cooper 1992, 44; Green 1992, 122-23.
[10] Kluger 1991, 79-137.
[11] Cooper 1992, 42.
[12] Johnson 1988, 316-17.
[13] Cooper 1992, 44.
[14] Ibid.
[15] Jung 1984, 25.
[16] Gimbutas 1989, 266.
[17] Aeppli 1943, 364; Jung 1984, 37.
[18] Jung 1978, 10: 448.
[19] Jung 1976, 1: 169.

BULL

Family: Bovidae.

Size: The Cape Buffalo's head-body length is 240–340 centimeters (95–134 inches).

Weight: The Cape Buffalo weighs approximately 800–1200 kilograms (1750 pounds).

Gestation: Approximately 9–11 months for the wild oxen, depending on the species.

Longevity: Maximum longevity of the oxen in captivity is 30 years.

Distribution: Wherever there is suitable vegetative food.

Habitat: Alpine tundra to tropical forest, usually near water.

Butterfly

One simply cannot help being struck by the fragile, vulnerable beauty of the butterfly as it flutters by in the final, winged, stage of its development. It is the archetype of metamorphosis — the profoundest sort of physical change — and the inescapable symbol of resurrection, as the worm-like caterpillar, a creature of the earth, transforms in its quiescent pupa stage and emerges from this still and death-like state as a gaudy, gossamer creature of the air.[1] The order Lepidoptera, which includes moths as well as butterflies, is one of the largest among the insects. Though the classifications are complicated, moths are predominantly nocturnal creatures, whereas butterflies are creatures of the sunlight.[2]

The developmental cycle of the butterfly occurs in four stages: egg, larva or caterpillar, pupa, and adult (also called imago). The larval stage, depending on variables such as weather and food supply, can last as long as three years, but is generally much shorter. The pupa stage, which can be anywhere from a week to several months in length, produces the most dramatic changes. The organs are dissolved, and the very substance of the caterpillar is re-deployed to create, as if from scratch, the moth or butterfly.[3]

Both butterflies and moths have their taste organs on their legs, making those appendages handy probes for determining if there is food value in the plants on which they land. Between the thorax and the abdomen are auditory organs capable of detecting the ultrasonic echolocating signals of the bats that prey on them.[4]

In orange and black, monarch butterflies, perhaps the most familiar of their kind in North America, are utterly dependent on the milkweed plant, which is their shield and sustenance. The monarch butterfly has developed immunity to certain toxic substances in the plant, which remain poisonous in its body and discourage predators, quick to learn its distinctive markings. Probably to ensure an adequate supply of milkweed, the monarch butterfly undertakes a unique yearly migration of as much as four thousand kilometers (twenty-five hundred miles) between summer breeding grounds in the northern United States and Canada and winter habitat in Mexico. This is extraordinary because monarch butterflies live less than a year, so the epic journey is made entirely by inexperienced individuals equipped with the most rudimentary nervous systems. The only conclusion that one can draw is that they are guided by instinct.[5]

The metamorphosis of lepidopterans is profoundly striking, with obvious intimations of immortality. So it is not surprising that the human spirit or soul assumes the form of a butterfly in many myths across the world. Especially in Eastern religions, with their emphasis on meditation, the utterly still, but profoundly changing pupa seems the very model of spiritual evolution through serene contemplation.[6] In Japan, the butterfly is symbolically identified with the blossoming of young womanhood,[7] while in China, it is associated with immortality, leisure, and the joyfulness of a young man in love.[8] The butterfly was an attribute of Xochipilli, the ancient Mexican god of vegetation. Its fluttering motion suggested the flicker of firelight. And the goddess Itzpapálotl was portrayed as a butterfly surrounded by stone knives. She was a night spirit associated with the stars, which also flicker or twinkle, and a symbol of the souls of women who had died in childbirth.[9] In Christian symbolism, this insect's metamorphosis represents the earthbound body of Jesus transformed into the luminous transcendent entity who rose from the tomb. For this reason, the butterfly is sometimes depicted on the hand of the infant Jesus. Christians of a bleaker, more pessimistic bent were inclined to point out the terribly short life and fleeting beauty of the butterfly, seeing it as a symbol for the emptiness of vanity and the ephemeral quality of life.[10]

The shortness of life, and the inevitability of death, does indeed give poignancy to the brief beauty of the butterfly. Like the great goddess who was worshiped in many cultures and known by many names, the butterfly has a deeply ambivalent symbolic significance. It is a vehicle of transformation that can not only raise us up magically but also stab us in the heart. Thus, in European folklore, the butterfly frequently shows a surprising demonic aspect. In Serbia, where belief in witches can be understood as a debased remnant of an earlier worship of the goddess in her destructive aspect, it is said, "Kill a butterfly and you kill a witch."[11]

On the one hand, the butterfly has positive connotations, often appearing in dreams as the return of "spirit" and "soul" — a revitalized sense of an inner life and purpose — that might have been missing amidst difficult life experiences, such as depression or anxiety. The butterfly can betoken the emergence of new parts of the personality, especially feminine aspects, and it may signify the constellation of a deep, self-healing process. On the other hand, the image of a butterfly also has negative implications that need to be taken into account in assessing its significance in a dream. We think of the "social butterfly" as flitting thoughtlessly from one place to the next — a beautiful creature, but lacking depth, focus, and endurance, thus implying an overly superficial attitude.

Notes
[1] Johnson 1988, 194.
[2] Grzimek 1984, 2: 316.
[3] Grzimek 1984, 2: 316-20.
[4] Grzimek 1984, 2: 320.
[5] Stevens 1990, C1.
[6] Johnson 1988, 194.
[7] Biedermann 1994, 53.
[8] Cooper 1992, 45.
[9] Biedermann 1994, 53.
[10] Charbonneau-Lassay 1991, 346; Becker 1994, 50.
[11] Gimbutas 1989, 275.

BUTTERFLY
Family: Lepidoptera (112,000 known species of butterflies and moths).
Size: The smallest adults are moths of the family Nepticulidae. The largest are the South American owlet moths.
Wingspan: The smallest nepticulidae measure barely 2 millimeters (0.08 inches); South American owlet moth measures approximately 32 centimeters (1.1 feet).
Weight: Large swallowtail weighs from 0.3 grams; the world's smallest butterfly, the Pygmy Blue, weighs only a few thousandths of a gram.
Longevity: Most butterflies, particularly those of temperate regions, rarely live for more than a week or two.
Distribution: Worldwide except Antarctica.
Habitat: Where plants grow to provide food.

Camel

Known to us primarily as the exotic mount of desert nomads, or as a plodding and imperturbable beast of burden in desert caravans, the camel once lived exclusively in North America. For the past ten thousand years, it has been extinct, outside of zoos, in the western hemisphere, although its close relative, the llama, remains native to South America.[1] Today, wild camels are found only in the arid steppes and deserts of Asia; in North Africa domesticated breeds are still the "ships of the desert." The bactrian, or two-humped camel, is of Asian origin, and the one-humped dromedary is primarily known in Africa.[2] With feet well adapted to walking on desert sands as well as rocky terrain, and the ability to go for extended periods without water, both species are unusually suited to hot, dry climates.[3] For perhaps as long as six thousand years, they have been invaluable transportation to humans wanting to cross the desert.

Camels are kept primarily for carrying loads, and to a lesser extent for riding, but their wool, meat, milk, skin, and even dung (an important source of fuel) are also valuable.[4] They are docile and trainable when properly handled, and they are said to bear their loads uncomplainingly if not overburdened by the proverbial "last straw." However, they are liable to fits of rage in the rutting season, and they will spit or even kick and bite when annoyed.[5]

A camel can lose as much as a quarter of its body weight in the hot desert sun without being in danger of death from thirst. How it manages such a feat has been the subject of much research and debate. One current theory is that the camel's fatty hump acts as a kind of thermal regulator, storing heat in the daytime and releasing it slowly at night, thereby avoiding the water loss that comes from more normal forms of regulation such as sweating or panting.[6]

Camels have a good sense of smell and the ability to close their nostrils against the dust and flying sand of desert winds.[7] They also have excellent hearing, but are said by their handlers to pretend not to hear commands.[8] Their highly flexible diet often consists of the kind of thorny plants, leaves, twigs, and dried grasses that other animals would refuse, although they will take the best of whatever they can get.⁹ Camels may live as long as fifty years.¹⁰ They mate throughout the year, preferring to copulate lying down, and pregnant females give birth to a single calf.¹¹

As with all animals, people tend to project qualities onto the camel suggested by some aspect of the animal's being, whether true or not. Thus, the face and carriage of the camel suggest haughtiness to some people and stupidity to others. Its minimal needs have in general made it a symbol of moderation and sobriety. For its willingness to shoulder burdens without complaint, St. Augustine (354-430) made the camel a symbol for the humble Christian. Because the camel was said to accept no load heavier than it could carry, it became a symbol of discretion to some people, and of laziness to others.¹²

Although camel drivers universally regard their charges as sly and stubborn beasts, intransigent in the extreme, filthy and sexually irrepressible, the word "camel" is a term of endearment in much of the Arab world.¹³ After all, the camel was the blessed mount of the Prophet. Elsewhere in the world, the word (or its cognates) is used to denote a large, stupid, lumbering or loutish person. The camel's size no doubt suggested the biblical proverb (Matthew 19:24): "It is easier for a camel to go through the eye of a needle, than for a rich man to enter into the kingdom of God."¹⁴

The desert, an unforgiving place offering little support and nourishment, can represent psychic states of feeling deprived and endangered without the waters of life, exposed without defenses to one's inner demons. Symbolically, the camel represents a capacity within a human being to traverse the "inner desert." The inner demons can be the cloudy, darker, less acceptable depths of one's personality, including instincts and passions, which can lead to depression. Thus, the desert is frequently associated with depression, and the camel stands for the ship of the desert. However, in a more positive light, the camel can also stand for the inner resources necessary to persevere with one's life and/or with creative work, tolerating and challenging the depression, irritability, and negative states of mind that inevitably emerge.

Dreams of a camel usually evoke the associated symbol of the desert and often represent a capacity to go through deep states of abandonment, loss, and loneliness — a process essential for maturity. Such states are commonly denied — literally pushed away from conscious thought, only to return and take their toll in the form of depression. A camel appearing in a dream may make the dreamer aware of such negative states, while stimulating the capacity to seek resolution and move on to a new consciousness.

Notes

1 Macdonald 1987, 499.
2 Grzimek 1984, 13: 139.
3 Burton 1981, 592.
4 Grzimek 1984, 13: 138.

[5] "Camel." *Encyclopedia Britannica*, 1997.
[6] Grzimek 1984, 13: 141-42; McFarland 1987, 563.
[7] Arnold 1992, 33.
[8] Lavine 1979, 43.
[9] "Camel." *Encyclopedia Britannica*, 1997.
[10] Nowak 1991, 2: 1357.
[11] Macdonald 1987, 513-14.
[12] Biedermann 1994, 56-57.
[13] "Camel." *Encyclopedia Britannica*, 1997; *Funk & Wagnalls Standard Dictionary* 1972, 184-85.
[14] Jobes 1962, 1: 280.

CAMEL
Family: Camelidae.
Size: Head–rump length is 225-345 centimeters (88-135 inches); body height with the hump is 190-230 centimeters (75-90 inches).
Weight: 450-650 kilograms (990-1430 pounds).
Gestation: 390 to 410 days.
Longevity: Up to 50 years.
Distribution: Asia and North Africa; llamas in South America.
Habitat: Arid steppes and deserts. Llamas are found in high–altitude plains, dromedaries in hot dry climates.

Cat

Elegant, poised, even regal of bearing, aloof and serene in repose, stealthy on the hunt, the cat has been dom-domesticated for more than four thousand years. Just as the ancient Egyptians worshipped cats as gods,[1] our modern Western society has expressed its devotion by treating its feline pets as beloved family members.

Probably descended from a small wild cat, *Felis sylvestris*, the common house cat, has been bred into more than thirty recognized forms ranging from the tiny Mexican hairless to the rather substantial and fluffy Maine Coon cat, with a myriad of promiscuously generated variations in between.

Even thoroughly domesticated cats, like dogs, can turn feral if abandoned, surviving in most climates through their enduring hunting skills. Indeed, in rural areas cats are often kept less as pets than as live rodent control. Even humans, especially if careless or thoughtless, can come out second best in a wrangle with a frightened or cornered cat, whose teeth and razor-sharp claws can be deployed with bewildering speed.

Cats have almost eerily acute senses, with powers of smell, and especially hearing and sight, far beyond human limits — not to mention extraordinary balance and lightning reflexes. Because their sensitivity to short wavelengths of light is six times that of humans, cats can hunt with great effectiveness at night. Their tactile sense is enhanced by feedback from their whiskers and the long sensitive hairs above their eyes and elsewhere, which help them maneuver in the dark. Their ears are highly mobile, almost instantly and reflexively so, which allows them to pinpoint the source of a sound with great accuracy. The position of the outer ear is also highly expressive. Turned-back ears are a sure sign of displeasure, if not anger.[2]

Persistent stories about a cat's ability to survive a fall by always landing on its feet are, within reasonable limits, justified. Cats are amazing athletes, capable of jumping and/or scaling great heights and performing acts of remarkable acrobatic prowess.[3] Domestic cats and some of their wild cousins at times create a kind of vibrating murmur in the throat, which we know as purring. It is widely thought that cats purr as an expression of pleasure or satisfaction, and indeed various humans take pleasure in just hearing (and feeling) a cat's purr. Nevertheless, this phenomenon is little understood.

Female cats may come into heat as many as five times a year. They can be quite active in attempting to initiate copulation. Tomcats respond to the female's wailing calls and hormonal scent with great alacrity and intense interest, but after coupling, they go their solitary way, playing no part in raising the kittens.[4] Females have highly developed maternal instincts, fiercely protecting, cleaning, and caring for their kittens. Indeed, mother cats have been reported rearing the young of other species, such as dogs, rabbits, and even mice.[5]

The Egyptians, who no doubt valued the cat for practical reasons, were the first to domesticate them. As one of the earliest urban peoples, they most likely had a rodent problem on their farms and in their granaries, as well as a problem with poisonous snakes. The cat became associated with the goddess Isis and closely identified with Bastet, a goddess of music, dance, joyous festivals, and other pleasures. Bastet also protected people from disease and contagion. Hundreds of thousands of carefully preserved cat mummies reflect the honor that was paid to cats as well as the significance of Bastet (or Bast, or Ubasti) in the Egyptian pantheon.[6]

From Egypt, cats made their way to Greece and Rome, where they were viewed as attributes of the goddess Artemis, or Diana.[7] Both the Greek goddess Hecate and the German goddess Hel had a black cat for a mount,[8] while the Norse goddess Freyja was pictured in a chariot drawn by cats. In Welsh mythology, an enchanted human in the form of the sow Henwen gave birth to the Great Cat, a terrible creature that could eat nine score warriors. Zoroastrianism puts cats in the service of the evil Ahriman, just as Christianity connects the cat with Satan, finding it an embodiment of lust and sloth.[9] In China, on the contrary, cats were thought to ward off evil spirits, and their images were often employed as a talisman for good luck.[10]

Like all nocturnal hunters, the cat has long been associated with the moon,[11] and therefore with the feminine aspect of things. The negative side of this is witchcraft; the cat has certainly suffered slander as well as slaughter for its supposed service as a familiar to witches.[12] In the Middle Ages, fearful, devil-hating Europeans ironically contributed to the spread of plague by burning cats in such vast numbers that the rat population skyrocketed, spreading fleas and therefore contagious disease in their wake.

Perhaps because cats can be observed "playing" with their victims (in reality just a manifestation of their innate, reflexive hunting skills), and because their sexual contacts are often bawdy, brazen, and loud, they came to be considered cruel, depraved, and evil. Even today the large eyes and unblinking gaze of the cat, its whole self-possessed manner, make some people extremely uncomfortable.[13] Ailurophobia, the fear of cats, is among the most common phobias in the world. The superstitiously inclined ascribe to black cats an extra degree of inauspiciousness. The notion that cats have nine lives, along with the similar idea that they always land on their feet, underscores the human feeling that they are, above all, resourceful and resilient.

Dreams of a cat can symbolize a self-centered attitude that can suddenly turn hostile when disturbed. It can also represent the capacity to enchant hypnotically or to beguile through visual contact. Because of its aloofness, the cat can portray a tantalizing, seductive object, something a person might want but cannot obtain. But it can also symbolize self-containment and contentment, even in an isolated condition. Perhaps the most significant meaning of the symbol of the cat in a dream is its capacity for ruthlessly and relentlessly getting what it needs or wants. Thus, to dream of a cat could stimulate the dreamer to think about his or her own needs and exactly how to gratify them.[14]

Notes
[1] Biedermann 1994, 59.
[2] Grzimek 1984, 12: 281-85.
[3] Dale-Green 1983, 17.
[4] Grzimek 1984, 12: 287.
[5] Hannah 1992, 66.
[6] Dale-Green 1983, 2, 72.

[7] Biedermann 1994, 59.
[8] Dale-Green 1983, 72.
[9] Cooper 1992, 48-49.
[10] Dale-Green 1983, 48.
[11] Dale-Green 1983, 12.
[12] Biedermann 1994, 59.
[13] Biedermann 1994, 59; Dale-Green 1983, 21.
[14] von Franz 1976, 186.

CAT

Family: Felidae.

Size: Males may reach 71 centimeters (28 inches), but 51 centimeters (21 inches) is a more usual length for females.

Weight: An alley cat may weigh up to 13 kilograms (28 pounds), while most domestic cats weigh 2.5-4.5 kilograms (6-10 pounds).

Gestation: Approximately 63 days, with an average litter containing four kittens.

Longevity: Up to 20 years.

Distribution: Cats have penetrated almost every continental habitat, including rain forest, desert, cold steppes, and mountains. They are not found in the treeless tundra region or on polar ice.

Habitat: Worldwide.

Caterpillar

In Lewis Carroll's *Alice in Wonderland,* the caterpillar is an enigmatic character who knows (as do all lepidopterans) the great secret of metamorphosis. The eggs of moths and butterflies hatch into caterpillars, simple creatures whose main function is eating to store up fat and protein in preparation for the eventual transformation into a fully formed adult moth or butterfly. Although the caterpillar is sometimes a symbol of lowliness because of its wormlike appearance, its metamorphosis can represent the reincarnation or transmigration of souls.[1]

The sense organs of caterpillars are rudimentary, but their mandibles are large and powerful. On their mouthparts are spinnerets from which they spin the silk for their tents and cocoons. Some caterpillars produce these silk threads more or less constantly, using them as mountain climbers use ropes, to climb where they could not otherwise go and to recover their position when they fall.[2] When the weather turns cold and food becomes scarce, the caterpillar establishes itself in a sheltered place.[3] Its body contracts, pulling in the feet, and from an opening at the top of its head, it spins silk thread in which it carefully winds itself. It then secretes a liquid that binds the silk into a seamless and impervious cocoon as it dries and nests in a kind of sarcophagus where the pupa will prepare for metamorphosis.[4]

Caterpillars are often strikingly colored and sometimes oddly adorned with warts or thorn-like projections on their bodies. Some are quite hairy, while others are quite smooth; some are well camouflaged, while others are difficult to miss. Camouflaged or not, they suffer a high mortality rate, falling victim to bad weather, birds, and other insects.[5] Those that survive the summer spin themselves a cocoon in the fall, within which they reorganize the constitution of their bodies and become a fully formed adult moth or butterfly.[6]

The ancient Egyptian religion, with its emphasis on reincarnation, was fascinated by the caterpillar, and it is not hard to imagine that mummification rituals were developed with an eye toward the creation of the cocoon. Similarly, the ancient Greeks were inspired by this transformation, placing representations of butterflies in their tombs.[7]

Because of its remarkable capacity for changing form, the caterpillar symbolically can represent transformation, development, and growth in the human being, or, in Jung's terms, the process of individuation. In this psychic journey old ways, attitudes, patterns of thought, and behavior lose energy and value (in effect, dying) and a new sense of inner life and psychic reality comes forth, symbolized by the butterfly/moth about to emerge. The conscious personality, or ego, must usually attend to this process through creative introversion. Thus, the caterpillar's retreat into the dark silence of the cocoon has been seen as a model for quiet withdrawal, spiritual focus, and meditation. Consequently, the caterpillar in dreams can be an image for an intermediate stage of personal development, characterized by the death of the old and the birth of new patterns of conduct and attitudes. Usually this image is accompanied by feelings of depression and despair, which in turn are signs that the conscious personality must embrace more introversion and revert to a state of "being" instead of "doing." The caterpillar signifies the remarkable, creative potential within the human being, out of which, like the butterfly/moth, a sense of soul is born.

More can be learned about the unique physical characteristics and symbolic significance of caterpillars by referring to butterfly and moth.

Notes
[1] *The Herder Symbol Dictionary* (1986), 33.
[2] Grzimek 1984, 2: 321-22.
[3] Grzimek 1984, 2: 316.
[4] Charbonneau-Lassay 1991, 345.
[5] "Caterpillar." *Encarta 97 Encyclopedia*, 1997.
[6] Charbonneau-Lassay 1991, 345-46.
[7] Charbonneau-Lassay 1991, 347-48.

Cheetah

Long of leg, small-headed, streamlined to a spotted blur when it makes its fatal dash, the cheetah is impressively athletic in general and extraordinarily well built for speed. Judging from fossil remains, it is little changed from its first known ancestors, which lived and died in the early ice ages.[1] Trained cheetahs were used for hunting for more than three thousand years by the ancient Sumerians, Egyptian Pharaohs, Mongol Khans, Mogul conquerors, and, more recently, European royalty with a special desire to hunt in pompous splendor. Cheetahs are extremely difficult to breed in captivity, so young adults were taken from the wild for this kind of training. The cheetah became extinct in India in the 1950s. The African cheetah still roams wild, but the now familiar loss of habitat to encroaching human land use and the wholesale slaughter for pelts in the 1960s has put this magnificent animal at the head of most endangered species lists.[2]

Because cheetahs are large, feline, and spotted, they are sometimes called hunting leopards — incorrectly, since they are classified in a sub-family apart from the big cats (lions, tigers, jaguars, and leopards). Despite their substantial size, they share several physical characteristics with smaller cats. Adults lose the ability to retract their claws, making their rather narrow paw prints unique among large cats. Their faces are marked by distinctive black stripes extending from the eyes to the corners of the mouth.[3] Cheetahs do not roar as the large cats do, nor do they mew like small cats. They make a surprisingly delicate chirping sound, among other vocalizations.[4]

The cheetah lacks the strength, weight, and crushing jaw power of its big cat cousins, and it succeeds as a hunter primarily by its ability to run down any prey — not necessarily over long distances (its stamina is not sufficient for that), but in short bursts. The extraordinary flexibility of its spine imparts a springing action to its stride that allows maximal extension of its already long limbs, making it the fastest animal on land — 75 kilometers an hour with a top speed of 110 kilometers for very short periods. It can accelerate from zero to 96 kilometers an hour in just three seconds — a feat few sports cars could match.[5]

Stalking with sharp vision as well as a keen sense of smell, cheetahs can take prey as large as wild ass, antelope, and zebra. More often, they take medium to smaller animals such as impala, dwarf antelope, blackbuck, or even rodents and rabbits. They will not eat carrion unless starving. Somewhat idiosyncratically, the cheetah will not pursue an animal that has escaped from its grasp.[6] Cheetah groups are not territorial in the usual sense, but family and *ad hoc* hunting groups do keep apart, marking "temporal territories" with their urine. Sexually paired cheetahs stay together for extended periods, sometimes for life. Cubs are raised and, after weaning, fed by both parents, who bring them food for a few weeks, then lead them to fresh kills to feed for themselves. Cubs have a high mortality rate — fifty percent in the first eight months — and are often killed by lions, though not necessarily for food.[7]

Because the cheetah's main distinction is its remarkable speed, which can symbolize a suddenness of attack from which flight is futile, to dream of a cheetah may call attention to the dreamer's capacity for sudden attacking behavior. These acts may be so quick and subtle — for example, quick sadistic repartee or a subtle envious undermining — that the victim may not even be aware of them. However, the cheetah can also represent the potential for quick and decisive action and might indicate, to someone who is particularly indolent or operates far too slowly in some situations, the need to respond more instinctively and with less reflection.

Notes
[1] Grzimek 1984, 12: 363.
[2] Grzimek 1984, 12: 363-69.
[3] Grzimek 1984, 12, 364.
[4] Nowak 1991, 2: 1094.
[5] Grzimek 1984, 12: 364-65.
[6] Grzimek 1984, 12: 365.
[7] Grzimek 1984, 12: 369-70.

CHEETAH
Family: Felidae.
Size: Head-body length is 112-150 centimeters (45-60 inches); tail length is 60-80 centimeters (25-30 inches); shoulder height is 70-90 centimeters (28-35 inches). Males are usually larger than females.
Weight: 35-72 kilograms (77-160 pounds).
Gestation: 91-95 days.
Longevity: Up to 12 years in the wild; up to 17 years in captivity.
Distribution: Africa, southern Asia, and the Middle East.
Habitat: Semi-desert, open grassland, and thick bush. Activity is mostly diurnal, and shelter is sought in dense vegetation.

Chicken/Hen

A domestic fowl in every sense, the highly social, gently clucking, broody hen is a cliché of the barnyard, not to mention an ubiquitous element of the human diet. Chickens belong to the order of gallinaceous birds, which include pheasants, partridges, quail, peafowl, turkeys, guinea fowl, and grouse. Descended from a wild fowl of India, they have been domesticated for at least four thousand years, but only in the past three hundred years have they been mass produced for their meat and eggs. In that time, many dozens of breeds and hundreds of varieties have been developed with an impressive range of body types, plumages, crests, wattles, and other physical features.

Though most breeds are capable of short flights, the chicken, with its heavy body and stubby wings, is essentially earthbound. Indeed, its feet are well adapted for digging or scratching up insects, worms, seeds, and the like.[1] Like many other animals, chickens in groups have a strict hierarchy of ranking, wherein more dominant birds will scratch or peck at the more submissive ones that trespass on their food, space, or reproductive prerogatives.[2] This famous "pecking order" aptly describes any number of human situations as well. In terms of intelligence, chickens are considered rather dim. Every chicken farmer can tell tales of nearly (or actually) losing a large number of birds in a storm because the poor things, gaping up at the rain, did not have the wit to shut their mouths and avoid drowning.

The reproductive system of the hen is highly developed. As with most domestic animals, human husbandry has altered and enhanced the thrust of evolution, resulting in birds that can produce as many as 250 eggs a year.[3] Periodically domestic hens turn "broody," stop laying and seem to want nothing more than to sit on their nests and hatch chicks. The male chicken or rooster has only a rudimentary copulatory organ, which is nevertheless adequate to impregnate a female. Indeed, one rooster may cover and fertilize a large number of hens.[4] Combined with the swaggering aggressiveness of the male, this may account for his strong association with male sexuality.

Chicks are physically precocious — they are able to walk and find food almost immediately upon hatching — and, at the same time, vulnerable — naked of feathers and dependent on the mother hen for warmth and protection. A mother hen, puffed up in her "broody" feathers and sheltering a clutch of chicks, may be the image of maternal devotion. Yet at some point, she will simply fly up to her roost and leave the chicks utterly to their fates. For their part, the chicks seem neither to miss or nor to recognize their mother.[5]

The adage "what comes first — the chicken or the egg?" links the two together; the symbolism of one is shared by the other. Eggs are traditional symbols of rebirth, creativity, and potential, and thus the chicken shares those qualities, sometimes betokening the birth of something new and significant. The fertility of the hen and the sexual aggressiveness of the rooster make them potent symbols of sexual union, especially when seen together. This may explain why at one time a rooster and a hen were carried before the Jewish bride and groom on their wedding day.[6] Jung connects the cock and hen to Mercurius' lustfulness, and thus they can also represent sexual passions that are lascivious and totally uncontained and which do not necessarily lead to union.[7]

As does any animal, the chicken/hen has both positive and negative symbolic connotations. For a person who is particularly flighty, the nearly flightless chicken may symbolize a positive kind of groundedness. However, for someone who is stuck in material things, it could represent a grounding inertia and the stifling of spiritual or intuitive impulses. While these are usually the most significant meanings of the chicken as a dream symbol, there are also others. We speak of a fearful or cowardly person as being "chicken," perhaps unable to rise to higher ideals of courage or loftier spiritual states, which may be one of the issues that the dreamer needs to face. The chicken can also symbolize particular aspects of a person's relationship to the maternal — a notion that may have prompted the creators of medieval bestiaries to liken the mothering hen and her brood to Christ and his flock.[8] Furthermore, the chicken and egg link could alert the dreamer to possible creativity issues and how he or she is relating to them.

Notes
[1] "Fowl." *Encyclopedia Britannica*, 1997.
[2] Smith 1975, 328.
[3] *Encyclopedia Americana* 6 (1991): 441.
[4] Smith 1975, 329; *Encyclopedia Americana* 6 (1991): 442.
[5] Smith 1975, 324.
[6] Hastings 1910, 1: 516.
[7] Jung 1976, 13: 278.
[8] Cooper 1992, 125.

CHICKEN/HEN
Order: *Galliformes*.
Size: Various breeds show great diversity in size and shape.
Weight: The Brahma cock weighs approximately 5 kilograms (12 pounds).
Incubation: The hen incubates the eggs for 21 days, getting up for only 15-20 minutes to forage for food. Eggs incubated artificially need to be cooled for the corresponding 15-20 minutes.
Longevity: 10 years.
Distribution: Worldwide.
Habitat: Ground.

Cockroach

Relentlessly invasive, pervasive, gluttonous scavengers, cockroaches are among the most primitive winged insects and have survived more or less unchanged for over three hundred million years. They are among the oldest fossil insects yet discovered.[1] Today, there are nearly four thousand separate species, most of which live in the wild. However, the shiny black common cockroaches, as well as the brownish American and German cockroaches, have established themselves among humans. Small, quick, omnivorous, and highly adaptable, they are very difficult to keep out of food and waste. Though neither poisonous nor parasitic, they are well established as carriers of human disease.[2]

The German cockroach is now the most common in areas occupied by humans, in part because the female may lay three or four egg capsules annually with nearly thirty eggs in each. When the eggs are hatched, the new cockroaches will reproduce within four to five months. Given an adequate food supply and an absence of predators (such as lizards, toads, and skunks), populations can multiply rapidly.[3]

Cockroaches vary widely in size, ranging from eight to forty millimeters (0.3 to 1.5 inches) in length for large tropical varieties. All have wings, and some can fly, but very few actually do so. Colors vary from pure white or colorless in cave-dwelling or otherwise subterranean species to striking shades of deep red, lime green, or even cobalt blue. Most move about by nimble scurrying. One species, *Diploptera punctata,* gives birth viviparously (most unusual for insects), even secreting a milk-like liquid that the embryos drink while still in the uterus.[4] When disturbed, some cockroaches secrete an odorous substance, which warns other roaches of danger; in addition, they may make warning noises by scraping the spurs on their feet along the ground.[5] Cockroaches, like many insects, have hairlike sensory organs called setae on nearly all parts of their bodies. The setae are exquisitely sensitive to vibrations and are one of the reasons it is so difficult to exterminate these pests.[6]

In some parts of Europe (notably France and Russia), the cockroach (much like the cricket or grasshopper) is considered a protective spirit; its presence in the house is welcomed as a portent of good luck, and its departure is considered an ill omen. Irish folklore includes tales of witches taking the shape of roaches. In certain cultures, the cockroach was used in folk medicine preparations for the treatment of urinary disorders, worms, and epilepsy, among other ailments.[7]

The cockroach, considered offensive because it feeds on waste, often represents unconscious thoughts or impulses that, because they are seen as repulsive or dangerous, have been deeply repressed. Yet cockroaches are themselves profoundly irrepressible. The adaptability of this very primitive creature, its fecundity, and its resistance in the face of determined efforts to eradicate it make it a very powerful symbol for the way intensely rejected fantasies or memories live on in the depths of the unconscious, deeply disowned by conscious awareness. Some scientists have hazarded the guess that cockroaches might well be the only macroscopic land animals to survive a nuclear holocaust. Consequently, this ancient insect becomes a paradoxical symbol of those parts of the life force that are both repellent and remarkably enduring.

Representing the reprehensible and discarded, the cockroach can stand for rejection of dark, shadowy elements of the psyche, or else extremely creative ones that endure for years, even though severely repressed. The cockroach might stand for very important, persisting truths that a person has disowned, neglected, and denied. Sometimes, these rejected feelings can cover a multitude of states, including envy, sexuality, union, a spiritual attitude, and deep creative ideals. When a person can sit and meditate on these feelings and allow them to germinate like the seeds of a flower in dark, damp soil of the soul, he or she may find that deeply held values and long-buried positive qualities begin to return. Accepting the distasteful feelings lets these personal values begin to return and effect needed change. The cockroach as a dream symbol can represent the psyche's readiness for such reflections.

Notes
[1] "Cockroach." *Encyclopedia Britannica*, 1997.
[2] Grzimek 1984, 2: 124.
[3] Grzimek 1984, 2, 127.
[4] Angier 1991a, C1, C8.
[5] Wootton 1988, 159.
[6] Wootton 1988, 48, 160-61.
[7] *Funk & Wagnalls Standard Dictionary* 1972, 240-260.

COCKROACH
Class: Insecta.
Size: The most common cockroach found in human dwellings through-out the world is the German cockroach, which has a length of 8-13 mil-limeters (0.30-0.50 inches); other species can be as large as 6 centimeters (2.4 inches).
Weight: Varies from 6-8 grams (2-3 ounces).
Incubation: 24-40 days.
Longevity: Over four years, during which time a female may lay more than 1,000 eggs.
Distribution: Cosmopolitan, not found in Polar regions.
Habitat: Warm, humid, and sheltered environment.

Cow

Huge grazing, ruminant beasts, placid and docile, cows are wet nurses, if not substitute mothers, to millions of people all over the world — a source of milk, cheese, leather, and meat. Kept domestically for perhaps eight thousand years (at first strictly for ritual purposes, later for meat, and only thousands of years later for milk), cattle are descended from wild aurochs. They currently number approximately 1.2 billion, widely distributed on the plains and savannas of subtropical and temperate climate zones.[1] A number of breeds have been developed specifically for dairy production; under ideal conditions a dairy cow may produce sixty-five hundred to ten thousand liters of milk in a year.[2]

Definitively gregarious, cattle will spread out to graze more or less randomly for up to eight hours a day.[3] They instinctively herd together when they sense danger and for warmth and security when they bed down for the night. They have an excellent sense of smell; their sight and hearing are adequate.[4] Cows have four stomachs — rumen, reticulum, omasum, and abomasum — an arrangement that allows them to derive maximum nutrition from a diet that consists almost entirely of grasses. Cuds, balls of partially digested food from the rumen and reticulum, are regurgitated and chewed a second or third time. The process is called ruminating.[5] Cows may come into estrus and mating may occur at any time of the year (a cycle lasting approximately twenty-one days). Bulls make hundreds of genital inspections each day, ever vigilant for receptive cows.[6]

Cattle society is hierarchical and quite stable, especially in free-ranging herds. Newly matured or arrived individuals must find their place in the pecking order, generally by means of pushing or shoving matches that are over in a matter of moments with no harm done. Obviously weaker individuals often submit without a fight, and amity is the general rule, although the more primitive subspecies are often more aggressive with one another. Animals of roughly equal status in the hierarchy will lick one another as a form of social grooming.[7]

Because of its value to humans, the cow has a major role in the mythology of many nations. The fertility rites of the Greek goddess Hera involved the sacred marriage of the lunar cow and the solar bull, a celebration of agricultural renewal. Sacred herds of cattle were kept at her temple at Argos. In the *Iliad,* Hera is described as ox-eyed, and she took the form of a white cow when she fled from the monster Typhon. She is also associated with the Moon Cow, Io, and early Greek travelers to Egypt closely identified Hera and Io with the Egyptian mother goddesses Isis and Hathor, who are also prominently associated with the cow.[8] In the Norse creation myth, a cow called Audumla was the first creature to emerge from chaos. Four rivers of milk flowed from her udders. The cow shaped the first man by licking salty blocks of ice. Celtic myth also honors the cow as a provider of nourishment and describes the magic cows of Manannan, which were always in milk.[9]

In Hindu tradition, the cow is sacred, revered as a provider of nourishment and associated with sacred fire. No one dares to harm the cows that wander freely in some areas of India, even if they create havoc in the streets and marketplaces. Buddhists find a parallel between cow and man in their progress toward enlightenment.[10] In China, the cow is symbolic of the earth and is therefore considered yin.[11] At the New Year, she represents the passing year, and her calf stands for the year to come.[12] For Native Americans, White Buffalo Cow, a figure of powerful medicine, brought the sacred pipe to the people for their rituals.[13] The children of Israel turned away from Yahweh to worship the golden calf, and since then, the cow has become symbolic of false gods — a political development that is common wherever matriarchal societies with female gods have given way to patriarchal dominance. Christian writers later reinterpreted the golden calf as a mammon or "demon of riches."[14]

Despite all its nourishing qualities, the cow, with its docile ways and placid, contented stare, has at times been made as the symbol of stupidity. However, while the cow processes food slowly in its ruminative way, it does so methodically and derives great nourishment from it.[15] Thus, the cow can psychologically represent an inner state of contentment and nourishment — passive being, rather than active doing. For someone who is too passive, the cow may be regarded as a negative symbol, representing a regressive, vegetative consciousness. In mythologies everywhere, the cow is associated with goddesses of death as well as birth, suggesting that the cow's peaceful, unintelligent gaze may carry a regressive hint of morbidity as well as of fecundity. The appearance of a cow in the dream of an excessively passive person would thus signify a need for more active behavior. However, where the individual is sufficiently active and inquiring, a cow could represent creative power that the dreamer can contact by exercising more patience and meditative restraint.

Notes

[1] Grzimek 1984, 5: 409-12.
[2] "Food Processing, Milk." *Encyclopedia Britannica*, 1997.
[3] Nowak 1991, 2: 1428.
[4] Macdonald 1987, 544-48.
[5] Encyclopedia Americana 1991, 6: 79-80.
[6] Grzimek 1984, 5: 412-13.
[7] Grzimek 1984, 5: 417.
[8] Johnson 1988, 277.
[9] Green 1992, 92; "Ancient European Religions." *Encyclopedia Britannica*, 1997.
[10] Becker 1994, 69.
[11] Cooper 1992, 62.
[12] Jobes 1962, 1: 376.
[13] Cooper 1992, 62.
[14] Charonneau-Lassay 1991, 63.
[15] Charonneau-Lassay 1991, 66.

COW

Family: Bovidae.
Size: Shoulder height of 90-110 centimeters (3-3.5 feet).
Weight: 450-1,000 kilograms (990-2,200 pounds).
Gestation: 277-290 days.
Longevity: May live more than 20 years.
Distribution: Worldwide — wherever there is suitable vegetative food.
Habitat: Savannas, subtropics, and temperate climate zones.

Coyote

Nearly ubiquitous in North America (although unknown elsewhere), the coyote is a canine predator, substantially smaller than the wolf, which is its natural competitor and sometimes its enemy. However, what the coyote lacks in size and strength, it more than makes up for in persistence, cleverness, and adaptability.[1] Like all predators, the coyote helps keep the animal population in balance; like all scavengers, it "cleans up" the environment, removing carcasses that might otherwise become a source of infectious disease. Akin to the wolf and jackal, the coyote can breed with domestic dogs, producing fertile hybrids, called coydogs.[2]

Like other canids, coyotes are social animals, using expressive postures, behaviors, scent marking, vocalizations (including howling), and even facial expressions to communicate among themselves. Although coyotes' howling is shorter and sharper than that of wolves, it is a haunting and lonesome sound.[3] Less shy of people than wolves, coyotes are wily scavengers, eating refuse, carrion, certain fruits, and grasses when they cannot catch small mammals, frogs, crustaceans, or occasionally fish or snakes. They are generally good swimmers and will take ducks and other waterfowl when they have the opportunity.[4]

Sometimes other predators like wolves, mountain lions, or golden eagles kill coyotes. Coyotes do not run in packs, but they will hunt cooperatively, chasing down prey in relays to conserve energy. There are reported instances of coyotes and badgers hunting together as a team.

As mammals go, coyotes make devoted couples, remaining paired for years and sometimes for life. Females fight more often than males, and when males do fight, it is inevitably over a female, which may then choose to have nothing whatever to do with the winner.[5] The mother gives birth to two to twelve blind and helpless pups, which she will nurse for ten days or more before

beginning to wean them to regurgitated meat. The father is protective and attentive, bringing food for the female and the pups until the female is able to resume
hunting. The pups begin to learn to hunt within two months of their birth, and
at around ten months they will start to leave home, finding their own way in
the world.[6]

In myth and folklore, the coyote is the consummate trickster — a figure of
humor and absurdity, sometimes a buffoon or a clown, an irrepressible and
ridiculous creature with special powers that invariably backfire. The popular
television cartoon character Wiley Coyote is a modern rendition of this image.
The coyote can also appear as a satyr-like sexual rascal, a four-legged Falstaff
and a bigger-than-life bad example, ready to take on every available female —
human or otherwise. It can be a creative force that steals fire for humanity and
reveals the secrets of sex. The coyote is a night-spirit that brings floods, death,
pain, and evil into the world — all in all a troublesome, deeply ambiguous figure, scourge and savior both.[7]

Coyote, as the Native American trickster figure, challenges the inevitable
rigidity of established order which can block the creative process, with spontaneity, humor, contradiction, and ridicule. With all its complexities, the coyote
represents a remarkable caricature of the creative artist, almost as if it embodies
not only creativity but also the disorder that accompanies creativity. Generally,
such trickster-like figures are very powerful indicators that an imaginative and
visionary impulse that flies in the face of existing morals and wisdom must be
recognized and engaged. If this impulse is not dealt with in a positive way, the
coyote image can take on an extremely negative quality and can lead to self-
destructive behavior, such as tricking oneself into feeling safe while engaging
in dangerous sexual, aggressive, or immoral acts.

If a person dreams of a coyote, perhaps he or she is shying away from a particular creative effort, fearing condemnation by the moral collective. Or it may
be that the person's creativity is being blocked by a too-rigid compulsive attitude. The coyote image could also suggest anxiety about sexuality, being excluded,
or being made to feel ridiculous by the "wisdom" of ordinary people, who
seem to know how to get on in their lives without new thoughts.

Notes
[1] Grzimek 1984, 12: 228.
[2] Grzimek 1984, 12: 234-35.
[3] Andrews 1993, 261.
[4] Grzimek 1984, 12: 228; Pfeffer 1989, 103.
[5] Pfeffer 1989, 103.
[6] Grzimek 1984, 12: 223, 228.
[7] Cooper 1992, 62-63.

COYOTE
Family: Canidae.
Size: Body length is 95–125 centimeters (35–50 inches); shoulder height is 45–53 centimeters (15–20 inches).
Weight: 15–20 kilograms (30–45 pounds), but in exceptional cases, coyotes can weigh almost 30 kilograms (66 pounds).
Gestation: 60–65 days.
Longevity: Up to 14.5 years.
Distribution: Throughout Alaska and Canada and most of North America extending down to Costa Rica.
Habitat: Open country and grassland; also occupy deciduous, mixed coniferous, and mountain forests.

Crab

The distinctive sidewise scuttling of crabs is among the oddest forms of pedal locomotion in the entire jointed world of arthropods, and it contributes (along with their armored exoskeletons) to the strange and somewhat unsettling impression that they make on us. Crabs, along with lobsters, crawfish, shrimp, and the like, are crustaceans — meaning that they have a crusty integument, a hardened skin, as opposed to a true shell. Most crabs also have a massive, bony, and shield-like carapace on their backs. Varying in size from the tiny long-beaked spider crab (half an inch in diameter) to the gigantic, forty-pound Japanese giant crab, which can be fifteen inches across the body and more than ten feet stretched out from claw to claw,[1] crabs

have adapted to a number of environments — from the deep sea to coastal waters
and from tide pools to dunes. Some land and fresh-water crabs never venture
near the sea at all.[2]

The majority of crabs burrow in sand or sediment, to lay eggs, to escape predators, or to lie in ambush for their own prey. The helmet crab has evolved a
second set of antennae that are modified to form an air tube for its gill chambers, enabling it to remain buried in the silt for extended periods. Other crabs
have evolved paddles on their hindmost legs to aid in swimming.[3] Although
not particularly appreciated for its intelligence, the spider crab festoons itself
with small green plants, sponges, or anemones, carefully choosing textures and
colors for maximum camouflage. If the crab is moved to a different environment, it will painstakingly and immediately strip off its "do" and redo it.[4]

Crabs must unite sexually to reproduce, but the female's hard shell lacks an
appropriate aperture. In order to mate, the female must first divest herself of
the old shell. The male then has a small window of opportunity to enter her
before the hardening of her new shell. The chosen male, tipped off biochemi-
cally by the female's secretions, jumps on her back and fends off rivals. He then
clings precariously to her carapace until the time is ripe for copulation.[5]

Like all crustaceans and many insects, crabs have compound eyes; they can
discern shape and color as well as orienting themselves toward the light. A particular sensitivity to polarized light allows them to navigate even on cloudy days,
and their field of vision, horizontally, approaches a remarkable 360 degrees. Some,
like the eerie-looking ghost crab, have eyes at the end of flexible stalks. Most
crabs are highly receptive to vibrations, whether at acoustic or mechanical frequency. Minute organs on the antennae, feet, and mouthparts are chemically
susceptible to taste and smell.[6]

Because nearly all crabs are creatures of inter-tidal habitat and nocturnal habit,
they are often widely associated with the governess of tides and mistress of the
night, that is, the moon. For the Incan people, the crab was an aspect of the
Great Mother figure who devours time and the ebbing moon. Like many animals that periodically shed their skins or shells, the crab symbolizes resurrection
and/or reincarnation. In Buddhist traditions, it is associated with the sleep of
death, the limbo state between one life and the next.[7] One of the more colorful beliefs of the ancient Babylonians was the notion that when the planets
lined up just so in the constellation of the Crab, the world would dissolve into
its primordial elements. Similar notions occasionally arise in various cultures
of India, Egypt, Persia, China, northern Europe, and pre-Columbian Central
America.[8] The authors of the Christian bestiaries, imagining that the crab tricks
the oyster by placing a pebble in its open shell, make the crab a symbol of
cruelty and deceit.[9]

The Latin word for crab, "cancer," became the name of the dreaded disease
since the swollen veins surrounding a tumor were thought to resemble the legs
of a crab. The crab's burrowing and hidden ways, its surreptitious speed, and its

methodical, tenacious, piece-by-piece consumption of scavenged food, suggest the deadly agency of the disease.

Concealment and regression dominate the psychological symbolism of the crab. Burrowed in the sand, hidden and armored in its shell, elaborately camouflaged, sidling and scurrying on tiptoe in a kind of ballet, the crab can be a caricature of a furtive soul with a secret. An animal of the margins between sea and land, breathing as well under water as above, the crab is a primitive creature, highly alert, sensitive, reactive, thrown up on our shores amidst the chaos of spume and surge, seeming to come from the very depths of the human unconscious. To dream of a crab, with its periodic molting and re-armoring, usually calls the dreamer's attention to the need for a rallying of strength, energy, and discipline as well as to the positive significance of regression and rebirth.[10]

Notes
[1] Jung 1975, 8: 241-43.
[2] Banister and Campbell 1988, 240.
[3] Ibid.
[4] Hillman 1983, 286-87.
[5] Banister and Campbell 1988, 241; Attenborough 1990, 300.
[6] Grzimek 1984, 1: 477-79.
[7] Cooper 1992, 63.
[8] *The Herder Symbol Dictionary* (1986), 48; Walker 1983, 183.
[9] Cooper 1992, 63.
[10] Hillman 1983, 286-87.

CRAB
Subphylum: Crustacea (with a large variety of sub-super orders and families).

Size: The Australian Tasmanian crab's main claw may be 43 centimeters (17 inches) long; the carapace of a very large specimen may measure 46 centimeters (18 inches) across. The giant crab, near Japan, occurs at depths of 50-300 meters (150-1,000 feet), and may be up to 3.7 meters or more from the tip of one outstretched claw to another. The body is about 37 centimeters (15 inches) across. The long-beaked spider crab has a body of about 1 centimeter (0.25 inches) in diameter.

Weight: Tasmanian crab weighs over 9 kilograms (20 pounds); Japanese crab weighs more than 18 kilograms (40 pounds).

Incubation: Little is known, but they probably pass through the zoea larval stage, and after several molts they reach the megalopa larval stage, which metamorphoses into juvenile crabs.

Longevity: Large specimens are probably more than 20 years old.

Distribution: All oceans, rivers, in fresh water, and on land.

Crocodile/Alligator

With their gaping, saw-toothed jaws, armored skin, and cold-blooded reptilian stare, the crocodilians (crocodiles, alligators, caimans, and the single species of Indian gavials) remind us of the terrible but long-gone flesh-eating dinosaurs of the Jurassic and Cretaceous eras. They are the largest and most dangerous of living reptiles.

Once classified together with lizards as saurians, crocodilians are lizard-like in shape but distinguished by protective armor of partially ossified plates that cover the skin. One distinction between alligators and crocodiles is that the former live almost exclusively in the western hemisphere (the exception is the rather smaller Chinese alligator). Alligators have broader, blunter snouts. Crocodiles have narrower heads, more pointed snouts, and at least two overshot lower teeth, which protrude when their jaws are closed.[1]

In the water, using their laterally flattened tails as paddles, crocodilians are powerful swimmers; on land, although they may look awkward crawling about on their bellies, they can manage surprising speed by raising themselves up and trotting along with legs extended. By regulating their buoyancy and center of gravity, they can float in the water with only their bulging eyes and prominent nostrils exposed. Most crocodilians have both upper and lower eyelids, as well as an inner, semi-transparent eye covering called a nictitating membrane. Pupils are vertical slits, a feature common among nocturnal predators. Uniquely among reptiles, they have external ears, though these are little more than a fold of skin that can protect the eardrum when the animal is submerged.[2] Crocodilians are air-breathers and spend time on dry land to bask in the sun, regulating their temperature (as all cold-blooded animals must). But water is their natural habitat, and they are capable of remaining submerged for as much as an hour.[3]

Crocodilians procreate, hunt, and feed primarily in the water. In a nest of decaying vegetation, females deposit a number of hard-shelled white eggs, which they coddle tenderly and protect fiercely for the eight to fourteen weeks before hatching.[4] They hunt fish, turtles, and other aquatic animals; they scavenge on larger mammals like hippopotamus and even elephants that may happen to die in or near the water. They are also capable of leaping out of the water with such explosive suddenness that they can seize and drag under animals many times their weight. Alligators do not generally attack humans, but crocodiles are notorious man-eaters.[5]

Fearsome as they are, the teeth of crocodilians are ill-suited for tearing their prey apart or even for chewing. Combined with the awesome closing power of the jaws, they are, however, perfect for clamping onto and holding their victims. Small prey is swallowed whole, but larger animals are often dragged underwater and stashed there until decay begins to soften the skin and flesh. The crocodile butchers its prey by clamping onto a piece of flesh and violently twisting over and over until a mouthful is torn loose from the carcass. Lacking a tongue, it must engulf its food with a series of jerks and tosses of the head.[6] Full-grown crocodilians have relatively few predators except large cats, especially jaguars, and human beings, who use them only occasionally for food but find them almost irresistible for stylish shoes, handbags, and stuffed souvenirs. Elephants or rhinoceroses defending their young also occasionally kill them.[7]

The American alligator is famous for its loud, sometimes individually distinctive roaring, which is most common among males at the breeding season. A round of calling may also be set off by thunder and (as was reported during the Battle of New Orleans) by cannon fire.[8] Non-vocal methods of communication include head slapping — a loud noise made by snapping the jaws together just at the surface of the water — and tail thrashing. Both produce sounds that carry over surprisingly long distances. Subtle twitching produces ripples and waves in the water that may also constitute a form of communication.[9]

No doubt because of the snap-jawed, dagger-toothed, big-mouthed orality of crocodilians, the anxious notion of the "vagina dentata" often creeps into crocodilian folklore, especially in the Western Hemisphere. In various Native American myths, the hero meets a woman who wants to have intercourse with him, although she has killed many men before him because of her toothed vagina. Being a hero, he overcomes this threat by putting sticks into her vagina, eventually knocking out her teeth. This can represent the capacity to actively confront castration anxiety and fear of the feminine and overcome them.[10]

The crocodile, for ages a significant player in the ecology of the Nile River, had special significance in ancient Egypt, where it was worshipped as Sebek, a powerful deity associated with the sun. Sebek is also connected with the demonic Set, the murderer of Osiris, who after his great crime hid from justice in the body of a crocodile. At times, the crocodile was associated with Ra, the sun god; Am-mit, the monstrous creature which is said to devour condemned souls, is depicted with the head of a crocodile. This transformation of the devouring, dangerous forces of the psyche into creative, protective ones is found in other cultural myths as well.[11] In Hindu mythology, the water god Varuna has a crocodile for a mount.[12] In Aztec mythology, where the power of the negative mother is especially extreme, a giant crocodile, Tlaltecuhtli, is considered "lord of the earth."[13]

Crocodilians are excellent mothers, as reptiles go, but in the paradoxical world of symbols and archetypes, they are associated with the dark, destructive side of creative energies and often represented as swallowing their young. The mundane allusion to "crocodile tears" denotes hypocritical remorse or a false show of tenderness.[14]

Crocodilians can also have positive connotations. Like all amphibians, they are creatures of transition, inhabitants of the fecund, muddy margins between earth and water, and thus, symbolically, between extremes like birth and death. As a result, they are often imagined as keepers of special knowledge and are strongly connected with the feminine principle.[15]

In areas of tribal Africa, the crocodile is sacred, considered by some to be the protective spirit of dead ancestors, and shamans use its various parts in ritual magic. In some regions, crocodiles were associated with notions of reciprocal justice; killing one was taboo unless it had killed a human. In Southeast Asia the reincarnated spirit of a dead ruler was believed to take the form of a crocodile, continuing to impose its authority through the fierceness of the reptile. In many places, crocodiles were thought to have special powers as the keepers and protectors of all knowledge and as guardian angels that could drive away evil spirits. In Indonesia, young girls were apparently sacrificed to them.[16] In a medieval Europe the crocodilians were associated with dragons, creatures of ambivalent significance — sometimes ravagers of damsels, destroyers of men, but also guardians of treasure, representing a person's deepest and most powerful psychic values.[17]

In dreams, a crocodile could symbolize a powerful, dangerous drive — cold-blooded both literally and in the sense of being emotionless — well beyond the governance of will, to drag down and destroy consciousness and feeling. It is a reminder of unspeakably ancient and unmediated instincts, voracious and brutal, which still lurk in the darkest recesses of our unconscious. On the one hand, images of alligators and crocodiles may denote a drain of energy, a loss of will, lethargy, a flooding of emotions, and represent the primal regressive pull to unconsciousness that the heroic impulse must overcome. On the other hand, these same impulses that the hero battles are often also divine, as in the mythology of ancient Egypt and in many so-called primitive tribes. In a human being, seemingly negative, destructive attitudes, upon closer examination, often turn out to be protectors. Always a terrifying image, yet often proving to be a protective one, the alligator or crocodile needs to be approached with a capacity to embrace its symbolic ambivalence.[18]

Notes
[1] Burton 1981, 197.
[2] Grzimek 1984, 6: 127.
[3] Ibid.
[4] Grzimek 1984, 6: 127, 138-41; "Reptile." *Encyclopedia Britannica*, 1997.
[5] Grzimek 1984, 6: 124-27.
[6] Grzimek 1984, 6: 136-37.
[7] Alderton 1991, 77.
[8] Alderton 1991, 73.
[9] Alderton 1991, 73-74.
[10] Gillespie and Mechling 1987, 81.
[11] Becker 1994, 72; Budge 1969, 1: 286.
[12] Andrews 1993, 354.
[13] Bonnefoy 1991, 1184.
[14] Jung 1984, 327.
[15] Andrews 1993, 354.
[16] Ross 1989, 161-62, 166.
[17] Andrews 1993, 355.
[18] Jung 1984, 327, 426, 645-46, 649.

CROCODILE/ALLIGATOR
Order: Crocodilia.
Size: Crocodiles up to 6 meters (19 feet). The American alligator up to 5.5 meters (18 feet).
Weight: A newborn saltwater crocodile weighs about 100 grams (3.5 ounces). An adult can reach almost 1,000 kilograms (2,200 pounds). Most adults weigh only 200-300 kilograms (440-660 pounds). The weight of the alligator depends on its captive or wild status, and on its geographical distribution. A 14-foot adult can weigh over 300 kilograms.
Incubation: 2-4 months, depending on region and species, for crocodiles; about 63 days for alligators.
Longevity: Maximum life span of the American alligator is 56 years.
Distribution: Tropical and subtropical regions.
Habitat: Crocodiles are mainly inhabitants of swamps, lakes, and rivers, although some species make their way to brackish water or to the sea.

Crow/Raven

Vaguely foreboding, even intimidating, with their challenging stare, inscrutable demeanor, and uncanny intelligence, the crow family includes the crow, rook, raven, and jackdaw. These are large, nonmigrating birds, most with glossy black plumage and a distinctive, harsh call that carries over great distances.[1] They typically have strong, substantial bills with bristly feathers at the nostrils.[2] Crows and ravens of the genus *Corvus* are nearly omnivorous, but favor carrion, which they reportedly have a mysterious ability to find. Often driven from a corpse by eagles or vultures, for which they are no match on the ground, ravens (the largest of the crow family) frequently turn the tables in the air, harassing golden eagles and other larger predators.[3]

Extremely intelligent, crows have been observed in South Pacific rain forests shaping twigs into hooks, which they use to extract worms and grubs from holes in trees and logs.[4] Sexually monogamous, crows live among an extended and cooperative family that may number fifteen or more and include as many as five generations. These family groups are territorial, but individuals from many families may mass in huge communal roosts to feed and socialize. They are quite playful among themselves, indulging in games of tug-of-war and other antics.[5]

The raven appears as a significant spirit for the Thlinkets and other Native American tribes of the Pacific Northwest coast.[6] It is an ambivalent figure, a greedy and deceitful trickster on the one hand, and a Promethian helper of mankind on the other. In various Native American traditions, Crow is a master of illusion and reality, a harbinger of change, and a shape-shifter capable of being in two places at once. In one story, the people are living in darkness until Raven steals light from the spirit people and brings it to man. In other stories, Raven brings fire to man and is the source of celestial fire — the sun, the moon, and the stars. To the Algonquin, Crow brought grains and beans, the first fruits of the earth.[7]

As shown by Edgar Allan Poe's nineteenth-century poem *The Raven,* crows give humans an eerie feeling. Being scavengers, both ravens and crows are bold and patient — a raven waiting for humans to walk away from the scraps of a picnic may stare in a most disconcerting way. Crows massed in a tree may jabber raucously, even taunting unarmed humans.[8] But just one shotgun blast can disperse them with eerie speed. Being natural consumers of carrion, ravens and crows are associated with death. The familiar banshee of Irish myth supplanted an earlier Celtic goddess of death called Morrigan, who had a terrible carrion-crow aspect, rending bodies to pieces, notably those fallen in battle.[9] Another battle goddess, Badb, whose name means crow or raven, symbolized war, violence, and evil.[10] In Roman myth, ravens and crows, then white as swans, were sacred to Apollo and watched over his lover at Delphos. But one day the crow brought bad news to the god, and all crows were turned black.[11] In ancient Greece, crows were considered unlucky, and although they were sacred to Athena, it was thought to be a sign of impending death if a crow alighted on a roof.[12]

The notion of the raven as a messenger is common. Noah released the raven to seek land after the flood, and the raven flew back and forth until the waters dried up (Genesis 8:9). In Japan, although the crow may be a token of bad luck, it is also depicted as a messenger of the gods.[13] Ravens are sometimes portrayed as the familiars of witches, and in Egyptian mythology, the crow was associated with evil and destruction. The ancient Hebrews considered it unclean and deceitful, associating it with death and destruction.[14] In alchemy, the raven represented the dark side of the soul, and alchemists used it as a symbol of the devil.[15] Ravens were thought to incarnate the souls of wicked priests, the damned, and those denied Christian burial. In some cultures, black can symbolize the void and the seeking of spiritual answers. Thus, nearly everywhere ravens and crows are suspected of preternatural knowledge, either of the future or of occult truths. In the Zoroastrian tradition, ravens represented purity and were sacred to the god of light and the sun.[16] A three-legged crow was worshiped in China as a symbol of solitude.[17]

When the crow or raven represents the trickster-like quality of Native American folklore, where it can change shape and be many different entities,[18] it can stand for deep aspects of our being that do not have the clarity of consciousness. It can represent hidden potentials within us, ambiguous but essential to the creative process. The crow, like other animals, can also stand for deep psychic life — far from consciousness, far from the world, an essential instinctive quality in the human being. Consequently, it may portray patterns that have not undergone the human capacity of separating, differentiating, and valuing.

When crows and ravens appear in dreams, they can come as enigmatic messengers or as harbingers of a need for introspection that may have a melancholic quality. Their presence can represent an inner change in which certain attachments of desire have been released, and bring a kind of gloominess, which can help the dreamer understand that there is meaning in a process that might appear to be just despair or depression. The crow/raven in dreams can also represent an emerging intuition or awareness, or else a dark, dangerous thought or fantasy that could be destructive if acted upon. In addition, the crow/raven can portray the need for the conscious personality to be more of a thief, for the person to dare to engage and nurture the creative process within. The bird's appearance in a dream can also be a signal that something deeply traumatic from the person's past is emerging. But it can bring to life a spiritual fire of warmth, emotion, and creativity, pulling the person out of the depths of darkness and into consciousness.

Notes
[1] Grzimek 1984, 9: 519.
[2] Perrins and Middleton 1989, 444.
[3] Grzimek 1984, 9: 519.
[4] Browne 1996, C1.
[5] Brody 1997, F1.
[6] Hastings 1910, 510.
[7] Cooper 1992, 69; Hastings 1910, 510.
[8] Andrews 1993, 130.
[9] Neumann 1963, 164; Gimbutas 1989, 209.
[10] Cooper 1992, 193.
[11] Andrews 1993, 130.
[12] Cooper 1992, 68.
[13] Ibid.
[14] Cooper 1992, 192.
[15] Jung 1976, 14: 734 note, 741.
[16] Cooper 1992, 192.
[17] Andrews 1993, 131.
[18] *Funk & Wagnalls Standard Dictionary* 1972, 266.

CROW/RAVEN

Family: Corvidae (Raven is the name for the largest and most characteristic of the crow-like birds).
Size: 15-65 centimeters (6–26 inches) long.
Wingspan: 91 centimeters (36 inches).
Weight: Approximately 1,250 grams (2.7 pounds).
Incubation: 16-22 days.
Longevity: Maximum recorded in captivity is about 29 years; other adults of the crow species do not live to be older than 10 years.
Distribution: North America, northern Europe, the Near East, and Africa.
Habitat: Varied, including forests, farmland, grassland, desert, steppes, and tundra.

Deer/Moose/Reindeer/Elk

Swift in flight and subtle in hiding, deer are the hunts- man's classic quarry, both the sweet-eyed doe and the proud stag. Creatures of wood and plain, swamp and tundra, cervidae range in size from the stately moose and mighty elk to the diminu- tive mouse deer, no bigger than a rabbit. All are ungulates, having evolved hooves in place of claws, and rumi- nants, having a multiple-sectioned stomach to help in digesting cellulose fiber. Deer are capable of leaps 3 meters (9.3 feet) high and up to 12 meters (39.6 feet) long, and they are excellent swimmers.[1] Most are social to some degree, and some undertake seasonal migrations. Their diet is completely herbivorous.[2] Before giving birth, eight and a half months after copulation, the pregnant doe will chase away her young from the previous year, separating herself from the herd for the actual birth, which may take less than ten minutes. She will then keep her newborn hidden in a thicket for several days, coming to it only for feeding.[3]

Although some species lack antlers, they are a distinguishing characteristic of most male deer. In reindeer (caribou), they are found on both sexes. Sexual orna- ments as well as weapons, the antlers are not horns, but twin sets of branched, bony outgrowths from the forehead that in most cases are shed annually.[4] The deer's antlers are much prized as trophies, as well as for medicinal properties ascribed to them by various traditional cultures. Antlers, especially new antlers in the so-called "velvet" stage, are considered potent medicine in the Orient; in various forms they are used for a wide range of cures and therapies — so much so that a number of species have been threatened with extinction. Unlike rhinoceros horn, which is falsely supposed to have aphrodisiac powers, the "velvet" of new deer horn holds powerful hormones that evidently have a heal- ing effect.[5] When a stag fights for dominance, his antlers are used less as weapons than as a kind of grapple with which the two competitors push and pull in a contest of strength. If antlers become locked and they cannot be separated, both parties will die of starvation.[6]

Ranging over polar regions, tundra, and northern woodlands of Europe, Asia, and North America, reindeer are forced to migrate seasonally because of the severity of their habitat. Males are larger and heavier than the females. Reindeer antlers are distinctive for their flattened cross-section, light color, and asymmetrical shape. Reindeer are the only truly domesticated species of deer.[7]

The North American moose is the largest and probably the most distinctive deer extant today. This often solitary beast has an uncanny ability to camouflage itself standing motionless in a marshy pond or, even more remarkably, moving silently and speedily through the woods. Although its large size and long spindly legs make it appear awkward, the moose is remarkably agile and well adapted for moving through deep marshes and heavy snow. The moose's short but broad antlers, flattened into a form that is almost like the palm of a hand, with many finger-like tines or snags,[8] are used both as offensive and defensive weapons. It has just two enemies: the grizzly bear, which it can outrun, and humans.[9] Because it can charge aggressively at forty miles per hour, the moose can be dangerous, much feared by people who live in its vicinity. When a deer and an automobile collide, the deer is invariably killed, but when a moose and an automobile collide, the driver is more likely to be killed or seriously injured and the car is surely demolished.

The European elk *(Alces alces)*, the largest existing deer of Europe and Asia, resembles the moose. While it prefers to congregate with its own gender, the elk lives in herds and interacts with others of its species. Speed enables it to escape predators. The elk is herbivorous, with substantial fur that keeps it warm during extreme cold weather.[10] While it stands for endurance and hardiness, supernatural powers are also attributed to it. The elk was a totem of the Native American Omaha people.[11]

As a favored prey of early man, the deer has always had a certain mystical potency. Stags, and humans dressed as stags, appeared in Paleolithic cave paintings; as part of the magical rituals attending the hunt, the identities of hunter and hunted merged.[12] Symbolically, the proud antlers of the stag seem to embody male strength, domination, and power to command. Thus, the magic wand and the scepter were made of stag horn in the very oldest human societies, and kings often wore crowns of horn.

The deer's antlers have important, multifaceted meaning for numerous cultures, and they can represent various conditions that are beyond the factual life of the animal. The tree-like antlers of the stag connect it with the "Tree of Life" and with fertility as well as spiritual growth.[13] In Norse mythology, Yggdrasil is the world-tree, and in its four branches, stags graze, eating buds representing the hours, blossoms representing the days, and branches representing the seasons.[14] Thus, early humanity saw a remarkable quality of life and its renewal in the antlers of the stag.

The symbol of the deer also has a strong connection with the feminine. Myths of deer-women who rule the world still have some currency among the more traditional hunting people of northern Europe. The image of the gentle-eyed doe is often used for adult female animals such as the rabbit or kangaroo, where the male is called a buck, and is sacred to various goddesses associated with birth.[15] In Greek myth, the deer was sacred to the goddess Artemis, the legendary huntress, who was often transformed into a deer, giving credence to the idea that the hunter and hunted are frequently the same.

The deer is also a powerful image in alchemy, representing the alchemical mercury, which can stand for the fleeting, changing, and illusory quality of unconscious fantasy. In the ancient world, as recorded by the Roman author Pliny and others, one finds the notion that a deer struck by an arrow would find the curative herb "dittany," which would cause the arrow to fall from its side.[16] The struggle of the stag is a recurrent theme in European lore. The *Physiologus* speaks of ancient beliefs that the stag (represented by "flowing waters of wisdom," which became symbolic of Christ) killed the dragon/serpent/snake, symbolic of the Devil. The image of the stag as the enemy of the serpent continues today.[17]

The deer's home is the wilderness, which is as unfathomable as the sea and an equally appropriate symbol for the unconscious. As the hunter stalks the innocent hind or hart, that gentle creature, sure-footed and elusive, draws him farther and farther into the wild, and so becomes, in psychological terms, a psychopomp — a soul-guide. The organized nature of the hunt, its highly focused intent, seems to suggest a salient consciousness, which through the mediation of the deer image invades or probes the unconscious with purpose. Moreover, this excursion into the wilderness, led on by fleeting glimpses of the quarry, increasingly isolates the hunter from civilization — from the collective wisdom and security of society — until finally, he or she is in peril. The full metaphorical significance of the deer lies in the crucial ambiguity of its pursuit — one may achieve one's goal and expand consciousness, or else be overwhelmed by the wilderness and die.[18]

The guiding quality of the deer is probably its major symbolic significance. When this animal appears in a dream, it is important to consider whether the dreamer needs to make a deeper journey into his or her unconscious. Possibly this person has been too focused on solid reality and scientific ways of being, avoiding the guidance of swift insights. A deer appearing in a dream could imply that his or her life requires renewal — that it has reached a point where attitudes, like the antlers of a deer, must be allowed to die or change. Thus, the deer can be an extremely important symbol of revitalization through deeper exploration of the unconscious.

The image of a moose implies different qualities. Unlike the deer, it is a solitary animal, and consequently represents the loneliness commonly associated with the process of individual growth, often associated with depression. Hence, the appearance of a moose in a dream could signal that depressive feelings need to be understood as a call for creative introversion rather than as a manifestation of pathological disorder. The moose, dangerous and quick to aggression, would represent these powerful forces often associated with depression and which the dreamer must assimilate into his or her own conscious personality.

An elk appearing in a dream would not have the same dangerous quality, but it does represent extremely potent energies that can be helpful or harmful. In many Native American Indian mythologies, the elk has to be vanquished; in some stories the elk guides the hero into the forest or carries him on a journey. The elk could thus represent an effective guide in the process of individuation, in contrast to the moose's solitary and more introverted disposition.

Notes
[1] Burton 1981, 596.
[2] Nowak 1991, 2: 1362.
[3] Grzimek 1984, 13: 154.
[4] Nowak 1991, 2: 1362.
[5] Grzimek 1984, 13: 155-56.
[6] Grzimek 1984, 13: 181.
[7] Grzimek 1984, 13: 238.
[8] Grzimek 1984, 13: 230-31; Andrews 1993, 286-87.
[9] Attenborough 1990, 199-201.
[10] Andrews 1993, 270-71.
[11] Cooper 1992, 95.
[12] Becker 1994, 279.
[13] Becker, 1994, 279-280.
[14] Biedermann 1994, 92.
[15] Gimbutas 1982, 171.
[16] Cooper 1992, 70.
[17] Curley 1979, 58-60.
[18] von Franz 1975b, 86-87.

DEER/MOOSE/REINDEER/ELK
Family: Cervidae.
Size: Shoulder height ranges from 38 centimeters (15 inches) in the Southern pudu to 230 centimeters (90 inches) in the moose.
Weight: From 8 kilograms (17.5 pounds) for the Southern pudu to 800 kilograms (1,750 pounds) for the moose. The antlers of the moose can weigh more than 20 kilograms (44 pounds).
Gestation: 24-40 weeks, according to species.
Longevity: Normally 12-15 years for reindeer and caribou (over 20 years in some rare cases) and 20-25 years for moose.
Distribution: North and South America, Eurasia, and northwest Africa (introduced to Australasia).
Habitat: Mainly forest and woodland, but also arctic tundra, grassland, and mountain regions.

Dog

Not exactly the nearest neighbor on the taxonomic tree of life but reputedly "man's best friend," the domestic dog comes in a stunning range of sizes, shapes, traits, and personalities. From the enormous English mastiff to the tiny Mexican hairless, all are descended from the wolf, which can, theoretically, breed with any of them.[1] Dogs have no doubt benefited from their ancient partnership with human beings, but, evolutionarily speaking, they have paid a price as well. Their brains are thirty-one percent smaller than those of wolves, and their sensory acuity is much diminished.[2] Dogs, like wolves, are territorial, hierarchical, and social animals, instinctively deferential to the dominant or "alpha" dog.[3]

The association of dogs and humans is ancient, going back perhaps fifteen thousand years. Dogs scavenging at the periphery of human hunting camps and habitations were probably tolerated for their alertness to approaching game or danger. Semi-domesticated dogs were certainly used for hunting long before they were fully domesticated, and later they were trained to herd and protect livestock as well as to defend homes. Smell is their forte, although they hear almost as well as cats and have a notable sensitivity to sounds in the twenty-kilohertz range, which are inaudible to humans. Their vision is not particularly sharp, and they are not very good at recognizing motionless animals or objects.[4] Female dogs come into heat twice a year, bearing litters that range from three to ten puppies — born blind and more or less helpless.[5] With billions of dollars spent annually on the care and feeding of dogs, the integration of dog and human society has never been more thorough. There are guard dogs, attack dogs, seeing eye dogs, police dogs, hunting dogs, bomb-sniffing dogs, drug-sniffing dogs, dog movie stars, dog hotels, dog fashions, and even dog cemeteries.

Dogs have often been symbolically linked to the concept of healing. Aesculapius, the Greek god of medicine, had a dog for a companion; the Sumarian goddess Gula, who as a healer restored life to the dead, was depicted with a dog beside her throne.[6] Like many animals, dogs will lick their wounds when they are hurt, and there is a widespread folk belief that a dog's tongue (or saliva) has healing qualities. Dogs will also attempt to heal themselves by eating grasses when they are sick, and they have even been credited with an herbalist's knowledge of just which grasses will do the job.[7]

Since animals usually represent instinctive life, those that willingly consort with humans, such as dogs or cats, have historically been accused of being familiars — creatures of witches, necromancers, or the devil.[8] The Black Dog, a spectral canine with fiery eyes, is a perennial motif in tales of hauntings, and usually a portent of death.[9] The Greek deity Artemis, called Diana in Roman mythology, was the goddess of wild animals and childbirth. She hunted with her dogs, which metaphorically represented her relationship to the creative and instinctual life. When the Boeotian hero Actaeon offends her by spying at her bath, thus showing a lack of deference toward the great goddess, she causes his own hounds to tear him apart.[10] In psychological terms, Actaeon fails to understand boundaries and allows himself to become too drawn into the sphere of the gods. This is an inflation, a grandiosity and lack of discrimination, which leads to his death, through the psychotic disintegration that can follow from inflation.

Given their instinct to guard, dogs have long been associated with guarding real thresholds. So, it seems symbolically apt that one be placed at the boundary between the world of the living and that of the dead. In Persian mythology, two four-eyed dogs guard the Chinvot Bridge between those worlds. In Hindu myth, the sun and moon dogs of Indra are guardians, and several Native American peoples incorporate similar notions in their mythologies. Another Greek goddess, Hecate, who had power over heaven, earth, and sea and presided over magic and spells, is associated with dogs; she is identified with the original hellhound, Cerberus, the three-headed dog that guards the gates of Hades. In Norse mythology, a dog Garm, guards the entrance to Niflheim, the dark realm of the goddess Hel, and bars the entrance of any living soul.[11] Anubis, the Egyptian god of the land of the dead, is pictured with the head of a dog.[12]

Judaism and Islam do not hold the dog in much esteem. Both consider it an unclean scavenger, ritually taboo. In Islam, "dog" is a term of shame and dishonor for unbelievers. In Christian culture, the dog represents faithfulness. Fido, a favorite pet name for dogs, means "I am faithful" in Latin.[13]

Occupying a threshold between the world of the living and the dead, a faithful friend and guardian of Hades, the dog can symbolize a connection between consciousness and the unconscious.[14] Dogs are extremely sensitive to how they are treated, so a person's abuse of his or her body — a chronic refusal to listen to bodily feelings, symptoms or other forms of the language of the body such as anxieties or energies — can take the dog-image into a negative form. The notion of a dog that "turns" on his master remains particularly potent and disturbing because it powerfully underscores how a wrong attitude can have a devastating effect on one's bodily life, something that one expects to be able to rely upon most deeply.[15] The dog can become "mad," a carrier of hydrophobia (rabies), which results in a short period of excitation characterized by restlessness, nervousness, irritability, and viciousness, followed by depression. In humans, this may represent fear of the unconscious, that part of a person that he or she knows is there but cannot yet understand.

Dreams about dogs can have a wide-ranging significance. On the one hand, one should always be aware of the possible sexual significance of the animal and its effect on the dreamer's life. The appearance of a dog in a dream might suggest a need to listen with more attention to personal instincts rather than to take a rational, scientific approach to daily actions and attitudes. Since the dog is closely related to bodily knowledge, dreamers might consider how they need to be more aware of the wisdom of their bodies and their physical symptoms and to engage the body's healing potential, allowing imagination free rein.

Notes
[1] Grzimek 1984, 12: 199.
[2] Grzimek 1984, 12: 211.
[3] Grzimek 1984, 12: 196.
[4] Grzimek 1984, 12: 196-223.
[5] Grzimek 1984, 12: 223-27.
[6] Woloy 1990, 24-25.
[7] Hannah 1957-58, 104-05.
[8] Biedermann 1994, 97.
[9] Cooper 1992, 78.
[10] Jung 1976, 14: 188.
[11] Woloy 1990, 36-37.
[12] Hannah 1992, 97.
[13] Cooper 1992, 74, 77.
[14] Schwartz-Salant 1982, 118, 123.
[15] von Franz 1975b, 95.

DOG

Family: Canidae.
Size: The fennec fox has a minimum adult head-body length of 24 centimeters (9.5 inches), while the gray wolf is up to 200 centimeters (6 feet, 7 inches) in overall length.
Weight: 0.8 kilograms (1 pound) for the fennec fox to 80 kilograms (175 pounds) for the gray wolf.
Gestation: 9 weeks.
Longevity: Dogs enter old age when they are about 12 years old. Sometimes, they live up to 20 years.
Distribution: Worldwide.
Habitat: Evolved in open grasslands but now adapted to an exceptionally wide range of habitats.

Dolphin

Benign, friendly, intelligent, and graceful, the dolphin is an aquatic mammal with which perhaps humans feel a special affinity, more than with any other wild animal. Like children, dolphins frolic and jump in the ocean, seeming to laugh and invite us to play with them in the great waves. However, recent observations have revealed a dark side to this playfulness and the benign image of the dolphin. They can and do slay their fellow mammals, attacking people by using their beaks as cudgels and ripping them apart with their sharp teeth. These destructive impulses seem to be independent of the need for food. In addition, dolphins have been observed in recurring acts of infanticide.[1]

Dolphins belong to the suborder of toothed whales (Odontoceti), which includes whales, dolphins, and porpoises.[2] Some confusion exists concerning names, with a popular tendency to call any large dolphin a whale and any small whale a dolphin. It is the bottle-nosed dolphin that most of us have in mind when the word "dolphin" is used.

Dolphins are highly social animals, often gathering in large herds. They seem to be attracted to ships and are famous for their playful, leaping antics as they circle, chase, and lead. Like bats, they use focused "beams" of sound to navigate; there is evidence that failures of their "sonar" are responsible for the well-publicized groundings of large numbers of dolphins. Their clicks, whistles, and other high-pitched vocalizations are also used for sophisticated communications, which may help the social groups coordinate travel, hunting, and defense, and perhaps serve other purposes. Dolphins have a very large and highly developed brain, and some scientists have gone so far as to suggest that in many ways their brain is superior in development to our own.[3]

Groups of dolphins may temporarily split up into smaller "clans," and then merge back into the herd at large. These divisions may help the dolphins evade sharks (their primary enemies now that they are rarely hunted by humans) and forage more effectively for fish. Recent research has also shown that male dolphins form teams that seem designed to "rape" or seduce fertile females belonging to rival groups. Once the females are separated from their groups, the males perform a kind of synchronous and highly athletic ballet to impress them. Females often play along, but if they attempt to flee, they may be "mobbed" — treated quite roughly and sometimes even seriously injured. Eventually, the female will copulate with one or more of the males. Females also form groups that seem meant to foil male plans, sometimes managing to free their beleaguered sisters. Such dynamically changing social alliances may have been a spur to the evolution of the dolphin's high intelligence.[4]

The dolphin has an extraordinarily positive reputation. In myth and legend and persistent anecdotes, shipwreck victims or other helpless swimmers have been saved from sharks and/or drowning by dolphins. Telemachus, the son of Odysseus, was saved in this way, prompting his father to place a dolphin emblem on his shield.[5] The Roman author Pliny tells of a friendship between a young boy and a dolphin, somewhat similar to the enormously popular *Flipper* movies of the 1960s. Recent scientific studies have given such stories more credibility, and at aquariums and Marinelands all over the world, people can see the level of training or "cooperation" these mammals can achieve. Some researchers even believe that unparalleled levels of interspecies communication may eventually be possible between dolphins and humans.

The dolphin was an attribute of Poseidon, the Greek sea god, and Aphrodite, Greek goddess of sexual love and beauty, was born from the sea foam and often depicted with dolphins.[6] The Greek god most closely associated with dolphins was probably Apollo. Known as Phoebus Apollo, the sun god, he was also called Apollo Delphinos, because he could take on the form of a dolphin; as a result, his famous oracle was called Delphi. The connection brings together the symbolism of the masculine sun god with the feminine significance of water. The story of the Greek bard Arion's rescue by dolphins was used by Christians to create a parable of converts saved by the waters of baptism.[7]

A mammal, an air-breather like humans, a land-dweller that reversed the usual trend of evolution and returned to the sea, the dolphin is a rescuer of people in myth and fact. Psychologically, the dolphin can represent the inner capacity to buoy up a person, nudging and directing him or her to a safe shore. The dolphin also represents the remarkable, spontaneous order-producing quality of play, especially the capacity to be playful amidst terror and extreme emotion. Therefore, a person dreaming of a dolphin may need to expand awareness to include the powers of play and imagination. They may need to experience how "non-serious," yet active and focused behavior can bring the self — the innate organizing principle of the psyche — into relationship with consciousness. The dolphin must also be considered in terms of its dark side. The person dreaming of the dolphin must consider whether he or she is secretly a predator, imaginally tearing others to pieces through envy or deep-seated hostility. Psychic health always requires a balance between opposites, such as the creative and destructive potential of the dolphin.

Notes
[1] Broad 1999, C1.
[2] Grzimek 1984, 11: 542-43.
[3] Angier 1995, 32-33.
[4] Ibid.
[5] Grzimek 1984, 11: 508.
[6] Biedermann 1994, 99.
[7] Cooper 1992, 79.

DOLPHIN
Family: Delphinidae (with 14 genera and about 32 species).
Size: 1 to 4 meters (3-13 feet long).
Weight: The male *Coryphaena hippuras* can weigh up to 30 kilograms (70 pounds).
Gestation: 10-12 months.
Longevity: The bottle-nosed dolphin lives for 20-25 years.
Distribution: Throughout the world's oceans and some rivers.
Habitat: Rivers and oceans.

Dove/Pigeon

Whereas doves are lovely and innocent — avatars of peace and love — pigeons are considered by some to be dirty, disgusting birds — avatars of nothing except perhaps the defacement of public statuary. Yet doves and pigeons share a wide range of physical characteristics, and both belong to the avian family Columbidae. Their small heads, full, large-breasted bodies,[1]

and distinctive, cooing call make them easily recognizable. While the word "pigeon" is inclusive, smaller species are generally called doves and larger ones exclusively pigeons. In practice, the usage overlaps substantially.

These birds have two unusual physical characteristics. Both male and female secrete a so-called "crop milk," chemically similar to mammalian milk, on which they feed their hatchlings.[2] They also drink by immersing their bills and sucking, like a person with a straw, rather than by scooping water in their bills and then tilting their heads back to swallow, as most birds do.[3] Doves and pigeons are monogamous, incubating and feeding cooperatively, males sitting by day, females at night. To varying degrees, most species tolerate or live with humans,[4] and pigeons are a common sight in most cities. Humans (who eat them as food and call them squab) are their natural predators, along with martens, weasels, cats, rats, hawks, and owls. There is speculation that the North American Passenger pigeon's extinction was due to inefficient reproduction and the bird's slaughter in great numers in the last part of the previous century.[5]

Domesticated as early as 3000 BCE in Egypt, pigeons have a legendary homing instinct, leading to their use as messengers for the past thousand years. A pigeon postal system existed in twelfth-century Baghdad, and Genghis Khan used messenger pigeons in his thirteenth-century conquests.[6] Although pigeons are demonstrably sharp-eyed,[7] scientists have a number of complicated and inconclusive theories to explain their uncanny homing abilities. Research shows that they are unusually sensitive to infrasound, ultraviolet light, polarized light, and changes in atmospheric pressure, but no one can say definitively how these sensitivities are used for navigation.[8] With its unerring tendency to "home," the pigeon embodies the maternal and embracing quality of faithfulness and represents a return to one's essence.

The mild, pacific, and nurturing qualities of the dove, along with its soft, cooing voice and puffed-up breast, connect it to feminine aspects of the psyche and related aspects of Eros. The small gray Mourning dove is a devoted mate and so notoriously amorous that its other name, turtledove, is used to describe overenthusiastic lovers. Throughout history, the dove has been associated with a great number of female deities. It was an attribute of Aphrodite,[9] as well as such saints as Theresa of Avila, Gregory Basil, Thomas Aquinas, Catherine of Alexandria, and the four evangelists.[10] Holding an olive branch, the dove was an emblem of the Greek goddess Athena. Sacred to Adonis and Bacchus,[11] it was also connected to Astarte and Isis.[12] According to the Roman poet Virgil, two doves guided Aeneas into the valley where the Golden Bough (mistletoe) grew.[13]

Different cultures use the same animal to illuminate varying and often contradictory themes. A Slavic tradition holds that doves are the souls of the dead. The Pueblo Indians thought the dove called to people to show them where water might be found.[14] In India, the dove was a symbol of lust.[15] In Islam, it is regarded as holy for having protected Mohammed in his flight.[16] In China, the dove represents fidelity as well as longevity,[17] and in Japan it figures in ancient legends as a messenger of war.[18] Frau Holla, an ugly old witch in Germanic tradition, appears once a year in the form of a dove, a talisman of fertility.[19]

The dove is also curiously connected with castration. In ancient Mesopotamia, doves were associated with this practice ritually. The beautiful and legendary Queen Semiramis, founder of Babylon, whose name may be translated as "dove," was said to have castrated her lovers. Eventually, castration was supplanted by the symbolic act of circumcision. The Festival of the Circumcision of Christ had as its symbol a dove holding in its beak not an olive branch, but the Holy Prepuce.[20] In the Old Testament, Noah releases three doves after the flood. One returns with an olive branch — a token of reconciliation with God and a symbol of peace. The dove of peace is invariably white, for its stainless purity, and whoever injures the pure and harmless dove defiles and slanders the spirit and essence of innocence.[21]

Connected as it is with Eros, but being also a creature of the air and spirit, the dove may represent a link between physical and spiritual impulses, or between the conscious and unconscious. Thus, it is an apt symbol for the Holy Spirit, which in Christianity links or mediates the invisible God and the godhead embodied in the figure of Jesus. The dove usually represents a spiritual uplifting capacity through which one can imagine emotions and passions rather than identifying with them and acting them out. Consequently, someone who dreams of a dove may need to be more imaginative about his or her lust, drives, passions, or emotions. Rather than acting on them or repressing them, the dreamer may need to engage these states in creative fantasy. The dove can represent that psychic capacity for creative fantasy.

Notes
[1] Grzimek 1984, 8: 247-49.
[2] Macdonald 1987, 216.
[3] Grzimek 1984, 8: 247.
[4] Grzimek 1984, 8: 249.
[5] Abs 1983, 293.
[6] "Pigeon Racing." *Encyclopedia Britannica*, 1997.
[7] Abs 1983, 245.
[8] Abs 1983, 281.
[9] Johnson 1988, 30.
[10] Biedermann 1994, 101.
[11] Cooper 1992, 81-82.
[12] Andrews 1993, 133.
[13] Frazer 1979, 815.
[14] Andrews 1993, 133.
[15] Walker 1983, 252.
[16] Becker 1994, 86.
[17] Biedermann 1994, 102.
[18] Cooper 1992, 81-82.
[19] Gimbutas 1989, 195.
[20] Walker 1983, 253-54.
[21] Becker 1994, 86-87.

DOVE/PIGEON
Family: Columbidae.
Size: 15-82 centimeters (6-33 inches) in length.
Wingspan: Passenger pigeon measures 58-64 centimeters (23-25 inches); the mourning dove, 43-48 centimeters (17-19 inches).
Weight: 30-2,400 grams (1-85 ounces).
Incubation: 13-18 days.
Longevity: 35 years.
Distribution: Widespread except Antarctica and high northern latitudes.
Habitat: Mostly in woodland or forest; some in open country or on cliffs.

Duck

A familiar fowl, hunted for sport as well as food and sometimes the comical inspiration for cartoons, ducks are a varied group of web-footed, flat-billed water birds of the family Anatidae, which includes geese and swans, although ducks are generally smaller and shorter of neck than those birds. Technically, the word "duck" refers to the female, while the males are called drakes. The mallard, a well-known and familiar type of duck, is a forerunner of the domestic duck. The male of this species is particularly beautiful, and its subspecies is prevalent in Europe, Asia, and North and Central America.[1]

The duck's distinctive flat beak is very sensitive and perfectly adapted for finding, identifying, and seizing food under water, in marshy environments, or along the banks of rivers or lakes. Strong but not particularly graceful fliers (they cannot glide), ducks are excellent swimmers whose buoyancy results from the air trapped in their feathers. They are comfortable and mobile on land, but their short legs and wide, heavy bodies produce the distinctive side-to-side waddle of the "duck walk."[2] Some can dive to depths of one hundred feet.[3]

Konrad Lorenz, the noted ethologist, discovered in mallard ducklings the tendency to "imprint," that is, to fixate on the first sound that they hear (usually the mother) and follow its source. Duck mothers encourage their young to follow closely behind them in neat ranks, presumably to keep track of them,[4] and this may account for the expression, "get one's ducks in a row."

Ducks tend to gather in large flocks in the winter, pairing off in the spring for mating and nesting. They are, to varying degrees, monogamous. Hatchlings swim and feed themselves almost immediately. At some point after hatching, the drakes gather into flocks and migrate to a traditional molting ground, where they, and later the females, will shed their wing feathers and remain flightless for a time. During this period, the distinctive coloration of the males may be hidden or obscured, which is why this phase of plumage is called "eclipse." When the molt is over, the males again display their gaudier plumage. The females remain rather drab by comparison, presumably because of their need to remain inconspicuous and safe from predators while sitting on their eggs.[5] Male mallard ducks are rather aggressive sexually, consistently harassing and attempting to mount unwilling females. This tendency may or may not explain why in ancient Egypt, where ducks were first domesticated almost thirty-five hundred years ago, they were frequently depicted in contexts that, while stubbornly enigmatic, are clearly and graphically sexual.[6]

In China, the brightly plumed mandarin duck is considered a symbol of marital devotion because it mates for life. Among Romans, the duck was regarded as a weather prophet,[7] and among Hebrews it was thought to be a symbol of immortality.[8] The duck is sacred to the Greek goddess Aphrodite[9] and associated in Egyptian myth with Isis.[10] Native Americans saw it as a mediator between water and sky, and in some versions of their creation stories, the duck dives into the primal flood to bring up the first mud of the earth.[11] In today's world, ducks are often seen as benign, if excitable creatures (like the notable cartoon fowl Donald or Daffy Duck). Their cacophonous quacking and calling when gathered in large flocks give them an association with deceitful chattering and gossip (the French idiom for "false report" is *canard*, literally "duck").[12] In some folktales a beautiful woman is revealed as having duck's feet — exposed as evil, a creature of witches or the devil. In other folktales, the duck is the rescuer from evil.[13]

Ducks can be considered superficial creatures, floating and bobbing (metaphorically speaking) on the surface of the great unconscious. But symbolically, as von Franz points out, the duck is a remarkable bird. It can move on land, in the water, and in the air. It represents a principle that is at home in all realms of nature and often stands for the self, which expresses the unity of the personality as a whole.[14] Therefore it portrays the "transcendent function," that capacity of the unconscious psyche to transform and guide the blocked human being into a new situation.[15]

Thus, dreams of a duck should be considered an alert to the immanence of this imaginative capacity and an attempt to embrace it with reflection and openness to changes. In contrast, the duck can also represent the evil quality of gossip, along with a tendency to avoid depth and stay on the surface of life. This narcissistic quality is depicted in many tales where witches and devils have duck's feet.

Notes
[1] Grzimek 1984, 7: 313.
[2] Grzimek 1984, 7: 262.
[3] Andrews 1993, 135.
[4] Grzimek 1984, 7: 313.
[5] Grzimek 1984, 7: 260, 269; Gooders and Boyer 1986, 9.
[6] Angier 1995, 7; Biedermann 1994, 106.
[7] Cooper 1992, 87.
[8] De Vries 1976, 150.
[9] Birkhäuser-Oeri 1988, 103-04.
[10] De Vries 1976, 150.
[11] *Dictionnaire des Symboles* 1982, 161.
[12] Cooper 1992, 87.
[13] von Franz 1974, 223-24.
[14] Jung 1977, 6: 789.
[15] von Franz 1974, 223-24.

DUCK
Family: Anatidae.
Size: 32-74 centimeters (12.5-29 inches). The mallard, the most familiar duck, measures 50-65 centimeters (20-25 inches).
Wingspan: 25.2-30.7 centimeters (10-12 inches).
Weight: The mallard weighs 750-1,572 grams (1.65-3.45 pounds).
Incubation: The uniform eggs are laid, but not incubated until the clutch, which is often quite large (5-13 eggs), is complete. Incubation is 25-30 days.
Longevity: As long as 20 years in captivity.
Distribution: Worldwide except Antarctica.
Habitat: Chiefly coastal and freshwater wetlands.

Eagle

Great in size, fierce in aspect, proud and wild in spirit, the eagle is unquestionably the king of birds, ruler of the sky. It has never failed to make a deep impression on any culture that has known it. Eagles belong to the avian order of raptors, birds of prey that include hawks, falcons, vultures, buzzards, secretary birds, and kites. All have sharp, hooked beaks and taloned feet for seizing prey.[1] The golden eagle is the most common, although it has been driven out of its habitat in most of Europe and the eastern United States. The bald eagle, a familiar emblem of the United States, remains an endangered species. Other eagles include the white-tailed sea eagle and Steller's sea eagle.

The eagle sites its nest, or aerie, where it will be most inaccessible to intruders, generally on high crags or cliffs.[2] From this high perch, eagles can protect their young and survey a vast terrain for prey. Strong fliers, they soar majestically on thermal currents, swooping with astonishing speed when they spot prey and attacking with talons forward.[3] They usually hunt alone, preying mostly on small mammals, birds, and fish, although eagles have been known to take larger prey such as newborn lambs or to cooperatively tackle game as large as deer or antelope.[4] Tales of eagles carrying off human babies are mostly fanciful, albeit certainly possible.

We call someone with very strong vision "eagle-eyed" because eagles are famously sharp-sighted. In good light, they can make out subtly camouflaged prey at astonishing distances, but in dim light their vision is no better than human vision.[5] Eagles are sexually dimorphic — the females are larger than the males.[6] Couples pair for life, and courtship involves nuptial flights that sometimes include breathtaking aerobatics.

The eagle has had strong symbolic significance across a wide range of cultures and times. Its superior size and strength, regal bearing, and mastery of the skies have made it an inevitable emblem of gods, kings, emperors, hunters, warriors and the like.[7] Native Americans have revered it for its strength, courage, persistence, and skill as a hunter, and many tribes worshipped eagle deities.[8] Depictions of the eagle figure significantly in Native American art; for example, the Thunderbird of Northwest Indian culture is an eagle.[9]

In North America, as elsewhere, the eagle is associated with the sun because of its high-flying ways, and accordingly with the sun's energy and power, both mystical and physical, including influence over the weather.[10] Eagle feathers were used in costumes, adornments, and fetishes to symbolize the rays of the sun as well as the power of the eagle's spirit.[11] Eagle claws and bones were used in amulets and pouches for purposes of sympathetic magic or medicine in traditional cultures.[12]

The golden eagle of European heraldry has been intimately associated for millennia with *imperium,* that is, with command and sovereignty. Zeus, the chief Greek god, often took the form of an eagle and used the glorious bird as his battle ensign.[13] Likewise in Rome, the eagle was associated with Jupiter, and it crowned the battle standards of the Roman legions.[14] Symbolically, the eagle is widely associated with the vertical dimension of ascent. When a Roman emperor died, it was the custom to release an eagle, whose spiralling rise would symbolize or embody the ascent of the ruler's soul to join the other gods above.[15] The *Physiologus* identifies some of the eagle's attributes with the mythical phoenix, furthering its association with resurrection and helping ensure that Christian writers would see a symbolic connection between the eagle and Christ's Ascent.[16]

In the Old Testament, the eagle was considered an "abomination" and was among the birds whose flesh was regarded unfit for consumption by Hebrews (Deuteronomy 14:3, 14:12). In Eastern cultures, one of the mounts of Vishnu is Garuda, represented as half-man, half-eagle; the eagle is also an emblem of Indra, the Vedic god of rain and thunder. The Buddha rides an eagle, and in ancient China it was an icon of strength and power.[17]

Alchemists used the soaring eagle as a symbol of the liberated spirit and the double eagle as a symbol of their major theme of connecting opposites, also expressed by the hermaphroditic Mercury. Avicenna, an Arabian physician/alchemist (980-1037), linked the spiritual aspect of the soaring eagle with its opposite, the instinctual, unconscious earthbound toad, finding in that conjunction the whole of the alchemical work, namely the self.[18]

On the negative side, the eagle is sometimes associated with the sin of pride or arrogance.[19] Since the eagle is a deadly predator, in Christian tradition it became associated with the Great Destroyer, Satan. The fact that eagles are great takers of fish, and that the fish is a widespread symbol of Christ, strengthened this association.[20]

Psychologically, the eagle's high, soaring flight connects to spiritual seeking, and its clear-eyed vision links its spiritual aspect to intellect and the power of the imagination. Its mastery of the skies, strength, and fierceness tie the eagle to aggressive impulses that can be employed in service of spiritual drives and vision.

In dream imagery, it can thus compensate for a too stagnant, grounded point of view that requires an uplifted state and a more aggressive, active standpoint. On the other hand, for a person who readily soars into imaginal flight and excessive intuition, the eagle could signify a soaring attitude that obliterates an awareness of "innerness" of the soul.

Notes
[1] Grzimek 1984, 7: 336.
[2] Grzimek 1984, 7: 382.
[3] Grzimek 1984, 7: 337.
[4] Grzimek 1984, 7: 381-82.
[5] Downer 1989, 55.
[6] Perrins and Middleton 1989, 117.
[7] Waldman 1994, 69.
[8] Brown 1992, 42.
[9] Waldman 1994, 69.
[10] Ibid.
[11] Andrews 1993, 138.
[12] Waldman 1994, 69.
[13] Andrews 1993, 137; De Gubernatis 1968, 195, 197.
[14] Andrews 1993, 137.
[15] Walker 1983, 262.
[16] Becker 1994, 91.
[17] Cooper 1992, 91.
[18] Fabricius 1989, 55.
[19] Becker 1994, 91.
[20] Chardonnay-Lassay 1991, 30-31.

GOLDEN EAGLE
Family: Accipitridae.
Size: The male golden eagle has a length of 79-95 centimeters (31-37 inches); the female is approximately the same length.
Wingspan: 195-210 centimeters (77-83 inches) for the male and 210-215 centimeters (82.5-85 inches) for the female.
Weight: 3-4.5 kilograms (6.5-10 pounds) for the male and 4-6 kilograms (9-13 pounds) for the female.
Incubation: 40-45 days.
Longevity: Up to 48 years in captivity.
Distribution: Worldwide.
Habitat: Open country from barren areas to open coniferous forest; prefers cliffs and large trees with large horizontal branches for roosting and perching.

BALD EAGLE

Family: Accipitridae.

Size: The male bald eagle is 68-76 centimeters (26.5-30 inches) long; the female is 84-105 centimeters (33-42 inches) long.

Wingspan: The male extends 188-197 centimeters (74-77.5 inches); the female extends 211 centimeters (83 inches).

Weight: 4.1 kilograms (9 pounds) for the male and 5.84 kilograms (13 pounds) for the female.

Incubation: 35 days.

Longevity: Average life span in the wild is unknown, but 30 years is a reasonable estimate under natural conditions.

Distribution: Worldwide.

Habitat: Near water, rivers, lakes or reservoirs that provide a reliable food source and isolation from disturbing human activities.

Eel

With their sinuous, snake-like bodies, eels are among the most easily recognized fish; the order Anguilliformes includes more than 360 species, some of which, like the deep-sea dwelling gulpers, have bizarre, even fantastical shapes. Smooth-skinned (most species have no scales) and often slimy, eels lack pectoral fins altogether, and the dorsal and anal fins are generally merged into a continuous seam. Almost all adult eels are predators, feeding on worms, fish, snails, and crustaceans.[1] They vary in size from under four inches to over eleven feet in length (in the case of some moray eels). Eel blood contains a potentially dangerous ichthyotoxin that damages mucous membranes but is quickly destroyed in cooking. This presumably evolved as a discouragement to non-human predators.[2]

All eels are marine creatures at some stage, and the so-called freshwater eels return to the sea to spawn. Many species undergo a metamorphosis, including a larval stage that may last for up to three years.[3] In the case of the most economically significant of the species, the European eel, mature adults migrate thousands of miles to lay their free-floating eggs in the Sargasso Sea, and then die.[4] The tiny larvae make their way (at first passively in the Gulf Stream, then more actively as they mature) back to European rivers over the course of three years. During that time, they metamorphose to a juvenile or elver stage in which they are known as glass eels, because they are quite transparent until they reach their freshwater habitats.[5]

The suborder Heterocongrinae, commonly called garden eels, use their pointed tails to dig themselves backward into the sand with astonishing speed. The front end of the animal sticks up from the sea floor like a flower. In typically tight-clustered colonies of several hundred individuals, they more than justify their common name. Members of another suborder, the moray eels, occupy the nooks and crannies of tropical and subtropical reefs and rock shelves. They are a skin-diver's nightmare — aggressive when disturbed, powerfully muscled, fearsomely toothed, and capable of secreting venom that, in several species, can kill a full-grown man.[6] The famous and peculiar electric eel *(Electrophorus electricus),* although technically not an eel, being classified in the separate order Cypriniformes, is sufficiently eel-like in appearance to fool most of the people most of the time.[7] Special organs within its tail can generate a substantial electrical potential, as much as five hundred volts, which it discharges to stun prey or predators, including humans.[8]

The eel is such a fascinating creature that a good deal of projection accrues to it, interfering with careful observation. In many parts of the world, the eel is an important source of food, and therefore closely observed. Ancient authors Aristotle and Pliny thought, more or less correctly in the case of freshwater eels, that large eels went down to the sea and small eels returned. But Aristotle asserted that eels sprang from "the entrails of the earth," while Pliny was equally convinced that elvers arose from residue scraped from the skin when adult eels brushed or bumped against rocks.[9] Eels were considered sacred, and sometimes kept for ritual purposes, by the ancient Greeks, Phoenicians, and Polynesians; the latter considered them animal ancestors associated with the mythology of a Great Flood. Particularly in China, and generally elsewhere, the eel's phallic shape is associated with sexuality.[10]

The unconscious is like the deep, unfathomable sea, and fish in general are — like unconscious thoughts, feelings, impulses, and emotions — a real aspect of our being that we do not normally see in our usual conscious life. Considering the eel's physical and mythological properties, it can often represent powerful, if unconscious, sexual and aggressive impulses. An eel manifested in a dream may mean that these essential aspects of human existence are trying to approach consciousness. Since sex and aggression are issues of extreme sensitivity in many modern cultures, the symbolic image of the eel would carry not only the vital energy and power of sexuality and aggression, but also the anxieties and fears that accompany these instinctual impulses. Depending on the way the conscious personality relates to these thoughts and feelings, they can also be experienced as potent, friendly, even helpful and supportive influences.

Notes
[1] Grzimek 1984, 4: 159-61.
[2] Banister and Campbell 1988, 27.
[3] Grzimek 1984, 4: 162.
[4] McFarland 1987, 387.
[5] Grzimek 1984, 4: 160.
[6] Grzimek 1984, 4: 164.
[7] McFarland 1987, 149.
[8] Grzimek 1984, 4: 296.
[9] Banister and Campbell 1988, 27.
[10] Cooper 1992, 92-93.

EEL
Order: Anguilliformes (24 families).
Size: At maturity, eels range from 10 centimeters (4 inches) to 3.5 meters in the deep sea Cyema atrum, and to 11.5 meters in the moray Thyrsoidea macrura.
Weight: Fresh-water eels weigh 140-170 grams (5-6 ounces); female fresh-water eels can weigh up to 6 kilograms (13 pounds).
Gestation: Larval stage can last 1–3 years.
Longevity: 6 years.
Distribution: Eels are found in all seas, from coastal regions to the mid-depths. One group, the fresh-water eels of the family Anguillidae, live in fresh water but return to the sea to breed.
Habitat: In seas and fresh water.

Elephant

Though dwarfed by the similar-looking but much larger mammoth, which became extinct in the last Ice Age, the elephant is the largest terrestrial mammal living today. Massive and strong, it possesses considerable intelligence and is capable of great agility and physical delicacy. There are two species of elephants: the larger African elephant (the one with the big ears) and the slightly smaller Asian elephant. Asian elephants have been tamed since approximately 3500 BCE, and they have been used for work, battle, and ceremonial purposes. African elephants are widely supposed to be untrainable, but it seems likely that the elephants on which Hannibal attacked Rome were African, and recent attempts to domesticate them have been at least partially successful.

Apart from its colossal size, the elephant's trunk is its most salient feature — a prehensile nasal extremity used for smelling, feeling, greeting, grasping, eating, drinking, bathing, and fighting.[1] Not all elephants have tusks, but those that do use them to pry, dig, fight, and lift. The tusks are vast incisors that grow outward continuously throughout life. The heaviest tusk on record weighed 103 kilograms (226 pounds).[2] Tusks have been used to make piano keys and jewelry. Elephants are also noted for their thick skin, which is actually quite sensitive. Thus, the elephant, like the rhinoceros and some species of pigs, is referred to as a pachyderm, derived from the Greek term meaning "thick skin."

Elephants are highly social animals, living in herds of eight to twenty cows, young adults, and babies. Full-grown bulls generally live in separate herds or roam alone. Cows, which can reach an age of sixty to eighty years, become sexually mature at nine to twelve years of age, and they can give birth well into older age. Mothers are gentle, protective, and very caring with their offspring — indeed, the whole herd is indulgent and protective toward calves.

Elephants use a number of vocalizations; they may trumpet loudly when attacking, surprised, or feeling lost from the herd. Individual members of the herd may contribute to a general rumbling, which seems to help maintain the group's sense of cohesion. The same deep sounds may be exchanged as greetings when elephants approach each other. They have good vision, although it is not ideally adaptable to changing light conditions, and their sense of smell plays an important role in their ability to recognize one another. Above all, their extremely keen hearing has most impressed hunters and the mahouts who handle trained elephants.[3] Forest-dwelling elephants in particular usually use their low rumble (at a frequency of fourteen to thirty-five hertz or cycles per second) which carries well through wooded environments where higher pitched vibrations are easily lost.[4] Elephants are also said to sense impending earthquakes — perhaps by reacting to minute electrical changes in the atmosphere that occur when rocks are stressed.[5] And, in spite of their large size, elephants are excellent swimmers.[6]

Strict vegetarians, elephants spend as much as sixteen hours a day foraging and eating. A large adult might consume 300 pounds of tree leaves, shoots, and grass, and perhaps 230 liters (50 gallons) of water.[7] They digest just over half of what they eat. The rest, having passed through the animal, not only fertilizes the earth but also disperses seeds. Overgrazing can cause problems, because elephants often kill more foliage than they actually eat. In areas of cultivation, they can cause serious crop damage. Full-grown elephants have no natural enemies except humans, who kill them for their ivory and disturb their habitat. Still, elephants have been known to bleed to death from crocodile bites, and big cats or packs of hyenas or dogs may set upon older animals if they are separated from the herd. Young elephants are quite vulnerable if the herd, for whatever reason, cannot defend them.[8]

Because elephants seem to be conscious of death, they are thought to be capable of emotion. Researchers have found considerable evidence of elephants gathering around a fallen comrade, even burying it with earth and branches. This remarkable ritual is a behavior anecdotally related to a mourning process. Persistent legends of elephant graveyards where the great animals go to die — a fabulous treasure trove for wishful ivory hunters — have never been substantiated, although large concentrations of elephant bones have been found, possibly the result of mass deaths from grass fire or human ambush.

That the elephant has a long memory is proverbial. Migrating over vast distances in their constant search for food and water, elephants apparently rely on the memories of older animals to guide them. There are also persistent reports of incidents in which particular herds, having been decimated by hunters, retain their enmity for humans across generations, suggesting some form of cultural transmission.[9]

In India, the elephant figures prominently not only as a domesticated animal in everyday life but also as creature in the country's highly developed religious iconography and folklore. In Hindu mythology, the elephant symbolizes the very deep and powerful creative processes in the human psyche. One of the legends depicts eight male elephants arising from an egg in the right hand of Brahma, and eight females from another in the left. All elephants, divine and real, are descended from these sixteen legendary beasts.[10] The divine elephant is called Megha, or "cloud," a poetic image that conjures the elephant's size, albeit not its weight. When it is properly worshipped, the elephant's symbolic affinity with real clouds is thought to give it a magical power to summon rain.[11] Also, the divine elephant Airavata became the mount of Indra, and the chief attendant of Shiva is Ganesha, god of writing and wisdom, who has the head of an elephant. Because of the connection of the elephant with clouds and rainmaking in Hindu mythology, the elephant can be seen psychologically as a symbol of the self, the far-reaching totality of the personality from which all inner fertility and consciousness proceeds.

The Chinese saw the elephant as a symbol of strength and cleverness. The Romans associated the elephant's intelligence with the god Mercury. Because the elephant can live longer than most animals, it is considered in many cultures a symbol of longevity and victory over death.[12] Thus, the elephant is also a symbol of the deep-seated wisdom, knowledge, steadiness, and imagination that exist, although often hidden, in every person. In the long lifespan of this remarkable beast, in the evidence that the herd depends upon the knowledge and wisdom of the old cows, we can imagine, as people have done for eons, a reflection of our own capacity to grow and increase in value as we age.

Finally, elephants have a curious symbolic relationship to snakes. An ancient belief was that when the female elephant gave birth, the male elephant protected it from attack by deadly snakes. The snake in this case represents the universal and deeply backward pull of the unconscious, which leads ultimately to death, while the elephant represents resistance to that urge — the forward momentum of the life force.

The appearance of an elephant in a dream may represent stolid, determined resistance to negative or regressive psychological tendencies.[13] The elephant's sensitivity to atmospheric changes may be a compensatory image for the dreamer's too insulated, narcissistic attitudes and exhort him or her to seek a deeper connection to the wider scope of nature and the world. Its outstanding memory could suggest that the dreamer understand that he or she may have a genetic disposition to certain negative behavior, attitudes, and personal shadow sides, and that these are not of his or her own doing, but belong to a long familial line and can, with careful attention and diligence, be changed for more positive traits. The elephant's unusual size, amazing strength and superior intelligence conjure up an image of what may actually be available to the dreamer in the personal unconscious, and give that person the courage to face the world in a more positive way.

Notes
[1] Bonner 1993, 52; Grzimek 1984, 12: 478.
[2] Delort 1992, 24-25.
[3] Grzimek 1984, 12: 496.
[4] Brody 1993, C1.
[5] Downer 1989, 18.
[6] Grzimek 1984, 12: 489.
[7] Bonner 1993, 52.
[8] Delort 1992, 32.
[9] Slater 1987, 140.
[10] Zimmer 1974, 104.
[11] Zimmer 1974, 109.
[12] Biedermann 1994, 116.
[13] Biedermann 1994, 115-17.

ELEPHANT

Family: Elephantidae.

Size: Male African elephant measures 6-7.5 meters (20-24.5 feet) in head-body length and 3.3 meters (10.8 feet) in height; female head-body length is 0.6 meters (2 feet) shorter. Asian elephant measures 5.5-6.4 meters (18-21 feet) in head-body length and 2.5-3 meters (8.2-9 feet) in height.

Weight: Male African elephant weighs up to 6,000 kilograms (13,200 pounds); female weighs 3,000 kilograms (6,600 pounds). Asian elephant weighs up to 5,000 kilograms (11,000 pounds).

Gestation: 22 months.

Longevity: Both African and Asian elephants live about 60 years in the wild (more than 80 years in captivity).

Distribution: Africa (south of the Sahara), Indian subcontinent, Indochina, Malaysia, Indonesia, and South China.

Habitat: Savanna grassland and forest (African); forest (Asian).

Falcon

A wild spirit, never truly tamed, the falcon is a grand and impressive bird, with a smooth and elegant flight. Its name applied originally to all birds of prey used by humans for hunting. It now refers to those members of the order Falconinae with pointed wings, longer than their tails, most of which belong to their subfamily. Species of the so-called true falcons (genus *Falco*) are found worldwide. All are strong fliers and excellent hunters.

Falcons have holes with baffles for nares (noses), and short tarsi (lower legs) for impact absorption when they kill prey at high speeds. They have dark eyes and irises and black malar stripes on the face near their eyes. Their beaks are sturdy and strongly curved (the root of the word "falcon" means sickle-shaped) with a sharp, tooth-like spur on either side of the upper mandible. This so-called falcon's tooth is significant because, unlike hawks, which tend to kill with their talons, falcons kill with their beaks.[1] Some will seize birds of their own size or smaller on the wing. Others, such as the hovering falcons and kestrels, hunt mostly on the ground, taking rabbits, small rodents and reptiles, and larger insects. The hovering of kestrels is rare and remarkable among birds, a graceful and athletic ability that allows them to pounce when they are ready with great suddenness and accuracy.[2]

Falcons do not build their own nests, preferring to lay their eggs in tree cavities, rock ledges, abandoned nests of other birds, or even on the ground. The eggs are yellow and speckled with brown spots.[3] Like eagles, the female is generally thirty percent larger than the male, which, although more maneuverable in flight, cannot take the larger animals that the female can.

Many species have been used for the ancient art of falconry — the taming, training, and flying of birds of prey for sport and/or hunting. Falconry probably first developed in Asia as much as twenty-five hundred years ago and was a popular diversion for European nobility in the Middle Ages. Although its popularity waned as guns made fowling more efficient, falconry has nevertheless enjoyed several revivals since then.[4]

Five species comprise the list of so-called trained falcons: the gyrfalcon, hobby falcon, Eleonora's falcon, the merlin falcon, and, preeminently, the peregrine falcon. To "fly" the peregrine falcon, a truly astonishing flier, was once a royal prerogative, forbidden to all but kings and princes.[5] These are among the swiftest animals on earth; their top speed in a dive or "swoop" has been estimated at 100–250 miles per hour.[6]

In ancient Egypt, the gaze of the falcon was thought to paralyze its prey, and thus it was an attractive emblem for several pharaohs who no doubt coveted such a power.[7] It was sacred to the sun god Ra and to Horus, another sky god, who was often depicted either as a falcon or with the head of one.[8] Several lesser deities, including Mentu and Seker, were associated with it as well.[9] In China the falcon is associated with both the beneficent power of the sun and the destructive forces of war. In Japan it signifies generosity and victory.[10] Many Native American tribes considered the falcon the younger brother of the eagle, although for the Indians of the southeast woodlands the eagle was a symbol of peace and the falcon was considered the bird of battle.[11]

In the Christian tradition, most birds of prey, including falcons, were interpreted as ravagers of souls; in the elaborated symbolism of the Christian Middle Ages, the sparrow hawk was the figure of envy — perhaps because of the notion that envy tears the heart even as the hawk does its prey.[12] A trained falcon is an attribute of several saints, including St. Hubert, the patron saint of hunters.[13] Particularly in the Renaissance the hooded falcon was used as a symbol of the hope that light might follow darkness, whether in a religious sense or otherwise. The Norse god Odin, much given to shape-shifting, sometimes took the form of a falcon, as did the trickster god Loki.[14]

Most birds, like most principles of spirit, are elusive, autonomous, beyond command. The falcon's trainability — the notion that people can use such a free, wild, winged creature of spirit — gives the image of this bird much of its resonant power in the human psyche. For example, in dreams the falcon can represent a spiritual principle that can be tamed or employed for practical purposes; hence, it is a potent inner resource. Some people use this inner spiritual principle in their external lives, employing the positive imagery in situations where the power of will is necessary, such as in Twelve Step programs or athletic competitions. In these cases, one's inner imagery is trained, even as the falcon is trained, so that the power of symbolism can be marshaled in the service of almost any discipline.

Notes
[1] Grzimek 1984, 7: 419.
[2] Grzimek 1984, 7: 416-19.
[3] Grzimek 1984, 7: 419.

[4] "Falconry." *Encarta 97 Encyclopedia*, 1997.
[5] Grzimek 1984, 7: 416-25.
[6] Perrins and Middleton 1989, 108-09.
[7] Biedermann 1994, 125.
[8] Becker 1994, 107.
[9] Biedermann 1994, 125.
[10] Jobes 1962, 1: 546.
[11] Cooper 1992, 97.
[12] Charbonneau-Lassay 1991, 206-07.
[13] Biedermann 1994, 126.
[14] Ibid.

FALCON

Family: Falconidae.

Size: There are great size and weight differences between the smallest and largest members of the true falcons. The length of the true falcons can measure 25-50 centimeters (10-24 inches). The length of the peregrine falcon is 36-48 centimeters (14-19 inches).

Weight: The small American sparrow hawk weighs only about 100 grams (3.5 ounces), while the female of the large gyrfalcon weighs up to 2,000 grams (4.5 pounds). The peregrine falcon weighs 550-1,120 grams (1-2.5 pounds).

Wingspan: Gyrfalcon is 112-32 centimeters (44-52 inches); peregrine falcon is 29-38 centimeters (11-15 inches).

Incubation: About 30 days.

Longevity: Smaller falcon's average life span is approximately 3 years, but some may reach 10-12 years. All species live much longer in captivity, and the length of the life cycle is directly proportional to the size of the bird.

Distribution: Worldwide.

Habitat: Mostly open spaces.

Fish

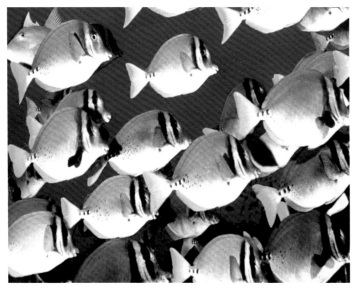

A momentary glint in the sunlight, a subliminal glimpse of shadow in the murky depths, a ripple, a sudden, surprising leap — in these fleeting ways we normally experience fish in their natural element. In the deepest trenches of the vast oceans, in great rivers and tiny streams, in lakes and modest ponds[1] live more than twenty thousand species of fish. Freshwater and saltwater varieties are mostly (although not completely) distinct.[2] Fish are carnivores and herbivores, luminous, transparent, electric, oviparous, viviparous, sexual, bisexual; some are only female, others only male. Some are gregarious; some swim alone; some are fatally poisonous, and some are delicious to eat. From the tiny guppy to the 50-foot whale shark, the variety of sizes, shapes, colors, habits, and habitats is nothing less than staggering. Fish range in adult length from less than 10 millimeters (0.4 inches) to more than 20 meters (65 feet) and in weight from about 1.5 grams (0.2 ounces) to many thousands of kilograms.[3]

Fish are referred to as the bounty of the sea because our first and perhaps primary connection with them is as food. But throughout prehistory the fish was also equated with fecundity and female reproductive powers, even with the female genitalia — especially in the stylized representations called "yoni."[4] The womb can easily be seen, functionally as well as symbolically, as an encapsulation of the fertile sea waters that gave birth to the very first life. It is not surprising, then, that far back in human history, the fish was an emblem of an urfertility goddess, and often represented as her uterus.[5] The first letters of the Greek phrase *Iesous Christos Theou Huios Soter* (Jesus Christ, Son of God, Savior) form "Icthius," the Greek word for fish. Awed by the magic of the acronym, and the fact that it was resonant with their interest in baptism, Christians made the fish their symbol. Christianity also co-opted symbolic connections between the fish and a number of lunar fertility goddesses, who seem to have a more essential as well as earlier claim to the symbol.[6]

Catholics were, until recently, required to eat fish on Fridays. Fish have been used as ritual food in many religions, particularly the cults of lunar goddesses connected with love and/or fertility such as Ishtar, Isis, Hathor, and Aphrodite/Venus. On the other hand, the Syrians considered fish sacred and refrained from eating them. Priests of the Sumerian sea god Ea-Oannes wore a costume with a fish head, the shape of which was later borrowed for the mitre worn by Christian bishops.[7]

In Hindu legend, the god Manu saved the holy books of the Vedas from the flood by transforming himself into a fish. In Buddhism, the fish represents asking refuge in the Buddha, the Law and the Sangha. In ancient Egypt, a likeness of a fish was worn as a talisman for abundance, domestic felicity, and prosperity. There, the fish was associated with Osiris, or more specifically with his phallus, which was eaten by a fish when Set cut it off and threw it in the Nile.[8] Individual species of fish were worshipped as divine or considered sacred. The whale that swallowed Jonah was regarded by most as a fish, although it is a mammal. The Torah likens the fish to the faithful believers of Israel and itself to the sustaining waters in which they live. In the Talmud, the Messiah is called Dag, which means fish.[9]

Jung notes that fish have been associated, often judgmentally, with every kind of concupiscence, especially sexual desire and earthly pleasures.[10] These attitudes may simply arise from patriarchs' arbitrary trashing of symbols formerly associated with feminine deities. Fish are usually elements of the sea, a symbol of the unconscious.[11] Such fish are distant, psychologically inaccessible, libidinous, and yet capable of surfacing briefly and spontaneously. And of course, one can fish for them, if one knows how. The fish is really quite a wonderful symbol of those elusive, inchoate elements of the unconscious which escape our awareness without an organized and conscious effort to relate to them.[12] Both the Buddha and the apostle Peter were, after all, called fishers of men.[13]

The image of fishing or diving in a dream might represent an attempt to connect the contents of the unconscious to conscious thoughts and processes. One must believe and imagine that symbolic fish, with their diversity (and thus the variety of psychological contents) embody unconscious processes, and that with patience one can catch them. These processes may be half-formed thoughts, feelings, impulses, and sensations, often more powerful and wiser than the conscious personality. Just as the sea is full of fish — beautiful and nourishing or monstrous and devouring — so the unconscious is full of such contrasting qualities. On the surface a person knows nothing of the unconscious — the fish — beyond knowing through faith that it is down there. To dream of fishes is to glimpse the living reality of unconscious elements, which meticulous attention can often bring to the surface and integrate into consciousness.

More can be learned about the unique physical characteristics and symbolic significance by referring to individual entries (dolphin, eel, salmon, shark, whale).

Notes
[1] Bannister and Campbell 1988, x.
[2] "Fish." *Encarta 97 Encyclopedia*, 1997.
[3] "Fishes — A Comparative Study." *Encyclopedia Britannica*, 1997.
[4] Walker 1983, 314.
[5] Gimbutas 1989, 258-60.
[6] Charbonneau-Lassay 1991, 300.
[7] Cooper 1992, 100-01.
[8] Ibid.
[9] Cooper 1992, 101; Jobes 1962, 1: 574; Goodenough 1956, 5: 53.
[10] Jung 1975, 9ii: 174.
[11] Jung 1976, 1: 172.
[12] von Franz 1977, 150.
[13] Cooper 1992, 100.

Fly

In human terms a fly certainly suffers from a negative image — a buzzing pest in every sense of the word, a carrier of pestilence, closely associated with the spoilage of food, corruption and decay, and an irksome distraction as well. Indeed, "a fly in the ointment" denotes an irritant that ruins one's pleasure. Yet the fly is just another highly successful wrinkle in the fabric of evolution — no less or more so than humans.

The housefly is probably the most familiar of the nearly ninety thousand species, because of its tendency to live and breed, in close proximity to humans. As the designation of their order (Diptera) indicates, all flies have just two wings; mouthparts are highly variable from species to species and are designed for feeding on fluids — blood, sap, or partially decomposed organic matter. The larvae, called maggots, are legless, worm-like grubs that undergo a complete metamorphosis to become adult flies.[1]

Flies reproduce in a variety of ways, including the parthenogenesis (single sex reproduction) of the greenfly. The mating of houseflies is a particularly curious affair in that the usual protocols of penetration are reversed; the female inserts her extended ovipositor into the vestibule of the male's reproductive chamber, where the eggs are fertilized.[2] She then lays a batch of up to one hundred eggs in or beside a source of food — feces, rotting garbage, or decaying flesh. The eggs hatch into maggots (small larvae) within twenty-four hours. These larvae molt several times, then pupate within a few days, and the resulting adults are ready to reproduce within approximately a week. The geometric progression is such that in less than five months, a single female could in theory have more than 5.5 trillion offspring, if all of them lived a normal life span (two months) and reproduced in average numbers. Of course, high mortality rates prevent this, but flies can reproduce prodigiously, especially in parts of the world where sanitation remains rudimentary.[3] Although houseflies clean themselves fairly constantly, they feed and reproduce in material rife with bacteria, quantities of which inevitably stick to their feet. Thus, flies become significant carriers of diseases such as typhus, dysentery, tuberculosis, and even polio.[4]

In eastern Asia, the fly's constant flitting caused it to be seen as a symbol of restless souls — from which, in turn, it came to be associated with sickness, death, and malevolent spirits. The word "Beelzebub" apparently conflates the Hebrew "Baal-zíbub" of the Old Testament ("Lord of the Flies") with the Greek "Beelzebul," once a Canaanite deity and thus inevitably a name for the Devil in the New Testament. The resulting confusion, along with the fly's undeniable connection with filth and decay, has helped establish a strong symbolic association between flies and evil.[5]

Loki, the devilish trickster figure of Norse mythology, often takes the shape of a fly.[6] Likewise Ahriman, the Persian principle of evil, enters into the world in the form of a fly.[7] The Romans, at the temple of Hercules Victor, made sacrifices to flies, as did the Syrians.[8] Medieval ascetics saw in the incessant, intrusive buzzing of the fly an analogue of the lustful, carnal impulses that bedevilled them; indeed, among Christians generally, the fly has often been considered an emblem of lewdness.[9] On the other hand, the Kalmucks, a Mongol people of northwest Kazakstan, revere and protect the fly as a soul creature; the Ashanti people of Africa worship a fly god; and the Navaho people of North America have a hero called Big Fly.[10]

Symbolically, flies can represent the dangerous aspects of collective attitudes — what Jung calls "psychic infection" — collective ideas that deter us from a more individual path. Dealing with the chapter in Nietzsche's *Thus Spoke Zarathustra* called "The Flies in the Market-Place," Jung speaks of the general idea of flies as an instrument of contagion, cross-pollinating pathogens as they swarm from one food source to the next, spreading collective or epidemic disease. This is a very effective schematic of the way dangerous collective fears, hatred, and prejudices are spread through the community.[11]

The fly's significance is indeed negative in most symbolic contexts. Not only do flies carry disease, but their buzzing intrusiveness is a good image of a dissociated psychological state that interferes with thoughts and destroys concentration. Dreams of swarming flies (as with dreams of other swarming insects) may indicate a severe mental fragmentation or psychotic process, and hence loss of a containing and supportive internal structure.[12] As a result, the fly has been almost universally associated with sorcery and demons, the Devil, and all that is poisonous, filthy, and repulsive. Yet a single fly flitting about in a dream can represent both the inner life of the soul and consciousness itself, the unnoticed witness, the "fly on the wall."

Notes
[1] O'Toole 1995, 80.
[2] Grzimek 1984, 2: 496.
[3] Grzimek 1984, 2: 495-96.
[4] Grzimek 1984, 2: 497.
[5] Becker 1994, 117.
[6] "Ancient European Religions." *Encyclopedia Britannica*, 1997.
[7] Becker 1994, 117.
[8] Jobes 1962, 1: 588.
[9] Charbonneau-Lassay 1991, 329-30.
[10] Cooper 1992, 104.
[11] Jung 1988, 606-07.
[12] Hillman 1988, 59.

FLY
Order: Diptera (with a variety of families).
Size: The housefly measures 0.55-0.75 centimeters (0.22-0.30 inches) in length.
Wingspan: One pair of membranous wings have a maximum span of 8 centimeters (3 inches); hindwings are modified as club-like balancers.
Weight: The housefly weighs about 0.014 grams (0.0005 ounces).
Incubation: The female housefly produces about 100 eggs at a time. They hatch in 12-24 hours into maggots (larvae), then transform into pupae and finally into adults.
Longevity: Depending on species and season, from several weeks to several months.
Distribution: Worldwide.
Habitat: All possible habitats.

Fox

Proverbially sly, physically nimble and elusive, the fox is surely hunted with more inflated pomp and ceremony than any other animal in the world. Indeed, Oscar Wilde said of the classic English fox hunt that it was "the unspeakable in pursuit of the uneatable." Foxes are smallish members of the Canid family with pointed snouts, relatively large ears, and a substantial, bushy tail. The range of the red fox extends over all of what is called the Holarctic region in North America, from the Plains north through the Arctic tundra, Europe, and Asia (except India, Tibet, and Indochina).[1] Localized subspecies include the small-eared arctic fox and large-eared, desert-dwelling fennec fox. Bodily extremities like ears and tails tend to be smaller in cold climates to preserve heat and larger in warm climates to disperse heat.

Foxes are generally solitary hunters, but they are social to the extent that several foxes may den together, often one vixen cohabiting with several males. Foxes often appropriate preexisting badger dens, which they may share with the badgers, wild cats,[2] rabbits or burrowing owls. Mating season is usually late winter, and litters average three to five "kits," born blind and helpless in the spring. By late summer they are fully independent.

Versatile predators, foxes combine stealth with dash-and-grab hunting techniques.[3] Unusually strong for their size, they are capable of seizing prey as large as a fawn and will certainly take wild fowl as well as domestic poultry, but they prefer small rodents like mice and voles.[4] The stealth of the fox, its nimbleness, and its vertical pupils (unique among canids) have led to the false inference that foxes are related to cats. That the fox can and does harrow the most seemingly secure henhouses gives it a reputation as a crafty thief and helps to define its relationship to humans. The fox's adaptability has made it, along with rats and humans, one of the most successful mammals on the planet.

Although the bright color of the red fox's coat is quite striking when the animal is away from cover, it is concealing in the brush. Similarly, the camouflage of the Arctic fox's white winter coat is nearly perfect in the snow.[5] In deep, loose snow, the fox's tail may sweep the snow as it runs, which has given rise to the notion that it intentionally "erases" its tracks to avoid pursuit.[6] Such beliefs stem from the fox's legendary reputation for wiliness. Some call it nothing short of uncanny, and others say that it is merely the result of an anxious disposition. The fox is swift and nimble, with keen smell, sight, and hearing. It is capable of running up trees, and it can swim, although it does so reluctantly.[7] The fox's main enemies are humans, yet even determined efforts to eliminate it have been unsuccessful. Larger raptors such as eagles, hawks, and owls have been known to prey on foxes.[8]

In ancient China, foxes were thought to be excessively lascivious. Thus, a maceration of their testicles was a traditional aphrodisiac; foxtails worn on the arm were considered helpful in amatory pursuits. Shape-changing is another common feature of the fox's mythology in Asia. In folktales, the fox lives for a thousand years and becomes a master of seduction, with no fewer than nine big, long bushy tails.[9] Stories tell how a fox may seduce a woman during the night. As the woman reaches orgasm and the fox does not, the animal builds up power until eventually it gains the ability to shape-shift to human form. In other stories, the fox can become human after fifty years, and after a hundred years, it may become either a wizard or a true *femme fatale* who brings doom to her lovers.

In Native American myths and stories, the fox is also a shape-shifter, but more universally he is a trickster. In Sumerian culture, the fox was associated with the trickster god Enki, having revived him when Enki ate poisonous plants. In Zoroastrian myth, the fox is imagined to have supernatural powers. In the Bible, the fox is a model of deceitful guile, and consequently a symbol of the Devil for Christians.[10] In Aesop and other Greek and Latin fables, nearly every kind of animal is deceived by the fox, which may even deceive itself.[11] In the Alps and in Austria, as well as Japan and China, the connection between the fox and witchcraft is strong, and much lore has evolved about witches (not to mention hysterical and epileptic women) abroad on their errands of mischief in vulpine form. Like the cat, the fox seems to represent primitive, instinctive female nature, although it is often personified as "Monsieur Reynard" in the *Roman de Renart*.[12]

Psychologically, the fox is our very own trickster, which cleverly evades a difficult situation — much the same way the sexual impulse pops up, often masking or camouflaging anxieties, aggressions and fears. In dreams, the fox, a master escapist, can be an apt symbol of the impulse to avoid potentially painful insights. This tendency is often seen in people with dissociative disorders, who displace true pain onto other, often painful situations, yet evade facing truly traumatic issues. More positively, the dream fox can represent imaginal perception, especially a capacity to weave one's way among seemingly conflicting messages or emotions. The fox can also be an inner instinctual guide that does not necessarily follow collective norms, values, or ways of thinking, but is nevertheless in the service of life and growth. It may indicate an emphasis on slyness, cleverness, and imagination to compensate for an overly intellectual viewpoint or a mechanical attitude toward sexuality that undervalues its deeper mysteries.

Notes
[1] Grzimek 1984, 12: 245.
[2] Grzimek 1984, 12: 247.
[3] Macdonald 1987, 68.
[4] Grzimek 1984, 12: 248.
[5] Andrews 1993, 273.
[6] Grzimek 1984, 12: 246.
[7] Andrews 1993, 276.
[8] Grzimek 1984, 12: 250.
[9] Biedermann 1994, 143.
[10] Cooper 1992, 105-06; Biedermann 1994, 144.
[11] De Gubernatis 1968, 2: 139.
[12] von Franz 1975b, 14, 140.

FOX

Family: Canidae.

Size: The red fox has a body length of 60-90 centimeters (23-35 inches) and a tail length of 35-40 centimeters (13-15 inches); its shoulder height is 35-40 centimeters (13-15 inches).

Weight: The fennec fox, smallest of all canids, weighs scarcely 1.5 kilograms (3.3 pounds). The red fox averages 7 kilograms (15 pounds). Individual animals have been known to reach much larger sizes and weights.

Gestation: 60-63 days for the red fox.

Longevity: Up to 6 years (13 years in captivity).

Distribution: North and South America, Europe, Asia, and Africa.

Habitat: Wide-ranging, from Arctic tundra to city center.

Frog

By any pond on a summer night a concert of mating calls, commonly called the croaking of the frogs, breaks the nocturnal silence, and their awkward, dissonant "music" touches a part of our humanity. Frogs and toads belong to the order Anura, comprising more than 2,600 species. The name signifies that they are tailless amphibians, at least in their adult stages. An alternative name, Salientia, means leaping or jumping, a reference to their strong hind legs and their bouncing capacity.[1]

The distinction between frog and toad is not easy, taxonomically. Divergent species can and do converge under similar ecological pressures. In general, frogs are more aquatic or semiaquatic, while toads are more comfortable on land.[2] Nevertheless, some frogs are almost exclusively arboreal, while others burrow in the earth, or remain always in the water.[3] Although there are a number of notably venomous frogs, toads are the more venomous of the two — even the eggs of the neotropical toad are highly toxic. Anurans, like most amphibians, have soft and moist skin, used to varying degrees as organs of respiration, to augment or in some cases replace the function of the lungs.[4]

Frogs interact with the world in many crucial ways. They will attempt to eat anything within a certain size range, so long as it is moving — even their own young.[5] Conversely, they will flee anything in motion that is larger than they are. Males will mount anything in sight, including other males, finding a pregnable female more or less at random. Their range of hearing seems to be limited to the frequencies of other frogs and of potential enemies. All other frequencies or patterns of sound are, in effect, edited out before they reach the brain.[6] Frogs are sensitive to colors, which are processed visually by the eye itself. The frog is very responsive to blue; to increase its chances of survival when in danger, it instinctively leaps toward the nearest blue spot, which in most cases is water.[7] As is common among predators, motion seems to be a significant facilitator of sight. It is said that a frog would starve to death within inches of a fat, juicy fly if the insect did not move.[8]

Frogs and toads undergo a dramatic metamorphosis as part of their development, though the enormous variety of species makes generalizations difficult. European common frog tadpoles hatch from egg masses deposited in still and shallow water, feeding at first on the remnants of their yolk sacs. Forelimbs appear within a few weeks, followed by hind limbs. Next the tail is absorbed, lungs develop, gills disappear, and the transformation is complete. The tadpole has become a frog, fully functional on land as well as in the water.[9] In what must surely be the most bizarre variety of the birth process, the tadpoles of *Rheobatrachus silus* and *R. vitellinus* actually develop in the stomach of the female, which gives birth by spewing up a litter of fully-formed and active little froglets, that then hop away.[10]

Frogs play a significant role in the food chain, helping to keep insects in general, and mosquitoes in particular (and therefore malaria), in check. In turn, frogs provide food for a wide range of fish, fowl, mammals, and reptiles.[11] For reasons not yet fully understood, but perhaps having to do with their extremely permeable skins, frogs are highly sensitive to ecological conditions;[12] the current dramatic disappearances of many species from certain areas of the world raises a specter of future environmental crises.

In Egyptian mythology, Heket (or Heqet), a frog goddess, was the midwife at the birth of the world, and she was invoked as a guardian of mothers and their newborn. Later Isis and Hathor, both goddesses of fertility and birth, had the frog as their emblem, and several very early gods were depicted as frogs.[13] In German tradition, a frog spirit or goddess, Holla, haunts the bogs and fens, ponds and wet places, retrieving a red apple, a symbol of life, when it falls down a well.[14]

The *Physiologus* compares righteous people to the land frog, which endures the fire of temptation, and worldly people to the water frog, which (the author supposes) plunges into lechery if touched by even the slightest fascination and craving.[15] Some anurans are sexually ambiguous in the biological sense, so perhaps it is not surprising that people perceive in them the sexual symbol of their choice — some seeing in their slimy bodies, darting tongues, swelling shapes, and sudden jumps an unmistakable phallic symbol. Others see in their fecundity and general shape a suggestion of the uterus. Perhaps for this reason, anurans are often connected with female magic, especially where it concerns birth and giving birth. However, in mythology, frogs are generally depicted as masculine and toads as feminine.[16] In some countries, the vernal chorusing of frogs is imagined to sound like, and symbolize, the crying of unborn children.[17] In many countries, the frog is associated with witches and shunned as poison. While some frogs are quite edible, others, like certain tree frogs of South America, have a poison in their skin so virulent that 0.0001 grams (0.0000035 ounces) is enough to kill a man.[18]

Although many frogs (and, more obviously, toads) thrive in habitats far removed from lake or stream, they have always been symbolically associated with water, sharing in the figurative as well as literal qualities of water creatures. Another salient characteristic is frogs' tendency to leap. Taken with its metamorphosis — an ontogeny that seems to recapitulate the phylogenetic emergence from water-breathing sea creature to air-breathing land creature — makes the frog an excellent symbol of the progressive, intuitive leap of the unconscious to the conscious. Frogs' metaphoric development recalls human maturation, and their shape, especially their articulated "fingers," is sufficiently homuncular to suggest a kind of lower-order caricature of the human personality.[19]

Frog images appearing in dreams often have nearly explicit sexual implications, a projection of sexuality, spontaneity, and quickness to joy. Not surprisingly, in a sexually repressed society, frogs and toads are considered archetypally repulsive and loathsome — objects of ambivalent fascination and revulsion. For example, in fairy tales, the prince (symbolic of a new emerging consciousness) cannot be redeemed until the princess overcomes her physical squeamishness and accepts his "animal" nature. Only then can the new consciousness become effective in the world. Thus, when a person dreams about a frog, he or she would usually be confronted with a need to relate to negative feelings about sexuality and spontaneity.

Notes

[1] Grzimek 1984, 5: 357.
[2] Duellman and Trueb 1986, 264-65.
[3] Grzimek 1984, 5: 357.
[4] Burton 1981, 269.
[5] Downer 1989, 43.
[6] Downer 1989, 72.
[7] Downer 1989, 52.
[8] Downer 1989, 43.
[9] Burton 1981, 274.
[10] Duellman and Trueb 1986, 137.
[11] Yoffe 1992, 36.
[12] Burton 1981, 268-69.
[13] Cooper 1992, 107.
[14] Gimbutas 1989, 255, 319.
[15] Curley 1979, 60-61.
[16] von Franz 1975b, 53.
[17] von Franz 1976, 23-24.
[18] Attenborough 1990, 88.
[19] von Franz 1976, 24.

FROG

Order: Salientia/Anura (with many suborders and family classifications).
Size: Range is from 2 centimeters (0.8 inches) for the Eastern narrow-mouthed frog to 15 centimeters (6 inches) for the Marsh frog, the average ranging from 2.5 centimeters (1 inches) to 6 centimeters (2 inches). The largest frog in the world, the Goliath frog of Africa, has a body length of 40 centimeters (16 inches).
Weight: Up to 3.3 kilograms (7 pounds).
Incubation: The development of frog eggs can take from 1–270 days, depending on species.
Longevity: Little is known about the longevity of amphibians in nature, while in captivity their life expectancy can be up to 36 years. A bullfrog can live up to 16 years in captivity.
Distribution: Worldwide except Antarctica.
Habitat: Arboreal, terrestrial, and aquatic.

Giraffe

The tallest animal in the world, the giraffe is a doe-eyed creature, gentle and silent, with an astonishingly long and elegantly arching neck and awkward, stilt-like legs. It surveys the world from a lofty perspective — as much as nineteen feet from the ground — among the leaves and branches of the trees on which it grazes with its long, nearly prehensile lips and tongue. Its natural range being limited to sub-Saharan Africa, this surprising-looking creature is a zoological as well as anatomical curiosity, seen by most of us only in captivity or pictures. It was known for centuries in the wider world only because it was considered so rare, exotic, and beautiful as to make it a fitting gift for princes and pashas, emperors, sultans, rajas, and potentates.

Despite its almost preposterous proportions and great bulk (males can weigh as much as four thousand pounds), the giraffe moves with stately grace. When threatened it can outrun most predators with long, loping strides, but if forced to stand and fight, it is fully capable of staving in the head of a lion with a single kick of its front legs.[1] Giraffes' mouths are adapted for tearing foliage and buds from trees. With their long necks and tongues, they easily reach high branches and get even the last leaves from the tops of the thorniest acacia tree.[2] Thus, they do not compete for food with grazing animals and can share their habitat with a wide range of creatures. Their vision, hearing, and smell are acute.[3]

The giraffe has a few notable physiological anomalies. Its extraordinarily long neck has only the ordinary number of vertebrae, although the individual bones have evolved to unusual length and strength. The extreme arterial pressure required to raise blood to the level of its elevated head is managed by a unique arrangement of valves in the cervical blood vessels.[4] The horns of a giraffe — blunt, bony knobs, covered with skin and hair — appear on both males and females, and may number anywhere from two to as many as five. A common but false notion is that a giraffe can never regain its feet once it lies down, and as a consequence must sleep standing up. Giraffes, like horses, will "nap" on foot, but they spend an average of eight hours a day lying down if not threatened.[5]

Of course, they are vulnerable in such a position, just as they are when bending down to drink. Because their front legs are longer than their hind legs, to drink they have to awkwardly splay and extend the front legs outward so that their heads can reach the water.[6]

Giraffes live in small groups, usually led by a dominant male. Rank is recognized within the groups, but gestures of dominance are few and subtle. Males fight only by butting heads and thumping necks, never with their deadly hooves.[7] Never domesticated as beasts of burden, nor raised for food or leather, too meek to make much of a hunting trophy and too large to stuff and mount, giraffes conflict with humans only as people reduce their natural habitat through conversion to agriculture.

The Arab word from which giraffe is derived is *zerafah,* which can be translated as "the lovely one."[8] With its exotic beauty, graceful shape, quiet, non-aggressive ways, shy, elusive manner, and long eyelashes, the giraffe, has an unmistakably feminine quality. In an Arab dream book by the Muslim theologian Damiri (1341-1405), the giraffe is said to signify a beautiful woman.[9] To the African Bushmen the giraffe was a cult animal and a vehicle of supernatural power.[10]

The lofty quality of the giraffe, the literal and symbolic distance between its aerial point of view and the touch of its hooves on the solid ground, suggests a kind of head-in-the-clouds otherworldliness. Roy Campbell expresses this view in his poem "Dreaming Spires."

> The City of Giraffes! — a People
> Who live between the earth and skies,
> Each in his lone religious steeple,
> Keeping a light-house with their eyes

By virtue of its height, the giraffe's capacity to see the world from a broad perspective is unique among land animals. With the rare symbolic quality of being linked both to the earth and to a higher, possibly spiritual level, the giraffe can represent the capacity to have an overview of life that remains earthbound and thus connected to reality. If somebody were to dream of a giraffe, that person might want to reflect on what he or she was doing in life that needed more of an overview or wide-ranging viewpoint. In this way, a dream of a giraffe might balance or compensate operating in a particularly hard-driving, focused, and goal-oriented way in the world. It should also be noted that, because of its forceful, defensive kick, the giraffe can characterize a necessary, albeit harsh, self-protective attitude.

Notes
[1] Hillman 1983, 300.
[2] Grzimek 1984: 13, 259.
[3] Macdonald 1987, 535.
[4] Grzimek 1984, 13: 265-66.

[5] Grzimek 1984, 13: 265.
[6] Grzimek 1984, 13: 256.
[7] Grzimek 1984, 13: 256-57.
[8] Hillman 1983, 229.
[9] Hillman 1983, 300.
[10] Cooper 1992, 111.

GIRAFFE
Family: Giraffidae.
Size: 2.5-5 meters (8-16 feet) long, 1.8-5.8 meters (6-19 feet) to crown of head.
Weight: Male weighs 800-1,930 kilograms (1,765-4,255 pounds); female weighs 550-1,180 kilograms (1,213-2,601 pounds).
Distribution: Africa, south of the Sahara desert.
Longevity: Up to 25 years in the wild; up to 28 years in captivity.
Gestation: 453-464 days.
Habitat: Open woodlands and wooded grasslands.

Goat

Funky, rank, and lustful, the goat is often portrayed in popular culture as the cranky cartoon creature that eats tin cans. Real goats, of course, bear little resemblance to this picture, although the males, or billygoats, can be rambunctious and possess scent glands that are somewhat malodorous. The goat genus, *Capra,* includes the ibex, the markhor, and the wild goat, from which all domestic goats are descended. All are old world animals; the American mountain goat, although related, is not really a goat at all, but rather a kind of chamois or antelope. Domestic goats have been kept for meat, leather, wool, milk, and cheese for most of recorded history (at least since the seventh century BCE).[1]

The wild goat originally inhabited the mountains of Asia Minor and the Greek islands. It prefers hilly terrain, from gentle slopes to steep, rocky inclines. Its numbers are now greatly reduced, and in many regions it has become extinct, although in some areas feral domestic goats still range. The males have beards and horns; most females lack beards and have considerably smaller horns. One or two births at a time are normal — the udder has just two nipples.[2]

Despite stereotypes, goats are clean and fastidious, choosing their food carefully and testing its scent and taste before eating. Although they will take household scraps and vegetables of almost any sort, they prefer grass and leaves. They are friendly, gregarious creatures that seek contact with conspecifics in the wild and are comfortable in the presence of people or other farm animals.[3]

The virility of the male goat may have inspired its association with various gods. It pulled the chariot of Thor, the Norse thunder god, and carried Agni, the Hindu fire god. Satyrs and fauns, notoriously lecherous demigods, are composite creatures with distinctly goat-like features. As sexuality fell into disrepute at the beginning of the Christian era, animals noted for their sexuality were considered particularly "beastly," and gods associated with them were demonized. Goats were scapegoated, as it were, taking on the burden of human ambivalence about sexuality to become the hypersexual mounts of witches. The Devil was portrayed with goat horns, especially when dallying at witches' sabbaths. The Knights Templar were at one time supposed to have worshipped a goat idol called Baphomet.[4]

The scapegoat ritual of the ancient Hebrews mentioned in Leviticus 16:8-10, one of expiation and atonement, involved two male goats; one was sacrificed to God, designated "for the Lord," and the other — the escape goat, called "Azazel" — was released and allowed to wander off, carrying with it the confessed sins and transgressions of the community. The word "Azazel" has widely different connotations. It can be the scapegoat itself, the place in the desert where the goat was sent, or a desert demon to which its fate was left. Azazel is also one of the Islamic names for the Devil. Christ would often be portrayed as the scapegoat, because a basic tenet of Christianity was that he took away the sins of humanity.[5]

In Arabic culture, the goat at the head of the herd is emblematic of dignity, but goats can also symbolize lawlessness and headstrong independence.[6] In medieval bestiaries, the lechery of the goat was imagined to reside in its blood. The goat's blood was thought to be the essence of sensuality and lasciviousness, so strong as to destroy anything but the "adamant," a fabulous substance with the characteristics of diamond. This fantasy substance was an incorruptible mineral that could dissolve anything. The physiology imagined here is obviously a projection of psychological evidence; the diamond within a person able to contain the extreme passions is the self as a mature structure.[7]

In ancient Greece, the goat was sacred to Aphrodite, Hera, and Artemis, and it was an attribute of Dionysos, who took the form of a goat when fleeing from the devil Typhon.[8] Minoan ceramics and stone seals depict goat figures in conjunction with moons, plants, and the tree of life. Female initiates of the Dionysian cult appear in frescoes accompanied by two little goats, underscoring the god's connection with sexuality.[9] In ancient Babylon, Ishtar was the goddess of war and sexual love, and Tammuz was her son-lover; the kid, a young goat, was used to symbolize those initiated into their cult, as possessor of secret revelations regarding the mysteries of passion.[10] In India, the spirit of the goddess Kali is said to inspire the oracular utterances of a priest who sucks the blood from the cut throat of a goat.[11]

The zodiacal constellation Capricorn (Latin: goat-horned) was often depicted as a hybrid — a goat with a tail of a fish. Jung said, "The sun mounts like a goat to the tops of the highest mountains, and then plunges into the depths of the sea like a fish." In astrology, Saturn is considered the ruler of Capricorn and can express itself in positive qualities of steadiness, perseverance, and discipline, as well as negative qualities of darkness, depression, and stubbornness.[12]

Psychologically, the reputed lewdness of the goat connects it to a wild instinctual life that, until tamed, is generally in opposition to spirituality or consciousness. In the context of nature, the worship of the goat-footed Pan can lead to renewal, but in the context of civilized life and its need for structure, Pan brings rape, sexual harassment, and all manner of sexual havoc. Thus, the responsible management of unruly, "goatish" sexuality is, in one sense, an essential part of human development. Yet in its proper place and perspective this sexuality is life-positive and even a link to passionate spirituality.

To dream of a goat may indicate that the dreamer requires a greater steadiness and firmness in his or her life pursuits, as opposed to a flighty, imaginal, intuitive approach to conflicts. Another interpretation, leaning toward the lascivious, sexual nature of the goat, could indicate either that the dreamer is cut off from sexuality or any kind of spirit of wildness and requires connection to that energy, or that there is too much indulgence, passionate sexual life in danger of engulfing the conscious personality and draining energy from other necessary values. A different option would be to address the issue of scapegoating. Many individuals have been severely scapegoated in their lives, which leads to distressing inner states, notably feeling guilty about whatever may be happening within their surroundings. Or they may be scapegoating others, blaming them for their own shortcomings and failures. At such times, the goat can signal the need to be aware of this scapegoat complex and to gradually desensitize its power.

Notes
[1] Grzimek 1984, 13: 490-91.
[2] Grzimek 1984, 13: 486-91.
[3] Grzimek 1984, 13: 491.
[4] Biedermann 1994, 153.
[5] Cooper 1992, 13; Frankel and Teutsch Platkin 1992, 61-62.
[6] Cooper 1992, 113.
[7] von Franz 1980c, 171-72.
[8] Cooper 1992, 112.
[9] Gimbutas 1989, 234-35.
[10] de Vries 1976, 217; Charbonneau-Lassay 1991, 87.
[11] Frazer 1979, 109.
[12] Fontana 1994, 166; Jung 1976, 5: 290.

GOAT
Family: Horned Ungulates (Bovidae).
Subfamily: *Caprinae*
Tribe: *Caprini*
Size: The wild goat, *Capra aegagrus*, has a body length of 120-160 centimeters (47-63 inches), a tail length of 15-20 centimeters (6-8 inches), and a shoulder height of 70-100 centimeters (27–39 inches).
Weight: The wild goat weighs 25-40 kilograms (55-88 pounds).
Gestation: 7 months.
Longevity: 18 years.
Distribution: Asia, Central Europe, North and Central America, North Africa.
Habitat: Steep terrain from hot deserts and most jungles to Arctic barrens.

Goose

A large, impressive bird, well known in both domestic and wild varieties, the goose is somewhat awkward on land, but awesome in flight. Alternately thought of as sweet and silly, or nasty and quite aggressive, it presents us with a jumble of contradictions. Among the three orders of flat-billed, web-footed waterfowl, geese are larger than ducks and smaller than swans. They are mostly monogamous birds, and emphatically (sometimes spectacularly) gregarious, gathering in flocks that may number in the hundreds of thousands and migrating *en masse* across great distances, generally in long chevrons or skeins. Steady and tireless fliers, they can cruise at extraordinary heights, taking advantage of the jet stream at altitudes as high as eight thousand meters (26,200 feet). Their honking calls carry for great distances, and a passing flight of geese in the fading autumn light is as haunting to the ear as to the eye.[1]

Geese feed primarily on vegetable matter — grass, sedges, herbs, and mosses[2] — which they tear up and chew with horny lamellae (tooth-like structures that line the beak) and a spur or "nail" at the tip.[3] They are raised for their flesh, and particularly their livers, which, when they are force-fed, are known as *foie gras*. This practice of force-feeding geese to enlarge the livers is now primarily associated with France (Strasbourg in particular), but it was practiced widely in Europe and the Middle East for millennia. In the past, there was also a lively demand for goose quills, which were used for pens and for fletching arrows and shuttlecocks, and of course goose down is still widely used to stuff quilts, featherbeds, pillows, and winter garments.[4] The domestic varieties in Europe are descended from the greylag goose, while those in Asia were probably bred from the swan goose.

We say "silly as a goose," and indeed, with their waddling walk and constant, senseless honking, geese can appear quite inane.[5] But they are also very sharp, alert, wary, and capable of astonishing fierceness. Their bite is quite painful.[6]

Famously aggressive, geese are so sharp-eyed and keen of hearing that they are often kept and counted upon to sound a noisy alarm at the first sign of intruders. In 390 BCE, a gaggle of geese is said to have saved Rome by alerting the guard to a Gaulish attack; from that time, sacred geese were kept in the capitol, becoming virtually an emblem of Rome itself.[7] They were sacred in the temple of Juno,[8] and, perhaps because of their fierceness, they were associated with Mars, the Roman war god.[9] Geese were also identified with Greek gods — Eros, the god of love; Apollo, the solar god; and Hermes, the messenger of the gods. As an attribute of Hera, the goose signified watchfulness and wifely duty.[10] It was also linked with the Greek nature goddess Nemesis, who was the instrument of divine or natural justice.

In ancient Egypt the goose laid the world egg,[11] and with her raucous call she announced the beginning of time and the advent of the sun. In a variant of that story, Hathor, worshipped as the Nile goose, gave birth to Ra, the sun, in the form of a golden egg.[12] Geb, the Egyptian god of the earth and the physical support of the world, was one of the original forms in their mythology and had the head of a goose.[13] The creative quality of the goose is further seen in India, where the goose and swan — not differentiated in various cultures — are both associated with the sun. Brahma often rides a magnificent gander, which is seen as an aspect of the god's creative principle.[14] In Native American cultures, the Snow goose is a totem of the winter solstice, and migrating geese are seen as arrowheads pointing out new paths, new possibilities, another indication of the creative quality of the goose.[15]

The goose appears in many rhymes and fairy tales. The old Greek fable "The Goose That Laid the Golden Egg" is an interesting parable of insight and spiritual loss, with gold a paradoxical symbol of both inner (spiritual) wealth and crass, material value. This potential spiritual loss may well be the source of the expression "to cook one's goose," meaning to be in a hopeless situation and/or to do oneself grievous harm. In European culture the goose appears as a symbol of stupidity, although in the Middle Ages geese were sometimes considered the familiars of witches, who were imagined riding them (if not broomsticks) on the way to their sabbath.[16]

Accordingly, the image of the goose in a dream can have a variety of symbolic meanings, depending on the context and the dreamer's present situation. For someone who is operating in a creative way, or needing to do so, the goose can symbolize a powerful creative process that may already be potentially in place. For somebody who is too stuck in material pursuits, and not sufficiently forward-looking, the goose can appear as a spiritual messenger, trying to orient the person to deeper values. For a person who may be too naive or wishful about life, the goose can appear as a force of "natural justice." If someone is not sufficiently protecting his or her territory, the goose can appear as a figure of aggression. For the dreamer who is "winning the battle but losing the war," the goose can represent an aspect of stupid self-destruction. In addition, the appearance of the goose in a dream may demand making peace with deep aggressive and violent fantasies, by facing and recognizing them, thus transforming them into a creative rather than a destructive potential.

Notes
[1] Hoyo 1992, 545–49.
[2] Hoyo 1992, 552.
[3] Grzimek 1984, 7: 258.
[4] Hoyo 1992, 564.
[5] Cooper 1992, 114.
[6] Hoyo 1992, 564.
[7] Ibid.
[8] Andrews 1993, 144.
[9] Cooper 1992, 114.
[10] Ibid.
[11] Becker 1994, 13.
[12] Walker 1983, 349.
[13] *Funk & Wagnalls Standard Dictionary* 1972, 459.
[14] *Funk & Wagnalls Standard Dictionary* 1972, 460; Cooper 1992, 114.
[15] Andrews 1993, 349.
[16] *Funk & Wagnalls Standard Dictionary* 1972, 460.

GOOSE
Family: Anatidae.
Size: Canadian goose is 55–110 centimeters (22–43 inches) in length. Other subspecies have a variety of sizes.
Wingspan: 122–183 centimeters (48–72 inches).
Weight: 3–6 kilograms (7–14 pounds).
Gestation: Approximately 28 days.
Longevity: 10–15 years in the wild, more than 30 years in captivity.
Distribution: Worldwide except Antarctica.
Habitat: Tundra to semi-desert, in both wooded and open country, invariably near water.

Grasshoppers/Locusts/Crickets

The orthopterans — grasshoppers, locusts, and crickets — are wonderful jumpers. Their highly developed hind legs launch them into sudden flight, for leaps nearly twenty times the length of their bodies.[1] When they are not swarming or jumping, they are noticeable primarily through their repetitive chirping sounds, made mostly by the males. Variations of rhythm, and to a lesser extent pitch, distinguish individual species as well as various intentions, such as courtship, rivalry, and flight.[2]

Of the two main types of grasshoppers, the Ensifera, including the long-horned species as well as the crickets and katydids, share a distinctive sword-shaped ovipositor. They make sounds by rubbing their modified wing covers, called tegmina. The short-horned species (Caelifera), some of which are referred to as locusts, make sounds by rubbing a comb-like structure on their jumping legs against a scraper on the tegmina. The former group eats other insects as well as plants; the latter are strictly vegetarian. For both, the noise-making apparatus is known collectively as the stridulatory organs — stridulation being the Latinate word for what people normally call chirping.[3]

Of the five thousand species of Caelifera grasshoppers, most are more or less solitary creatures, and only nine are known to form migratory swarms. (In the 1870s, North America experienced two devastating locust plagues that included swarms estimated to contain 124 billion insects.) Curiously, migratory species do not always swarm. They sometimes enter solitary phases that may last for a number of generations, until conditions, not yet fully understood, cause changes in their physiology as well as their behavior. Then great voracious clouds begin to gather. The "seventeen-year" locust, although it bears a superficial similarity to the true locust and does swarm, is not an orthopteran, but a cicada, a member of the order Homoptera.[4]

Females lay 2 to 120 eggs at a time, generally in holes in the ground, which they have dug with their ovipositors. The sticky egg masses, called pods, remain underground for the winter, until the hatching of the nymphs, which look like small adults without wings.[5] As they grow, they literally burst their tough, inelastic skins, which they shed or molt in a process that takes up to an hour. After forty to sixty days and five or six molts, the immature hopper undergoes one last molt from which it emerges as an adult with wings. Through their molts, the nymphs exhibit some regenerative power; an individual that loses a leg may produce a new one at its next molt, although the new limb is likely to be (and remain) diminished in size and function.

Some species of grasshopper accumulate toxic, or at least bad-tasting, substances in their tissues and blood, thereby discouraging predators. Some of these species even void or squirt their blood through mouthparts or leg joints.[6] A number of animals prey on grasshoppers, including beetles, birds, lizards, mice, snakes, spiders, and, in some parts of the world (Africa in particular), humans. Grasshoppers are an excellent source of nutrition, high in fats and proteins.[7] John the Baptist is said to have sustained himself in the desert for forty days on a strict diet of locusts and honey.[8]

In myth, folktale, cultural tradition, and symbolism, people have tended to be casual and sometimes confused about taxonomic distinctions among grasshoppers, locusts, crickets, and cicadas. Often considerable guesswork, local custom, mistranslation, and overlap are involved assigning these names to actual creatures and their symbolic representations. Crickets, for instance, are widely considered good luck, and one's presence in the house is considered a cheerful omen. In China, this belief seems to apply to grasshoppers as well as crickets.[9] Too, the plagues called down by Moses on the Egyptians or trumpeted in the Apocalypse are more apt to be identified as swarming locusts rather than grasshoppers, a much more benign and friendly-sounding designation. A farmer whose fields are being consumed, however, is unlikely to care what they are called; he just wants to be free of them.[10] The Old Testament god sent locusts, but Christianity's, kinder, gentler god generally made the pernicious locust an instrument of the Devil. The grasshopper's molt is reminiscent of rebirth, and a symbol of resurrection.[11]

Children intuitively delight in the leaping antics of the grasshopper, so it can symbolize joyfulness for an individual. While the cricket, and to a lesser extent the grasshopper, are sometimes benign figures, swarming locusts are thoroughly associated with devastation (to the earth and to human enterprise on the earth). It is difficult to imagine a positive aspect of these insects, unless one is prepared to accept the notion of psychic cleansing as a symbolic analogue of devastation. Swarming insects in general are symbolic of dissociation, a splitting off or fragmenting of elements of the psyche. Grasshoppers/locusts in particular carry an additional emphasis on devouring impulses such as envy, greed, or any insatiable appetites that threaten to consume us.

Should the image of a grasshopper appear in a dream, it is important to look for the missing element of joy in the dreamer's life. If locusts appear one might look further into aspects of the dreamer's inner life that may be eating him or her up, destroying inner structure and resources. In the case of a person dreaming of a swarm, either of grasshoppers or locusts, the dream might represent an inner state that destroys cohesiveness and a sense of wholeness, leading to a feeling of fragmentation. Difficulty in concentrating, loss of focus and energy, anxiety and dread, and loss of the sense of personal identity may be associated with this fragmentation. Such extreme states can be dangerous to the person's stability and mental health. Multiplicity of any symbol, and especially grasshoppers, locusts, cicadas, or any insects, is a warning sign that the dreamer needs to carefully examine his or her life, attitudes, and behaviors to determine what overly rigid, excessively compulsive, or unduly self-destructive tendencies might have created such a negative image.

Notes

1. Grzimek 1984, 2: 99.
2. *World Book Encyclopedia* (1991), 9: 328.
3. Ibid.
4. "Locust." *Encyclopedia Britannica*, 1997.
5. *World Book Encyclopedia* 1991, 9: 328.
6. Wootton 1988, 153.
7. *World Book Encyclopedia* 1991, 9: 327-28.
8. Grzimek 1984, 2: 112.
9. Andrews 1993, 342.
10. Charbonneau-Lassay 1991, 353-55.
11. Heinz-Mohr 1976, 130.

GRASSHOPPERS/LOCUSTS/CRICKETS

Order: Orthoptera (which includes grasshoppers, locusts, crickets, and the "seventeen-year locust" also sometimes known as cicada).

Size: Some grasshoppers exceed 11 centimeters (4 inches) in length (such as *Tropidacris latriellei* of South America). Short-horned grasshoppers measure 5 millimeters (0.2 inches) to 11 centimeters (4.3 inches) in length. Crickets measure 3 to 50 millimeters (0.12 to 2 inches) in length.

Weight: Varies with species.

Incubation: Some of these insects pass from the egg to adult stage within a few days or weeks. Others spend the winter months in the egg or in diverse immature stages, and a few may require several years to become adults. The "seventeen-year" locust (cicada) is the exception, with a life cycle completed in 2-5 years.

Longevity: Cicadas live 14-21 days; grasshoppers live 51-52 days.

Distribution: All but the coldest parts of the world.

Habitat: Greatest numbers are in lowland tropical forests, semi-arid regions, and grasslands.

Hare/Rabbit

A plague to every gardener, prey to every predator, and cuddly bunny to every child, the lagomorphs, including hares and rabbits, are either native species or introduced in nearly every part of the world. Highly fecund, famously flop-eared, fuzzy, and bewhiskered, lop-tailed and hop-gaited, the rabbit as a figure of fun shows up in an extraordinary range of folktales and children's literature. Although it is not always immediately obvious, rabbits and hares differ in some ways. Young hares are more developed at birth, fully furred and open-eyed; rabbits are born naked and blind. Rabbits are generally burrowing animals and inhabit dens, to which they repair for safety; hares nest in depressions on the ground or in heavy brush, relying on their superior running ability to escape danger. Larger hares can reach speeds of eighty kilometers (fifty miles) per hour to escape danger.[1] Hares are better jumpers, but rabbits are more agile.[2]

Both lagomorphs are fast and clever, evasive runners; both have split upper lips and strongly haunched rear legs that are longer than the front legs, which causes their characteristic hopping gait. Both are preyed upon by just about every carnivore, including wolves, foxes, snakes, all kinds of cats, and birds of prey. Humans eat them, use their fur, kill them as pests, and carry their feet on key chains for good luck.[3] Behind their well-known "buck" upper front teeth, lagomorphs have a second pair of small, peg-like incisors. They are strict herbivores, feeding on grasses, leaves, bark, seeds, and roots. To get the maximum nutritional benefit from such a diet, they immediately re-consume some of their feces and digest the food a second time.[4]

The long and extraordinarily mobile ears of the hare and rabbit not only increase their sensitivity to sound, but also help to localize its source. Their sense of smell is well developed and plays an important part in finding food; for the male it also helps in the detection and pursuit of females, whose scent glands give off an attracting odor. Eyesight is poor in hares and slightly better in rabbits. Both are highly adaptable, living and thriving under many climatic conditions, but they do not roam far out of home territory except in very unusual environmental conditions, when they have been known to migrate *en masse.*[5]

Hares and rabbits have a well-deserved reputation for fertility. Eggs are shed not in regular cycles but in response to copulation, and females come into heat immediately after giving birth. In some species the pregnant female can even conceive a second litter before the birth of the first — a phenomenon known as "superfetation."[6] Gestation periods are short, and litter size is large; a female may bear up to seven litters, or an average of thirty young, in a year.[7]

The hare and the rabbit are hardly distinguishable in lore and symbolism. Night foragers, they are seen as lunar creatures. The rabbit's erratic scampering reminded people of the moon's seemingly unpredictable appearance in the sky. From Mexico to South Africa and across Asia, the "hare in the moon" parallels our "man on the moon" as a folkloric character.[8]

Hares have also been closely associated with earth goddesses since earliest times. In Greek mythology, the hare/rabbit was linked with the goddess Hecate.[9] No doubt because of its intense sexual activity and fecundity, the rabbit was imagined to be the favorite animal of the goddess Aphrodite. Its meat was thought to make sterile women fertile; its testicles were eaten to increase the chance of bearing a male child.[10] In alchemical symbolism, hares/rabbits stand for Mercurius — a symbol embracing both the swift messenger of the gods and the moon-bright and elusive metal called quicksilver.[11] Oestra, the Teutonic moon goddess who gave Easter its name, was hare-headed to symbolize the spring renaissance of life and fertility and the rebirth of the moon. The Christian appropriation of Easter still includes the egg-laying "bunny" to represent fecundity. In the Hebrew religion, eating the hare was prohibited because it has a divided and cloven hoof (Deuteronomy 14: 7). The Scandinavian goddess of love and fruitfulness, Freyja, was depicted with hares in attendance.[12]

In medieval Europe, the hare, like the cat, was feared as a witch's familiar,[13] and witches were suspected of taking the form of a hare to do malicious deeds. Originally a "lucky" hare's foot was carried to ward off witches' spells.[14] In Buddhist legend, a hare became the symbol of self-sacrifice by springing into the fire to provide food for the starving Buddha. In Native American myths, the hare is a trickster figure (like the irrepressible cartoon character Bugs Bunny), outwitting larger and stronger creatures and (Prometheus-like) stealing fire for humanity.[15] According to Black Elk's account of the Sun Dance of the Oglala Sioux,

> ... the men also put rabbit skins on their arms and legs, for the rabbit represents humility, because he is quiet and soft and not self-asserting — a quality which we must all possess when we go to the center of the world.[16]

Psychologically, the hare may be considered the messenger of the unconscious. With its elusive, zigzagging movement, it is visible only in fleeting glimpses, much the way we experience brief flashes of insight that can never be traced or tracked head-on. The rabbit's fabled sexuality certainly typifies the irrepressible procreative urge to multiply, as well as the general idea of cyclical regeneration and creativity. Symbolically, the hare/rabbit represents the connecting link between our normal conscious (ego-oriented) reality, with its logical reasoning processes, and the more "magical" lunar processes of inspiration, intuition, and imagination. Consequently, if a person dreamed of a hare or rabbit, it might represent the need to bring creativity more into his or her work, perhaps in contrast to more rational qualities that were being used.

Notes

1 Macdonald 1987, 714–16.
2 Grzimek 1984, 12: 426–28.
3 Lacey 1993, 29–32.
4 Macdonald 1987, 712.
5 Grzimek 1984, 12: 428; Macdonald 1987, 714.
6 Macdonald 1987, 713.
7 Grzimek 1984, 12: 447.
8 Cooper 1992, 120.
9 Andrews 1993, 303.
10 Biedermann 1994, 164.
11 Andrews 1993, 303.
12 Cooper 1992, 121.
13 Ibid.
14 Fontana 1994, 94.
15 Biedermann 1994, 165.
16 Hulbert 1994, 85.

HARE/RABBIT

Family: Leporidae.
Size: Old World rabbit has an overall length of 35–45 centimeters (14–18 inches) and a tail length of 6 centimeters (2 inches); the European hare is 40–76 centimeters (16–30 inches) long, and its tail is 3.5–12 centimeters (1–5 inches) long.
Weight: Old World rabbit weighs 1–2 kilograms (2–3 pounds); European hare weighs 1.3–5 kilograms (8–11 pounds).
Gestation: Approximately 40 days in hares and 30 days in rabbits.
Longevity: In captivity, both hares and rabbits live 5–7 years; in the wild, a little more than a year.
Distribution: Americas, Europe, Asia, and Africa; introduced to Australia, New Zealand, and other islands.
Habitat: Wide-ranging from seashore to upper mountainous regions, from arctic tundra to city center, from dry desert to swamp, from agricultural landscape to forest.

Hawk

Hawks are diurnal birds of prey, like raptors, including the condor, vulture, kite, buteo, buzzard, eagle, osprey, and falcon but excluding owls, which are primarily nocturnal hunters. Hawks in general are sharp-eyed and strong-legged, with sharp talons that they use to kill their prey. They also have a hooked beak that they use to tear and dismember. They have slots for nares (noses), long tarsi (lower legs) for forest hunting, dark eyes and light irises, and longer tails than wings.[1] The combination of short wings and a long tail makes hawks very skillful at swerving and lets them maintain high speeds for short distances while they track and then plunge onto their prey, taking it unawares.[2]

Goshawks usually nest in old cut-up trees, trenches, or waterways, so that they can fly nearer to the ground to hunt. A courting pair soars high above the breeding territory and often uses old existing nests, lining them with fresh green branches of conifers. The clutch contains three to five eggs and the female usually incubates them, being relieved by the male for only one or two hours a day.[3]

In Greece the hawk was, in Homer's phrase, "the swift messenger of Apollo." If an augur spied a hawk pursuing its prey to the right, it was considered an omen of success; if it appeared to the left, failure was foreseen. The hawk also represented the messenger in India. In the *Vedas,* the most ancient and sacred scriptures of Indian philosophy, the hawk was a mount of Indra; it was an attribute of Ahura Mazda, the god of light, in the Zoroastrian tradition, as well as of the Iranian god Mithra.[4]

In general, hawks symbolize fierceness and aggression (in the political sense, a "hawk" is someone eager for war), as well as keen-sightedness and all the shades of symbolic meaning connected with that ability. Ovid's *Metamorphosis* tells the story of Daedalion, who went mad because his daughter Chione dared to boast that she exceeded the huntress-goddess Diana in beauty and was subsequently killed by the angry goddess. Daedalion's grief prompted him to jump from the heights of Mount Parnassus, but he was saved when Apollo changed him into a hawk, which vented its rage on all other birds, "causing others to suffer by its suffering."[5] Connected to its fierceness, the hawk was commonly used as a symbol of death in the Christian Middle Ages, although it occasionally appears as an attribute of the Holy Spirit.[6]

The ancient Hebrews saw in the hawk an expression of the wise providence of the Creator, because of its migrations.[7] The ancient Egyptian creator god Amun Ra included a hawk among his valued possessions. The hawk is a solar bird, imagined flying as high as the sun and gazing upon it unflinchingly. Sun gods, notably Horus in ancient Egypt, are often depicted as hawk- or falcon-headed.[8] In many Native American myths, the hawk (along with the coyote and other creatures) helped to create the world after the flood, making the sun and setting it alight.[9] The red-tailed hawk represented leadership, deliberation, and foresight to the Ojibwa people, while the Pueblo Indians used its feathers in healing ceremonies and invoked its spirit to bring rain.

Psychologically, the hawk represents aggressive impulses in service of life and extremely keen intuition. It can stand for the capacity to see deeply into unknown realms and to grasp situations that might otherwise remain obscure. The hawk is symbolic of force and energy, the human potential that can oppose the darker shadow motifs, the primitive drives of aggression, lust, or envy — in essence, those powers of the human soul that would overwhelm and distort spiritual values. The hawk's combined fierceness and keen perception can be seen in its continual linkage with death — representing, psychologically and in dreams, a presentiment of the death and dissolution of old ways and structures and the emergence of new ones. Thus to dream of a hawk for a rather passive, too accepting person signals the existence of an inner, extremely aggressive power of thought and imagination that can firmly oppose passive attitudes inimical to growth. An already "too hawkish" person, however, might dream of a hawk so that he or she can reflect on the one-sidedness of these attitudes and the need for more receptivity and compassion. Or the symbol of the hawk may represent the person's keen and aggressive intuition about what he or she needs to integrate.

Notes

[1] www.Michael.J.Kennedy-5@tc.umn.edu; Perrins and Middleton 1989, 102-12.
[2] Grzimek 1984, 7: 360.
[3] Grzimek 1984, 7: 361-62.
[4] Cooper 1992, 123.
[5] de Vries 1976, 241.
[6] Becker 1994, 138.
[7] Jobes 1962, 1: 733.
[8] Cooper 1992, 123.
[9] Andrews 1993, 154-55.

HAWK
Family: Accipitridae.
Size: Goshawks and sparrow hawks measure 30-70 centimeters (12-28 inches) in length.
Weight: Goshawks and sparrow hawks weigh 100-2,000 grams (3.5 ounces to 4.5 pounds).
Wingspan: From 35 centimeters (14 inches) for the African sparrow hawk to 1.5 meters (5 feet) for the rough-legged hawk. The female of the northern goshawk has a wingspan of 110-118 centimeters (43-46 inches), while the wingspan of the male is 92-101 centimeters (36-40 inches).
Incubation: 38-40 days.
Longevity: Average 3 years, but some may reach 10-12 years. All species live much longer in captivity.
Distribution: Worldwide.
Habitat: Woods alternate with bush-grown areas, clearings, fields, and lakes or river shores.

Hippopotamus

Hippopotamus in Greek translates as "river horse," but the massive, fleshy, barrel-shaped, gape-mouthed, and snaggle-toothed hippopotamus is not related to the horse. Yet it is very partial to rivers, where it feeds and lazes, supporting its bulk in the buoying waters. It is a colossal creature, weighing as much as 3.5 tons (7,000 pounds or 3,182 kilograms). Nearly hairless, with copper brown skin fading to light purple on its underside, the hippopotamus is exclusively herbivorous, feeding on grass, reeds, aquatic plants, leaves, and fruit.[1] Its sense of hearing and sight is well developed, and although hippopotamuses do not often vocalize, they call in the morning and evening. Their extraordinary roar can be heard for miles, although experts are not sure of its meaning or purpose.[2]

Hippopotamuses do not migrate, even when food is temporarily scarce. They are sedentary animals, preferring habitats that include ponds or slow-moving streams with foliage-covered banks. They graze primarily at night, spending their days either sunning themselves on the banks or, if it is too hot, resting in the water. They are not particularly strong swimmers, preferring to wade in slow-moving water perhaps 1.2 meters (4 feet) deep.[3] While the nostrils of the hippopotamus can be fully underwater, its nostrils, eyes and ears are placed on the head so that all three can remain above water and function while the rest of the animal — almost the entire hippopotamus — remains below the surface. When it feels threatened, it can remain underwater for up to six minutes, finally surfacing under floating aquatic plants to survey the situation, grab a quick breath, and, if necessary, re-submerge.[4]

If hippopotamuses are unable to bathe regularly, glands under their skin secrete a reddish-brown liquid that can look like blood. This unusual substance, which has a high salt content like sweat, protects the animal from sunburn and apparently has an antiseptic function. Hippopotamuses, even those with large wounds, rarely develop infections, despite frequent wallowing in waters that are often filthy. Their skin is famously thick and tough, especially where it is most frequently exposed to attack by other hippopotamuses.[5] Bulls have huge canine teeth on their lower jaws that might more properly be described as tusks (the largest ever found measured sixty-three centimeters or twenty-five inches). The incisor and canine teeth are very large and grow continuously as they are worn away. A bull wanting to intimidate a rival displays these weapons by gaping its jaws most impressively. If mere display does not suffice, a fight will ensue that can, if the opponents are equally matched, go on for hours. Old bulls are almost always profoundly scarred, and the teeth can actually pierce to the heart.[6]

Hunters avidly seek the large canine teeth, which have a protective outer layer of yellowish enamel that must be removed with acid to reveal the actual ivory.[7] With a diet high in cellulose, hippopotamuses produce large quantities of excrement, which, when mixed with the water in which they wallow, fosters the growth of microscopic flora that the fish eat. On land, bulls also use their droppings to mark the territories in which they claim exclusive mating rights. Within these areas, submissive bulls may wander unchallenged, but they are not allowed to breed. Copulation and birthing occur primarily in the water.[8] All hippopotamuses, except the pygmy variety, are gregarious, with herds forming around adult females and their offspring. Males generally go off by themselves, although in some areas a few are tolerated in the main herd. These "matri-centric" groups allow other females to watch the young when mothers move off.[9]

Being strictly an African creature, the hippopotamus figured largely in the culture and mythology of the Egyptians, and through them (to a lesser extent) in Greek and Roman culture. The hippopotamus goddess was worshipped in ancient Egypt under a number of names, including Rert or Rertu, Ta-urt, Apet, and Sheput, and she was identified in one way or another with nearly every great goddess of Egypt. The hippopotamus goddess was at times considered the female counterpart of Set and the mother of the sun god.[10] In general, she was a benevolent creature, appearing in at least one version of the *Book of the Dead* as a chthonic deity and good-hearted guardian of the dead. Yet the fear-some monster Am-mit, which appears in the scene of the soul's final judgment in the underworld, has the hindquarters of a hippopotamus, and the hippopota-mus was sacred to the evil and destructive Set. The male animal was feared because of its fierce aggressiveness, but the female animal was revered as a symbol of fertility and a protectress of women.[11] Figures of Ta-uret (Thoèris to the Greeks), called "the great one," show a hippopotamus standing on its hind legs with a woman's breasts and supported by the Sa loop, a talisman and a symbol of protection. These were used as amulets or charms and placed on the beds of women in the throes of childbirth.[12]

In the Old Testament (Job 40:15), the hippopotamus is a symbol of over-whelming strength and power, frequently identified with the Behemoth, an immense beast that is the terrestrial equivalent of the Leviathan — a primeval monster expected to reappear during the apocalyptic final days.[13] The creature intrigued Christian artists enough to appear frequently in depictions of the creation of the animal world.[14] The symbolic importance of the hippopotamus certainly stems from its incredible mass and its life in the water, where it is often nearly submerged. Its size connects it to awesome and powerful levels of psy-chic life, which dwarf the human personality. To dream of a hippopotamus is to dream of affects and drives that are far beyond the coping capacity of the will and the conscious mind. To dream of a hippopotamus is to dream of the "power of God."

On another level, the hippopotamus, with its swollen, pregnant-looking form, is a symbol of the Great Mother in both positive and negative forms, linking (more than most animals) the opposites of life and death. It thus can represent birth, with all its promising and life-giving implications, but with its great, yawning chasm of a mouth, it can also denote the devouring impulse, a compulsive drive to possess by engulfment. The reconciliation of these two great poles of existence is the work of all psychological and spiritual develop-ment. The poles may manifest as ongoing development and the embrace of new life situations versus regression and a backward motion to old forms and acquiescence.

The hippopotamus as a dream image offers the conscious personality a remarkable opportunity to gain harmony between the opposites of life and death, progression and regression. Since it is also a gregarious creature, the hippopotamus might reflect the dreamer's social involvement. He or she may be too isolated and need additional social contact to stimulate inspiration, motivation, and creative activities. Meditating upon the image, and feeling its awesome power, can enliven its significant capacity to hold such opposites together, and thus compensate for the one-sidedness of conscious life.

Notes
[1] Grzimek 1984, 13: 109, 116.
[2] Grzimek 1984, 13: 118.
[3] Grzimek 1984, 13: 117.
[4] Grzimek 1984, 13: 118.
[5] Ibid.
[6] Grzimek 1984, 13: 118-19.
[7] Ibid.
[8] Grzimek 1984, 13: 120; Macdonald 1987, 150.
[9] Grzimek 1984, 13: 122.
[10] Budge 1969, 2: 359; Jobes 1962, 1: 774.
[11] Budge 1969, 2: 359; Becker 1994, 143.
[12] Biedermann 1994, 174.
[13] Becker 1994, 143.
[14] Biedermann 1994, 174.

HIPPOPOTAMUS
Family: Hippopotamidae.
Size: Head-body length measures 3.3-3.45 meters (10.9-11.3 feet); height measures 1.4 meters (4.6 feet).
Weight: Male weighs 1,600-3,200 kilograms (3,525-7,055 pounds); female weighs 1,400 kilograms (3,086 pounds).
Gestation: Approximately 240 days.
Longevity: Approximately 45 years.
Distribution: West, Central, East, and South Africa.
Habitat: Short grasslands (night); wallows, rivers, and lakes (day).

Horse

Swift and powerful, spirited yet tameable, horses have a long and complex relationship with humankind. Often we abuse them as beasts of burden or as mounts — animal slaves, in effect. However, they are also comrades in battle, teammates in sport, and nearly equal partners in work; they can be a symbolic representation of the cultural process of transforming wild energy into useful forms. Although horses lived in North America until the end of the Tertiary Age, seventy million years ago, in historical times horses lived only in Europe and Asia. The first attempts at domestication probably took place around 4000 BCE, in Mesopotamia and China. By 2000 BCE domestic horses were a familiar sight over much of China. Brought to North America by the invading Spanish explorers and conquistadors, horses escaped and became feral. Called mustangs, their descendants were later caught and tamed by colonists and Native Americans alike. In the mid-seventeeth century there were an estimated two to four million mustangs, mostly in the Southwest. As of the early 1970s, fewer than twenty thousand survived.[1]

Among the many varieties of wild horses that once existed, those discovered in western Mongolia in the late 1870s by the Russian explorer N.M. Przhevalsky were probably the ancestors of at least some breeds of domesticated horses.[2] Once ranging from the Urals and Kazakhstan as far east as Mongolia, this breed survives today only in zoos, where they are kept in breeding groups. The stallion generally remains aloof from the rest of the herd. When they are on the move, he usually brings up the rear, sometimes urging slower members on and herding them together if they stray. The stallion will boldly attack intruders, but when the herd feels threatened by predators, the horses form a circle with heads toward the center, enabling them to strike out in all directions with their rear hooves. In this same formation, swishing tails are quite effective in keeping flies at bay.[3]

Although horses smell and hear much better than they see, their greeting behavior suggests that they cannot distinguish between another live horse and a stuffed dummy. Like elephants and rhinos, they can sleep either standing or lying down, although some individuals may do one or the other exclusively.[4] Horses have impressive pulling strength. Light horses are said to be able to pull seventy-seven percent of their body weight, and large draft animals sixty-eight percent. A thoroughbred racer can achieve a top speed of 60 kilometers (37 miles) per hour, and for short stretches of about 100 meters (328 feet) they may reach speeds of up to 66 kilometers (41 miles) per hour.[5] They have remarkable stamina as a result of a contraction of the spleen that injects additional oxygen-bearing red blood cells into the system. In just over a minute, the red blood cell count doubles, and aerobic capacity increases proportionately.[6]

In spring and summer, a mare comes into heat for approximately five days every three weeks. In estrus, she will urinate in small spurts, raise her tail, and flash her vulva to attract the attention of nearby stallions. If she accepts an interested stallion, she will brace, tail raised to one side, exposing her vulva. Veterinarians have noted that healthy mares usually give birth at night.[7]

The symbolic significance of any animal, including the horse, is often determined by how actual physical characteristics become hooks for unconscious projections, which enhance the physical image into a heightened symbolic or even fabulous form. Since horses are so influential in the development of society, they figure hugely in popular literature and entertainment. An uncanny sensitivity, everything from clairvoyance to prophecy, has been attributed to them.[8]

The power of the horse is evident in Greek mythology, which depicts stallions pulling the chariot of Apollo and black horses pulling the chariot of the great goddess Nyx (night) across the sky. The people of the Greek island Rhodes worshipped the sun by annually flinging a chariot and four horses into the sea for the sun's use. Similarly, kings of Judah dedicated chariots and horses to the sun, and Spartans and Persians sacrificed horses to the sun. In equestrian cultures everywhere, the horse was a most valued possession and, in the more primitive societies, among the most commonly sacrificed animals. In Nordic mythology, the father-god Odin (also known as Wotan) and his eight-legged horse, Sleipnir, noted for its speed, took on many attributes of a wind god. The custom in many places has also been to sacrifice a warrior's charger when the man died.[9]

In the Hindu religion, stallions pull the chariot of the sun god, Surya. Within that tradition, the body is a vehicle controlled by the spirit, as the rider controls the horse. When Vishnu, protector and preserver of the world and restorer of moral order, appears in his last incarnation to bring salvation and peace to the world, he is in the form of a white horse.[10] The horse is very important in Chinese mythology, representing vitality in their astrological system. Horses are emblems of freedom, and in the *I Ching,* the Chinese oracular text, they symbolize creative energy.[11]

The stallion is often seen as a symbol of sexuality, surely due to its strength and sexual dominance in nature. Consequently, the taming of a stallion can represent the taming of sexuality and wild abundant energy for the use of the conscious personality.[12] The horse's sexuality looms large in primitive rites and myths as well. For example, to sacrifice the stallion to those goddesses who were envisioned as mares represents conscious sacrifice of drives and compulsions to the greater good of fertility. The wildness of the horse is especially seen in the centaurs, half-men, half-horses of Greek fable that were considered a coarse, irrepressibly lustful breed of monster.[13] Some centaurs tried to rape the bride of their half-brother Pirithous — Persephone, the daughter of the goddess Demeter — and were driven off by Theseus. Yet from this crude, licentious dynamism, aesthetic and creative qualities emerge when these forces are properly tamed. One sees this potential in the centaur Chiron, the mentor of Achilles, Jason, and Aesculapius who taught them music, medicine, and morals. In the Middle Ages, the pervasive ethos of chivalry — touching on every aspect of manners, morals, honor, and obligation — was derived, etymologically as well as practically, from the horse. The word chivalry is derived from *cheval,* French for horse.

Rather like the dog, the horse has a special relationship with human beings, but with the important difference that a horse is much more powerful. The horse as mount represents our instinctual nature, an "under-riding" energy that supports and conveys our conscious selves, our egos. Freud, spoke of the ego riding the id.[14] Mastering these instinctual energies is vital to avoid impulsiveness, inappropriate sexuality, panic, and nightmares.

While horses can represent a forceful move toward consciousness, they can also symbolize libido moving firmly toward another world, death, taking the soul to another resting place. This symbolism is manifest in the use of horses in funeral ceremonies and is depicted vividly and movingly in Goethe's ballad of the *Erlkönig* (King of the Elves), in which the father rides through the forest into the night holding his dead child in his arms.

Generally dreams of a horse signify the emergence of the creative life of the unconscious in a form that consciousness can master. However, in a woman's dream, the horse usually signifies the sexual, creative undercarriage of her being, while in a man's dream the horse seems to indicate his own connection to potent energies of the unconscious available for more consciously directed effort and work.

Notes

[1] Grzimek 1984, 12: 562-75.
[2] Grzimek 1984, 12: 562.
[3] Grzimek 1984, 12: 567-68.
[4] Grzimek 1989, 12: 575-76.
[5] Grzimek 1984, 12: 575.
[6] Angier 1993, C1.
[7] Batten 1993, 178; Grzimek 1984, 12: 576.
[8] Hannah 1992, 108.
[9] Hannah 1992, 113-14.

[10] Cooper 1992, 131.
[11] Andrews 1993, 232; Wilhelm 1977, 273; Becker 1994, 145.
[12] Andrews 1993, 282.
[13] Becker 1994, 145.
[14] Gamwell and Wells 1989, 81.

HORSE
Family: Equidae.
Size: Head-body length measures 200 centimeters (79 inches); tail length measures 90 centimeters (35 inches).
Weight: 350-700 kilograms (770-1,545 pounds).
Gestation: 11-12 months.
Longevity: Usually 10-25 years in wild and up to 35 years in captivity.
Distribution: The first intensively domesticated horses were developed in Central Asia and then distributed worldwide.
Habitat: From lush grasslands and savanna to sandy and stony deserts.

Hyena

A scruffy, brutish, and primitive-looking scavenger and predator, the hyena, like the majority of carrion eaters, is mostly unloved by humans, especially when compared with dogs, to which it bears a resemblance but no relation. The hyena is a descendant of ferret-like animals from which civets, mongoose, and aardwolves also evolved. Spotted or laughing hyenas, native to sub-Saharan Africa, are distinct from striped hyenas, which are found in northern Africa, Arabia, India, and western Asia, although in many places they are endangered. In at least one regard the spotted hyenas, also called tiger-wolves, are unique; the females are larger and more aggressive than the males, and they have an exaggerated clitoris as well as a false scrotum, making them sexually ambiguous[1] to human eyes. The striped hyena has a ridge of erectile hair down its neck and back, and its tail is longer and bushier than that of the spotted hyena.[2]

With slightly longer front legs than back, more bulked up and powerful fore than aft, the hyena has a large head and powerful neck and jaw muscles. It is a marvel of orality, with fangs for seizing and shearing flesh, and back teeth that are ideal for breaking and crushing bone. It has keen eyes and particularly excellent night vision, as well as an extraordinary sense of smell.[3] Although they will take smaller animals (like rodents and snakes) alive, the brown and the striped hyenas are primarily scavengers.[4] For many years this was thought to be true for spotted hyenas as well. They were often seen waiting patiently at the periphery of a lion kill, for example, for their chance to snatch some leftovers. Current thinking is that these hyenas are actually very active hunters, although sometimes confounded by their own "laughing," a call they typically emit after a successful hunt. The purpose of the call is not completely understood, but it often attracts the notice of lions. The lions, of course, have no scruples about chasing off the hyenas, which must then scavenge their own kill.[5]

Spotted hyenas are highly territorial and social.[6] Packs of up to a hundred may occupy a territory, hunting together and sharing a labyrinth of underground passages and dens.[7] Cooperation is crucial. Although single hyenas may bring down young prey, it takes a pack to kill prey the size of a zebra or larger.[8] Brown and striped hyenas, in contrast, are primarily solitary.[9] Like the canids they resemble, they howl with heads bowed down to the ground, but not with head back and eyes skyward, like dogs and wolves.[10]

Like most large predators, hyenas elicit a certain macabre fascination in humans, who are often appalled at the spectacle of a large, peaceful ungulate brought down by a ravening pack. The length of time that it takes a stricken gnu to die, even as its viscera are consumed by snarling hyenas, may seem brutal to humans, but the hyenas are simply obtaining sustenance in the only way that nature has equipped them to do so. They are generally quicker and more efficient than lions, which often suffocate their victims.[11] Despite strong social bonds and a high degree of teamwork, hyenas can be very aggressive with one another, with serious injuries common when males fight over a female or when a pack competes for choice parts of the kill. Even newborn cubs (litters are usually no more than two) will attack younger siblings in a manner that frequently causes death, especially same-sex litter mates.[12]

In African mythology, the hyena is often closely associated with death. Some African peoples believe that, because hyenas eat the bones of the dead, their bellies are full of ancestral souls, and their ravenous whining and "laughter" is demonic. Hyenas are feared not as beasts but as ghosts and/or familiars through whose agency various mischief can be done.[13] In West African lore, a hyena trickster figure is invariably the dupe of the rabbit, another trickster.[14] A Sudanese people, the Dinka, tell a fable of a rope hanging from the sky, which old men could climb to heaven to be rejuvenated and return to earth young. One day, Hyena climbed the rope, and God, knowing that he might cause trouble, ordered that he not be allowed to return to earth. Inevitably, Hyena escaped, and as he descended, he cut the rope, so that ever after men had to die on earth at the end of their days.[15] In Asia, striped hyenas are considered the reincarnation of sorcerers, and in Arabic lore wizards are often imagined stealing the livestock of their enemies in the form of hyenas.[16] In European cultures, it was supposed that a precious stone (called a hyena or hyaenium) could be found in the hyena's eye or head and that this many-colored gem could inspire prophetic dreams.[17]

Psychologically, the hyena represents fantasies of extreme oral aggression, the tendency to want to bite and tear, which figures prominently in early life frustrations and in actual, mindless brutality. In the symbolic language of dreams, the hyena represents a very dark and terrifying shadow side of the personality. Since most hyenas live and hunt in packs, this animal can also represent violent group aggression that may be affecting the individual. Its demonic laughter, often a hysterical manifestation in human beings, may compensate for mental or emotional conflicts that the dreamer may be facing, which may need to be confronted with more seriousness, honesty, and depth.

Notes
[1] Grzimek 1984, 12: 185.
[2] Grzimek 1984, 12: 191–92.
[3] Attenborough 1990, 111.
[4] Grzimek 1984, 12: 191–92.
[5] Grzimek 1984, 12: 186.
[6] Grzimek 1984, 12: 193.
[7] Grzimek 1984, 12: 193.
[8] Grzimek 1984, 12: 189.
[9] Grzimek 1984, 12: 193.
[10] Grzimek 1984, 12: 189.
[11] Pfeffer 1989, 348–49.
[12] Grzimek 1984, 12: 189–90; Amin, Willetts, and Tetley 1989, 40.
[13] Jung 1988, 1: 180.
[14] Cooper 1992, 135–36.
[15] Parrinder 1969, 35.
[16] Cooper 1992, 135–36.
[17] Biedermann 1994, 180.

HYENA
Family: Hyaenidae.
Size: Spotted hyena's length is up to 165 centimeters (65 inches), its tail length is up to 33 centimeters (13 inches), and its shoulder height is about 80-90 centimeters (31-35 inches). Striped and brown hyenas have a body length of 90-120 centimeters (35-47 inches) and a tail length of up to 31 centimeters (12 inches).
Weight: Spotted hyena weighs 59-82 kilograms (130-181 pounds). Striped hyena weighs 27-54 kilograms (59-119 pounds).
Gestation: 84-110 days, according to species.
Longevity: Up to 40 years.
Distribution: Africa, particularly the Sahara Desert and Congo basin, Turkey and Middle East to Arabia, southwestern Russia, and India.
Habitat: Chiefly dry, open grasslands and brush.

Insects

Because of their amazing adaptability to conditions and habitats, the very ancient class of insects, largest in the animal kingdom, comprises more than 750,000 species, or approximately seventy percent of all animal species that have been catalogued. Wingless varieties show up in fossil records as early as the Devonian period (350-400 million years ago). In the Carboniferous period (280-350 million years ago), some insects developed wings, and for nearly 150 million years, they alone were capable of powered flight. Others developed the ability to survive in water.[1]

Descended from more primitive arthropods with paired legs on multiple abdominal segments (the centipedes and millipedes), insects have three more or less distinct parts — head, abdomen, and thorax — and three pairs of jointed legs attached at the thorax. At some stage of their development, most insects have wings and antennae. Spiders, although arthropods, have four sets of legs and are not insects.[2] The world's longest insect is the giant stick insect of Indonesia, which grows up to 330 millimeters (about 13 inches) long, while the smallest insect is the fairy fly, only 0.2 millimeters (about 0.008 inches) long.

The role played by insects in the complex ecosystems that maintain the earth is almost impossible to overestimate. Insects process and otherwise recycle vast amounts of animal and vegetable matter, putting nutrients back into the soil in usable form, and pollinate flowers the world over. Without them, many species of plants would quickly cease to exist, and indeed, human existence would be difficult to imagine. Despite human dependence on them and the largely benevolent nature of their impact on the earth, no other life form is so little revered or respected. Every other sort of animal has its human defenders, yet the diminutive insect excites people around the world to extremes of murderous rage and cold-blooded killing with little or no stigma attached. Most people abhor what they loosely call "bugs," the creepy, crawly things of the world, and they would, if they could, exterminate them all.[3] Many insects destroy our crops, and some actually feed on us; they invade our most intimate spaces; they plague us. We cannot control insects despite our best efforts and wishes, and at times we have even been willing to risk destroying the environment in the attempt.

So on the symbolic level, insects represent aspects of the human psyche that are rarely under the control of the will — persistent, intrusive, and hectoring thoughts or fantasies that, with their relentless capacity to invade, insist on being confronted.[4] Insects are marvelous reflections of our most unwanted and negative aspects — those we do not wish to acknowledge, and which we project, for example, onto cockroaches or flies, almost universal objects of disgust and revulsion. In Franz Kafka's story *The Metamorphosis,* Gregor Samsa changes into a gigantic insect. Some authors believe this insect to be a cockroach, which observes the world from a dejected and troubled perspective, yet is also a survivor *par excellence*. Others see it as the dung beetle, which, as the highly revered scarab of the ancient Egyptians, cleans up the world's waste.

In dreams, when insects appear in swarms or multiplicity, they often represent extreme states of mental fragmentation, and even areas of madness. Nevertheless, singly or in swarms, insects, with their sometimes complex social instincts, can also represent the most intense ordering process. Such positive significance is certainly carried, in slightly different ways, by ants and bees.

More can be learned about the unique physical characteristics and symbolic significance by referring to individual insects (see ant, bee, beetle, butterfly, caterpillar, cockroach, fly, grasshopper, moth, and wasp).

Notes
[1] Grzimek 1984, 2: 19-20.
[2] Andrews 1993, 330.
[3] O'Toole 1995, "Preface."
[4] Hillman 1997, 79-81.

Jackal

Synonymous with cringing sycophancy in the popular mind, the jackal is a far cry from the much-admired wolf, yet they are closely related in physique and behavior as well as classification. Both canids have rounded pupils (unlike the fox, whose pupils are vertical slits); jackals are smaller on average, with shorter legs and a more pointed snout; unlike the wolf, their tails are always held downward.[1] The jackal genus comprises three species: the widely distributed golden jackal (southeastern Europe to northern India and Africa), the black-backed jackal (Egypt, Somalia, and the Sudan to South Africa), and the side-striped jackal (western Africa and Ethiopia south to northern South Africa).[2]

Jackals have superb senses of sight, hearing, and smell.[3] Their ears, large and erect, are used for a wide variety of communicative gestures, as are the muzzle and tail. Highly social (although the black-backed species is distinctly less so), the jackal communicates through scent marking and an extensive range of vocalizations, which are often unique within subspecies.[4] Jackals are affectionate with one another, and sexual pairings may be lifelong. Males are helpful, although not crucial, in raising pups.[5]

The golden jackal likes low-lying, shrubby areas, preferably near water; coastal regions; and places near human habitation. Although given to appropriating dens dug by other animals, they will occasionally dig their own very simple lairs. Likewise, in areas shared with other, larger predators, like big cats, jackals will meekly accept leftovers, although they are capable of hunting alone for small animals, and in coordinated packs for larger ungulates. They will also scavenge refuse and/or wreak havoc among domestic animals, one of the reasons that humans consider them pests and hunt or trap them relentlessly.[6] Beyond the occasional competitive conflict with larger predators, the jackal has few natural enemies.

Many animals are, by long practice, more comfortable in their environments than humans, and their accustomed paths often show the easiest or least hazardous route across a particular terrain. Just as the American Plains Indians often followed the tracks of bison herds, various desert peoples of northern Africa used the jackal's paths as a kind of guide across the wastelands.[7] The jackal, as a scavenger, also has a reputation for haunting graveyards. Possibly these combined facts led people to think of the jackal as a psychopomp, or guide of souls from this world to the next.

Several civilizations make the jackal a culture hero, responsible for stealing divine knowledge from the gods and giving it to humans and for introducing death into the world.[8] The ancient Egyptian god Anubis, called "the Pathfinder" or "the Opener of the Way," is often depicted as jackal-headed or as a black jackal, although some say it is the visage of the similar-looking wild dog. Anubis receives the dead in the Hall of Judgment and weighs their souls to determine if in their lifetimes they sided with the powers of good or evil. Anubis also helps Isis find the pieces of her dismembered husband Osiris, and thus the jackal is connected to one of the central Egyptian resurrection myths.[9] Symbolically the jackal embodies the human ability to revitalize and re-integrate deadened or dissociated parts of the psyche. With its connection to death and the underworld and with its remarkable tracking capacity, the jackal is a symbol that mediates life and death and is particularly linked to the mysterious powers of regeneration that the unconscious possesses.

Because of its association with death, the jackal is a symbol of evil in some cultures. In Hinduism, jackals and ravens follow Kali in her terrible aspect as destroyer; in Buddhism, the jackal symbolizes the soul rooted in evil; in Zoroastrianism, it is the creature of the evil Ahriman. In Asian folklore, the jackal is a sycophant to the lion, scaring up prey for him and hoping for a taste of the remains. Perhaps because it usually does not kill its own food, jackal is a label used in Europe (and the New World, where it is not found) for someone who is a toady or a shill.[10] Some African peoples will not feed their children a jackal's heart, fearing that it would make them cowardly. On the other hand, in Hausa folktales, the jackal is the wise judge and called the "Learned One of the Forest." For the Hottentots, the jackal is a beloved trickster figure, not unlike Coyote of Native American lore. One African creation myth makes the jackal the first-born creature of the male sky god and the female earth. The earth receives the gift of language from subsequent children, but is incestuously ravished by the jealous jackal, which steals the gift of language and thus gains the power of divination.[11]

A dream of a jackal might signify that the conscious personality needs to relate more deeply to dissociated areas. Normally, these areas contain so many painful memories that it is extremely difficult to face them. These distressing recollections very often go unnoticed because they are split off throughout life. Focusing on this image, and the feelings and thoughts that emerge from it, can reveal the dreamer's shadow aspects (for example: jealous, sycophantic, cowardly, or manipulative).

Notes
[1] Grzimek 1984, 12: 236.

[2] Ibid.
[3] Grzimek 1984, 12: 239.
[4] Macdonald 1987, 67.
[5] Grzimek 1984, 12: 237-38.
[6] Grzimek 1984, 12: 236.
[7] Cooper 1992, 140; Jobes 1962, 1: 858.
[8] *Funk & Wagnalls Standard Dictionary*. 1972, 533-34.
[9] Cooper 1992, 139; *The New Larousse Encyclopedia of Animal Life* (1968), 19.
[10] Cooper 1992, 140.
[11] Parrinder 1969, 23-24.

JACKAL
Family: Canidae.
Size: 65-106 centimeters (24-42 inches); tail length 20-41 centimeters (8-16 inches); shoulder height 38-50 centimeters (15-20 inches).
Weight: 7-15 kilograms (15-33 pounds).
Gestation: Approximately 63 days.
Longevity: 8-9 years (to 16 years in captivity).
Distribution: Africa, southeast Europe, southern Asia to Myanmar.
Habitat: Depending on species, arid short grasslands, dry brush woodlands, high mountains, and moist woodland.

Jaguar

The jaguar (also called "el tigre" in Spanish), fierce and powerful, dispenser of abrupt death in the jungles of Central and South America, is the lion of the West, dominating the mythos and imagination of New World cultures from prehistoric times. Belonging to the order Panthera (along with the lion, the tiger, and the leopard), the jaguar is the only big cat in the Americas. (The puma, although sometimes larger, is for reasons of physiology appropriately classified with smaller cats.)

The jaguar's name comes from a Tupi-Guaraní Indian word that some take to mean "it kills with a bound."[1] Heavier and stouter than leopards, jaguars hunt mostly on the ground, taking more or less whatever they can get: turtles, frogs, or fish from the waterside; birds on the ground or even on the wing (if they can swat them); and mammals ranging in size from mice to deer and including capybara, tapir, peccary, agouti, monkey, and sloth. After a kill, the jaguar is likely to drag its prize to a place that it can defend easily.[2] Jaguars are basically solitary and rarely seen, being shy of people (and rightly so, as humans are among their only enemies). They make their presence known to other jaguars by scent-marking with urine,[3] and their hoarse roaring can be easily heard over substantial distances.[4] As with many cats, males and females get together for breeding, then go their separate ways. The female raises the cubs, usually two or three, which will hunt with their mother for two years once they are able to do so. Sexual maturity comes at three years; full adult size is sometimes not achieved until four years of age.[5]

Three thousand years ago in the Olmec culture of Central Mexico, the jaguar represented a terrible but central mythical figure, the embodiment of jungle mysteries, life, and death. It appeared in their carved glyphs in many forms: half-god, half-human, or half-child, and many stylized variations in between. Mayan cultures and others, including the Aztecs, incorporated aspects of the jaguar cult and identified it with the principle of fertility and the hidden secrets in the depths of the earth, as well as with the celestial fire of the life-giving sun. In Aztec myth, Tezcatlipoca, the god of warriors, was depicted as a jaguar. In some myths, the jaguar consumes both the sun and moon, either when they set or when they are eclipsed, making the animal a symbol of cosmological catastrophe. In other myths, the sun creates the jaguar as its proxy in the world, endowing it with a benevolent and protective role with regard to people and especially their homes.[6] Central and South American Indian cultures even now associate the jaguar with magic and sorcery. The jaguar is the familiar of the shaman, who sits on a carved jaguar stool and wears a ritual jaguar mask. The two may exchange shapes, or souls, to travel abroad — either one in the form of the other — and the shaman may read the future in the jaguar's eyes.[7]

Psychologically, the jaguar represents both the creative mystery of the unconscious and its dangerous, violent, and destructive aspects. In Indian myth, the jaguar swallows both the masculine sun, symbol of light and rational thought, and the feminine moon, symbol of the light of the unconscious, thereby extinguishing consciousness altogether. In this sense, it might herald the emergence of a truly catastrophic anxiety, a fear of losing one's entire world. Paradoxically, it also represents the positive principles associated with the life force: creativity, procreative power, courage, and vitality. The jaguar encompasses these opposites that are commonly found together in the process of creativity, in which old points of view are destroyed and new security and structure results.

To dream of a jaguar might signify that the individual needs to engage extreme and powerful currents of a creative process. Dreaming of a jaguar lends a special potency, even "numinosity," to this struggle. Experiencing the dream image of a jaguar, one might seriously recognize the fateful, destructive nature of unused creativity, while such awareness was previously only an intellectual curiosity, if considered at all.

Notes
[1] Pfeffer 1989, 205.
[2] Grzimek 1984, 12: 344
[3] Nowak 1991, 2: 1091.
[4] Benson 1977, 24.
[5] Grzimek 1984, 12, 344.
[6] Benson 1977, 24; Bernal 1969, 99.
[7] Cooper 1992, 140; Fontana 1994, 85.

JAGUAR
Family: Felidae.
Color: Black spots on head, neck, and limbs, and large black blotches on the underparts.
Size: Head–rump length is 112–185 centimeters (44–73 inches); tail length is 45–75 centimeters (18–30 inches).
Weight: 36–158 kilograms (80–350 pounds).
Gestation: 93–110 days.
Longevity: Over 20 years in captivity.
Distribution: From the southwestern United States to central Patagonia in South America. The smallest jaguars are found in Honduras, while the largest occur in Mato Grosso, Brazil.
Habitat: Jungle and scrubland, shore forests and reed thickets, as well as terrain with little shrub growth, as long as there is enough high grass or rocks to serve as cover.

Kangaroo

The bouncing, leaping marsupial marvel of the southern hemisphere, the kangaroo is an improbable creature to northern eyes. It is a deer-like herbivore with massively outsized hind legs which determine the distinctively antic, bunny-like hop of its casual locomotion and allow the truly impressive, bounding leaps of headlong flight. Its scientific name, appropriately enough, is Macropidae, which translates simply as "big foot." Kangaroos often stand erect, balancing on those large hind legs and a long, strong tail. Their forelimbs are very much diminished in size and better adapted for grasping than for ambulation. The more than forty different species of kangaroo range from the rather small wallabies to the large red kangaroo, nearly six feet tall. Some species can jump higher than ten feet and manage a horizontal jump of more than forty feet,[1] using their tails for balance and control.[2] They cannot step backwards; they always go forward, even when going around in circles.[3]

Nearly all kangaroos are herbivorous, and many species get along on sparse food and water.[4] They eat grass, shoots, and leaves, and they have a symbiotic relationship with a variety of gastrointestinal worms, which aid their digestion and apparently do them no harm.[5] Their predators are few, mostly snakes that can catch and kill young kangaroos and even adults of some of the smaller species.[6] Aborigines hunted kangaroos for their meat and used their skins for cloaks, water bags, and decorations. They utilized the sinews of the tail for sewing and binding, and teeth for making scrapers.[7] Since the late eighteenth century, human settlement has taken it toll on the kangaroo population by removing and thinning of shrubs and changes of feeding possibilities to the original habitat.[8] When cornered, kangaroos will defend themselves by kicking with their powerful hind legs, a blow that can cause considerable damage.

The fetus of the great red kangaroo, a hairless, embryo-like entity weighing perhaps one gram, crawls through the mother's thick fur and finds its way into her deep, warm marsupial pouch. There it attaches its mouth to one of the teats and stays for up to nine months, continuing its development until it is ready to crawl out into the world. Once out, it remains in close contact with its mother, growing and learning to fend for itself. When in danger even nearly grown joeys (as the young are called) may return to the pouch for an occasional drink of milk.[9] Mothers can give birth to a new generation before the previous one is fully weaned, and, remarkably, they can produce milk of different composition from different teats to suit the separate needs of the two generations. Kangaroos can control their own reproduction and cease to multiply when food scarcity or other environmental conditions militate against it.[10]

In Australian Aboriginal mythology, the red kangaroo, called "Kolakola," was the first beast of the species to make the unique and mystical Dream Journey across the land — a journey through "Dreamtime," a mythological past when the natural environment was shaped and humanized by ancestral beings.[11] The kangaroo was a tribal totem animal and was said to have given humans the first spear-thrower.[12] Symbolically, the female kangaroo appears to represent a paradoxical union of opposites. She has an extraordinary facility to jump and leap, actions often associated with spontaneity and spiritual life. At the same time, her marsupial pouch, a kind of externalized womb, makes her a symbol of mothering and nurturing qualities associated with steadiness and consistency. The varieties of milk at her disposal for her young can represent great adaptability to a diversity of needs.

Kangaroo dreams may be profitably examined in the context of those two often antithetical phenomena. Powerful leaps may remind us of leaps of faith, or of the spiritual and mental leaps that attend any creative endeavor, and the doe's physiology may remind us of all things nurturing, protective, and containing. Thus, the kangaroo symbolically holds together these powerful opposites. The phrase "kangaroo court"[13] may associate the animal (unfairly, of course) with precipitous judgment ("jumping" to conclusions). According to an unattested but persistent story, an early European explorer asked an aboriginal guide for the name of the extraordinary animal they had encountered, and he was told "kangaroo" — not realizing that this word was simply the local dialect for "I don't understand." That, too, may be relevant to kangaroo dreams. For we can never be reminded too often that questioning our "understanding" of what the dream means is always the beginning of grasping its elusive nature.

Notes
[1] Breland 1972, 13.
[2] Grzimek 1984, 10: 171.
[3] Morgan 1994, 99.
[4] Grzimek 1984, 10: 150.
[5] Facts About the Common Kangaroos by Dwayne Lake (internet).
[6] Croft 1991, 5.
[7] Macdonald 1987, 866.

[8] Grzimek 1984, 10: 150.
[9] Grzimek 1984, 10: 155.
[10] Morgan 1994, 99.
[11] "Aboriginal Narrative: The Oral Tradition." *Encyclopedia Britannica*, 1997.
[12] Cooper 1992, 142.
[13] Ammer 1989, 107.

KANGAROO

Family: Macropodidae.

Size: The male red kangaroo measures 130–160 centimeters (51-63 inches) from head to rump, with a tail length of 85–105 centimeters (33-41 inches); the female measures 100–120 centimeters (39-47 inches) from head to rump, with a tail length of 65-85 centimeters (25-33 inches).

Weight: 23-70 kilograms (50-154 pounds); the male is approximately twice as heavy as the female.

Gestation: 30-40 days. Young are born very tiny, fully formed, but continue their growth in the outside pouch (marsupium), where they attach themselves to the teats or mammary glands. The red kangaroo stays in the pouch for approximately 7 months.

Longevity: Approximately 17-18 years in European and American zoos.

Distribution: Tasmania, Australia, and New Guinea.

Habitat: Steppe and bush regions; grassy, arid plains.

Leopard/Panther

While the lion is widely hailed as the king of beasts, regally surveying his domain on the savannas and open plains, the leopard is the quintessential solitary prowler in the dark, forbidding jungle. The leopard and its New World cousin the jaguar are spotted members of the big cat family, and although they are physically different and geographically separate, they are both called "panther."[1] This confusion is exacerbated by the fact that all four "big cats" (leopard, jaguar, lion, and tiger) are classified in the genus Panthera. Leopards are a bit smaller, sleeker, more lithe, and more adaptable than other big cats and, as a consequence, more geographically diverse. They are found all over sub-Saharan Africa, the Arabian Peninsula, and from Asia Minor to East Asia and Java. Melanism is common, resulting in the so-called black panther, and there are a number of subspecies with more subtle variations of coat or markings.[2] The clouded leopard and snow leopard, although they are spotted cats of considerable size, are in some particulars of physiology and habit intermediate between small and big cats, although still classified into the family Felidae.

Solitary hunters, deadly effective night-stalkers, masters of the ambush and the sudden rush, leopards are also powerful climbers, capable of dragging a carcass half their weight up a tree to protect it from scavengers. Generally inclined to avoid confrontations with other predators, leopards can nevertheless be quite aggressive, especially if injured or desperate; under those circumstances, they have been known to take human prey. Like other big cats, leopards mark their territory with urine and defend it vigorously, although of course they are no match for humans with guns and/or bulldozers. Indeed, the species has been decimated by a combination of fur hunters, armed stockmen, and loss of habitat.[3]

The call of the leopard has been compared to the rasp of a coarse saw on wood; males use it to warn off other leopards from their territory, females to call their cubs or to attract a male when in heat. The males take no part in

L

raising cubs, which will remain with their mothers for eighteen to twenty months, after which female offspring will take over part of the mother's territory, while males will strike out on their own.[4]

The origin of the leopard fascinated early writers, who imagined the animal to be a cross between the "pard" or "panther" and the lion (*leo* in Latin).[5] Thus, "leopard" and "panther" are used interchangeably to refer to the same species (*Panthera pardus*), and the mythology surrounding this animal is somewhat similar. The *Physiologus* has an elaborate vision about the panther, which says far more about its symbolism than about its physiology. It states that the panther sleeps for three days after it eats, which was thought of as a symbol of Christ's death and resurrection. Upon awakening, the panther was believed to give off a pleasing fragrance that entices people to follow, which was believed to be like the heavenly wisdom of Christ.[6] In Isaiah (11: 6), the leopard which "shall lie down with the kid" is the very model of fierceness, and in the Old Testament, the cat is generally noted for its speed, cunning, strength, watchfulness, and perseverance. The famous rhetorical question from Jeremiah (13:23) — "Can the leopard change his spots?" — suggests a belief in a deep-seated darkness or evil that cannot be changed. The Christian Devil was occasionally depicted as a leopard, and it has also sometimes been identified with the Beast of the Apocalypse.[7]

In ancient Egypt, Osiris, as the Great Watcher, was represented as a crouching leopard with an open eye symbol, and his priests were often shown in leopard skins.[8] In China, the leopard is considered a lunar animal, symbolically representing bravery and the warrior spirit. In Africa, the leopard has the status of a cult animal in many places; it is associated with fertility rites among the Ibo people and honored by leopard societies and shrines; in West Africa it is sacred to the royal family of Benin; on the Gold Coast it is imagined as a mount of the storm god and considered an incarnation of dead spirits;[9] and it is associated in many parts of the continent with the light of the morning sun.[10] The leopard's grace and agility, as well as its wild leaping and fierceness, suggested to the Greeks the furious dances of the maenads, who acted like bloodthirsty leopards and who in certain myths were believed to be actually transformed into leopards, especially the celebrants of Dionysos. Dionysos and the leopard are closely connected, revealing the paradoxical convergence of death-dealing and life-giving qualities in the god. Thus, symbolically, the leopard embodies life and death simultaneously, whereas humans generally experience these states only as antitheses.[11]

The leopard is one of nature's quintessential "wild things," a dangerous predator, seldom seen, lurking in concealment, striking without warning, secretive, but powerful. Psychologically, it would be an apt model of the deeply potent and generally unseen aspects of our lives, which are normally hidden from consciousness — camouflaged, sometimes fleetingly glimpsed — but whose lurking, untameable presence we ignore at our peril. The leopard is also an apt model of the passionate, erotic and mad transformative aspects of our lives. It represents characteristics of the human self that are usually strongly resisted by collective life because of their intensely violent yet sensual qualities. Collective society wants stability and constancy, but the leopard represents a feature of the human psyche that dissolves that constancy and works against it so that new life and new forms can come into existence. Clearly, these powers are dangerous. If a leopard were to appear in a dream, it would represent precisely those dangerous energies that can lead to renewal, but would certainly require a very strong and humble attitude of the conscious personality if they were to prove creative rather than destructive.

Notes
[1] Andrews 1993, 315.
[2] Macdonald 1987, 45.
[3] Macdonald 1987, 47-49.
[4] Macdonald 1987, 44-45, 47.
[5] Cooper 1992, 147.
[6] Curley 1979, 42.
[7] Cooper 1992, 147.
[8] Cooper 1992, 147; de Vries 1976, 259.
[9] Cooper 1992, 147.
[10] *The Herder Symbol Dictionary* (1986), 119.
[11] Otto 1981, 110-11.

LEOPARD/PANTHER
Family: Felidae.
Color: Black spots on a fawn to pale brown background. Typically, the spots are small on the head, larger on the belly and limbs, and arranged in rosette patterns on the back, flanks, and upper limbs.
Size: Head-body length of 100-190 centimeters (40-75 inches); tail length of 70-95 centimeters (28-37 inches); shoulder height of 45-80 centimeters (18-32 inches). Males are about 50 percent larger than females.
Weight: 30-70 kilograms (66-155 pounds).
Gestation: 90-105 days.
Longevity: Up to 12 years in the wild, 20 years in captivity.
Distribution: From Africa south of the Sahara and South Asia (with a scattered population in North Africa) to Arabia and the Far East.
Habitat: Ranges from tropical rain forest to arid savanna, and from cold mountains to urban suburbs.

Lion

In the popular mind, the lion is considered the "king of beasts," perched in lordly preeminence at the very top of the food chain.[1] It is a magnificent creature, unique among cats, physically distinctive and a powerful carnivore. The lion is sexually dimorphic, the males alone having a mane, and it is highly social, living and hunting cooperatively in extended "prides."[2] Fossil remains show that lions once roamed most of the New and Old Worlds. They disappeared from North America about ten thousand years ago, from the Balkans about two thousand years ago, and from Palestine during the Crusades of the twelfth and thirteenth centuries.[3] Today, outside of wildlife preserves, they are found only in India. There they are all but extinct, as in Africa where several subspecies maintain a foothold in various wildlife preserves. Lions prefer tall-grass savannas, open woodlands, or scrublands, where they can stalk their largely ungulate, herd-animal prey from cover.[4]

Lion society has a highly developed dominance hierarchy, with even the weakest male outranking the strongest female. Nevertheless, the lioness does the vast majority of the hunting while the male lazes about eating, sleeping, occasionally fighting with other males, and having sex thirty to forty times a day.[5] The male lion's distinctive mane lends magnificence to its already imposing physique. This secondary sexual characteristic seems to inspire admiration among females in heat, and some people suppose that it protects the males from serious injury in contests over sexual privileges. One of the most impressive features of the lion is its roar, which is said to be audible at a distance of five miles and to be nothing short of soul shuddering at close range. Whether from sheer satisfaction, or for other unknown reasons, lions tend to roar just after sunset and may go on for an hour or more.[6]

Prides generally comprise one or two males, perhaps a dozen females, and their juvenile offspring. Adolescent males must leave the pride sometime in their third year, and they may roam over large territories, alone or in small groups. Eventually, they join other prides by challenging one of the resident males, remaining for a few years until displaced in their turn by more vigorous challengers. With the males coming and going, the lionesses provide the stability and continuity in lion communities, often remaining together for life, which in the wild averages fifteen years.[7] While there are documented instances of lionesses abandoning their young (especially if they have been disturbed *post partum),* family life in the pride is generally quite tranquil, with all the females scrupulously looking out for all the cubs, even nursing them if they have milk.[8]

Although they have an excellent sense of smell, lions track prey with their eyes and ears, pouncing individually on smaller prey. They work cooperatively to bring down larger game like wildebeests, adult giraffes, or even full-grown buffalo.[9] In the very earliest stages of history, when humans were hunters and nowhere near as close to the top of the food chain as now, people were invariably impressed with an animal of such enormous size and strength that could take any prey it liked, even humans. Such potency and seeming invulnerability would be sure to provoke fantasies of identification; indeed, royal families in particular seem to have felt justified in claiming the lion as an emblem, standard, or coat of arms.

The head of the male lion, with its great shaggy mane, may seem to have the radiance of the solar disk. In ancient Egypt the lion was associated with solar deities such as Ra and Horus, and a very early god in the form of a lion, Aker, guarded the gate of the dawn, through which the sun entered the visible sky.[10] The goddess Sekhmet, who epitomizes the devouring heat of the sun, was depicted with a lion's head; another goddess, Bastet, associated ambiguously with the cat or the lion, represented the more nurturing qualities of growth and life-giving warmth.[11] The lioness has also been associated with the Great Mother goddesses, lunar deities who were worshipped throughout Greece, Asia Minor, and India. In the Hindu tradition, the lion is identified with Durga, a destroyer of demons; in Buddhism, it is believed to be the Defender of the Law and the Buddha, representing wisdom, zeal, and enlightenment.[12]

In Tibetan culture, ancient goddesses are modeled after the lion, such as the beautiful, lion-headed Ka-gro-Mha, who danced naked over the fallen in battle.[13] In China and Japan, stone lions often stood guard at the portals of temples because the lion was thought to ward off evil demons.[14] In various parts of Africa, the lion is regarded as the reincarnation of dead ancestors or as an animal spirit or totem. In folktales, trickster characters like Jackal or Mongoose often outwit Lion.[15]

In the Old Testament, the lion is often invoked to symbolize the strength, vitality, and courage of the tribe of Judah (Genesis 49:9).[16] Christian writers heard in the lion's extraordinary call the analogue of the powerful, far-reaching call of Christ to those who would be saved.[17] Evidently, the now extinct cave lion thrived in the arid lands of the Middle East, and the Old and New Testaments make numerous references to it. In the Old Testament story of

Daniel, the King Nebuchadnezzar asks Daniel to interpret his dream of a mighty tree that grows beyond the heavens. Daniel says that the tree represents Nebuchadnezzar himself and his impious (inflated) sense of omnipotence. When the king has him thrown in the lion's den for his temerity, Daniel (4-6) survives through his persistent faith in divine power. Daniel's survival results from the combination of this faith and his awareness of his limitations, his acceptance of the overwhelming power and sovereign passion of the unconscious psyche — symbolized here by the lion.

Classical mythologies emphasize the enormous strength of the lion. Only Hercules, the legendary Greco-Roman hero, could kill the supposedly invulnerable Nemean lion, slayer of herds and men — not with his weapons, but by choking it.[18] Psychologically, this can be understood as Hercules wrestling in an intimate way with his own overwhelming power drive, defeating it as heroes in other myths wrestle and defeat powerful adversaries. When Hercules skins the lion and wears the pelt, he assimilates the powers of the lion that he has subdued.

In a dream the lion image may often represent the energy of the self — the totality and center of one's being — but in a compulsive form. Hence, one needs to look at areas in life where incessant "doing" excludes sufficient reflection, relatedness to others, and "being." When compulsive activity can be stopped (represented in alchemy by a lion with its paws cut off), the lion becomes a living symbol of strength and courage in service of the self. Yet in its "untamed" form the lion can stand for a variety of destructive behaviors, such as excessive pride, compulsive sexuality, arrogance, and an overwhelming need to dominate others.

Notes

[1] Dorst and Dandelot 1988, 143-44.
[2] Grzimek 1984, 12: 357-58.
[3] "Lion." *Encyclopedia Britannica*, 1997.
[4] Nowak 1991, 1092.
[5] Grzimek 1984, 12: 357.
[6] Grzimek 1984, 12: 357.
[7] Grzimek 1984, 12: 360.
[8] Grzimek 1984, 12: 358-60.
[9] Dorst and Dandelot 1988, 143-44.
[10] Budge 1969, 2: 360.
[11] Johnson 1988, 106.
[12] Cooper 1992, 148-50.
[13] Charbonneau-Lassay 1991, 7.
[14] Becker 1994, 179-80.
[15] *Funk & Wagnalls Standard Dictionary* 1972, 626.
[16] Biedermann 1994, 209.
[17] Charbonneau-Lassay 1991, 13.
[18] *Funk & Wagnalls Standard Dictionary* 1972, 787-88.

LION
Family: Felidae.
Size: Male body length is 1.7-1.9 meters (5-6 feet); female body length is 1.4-1.75 meters (4.5-6 feet).
Weight: Male weighs 150-250 kilograms (330-550 pounds); female weighs 120-180 kilograms (265-400 pounds).
Gestation: 100-119 days.
Longevity: Approximately 15 years.
Distribution: Sub-Sahara to South Africa, excluding Congo rain forest belt; Northwest India (a remnant population only in the Gir Forest Sanctuary).
Habitat: Grassy plains, savannas, open woodlands, and scrub country.

Lizard

As the first true land-dwelling creatures, reptiles are evolutionarily intermediate between primitive amphibians and higher terrestrial vertebrates such as birds and mammals. Reptiles look like miniature remnants of the ancient dinosaurs, the primal lords of the earth. Within this atavistic class, the suborder of lizards (Sauria) is even more primitive than snakes.[1] There are about three thousand species of lizards, including geckos, iguanas, skinks, and monitors.

Lizards can walk, run, swim, slither, burrow, creep, or even glide. Unlike amphibians, which must breathe in part through their skins, lizards are covered with scales, which sometimes are modified with horny or bony plates. Unlike snakes, which the legless varieties may strongly resemble, lizards have movable eyelids; another physiological fact that separates them from snakes and crocodilians (which were at one time classified as saurians) is that parts of the lower jaw are fused, making it impossible for most lizards to open their mouths wide enough to swallow large prey. Cold-blooded (ectothermic) lizards bask in the sun or on warm rocks to raise their body temperature. As all living creatures do, they shed their skin, not in one long piece like snakes, but rather in smaller pieces.[2]

While male lizards, like male snakes, have two penises (known as hemi-penises), females have no vagina at all, but instead receive sperm from the males into their cloaca — a chamber sharing the urinary, excremental, and generative functions. Some females, including the common lizards, are viviparous (produce living young), but most lay clutches of fertilized eggs having tough, brittle, or leathery shells in sand or earth. Perhaps the most unusual species from a reproductive perspective, certain rock lizards reproduce parthenogenically, that is, female lizards hatch from unfertilized eggs and produce more female lizards. A male rock lizard has yet to be found.[3]

Males of the Old World family Lacertidae, or true lizards, are highly territorial, fighting off any trespassing males that ignore their threatening display. True lizards have no dorsal crest or dewlap and cannot change color as the chameleon can. When seized by the tail they have the remarkable ability to detach the captured piece of anatomy, which by neuromuscular reflex goes on wriggling long enough to distract the attacker, while the rest of the lizard makes good its escape. A new tail is then grown, although many injuries of this sort can result in debilitating arrangements of multiple tails.[4]

Only two lizards, the Gila monster *(Heloderma suspectum)* and the closely related beaded lizard *(Heloderma horridum),* are venomous, although they use their venom only defensively, never aggressively. Nevertheless, humans are distinctly uncomfortable with lizards, as they are with many so-called primitive animals.[5]

The most dragon-like lizard, the monitor lizard (subgenus *Varanus*), varies greatly in size, reaching up to three meters (ten feet) in length. Monitors are diurnal, have sturdy legs, and are good climbers and swimmers. They have piercing teeth and pointed claws, which can seriously damage attackers. Depending on the lizard's size, prey can range from insects and the young of small mammals to fish, frogs, snakes, and even small deer and wild pigs. The monitor lizard has some of the characteristics of snakes (for example, the dropping of the lower jaw, an ossified skull, a long, deeply slit tongue, and the capacity to follow olfactory traces). It is more closely related to snakes than any other species of lizard. The most impressive monitor lizard of all, the Komodo dragon, is found only on the Sunda Islands, extending from the Malay Peninsula to the Moluccas southeast of the Asiatic mainland toward New Guinea (including Sumatra, Java, Borneo, Bali, and Timor).[6]

The common iguana lizard has a ridge of spikes running along its back from the neck (where it is largest) to the tail. They are nimble tree-dwellers and can also be excellent swimmers. They are herbivorous but defend themselves effectively with their sharp teeth and claws.[7]

Chameleons, famous for changing color to fit their environment, have laterally flattened bodies and heads that are often adorned with crests or horns. Their large, protuberant eyes can move independently, which helps locate insect prey. Like some frogs and toads, chameleons have a protrusible tongue, a kind of lingual lariat, which they can abruptly extend a full body's length with truly impressive accuracy. Insects are captured with the sticky pad at the tip of the tongue and retracted into the mouth in the wink of an eye.[8]

Geckos are soft-skinned and finely scaled, with flattened heads and, as befits nocturnal creatures, very large eyes. A permanently closed, transparent lid protects the eyes. The males have a loud, repetitive call, and they are among the loudest of the lizards, an order not noted for its vocalizations.[9]

One of the largest families of lizards, the skinks, comprises many hundreds of species. Most live on or in the ground and have long, thin, smooth-scaled bodies, tapering tails, and smallish limbs. Many lizard families include at least some species with minimal or absent limbs, but this tendency is particularly common among skinks.[10]

Some African tribes use the lizard as a totem as well as in magical practices. In East Africa, the lizard is believed to be a shape-shifter, transforming itself at will into a hyena. In West Africa the lizard is believed to turn into a leopard or lion.[11] In the Amazon basin, the Desana Indians believe that all animals are subject to a divine master of animals called *Vaí-mahsè,* who has a human form (a dwarf with red body paint and the odor of magical or medicinal herbs) but can appear as a small lizard. He is a patron spirit and protector of hunters, but he will try to bite or attack pregnant or menstruating women.[12]

Because of its habit of basking in the sun, the lizard is connected to the symbolism of light, especially in Christian art, where it is associated with seekers of knowledge. Like other animals that shed their skins, it is taken as a symbol of renewal and resurrection. Certain species of lizards hibernate, which the Romans saw as a suggestion of rebirth; its regenerative abilities (growing a new tail) add to this symbolic quality and may have earned it an association with Salus, a goddess of safety and health.[13]

Imaginary dragons generally bear a distinct likeness to some sort of lizard (although grossly exaggerated in scale), so the lizard may at times share in the ambiguous symbolism of those fabulous creatures. Both Greek and Egyptian myths depicted the lizard as a token of wisdom and good fortune; it was an emblem of Hermes, the fleet-footed messenger of the gods, and Serapis, a god of the underworld. In Zoroastrianism, the lizard was considered evil and associated with the devil Ahriman.[14]

On the evolutionary scale, the lizard is a transitional animal, evolving from water to earth, and hence a link between very deep levels of the unconscious and the mental functions that are related to reality. In addition, the lizard can represent the capacity to experience the unconscious through somatic reactions. Responsive to the subtlest sensations, the lizard can function as a symbol of heightened body consciousness — the back-of-the-brain sensitivity to elusive, barely perceptible cues and clues within our bodies and the world around us. While this level of perception is very far from consciousness, it joins symbolically with the world of clairvoyance or divination that the lizard can also represent.[15] In traditional cultures, hallucinogenic drugs are sometimes used to tap into the "lizard level" of the psyche, where understanding precedes verbally formulated thought. This kind of "power" can be used either for good or evil, white or black magic.[16] Consequently, in this context the lizard is symbolically ambivalent, capable of being a positive or negative factor depending upon how these perceptions are used.

In dreams the image of a lizard tends to manifest in the presence of very primal responses of the sympathetic nervous system — like flight, fear, anxiety, panic, and intense aversion reactions. These emotions might be linked to the creative process of renewal, a change of fundamental attitudes, a survival need, and to a much deeper level of the soul than simply a reflex action. To dream of a lizard would suggest emergence of a heightened sensitivity to emotions that are the result of processes very far away from consciousness. While the lizard is a very primitive symbol, it is less so than the snake, and consequently one is dealing with levels of consciousness that one can relate to more readily.

The lizard image is so deep in the body that one can feel its movement physically, but this feeling does not necessarily lead directly to mental images. For example, the image of the lizard may signify the need and growing capacity to connect to deeply somatic levels of the unconscious and the kind of body consciousness that can emerge from these levels.

Notes

1. Whitfield 1984, 402.
2. Burton 1981, 299.
3. Grzimek 1984, 6: 286.
4. Grzimek 1984, 6: 285-86.
5. *Encarta 97 Encyclopedia*, 1997.
6. Grzimek 1984, 6: 321-27.
7. Whitfield 1984, 416.
8. Whitfield 1984, 422.
9. Whitfield 1984, 424.
10. Whitfield 1984, 430.
11. Cooper 1992, 152.
12. Reichel-Dolmatoff 1971, 134-35.
13. Cooper 1992, 151; Biedermann 1994, 211.
14. Cooper 1992, 151.
15. Castaneda 1990, 107-58.
16. Ibid.

LIZARD

Suborder: Sauria.

Family: Lacertidae (True Lizards)

Size: True lizards are 10-75 centimeters (4-30 inches) long. The largest lizard, the Komodo dragon (Varanus Komodensis), or Monitor lizard, may grow to a length of 3 meters (10 feet). Although probably not the smallest, the little brown skink of the southeastern United States reaches a length of only 7 centimeters (2.8 inches) and weighs less than a nickel.

Weight: Monitor lizards in adulthood weigh from less than a gram (0.04 ounces) to more than 150 kilograms (330 pounds).

Incubation-Gestation: Some bear live young, others lay eggs. Variable timing is dependent on species.

Longevity: Geckos have been kept for as long as 20 years in captivity.

Distribution: Lizards are found in almost every terrestrial habitat, from the seacoast and the smallest offshore islands to mountain altitudes as great as 2,800 meters (9,000 feet). There is one species found above the Arctic Circle.

Habitat: Some are burrowing or terrestrial animals; others are arboreal or semi-aquatic. Iguanas are found in all three types of habitats.

Lynx

Fierce, secretive, and elusive, the lynx is a medium-sized cat, short of tail and long of leg, with a distinctive cheek beard and long, tufted ears. It is often confused with the bobcat, which it resembles, although the tip of the lynx's tail is black. In ancient writings, the lynx was sometimes mistakenly identified with a closely related animal that we call the caracal. The irises of the lynx are not greenish, as are those of wildcats, but yellow-brown to ochre-brown in color. Much better adapted to snowy regions than most cats, the lynx has thick fur padding on its large paws that not only protects its feet from the cold but also increases the surface area of the paws, preventing them from sinking into the snow.[1]

The lynx has excellent vision, and the long tufts on its ears act as antennae, enabling it to locate sounds with great accuracy. Its fur, which was once highly prized, varies with the geographic region it occupies, northern animals sporting a longer and more luxurious pelt than those from more southern climates. Even within one region coloration and patterning can vary considerably.[2]

Sleeping during midday and at night, they are most active in the early morning and late afternoon, hunting for mammals as small as mice or as large as deer. They also hunt birds, fish, reptiles, amphibians, and even large insects. In northern Europe, the most important prey is the reindeer, while in Canada it is the blue hare. Although lynx are sometimes hunted on the pretext that they threaten local game, like many predators, they actually strengthen prey populations, eliminating weak and sick individuals from the breeding stock and increasing the health of the remaining animals. Lynx treat wildcats as enemies to be chased off; wolves (everywhere) and leopards (in Asia) will prey on lynx.[3]

Solitary, like most cats, lynx range over territories that vary in size depending on the availability of food, and they mark those territories by defecating, usually in some specific and prominent place. They build their dens in hollow trees, beneath fallen tree trunks, in rock crevices, or in dense brush.[4] Lynx are generally not inclined to wander out of their territories; females will do so to find a mate during the rutting season, returning afterwards. In the course of that season (generally February and March), males are prone to fight among themselves before pairing up with females for mating. A female bears one to four young, which stay with her until the following mating season, when they seek out their own territories.[5]

The very name of the lynx is etymologically related to the idea of sight, and indeed, the animal's longstanding and well-deserved reputation for sharp vision has been inflated in some quarters to the supernatural level. As a result, the lynx was credited with the ability to see error and falsehood. The ancient Greeks, among others, believed it could see through solid objects. Perhaps for that reason, Italian scholars (including Galileo) formed the Academy of Lynxes in 1603, dedicated to searching for truth and fighting against superstition. Their symbol was a lynx battling with Cerberus, the gatekeeper of the underworld,[6] the implication being that clear vision would triumph over lack of consciousness, ignorance, and suffering. In northern mythologies, lynx were sacred to the goddess Freyja, in charge of love, fertility, battle, and death, and drew her chariot.[7] For Native Americans, the lynx is a keeper of secrets and occult knowledge, a revealer of mysteries.[8]

The image of the lynx can symbolize vision, particularly the kind of inner sight that is associated with shamanism. In a dream, the lynx could represent both the potential and the need for the dreamer to use a deeper and more penetrating vision in some area of his or her life. This perception could be an inner charge to see things "as they are," to see beneath the surface, or it could be a compensatory image for an unrecognized fear, a fear of taking hold of one's own "sight" and trusting it, while at the same time representing the capacity to do so. The fierceness of the lynx would give the dreamer the potential to be more heroic and aggressive in standing up for his or her vision. A more negative possibility is that the dreamer could be too tenacious about his or her insight — not flexible enough to listen to another person and seriously consider his or her perception.

Notes

[1] Grzimek 1984, 12, 307-08.
[2] Jobes 1962, 2, 1029.
[3] Grzimek 1984, 12: 309.
[4] Grzimek 1984, 12: 309-10.
[5] Grzimek 1984, 12: 307-08.
[6] Andrews 1993, 285.
[7] Ibid.
[8] Cooper 1992, 155.

LYNX
Family: Felidae.
Size: Head-rump length is 85-110 centimeters (33-43 inches); tail length is 12-17 centimeters (5-7 inches); shoulder height is 50-75 centimeters (20-30 inches).
Weight: 5-29 kilograms (11-65 pounds).
Gestation: 60-74 days.
Longevity: 12-15 years in wild, and over 21 years in captivity.
Distribution: Throughout Western Europe to Siberia, Alaska, Canada, and northern United States.
Habitat: Coniferous forest and thick scrub.

Monkey

Among primates, monkeys are not as close to humankind as the apes, from which they are distinguished by the presence of a tail.[1] Nevertheless, they are close relatives and share in the special significance that we attach to animals that remind us of ourselves. We use the expression "to carry a monkey on your back" to allude to addictions and "monkeyshines" as a term for fun and playfulness — for example, the famous organ grinder's monkey, amusing children and grown-ups alike. The first monkeys date from the Oligocene period, around thirty-five million years ago, and modern species are divided into two geographically distinct infraorders: Old World and New World monkeys.[2]

New World primates include tamarins, marmosets, and capuchin-like monkeys. They generally have nostrils that are wide open and further apart than those of Old World species. Their coat is fine, silky, and often colorful. Many species have ear tufts, mustaches, manes, or crests. All are strictly arboreal in habitat; most, if not all, have long tails, some of them prehensile.[3]

Old World monkeys include macaques, baboons, drills, and mandrills. They can be either terrestrial or arboreal, and all are quadrupeds (although some can walk on their hind legs for short periods). They have a narrow space between their nostrils, the nails on their digits are flattened, and their tails are not prehensile. Some have developed hard sitting pads on the lower buttocks.[4] Bodies are generally covered by hair, although the palms of the hands and feet are bare, as are the anal and genital regions of some species. Many monkeys use their long tails to help them balance and steer when they are climbing or jumping. In some species, the tail is prehensile in childhood but the ability to grasp is lost as the individual matures.[5]

Especially for arboreal species, orientation in space is crucial, and all monkeys have excellent binocular vision and good accommodation (the ability to focus selectively). They have well-developed tactile and auditory senses, and. although the olfactory sense is of less importance, many monkeys will sniff objects (or people) before accepting their presence.[6]

Although most mammals have one or more distinct breeding seasons, monkeys, as well as apes and humans, can mate at any time. However, females are only fertile during the estrous phase of their menstrual cycle. Many Old World monkeys show their fertility and attract the sexual interest of the male by a biological sign — the skin around the genital region swells and changes color.[7] Most monkeys produce single young, although in some species twins are common. Infants feed exclusively on mother's milk for the first few weeks, until they are gradually weaned to accept other foods.[8]

Monkeys, like most primates, live in fairly well-defined and exclusive groups within a specific territory. Intelligent, naturally inquisitive, and very active, they form complex relationships governed by rank and blood ties, as well as alliances and rivalries of a more or less fluid nature.[9] Members of a troop organize their collective moves through the forest by communicating with sounds and gestures, and particularly by simply observing the behavior of others. This inclination to imitate may have inspired the human schoolyard taunt, "monkey see, monkey do." Danger calls are quite loud and carry for long distances even in the dense forest, allowing for communication among large groups of monkeys.[10]

Although monkeys and apes are taxonomically distinct, this distinction is sometimes blurred in cultural or mythological contexts, and what is said of one is often said of the other. In the Hindu tradition, the monkey (and the ape) is associated with Hanuman, the monkey god, Rama's powerful assistant and emissary in the *Ramayana,* the great epic of India. The monkey represents benevolence and gentleness as well as strength, loyalty, and self-sacrifice. Some Buddhist writings have compared the frenetic activity of a monkey in a cage with the mental acrobatics people indulge in to avoid suffering unwanted emotions, such as boredom. Buddhists have called this frivolous activity "monkey mind."[11] Early Christians believed that the monkey represented every kind of evil, from the Devil, paganism, and heresy to lust, vice, malice, cunning, and slavish imitation. Throughout art and literature the monkey is used to caricature and satirize humans.

Compared to humans, monkeys seem childish and undeveloped, and every human weakness is projected onto them; they are imagined to be indecent, lascivious, vain, or greedy.[12] They are fascinating for the ways in which they resemble humans and disturbing for the ways in which they do not. Like apes, they symbolically represent a person's shadow side, the culturally rejected and repressed instinctual life. Jung primarily emphasized the foolish aspect of the monkey's symbolic and contradictory significance, the trickster-like qualities that both mask and satirize real wisdom — devilish or mindless and destructive one moment, yet god-like in the next.[13]

As an internal image, the monkey provides a kind of subversive balance, lest attitudes become too fixed and rigid. The monkey-like side of our nature may be inferior, imitative, or foolish, but must it be embraced on its own terms — in a playful, non-judgmental, and spirited way — if its wisdom is to be creatively useful to us. As a dream image, the monkey may indicate that too many "monkeyshines" are going on in the dreamer's life, a childlike foolishness that needs to be confronted. Or we may be prone to thoughtlessly imitate some behavior that is not in accord with our own convictions just to feel "accepted," as in the saying "monkey see, monkey do." Then again, the monkey might suggest a potentially creative, playful inner force that is attempting to challenge a too rigid conscious attitude.

Notes
1. "Monkeys." *Encyclopedia Britannica*, 1997.
2. Macdonald 1987, 340-41.
3. Macdonald 1987, 340-41.
4. Macdonald 1987, 340-41.
5. Grzimek 1984, 10: 313-15.
6. Grzimek 1984, 10: 316.
7. Grzimek 1984, 10: 319.
8. Grzimek 1984, 320-21.
9. Attenborough 1990, 216.
10. Grzimek 1977, 552-53.
11. Robert A. James. "Monkey Mind and Meditation." www.oaktree.net.
12. Aeppli 1943, 369.
13. Jung 1988, 2: 1394.

MONKEY
Superfamily: Cercopithecoidea (Old World monkeys).
Size: The largest, the drill and mandrill, have a head–body length of 70 centimeters (27.5 inches) and a tail length of 7-12 centimeters (3-5 inches). The smallest, the talapoin, has a head–body length of 34-37 centimeters (13.4-14.6 inches) and a tail length of 36-38 centimeters (14.2-15 inches).
Weight: The drill and mandrill weigh up to 50 kilograms (110 pounds). The talapoin weighs 0.7-1.3 kilograms (1.5-3 pounds).
Gestation: 5-6 months.
Longevity: 20-31 years according to species.
Distribution: Throughout Asia except at high latitudes, including northern Japan and Tibet; Africa south of about 15 degrees north (Barbary macaque).
Habitat: Habitat ranges from rain forests to mountains that are snowy in the winter, and also in savanna and brush.

MONKEY

Superfamily: Platyrrhina (New World monkeys).

Size: The largest is the lion tamarin monkey, with a head-body length of 34-40 centimeters (13-16 inches) and a tail length of 26-38 centimeters (10-15 inches). The smallest is the pygmy marmoset monkey, which has a head-body length of 17.5-19 centimeters (7-7.5 inches) and a tail length of 19 centimeters (7.5 inches).

Weight: Most species weigh 260-380 grams (9-13 ounces).

Gestation: 130-170 days.

Longevity: 7-16 years in captivity.

Distribution: South Central and the Northern half of South America.

Habitat: Chiefly tropical rain forest, gallery forest and forest patches in savanna.

Moth

Like pixies and other spirits of the night, the delicately fluttering moths that are drawn to our lights seem, in their pale, mute beauty, otherworldly and strange. Like the butterflies that they resemble, they are lepidopterans — creatures that have four stages of life: egg, larva (caterpillar), a dormant pupa, and a winged imago or adult. Many physical and behavioral characteristics overlap in the two genera, but a number of distinguishing generalizations can be made. Moths tend to be nocturnal, whereas butterflies are creatures of the day; moth bodies are thicker, their coloring generally (but not always) less vivid, their wings proportionately smaller, their antennae bushier, and their bodies sometimes hairier than those of butterflies.[1] Moths in flight also beat their wings more rapidly, producing a distinctive, whirring hum that butterflies generally cannot manage.[2]

These insects are famously sensitive to pheromones — airborne molecules with a powerfully attracting odor secreted by the female and detected by ardent males as much as several kilometers away.[3] The moth smells with its antennae, tastes with its legs, and hears with special organs on its thorax and abdomen. The hearing organs are unusually sensitive to ultrasonic frequencies and are used to escape the echolocation of their chief predator, the bat.[4] The New Testament speaks of the moth as a corrupting influence:

> Do not store up treasures for yourselves on earth, where moths and woodworms destroy them and thieves can break in and steal. But store up treasures for yourselves in heaven, where neither moth nor woodworms destroy them and thieves cannot break in and steal. For where your treasure is, there will your heart be also (Matthew 6:19).

The moth, like the butterfly, can be a symbol of the psyche. But, unlike the butterfly, it does not usually carry the sense of the psyche's rebirth. The moth's real (and proverbial) attraction to the consuming flame is its more commonly considered symbolic characteristic. Psychologically, this quality can be construed as a desire for consciousness or spiritual life, as implied by the symbolism of light itself. In reality, however, that light ultimately destroys the moth, and thus the moth evokes relentlessness or reckless compulsion that can accompany any quest for illumination. Such consciousness, untempered by an accompanying concern for life and relationship, can become self-destructive. The link between the moth and the flame alludes to the creative and dangerous quality of passion. As Jung says, "This passionate longing has two sides: it is the power which beautifies everything, but, in a different set of circumstances, is quite as likely to destroy everything."[5]

The potentially destructive aspects of consciousness and passion exist in any life and at any time. In symbolism, the moth is often associated with the Great Mother goddess, whose lover is eventually destroyed by his passion for her — as the flame destroys the moth. Sometimes symbols can have a simple, mundane meaning. For instance, moths will generally evoke the image of the destruction of that stored sweater in the attic, ruined by the lepidopteran. One can also speak of viewpoints being "moth-eaten." Hence, the moth can represent the process of slow, unseen destruction of the things we cherish most — our values, religious or mythical feeling, thoughts and emotions we hold dear.

In a dream, the moth image may compensate for a lack of steadfastness in a person's desire for consciousness. But the person who has too strong a compulsion to achieve a new kind of awareness, and yet fails to understand the recklessness and the calamity that can follow from such an effort, needs to consider the danger ahead. The dreamer might also be working with "moth-eaten," antiquated, and out-of-date attitudes, or might have to look for deep values that are in danger of disintegrating.

Notes
[1] "Moth." *Encyclopedia Britannica*, 1997.
[2] Grzimek 1984, 2: 318.
[3] Slater 1987, 67.
[4] Grzimek 1984, 2: 320.
[5] Jung 1976, 5: 165.

MOTH
Order: Lepidoptera (with 80-100 families).
Wingspan: From about 3-4 millimeters (0.12 inches) to a reputed 36 centimeters (14 inches) for the giant Hercules moth from the tropical rain forests of Australia and New Guinea.
Weight: Less than 1 gram.
Longevity: Some adult moths live, on average, 2-4 weeks. Many need to be able to eat for a longer period if their eggs are to have time to ripen. If a dormant period is entered, particularly one which lasts the winter, the life span can be extended to several months. Moths that do not eat at all live as males, only until they have mated or, as females, until eggs have been laid — that is, a few days or even, in extreme cases, only a few hours.
Distribution: All areas of the world.
Habitat: Where they can find a supply food and shelter.

Mouse

The mouse family, which loosely includes mice, voles, rats, lemmings, dormice, hamsters, gerbils, and several other small mammalian creatures, represents an astounding evolutionary diversity, comprising over a thousand different species. The European wood mouse and the American deer mouse, although not closely related, are both forest dwellers, and therefore probably most resemble the ur-mouse — the common ancestor of all the more specialized species that exploit so many different habitats and food sources. These tiny, timid, scurrying creatures, which are nevertheless bold enough to appropriate the margins of our homes for their own, are ambivalently imagined either as horrific pests or as cute, beguiling cartoon creatures on the order of Mickey Mouse.[1] Only ten to fifteen million years old, these rodents are among the most recent animal forms in evolutionary history. Strictly speaking, "mouse" refers to the house mouse, and "rat" refers to the black rat. But in common speech, any rodent under thirteen to fifteen centimeters (five to six inches) in body length is generally considered a mouse, and those over that size are called rats.

Many kinds of mice are pests, ruining stored grain and other gathered foodstuffs[2] and in some cases carrying disease, including typhus, spotted fever, salmonella poisoning, hantavirus, and bubonic plague. They are beneficial to humanity, however, because they constitute the primary diet of predators that would otherwise need to prey on valuable livestock. Mice have also long been used in laboratories to develop medications and to study genetics.[3]

House mice, as their name implies, are found mostly indoors, although some species or subspecies may spend part or even all of the year outdoors, depending on weather conditions. They are omnivorous (as any homeowner knows), and although more active at night, they do move about during the day, often alternating periods of rest and activity. Fleet and agile, they can run, jump, and climb, squeezing through surprisingly small spaces, often little bigger than their heads.[4] In houses, their self-sharpening incisors and their persistence allow them to gnaw through nearly any material.[5] They are quick to exploit local conditions and highly adaptable to their surroundings. The tonal range in mice is well beyond what humans can hear. Their equally excellent sense of smell is crucial in the search for food and in navigation (mice follow "scent paths" that have been marked with urine). In addition, it seems that mice recognize their relatives by smell. Females are more willing to share their nests with other females that are related to them and thus have a similar smell.[6]

House mice live in large families occupying a common territory, within which individual animals live in nests of their own. Mice are social animals to the extent that they share escape holes, eating and nesting places, and areas for elimination. The males in particular recognize an order of rank, and mutual grooming is common practice.[7] House mice mature sexually in just two to three months, produce an average litter of six and, if they are living indoors, reproduce more or less continuously throughout the winter — a situation that can lead to population explosions. However, house mouse populations have a fascinating form of self-regulation. When their numbers become too large for a given area, adolescent females become infertile; their sexual organs atrophy and birth rates drop. The process reverses itself when density decreases.[8]

Elusive nearly to the point of invisibility, mice have long been thought symbolic analogues of the soul. Secretive and partial to obscurity, mice were suspected of having dark, even demonic powers and uncanny abilities.[9] In Egypt, the mouse was sacred to Horus and to Isis, who took the shape of a mouse when she fled from Set.[10] In Switzerland and elsewhere, mice were considered creatures of the Devil. In the Old Testament, they were listed among the unclean animals.[11] Because of their fecundity, they were considered "lascivious" and associated with the Greek love goddesses, Aphrodite.[12] In Greek mythology, mice as well as rats were associated with Apollo, or, more specifically, with the dark or winter aspect of this sun god, called Apollo Smintheus. It has also been said that Apollo shot arrows bearing the plague, which suggests that the ancient Greeks understood that mice were carriers of disease. The cult of Apollo developed from the early cult of the mouse. Some have hazarded a guess that mice were associated with Apollo because they were kept in his temples as food for his snakes.[13]

Mice, in their role as invaders of pantries and carriers of disease and pestilence, are considered "spoilers," and thus are often viewed negatively. In psychological terms, the goods and stores being invaded may represent the valuable (but perishable) creative thoughts or energies that constitute mental wealth (and health), under siege by obsessive thoughts that creep in and destroy it. Mice can symbolize gnawing anxieties that eat away at one's peace of mind, or relentlessly invasive thoughts, often of an erotic nature, that disturb one's sleep at night or invade one's rest.[14]

Another salient quality of the mouse is its capacity to hide, to shun light and open spaces. Its elusiveness makes it an apt symbol of the soul and the unconscious — something animate and living whose existence we sense rather than perceive. The small size of the mouse, its timidity, and its instinct to retreat to the darkest corners when surprised reminds us of our own timidity and the speed with which our "bold" resolve can turn to withdrawal and fear.

If the image of a mouse were to appear in a dream, as always, the appropriate meaning would depend upon the dreamer's present, conscious circumstances. If the dreamer was denying his or her sexual feelings, the mouse could easily take on a sexual significance. If the dreamer needed to face a life situation that required courage, the person might dream of a mouse to illustrate his or her own timidity which needs to be seen, understood, and accepted. If the person was working on a creative problem or immersed in some relationship issues, the mouse image could signify too much obsessive thinking and the need for a symbolic cat, which would represent vigilance and a capacity to not dissociate into a flutter of incoherent or muddled thought.

Notes
[1] Macdonald 1987, 636.
[2] Whitfield 1984, 178.
[3] "Mouse." *Encyclopedia Britannica*, 1997.
[4] Grzimek 1984, 11: 362-63.
[5] "Mouse." *Encyclopedia Americana*, 1991, 19: 589.
[6] "Mouse." *Academic American Encyclopedia*, 1998, 7: 6.
[7] Grzimek 1984, 11: 363-64.
[8] Grzimek 1984, 11: 364.
[9] Biedermann 1994, 229-30.
[10] de Vries 1976, 330.
[11] Cooper 1992, 164.
[12] Biedermann 1994, 229-30.
[13] Cooper 1992, 164.
[14] von Franz 1975b, 63.

MOUSE

Family: Muridae.

Size: Old World mice head–body length is 4.5-8.2 centimeters (1.7-3.2 inches); tail length is 2.8-6.5 centimeters (1-2.5 inches). The house mouse, considered an Old World mouse, has a body length of 6-12 centimeters (2-5 inches); its tail is 6-11 centimeters (2-4 inches) long. The largest New World living species have a head–body length of 30 centimeters (12 inches).

Weight: 6 grams (0.20 ounces). The house mouse weighs 10-30 grams (0.35-1 ounce).

Gestation: 20-50 days.

Longevity: Up to 1 year in the wild and up to 6 years in captivity.

Distribution: The house mouse is distributed in all inhabited areas of the world.

Habitat: All terrestrial habitats (including northern forests, tropical forest, and savanna), excluding snow-covered mountain peaks and extreme high Arctic.

Octopus

An amorphous phantasm of grasping tentacles, sliding — almost literally oozing — about the ocean floor, squeezing and squirming through impossibly small crevices, obscuring itself in umbra clouds of ink, the octopus is a strange and mysterious creature. It is all head and feet, which is the literal translation of Cephalapoda, the class it shares with squid, cuttlefish, and nautiluses. The approximately 650 living species of octopuses are all marine dwellers.[1]

Octopuses have a fleshy mantle[2] that surrounds their internal organs, a respiratory funnel through which they can squirt water as a means of propulsion, and eight muscular, flexible appendages — usually referred to as arms — each equipped with two rows of suckers on the underside.[3] These limbs have substantial regenerative powers, often growing more than one replacement for a lost one.[4] Experiments have indicated that octopuses have an uncanny intelligence that surpasses all other invertebrates and even challenges many higher vertebrates.

Lacking both an internal and external skeleton, the octopus is able to insinuate itself into the narrowest cracks and crevices in search of food or shelter.[5] Using its arms for locomotion, it crawls about the rocky ledges of the sea floor, changing its coloration with remarkable ease to suit its environment.[6] In flight the octopus moves backward, using its funnel for jet-propelled escape or else swimming with its powerful arms; and like other cephalopods (except the nautilus), the octopus can squirt out a cloud of inky fluid, a visual and olfactory screen to confuse both its enemies and its prey. Enemies include conger and moray eels, dolphins, seals, and sharks; prey include almost anything the octopus can overpower, but particularly crayfish, crabs, and various bivalves.[7] Prey is seized with the tentacles and pulled to the mouth, where it is either crushed by the octopus's jaws or bored into by its radula, a specialized mouthpart with rough projections that functions somewhat like a drill. Salivary glands then secrete poisonous enzymes that not only subdue the victim, but also break down its tissues — a kind of external digestion. Some octopuses have been known to crawl up on the beach in pursuit of a crab.[8]

Octopuses are solitary creatures except at mating time, when the males gather together to fight for a female. The male extends a special tentacle, the hectocotylus, directly into the mantle cavity of the female, and his spermatophores, travelling along this tentacle, ultimately reach her genital opening.[9] The female takes unusual care of the grape-like egg clusters, using her arms to circulate water around them, cleaning and fussing over them so unceasingly that she will generally die of starvation shortly after the brooding period is done.[10]

The octopus image can be quite ambivalent, appearing either as a god or a devil. From Minoan times (3000-1100 BCE), funerary ceramics show a goddess in the form of an octopus, although not much is known about her. Not surprisingly, the octopus figures more prominently in the cultures of island peoples who are surrounded by the sea.[11] Polynesian myth tells how the octopus, rising from the primordial waters, begat Fire and Water, who warred against each other constantly until the world was finally destroyed by flood and only the octopus survived. In Hawaii, Octopus leads a revolt against the gods and is cast down to infernal regions. In the Society Islands it is a creator figure.[12] In a Samoan myth, the sea rises threateningly when the sacred ur-octopus breaks its ink sack.[13] In early Christian times, the octopus was likened to the Devil.[14]

When working with an octopus image, it is necessary to consider that, with its multiple arms and myriad suckers, the octopus is essentially a grasping thing. We often speak of tentacles metaphorically when we attempt to describe a force that is oppressive, far-reaching, unavoidable, and multifaceted. Another salient characteristic of the octopus is its profound elusiveness — shape-changing, color-shifting, elastic to the point of liquidity, a master contortionist, and an illusionist. There is hardly a trap from which the octopus cannot wriggle, almost no escape hole through which it cannot (almost literally) squirt itself. The octopus swims backward, withdrawing and obscuring itself in a cloud of ink; it is as difficult to confront as the vaporous dreams of a troubled unconscious.

Symbolically, the octopus can represent the psychic structure known as the great negative mother archetype, especially in her capacity to fixate and constrict, breeding anxiety at the thought (let alone deed) of any change. Furthermore, the inky secretions of the octopus, which obfuscate, can represent the destruction of consciousness, leaving a person disoriented and vulnerable to attack from many directions at once. The octopus can represent a psychological complex that is experienced in terms of feeling totally outnumbered. In speaking, a person may shift a point of view quickly again and again or may be pulled between different points of view until he or she is completely confused and disoriented. This conjunction of extremely negative and positive symbolic qualities is part of the paradoxical nature of the octopus. If a person can overcome chaos and unconsciousness, as represented by the octopus, this very intentional heroic act could reveal a hidden order. The octopus represents, *par excellence,* this connection between extreme chaos and fragmenting consciousness within which can lie an order that transcends this disorder.

The image of the octopus in a dream usually means that such exceptionally powerful and important issues must be confronted. Unless the person accepts the challenge to consciously enter the depths of his or her own being in which chaos appears to dominate, he or she will likely be left in chaotic and illusory patterns, inimical to life. Yet courageously (given the terror of the image of the octopus) and actively experiencing the resulting disorder can reveal the ordering capacity of the self.

Notes
[1] Banister and Campbell 1988, 269.
[2] Grzimek 1984, 3: 190.
[3] Grzimek 1984, 3: 218.
[4] Grzimek 1984, 3: 192.
[5] Pfeffer 1989, 89.
[6] Grzimek 1984, 3: 218.
[7] Grzimek 1984, 3: 220.
[8] Grzimek 1984, 3: 218-19.
[9] Grzimek 1984, 3: 220.
[10] Grzimek 1984, 3: 218.
[11] Gimbutas 1989, 277.
[12] Cooper 1992, 168.
[13] Jobes 1962, 2: 1194.
[14] Becker 1994, 218.

OCTOPUS
Family: Octopodidae.
Size: The common octopus has a length of up to 3 meters (10 feet).
Weight: Up to 25 kilograms (55 pounds).
Gestation: 4-8 weeks are required for the larvae to hatch.
Longevity: Smaller in-shore species may have a life span of no more than one year or, exceptionally, two or three. Nothing is known of the life span of the large oceanic squids, but it is presumed that giants such as Architeuthis attain their bulk only after a period of perhaps 4-5 years. In the smaller octopuses and squids, observational data indicate that many of the males die after mating and females after the first major spawning.
Distribution: Shallow coastal waters on both sides of the Atlantic (from the southern United States to Central America and from the English Channel to the Mediterranean Sea) and Indo-Pacific oceans. It has rarely been encountered beyond a depth of 150-200 meters (500-650 feet).
Habitat: Oceans with normal salinity content (3.2 percent-3.75 percent).

Opossum

A primitive-looking, somewhat rat-like creature, the opossum is one of the earth's oldest surviving mammals and North America's only marsupial. Like the kangaroo, the opossum does not develop a true placenta; a pouch on the female's abdomen covers the teats and serves to carry the young. The opossum is known, first and foremost, for "playing dead," and when threatened it enters a more or less self-induced state of shock. With lowered heart rate and barely detectable pulse, it seems to all outward appearances quite convincingly dead, even to the point of secreting a musky scent that suggests the odor of decayed flesh. This reaction is sufficiently confusing to put off most predators, at least long enough for the opossum to make good its escape.[1] The opossum will, however, respond more aggressively to less menacing intruders, hissing and baring fifty sharp teeth.[2] Of the approximately seventy-five species in North and South America, the majority are remarkably resistant to diseases such as rabies, and also to snake venom.[3]

Opossums can vary substantially in size from species to species, but most have long, almost naked, prehensile tails. They have five digits on all limbs, with claws on each except the first toe, which is opposable for grasping. The fur of the American opossum has long, projecting cover hairs.[4] Opossums are generally skilled climbers, and many species are extensively arboreal in habit.[5] Sharp of eye and ear, opossums are omnivorous, adaptable, and opportunistic in their diet, which includes fruit, insects, small vertebrates, carrion, and garbage. They generally forage in one area intensively, and then move on when food resources are depleted. The southern opossum may climb as much as eighty feet to feed on flowers in the canopies of tropical forests.[6]

Courtship is a fairly rudimentary affair. The male approaches the female while making a clicking sound with its mouth. If she is in estrus, she will allow him to mount; if not, she will either walk away or threaten. In any case, no further fraternization is to be expected. Gestation is short, twelve to fourteen days, and does not affect the estrous cycle.[7] At birth opossums are still in a more or less embryonic state of development; blind and tiny, they must wriggle their way, unaided, up the mother's belly to her pouch, find a teat, and fasten on. In many species, they remain there for several weeks, continuing their development outside the womb (but inside the pouch). With gradually decreasing dependence, they will stay with their mothers for several months.[8]

Opossums may make use of several nests within their range, sharing them (sequentially, never simultaneously) with other opossums. They are solitary animals, although they may congregate at common food sources during periods of food scarcity. There is no interaction unless other animals get too close. When two animals do meet, they generally just hiss at one another for a bit, and then continue on their way.[9]

The symbolism of the opossum follows from its fame for feigning death, which recalls similar tendencies in people — specifically the capacity or inclination to shut down and hide, emotionally and physically. Psychologically, this withdrawal is a defensive or protective measure, seen most dramatically in certain psychiatric disorders. However, the mechanism is operative in a number of common reactions to psychological stress, such as denial or dissociation, in which a person can become oblivious or insensitive — one might even say "dead" — to some particular situation or aspect of his or her life. When very intense emotional elements are suddenly touched in conversation or interaction with others, some people will almost instantly become sleepy or even actually fall asleep, thereby protecting themselves from the pain of emotional truth. In effect, they "play possum" with their feelings. To protect themselves, people as well as opossums may also become very aggressive.

Dreaming of an opossum often is a message from the unconscious that this tendency to "go dead" and dissociate is present and needs to be watched. Consequently, one would look for conflicts in the dreamer's life that have not been confronted or engaged and that result in "playing dead." In the event that dissociation is not the issue, the considerable aggression and self-defensive capability of the opossum can be seen as representing such attitudes and energies available to consciousness.

Notes
[1] Andrews 1993, 221-22.
[2] Macdonald 1987, 830.
[3] Grzimek 1984, 10: 57.
[4] Ibid.
[5] Macdonald 1987, 830.
[6] Ibid.
[7] Macdonald 1987, 830, 834.
[8] *Compton's Interactive Encyclopedia*, 1997.
[9] Macdonald 1987, 837.

OPOSSUM
Family: Didelphidae.
Size: Length is 7-45 centimeters (3-18 inches); tail length is 4-45 centimeters (1.5-18 inches).
Weight: 1-5.5 kilograms (4.4-12 pounds).
Gestation: 12-14 days.
Longevity: 1-3 years (to about 8 years in captivity).
Distribution: Throughout most of South and Central America, north through eastern North America to Ontario, Canada; Virginia opossum introduced onto the Pacific coast.
Habitat: Wide-ranging, including temperate deciduous forest, tropical forests, grasslands, mountains, and human settlements. Terrestrial, arboreal, and semi-aquatic.

Ostrich

At over three hundred pounds, easily the largest bird in the world, with its long, naked neck, powerful legs, and largely ornamental plumage, the flightless ostrich is remarkable. Ostriches are in the class of ratite birds whose sternum lacks a keel and therefore a point of attachment for strong flight muscles. They may have evolved from flighted birds from the steppes of Asia some fifty million years ago.[1]

The ostrich has just two toes on each foot, one large and clawed, the other small and clawless.[2] The male is visually striking, with black feathers and white accents at the wing tips and tail; the female is brownish overall, mimicking the colors of its natural habitats — the dry veldt of South Africa and the deserts of the north.[3] Ostriches feed on a wide variety of grasses and shoots, depending on the moisture in these plants for at least some of their water; they will also consume whatever small animals they can catch.[4]

Ostriches have rather complicated social lives, often gathering in large flocks, within which smaller groups remain distinct. Young males may group together for weeks at a time, and then merge back into the flock. In unusual instances, members of a different flock may adopt chicks, and even some young birds, apparently by mutual agreement. Generally (but not always) polygamous, males will typically mate with up to three females, then construct a nest — often just a scratched-out depression in the sand. The females will then lay their eggs, all in the same nest, but to be incubated only by the male and the most dominant female. The egg is enormous (often weighing more than half a pound) and extremely thick-shelled, although the African vulture has learned to break them with stones.[5]

Ostriches have excellent vision and hearing, and their survival depends in large part on their wariness. As the birds graze, one of their numbers will always remain with head high, alert to sound the alarm if a predator should appear. In addition to the deep alarm call, they can produce a wide range of sounds, from a near roar to a musical warble.[6] Their primary defense is speed. With their long legs, they can lope along for extended periods at fifty kilometers (thirty-one miles) per hour, and they can sprint, with strides up to ten feet long, at seventy-five kilometers (forty-seven miles) per hour, drawing upon their incredibly efficient hearts. When cornered, however, ostriches can deliver a powerful kick that could slice open a careless would-be predator in the blink of an eye.[7]

The ostrich's striking size and features attracted the notice of early peoples, with references in Egyptian and Mesopotamian art dating back to 5000 BCE. Various African cultures have used ostrich feathers for adornment since very ancient times, as did the Romans, whose imperial adventures often took them to Africa. The ostrich figures prominently in African ritual dances meant to keep the dead at bay. For the Kung Bushmen, ostrich eggs are a channel of supernatural power, and the bird's erratic undulating movements symbolize light and water for the Dogon people.[8]

For the writers of medieval bestiaries, the flight of birds was equated with the elevation of souls; thus, the flightless ostrich was seen as a symbolic analogue of the religious hypocrite whose soul had no loft. Another strange belief about the ostrich was that it incubated its eggs merely by staring at them, which led people to make the bird an attribute and exemplar of meditation. Yet another belief was that the ostrich used the sun for incubation; hence, it was considered a symbol of Jesus awakened by a solar father.[9]

In the mythology of the Semitic people, the ostrich is considered demonic and dragon-like. The ostrich feather was an attribute of Maat, the Egyptian goddess of justice and truth. It was the counterweight to the deceased's heart, which was weighed upon his or her death in the Judgment Hall of Osiris to determine the quality of the person's life and ultimate fate.[10] Among the practitioners of Brahmanism, urine is considered holy, and the ostrich is revered because it is the only bird that has the capability of urinating. In Greek and Roman myths, the ostrich was associated with the planet Saturn.[11]

Like many toothless birds, ostriches will swallow stones in order to aid in the maceration of food in the crop. No doubt observation of this tendency led to the idea, repeated throughout history by various "authorities," that the ostrich can eat and digest anything, including iron or fiery coals, which were believed to be good for its "cold" stomach.[12] The unusual conviction that the ostrich buries its head in the sand to avoid danger was already old when Pliny the Elder affirmed it in the first century BCE. The ostrich, of course, does no such thing; indeed, its speed, strength, and wariness make it a highly successful survivor in a world rife with predators.[13]

Nevertheless, to dream of an ostrich often suggests a blindness, a blocking out, or denial of some aspect of reality and/or danger. The dream image of an ostrich could also point to an area where imagination is stuck in a purely concrete understanding of the world, is too literalized and cannot soar, suggesting that the dreamer can see only the present reality and cannot envision the future outcome.

Notes
[1] Grzimek 1984, 7: 89-100.
[2] Grzimek 1984, 7: 91-92.
[3] Perrins and Middleton 1989, 18.
[4] Grzimek 1984, 7: 92.
[5] Grzimek 1984, 7: 91-93.
[6] Grzimek 1984, 7: 95.
[7] Grzimek 1984, 7: 95-96; Perry and Middleton 1989, 18.
[8] Perrins and Middleton 1989, 21; Cooper 1992, 171.
[9] Becker 1994, 221, 223; Charbonneau-Lassay 1991, 276-77; Biedermann 1994, 249.
[10] Cooper 1992, 170.
[11] Charbonneau-Lassay 1991, 275.
[12] Cooper 1992, 170.
[13] Pfeffer 1989, 270.

OSTRICH
Family: Struthionidae.
Size: 3 meters (10 feet) in height.
Weight: Over 150 kilograms (330 pounds).
Incubation: 42 days.
Longevity: Up to 70 years.
Distribution: Africa.
Habitat: Semidesert and savanna.

Otter

The otter is a kinetic creature, softly furred and comically bewhiskered, a mammal totally at home on land and in the water. It is so high-spirited and frolicsome that the appealing sight of one rarely fails to fetch a human smile. Known in the wilder, watery reaches of North and South America, Europe, Asia, and Africa, the otter is closely related to the weasel, badger, and skunk. But, unlike those land mammals, the otter is sublimely adapted to a largely aquatic life. Its webbed feet and sleek, flexible body make it an agile swimmer; its ears are closable; its fur is smooth and water repellent.[1] It can stay underwater for up to eight minutes.[2] Not surprisingly, its name is cognate with the Greek word "hydra," or water serpent, and ultimately with the word "water" itself.

Although not technically gregarious (not really a herd animal), otters are highly social. They live in small family groups, which are nuclear and exclusive but surprisingly unterritorial. Pups from different families will readily play together, and an antic sort of playfulness is one of their most striking characteristics. Mated pairs are affectionate with each other and tirelessly attentive to their young, although studies have shown that male sea otters are incorrigible thieves, snatching nearly a third of their food from apparently indulgent females. On shore, a mother will carry her young in her mouth, but on the water she will often float on her back, holding a cub to her chest with her forepaws in a beguilingly human fashion.[3]

Otters are very vocal, with a large repertoire of calls that vary distinctively from species to species. River otters have paired scent glands at the base of their tails that give them their typical, musky smell. These glands are used for scent marking, a common form of communication that not only stakes out territorial boundaries but also conveys a wealth of information about the claimant, including identity and sexual state.[4]

Otters lack the protective layer of blubber found in whales, seals, and other aquatic mammals, but they have a very high metabolic rate. This keeps them warm, energetic, and constantly looking for food. All otters have an outer and inner layer of warm, dense fur, but the fur of the sea otter is unique for its fineness and density (approximately a million hairs per square inch). The species-threatening trade in sea otter pelts ended in 1922 with the adoption of a nearly global ban on sea otter hunting. The partial re-establishment of sea otter populations is one of the great success stories of human conservation.[5]

River otters occupy dens on the banks of rivers, streams, lakes, and, occasionally, tidewaters. The larger sea otters may live among thick pelagic kelp beds in summer, but in winter, when such shelter from predators is less available, they stay closer to shore and land.[6] River otters dig dens amidst the shore shrubbery, with an entrance below the water line and an air passage leading out above it. They may also appropriate abandoned dens built by foxes, badgers, or rabbits. They hunt mostly at night, particularly when the moon is bright, taking fish, water voles, muskrats, and aquatic birds and their eggs.[7] Sea otters are picky eaters, generally preferring sea urchins, mollusks, crustaceans, and fish (in that order).[8]

The otter plays a minor role in some of the world's religions. In Zoroastrianism, the otter was considered to be among the clean animals, and it was a sin to kill it. In ancient Peru, it was a cult animal, associated with the ocelot that also haunted the stream banks and watersides. For Native Americans, it represents the feminine energy and the power of the earth and waters. Perhaps influenced by its playful and buffoonish character, Native Americans also considered the otter to be a trickster figure. The trickster turns all collective values upside down and encourages a re-evaluation of these attitudes.[9]

If the image of an otter appears in a dream, one may want to focus on the dreamer's relation to his or her unconscious psyche. One might ask if the person is too rigid and in need of the more playful, trickster-like quality of the otter. As an animal that moves with equal ease on land and through water, the otter can often be seen as a mediator between the conscious, reality-oriented world and the generally unseen patterns, emotions, fantasies, and desires usually thought of as aspects of the unconscious; and the dreamer may want to consider which of these parts need further attention to achieve a more unified attitude. The otter's strong and loving maternal instinct — the deep, positive, loving, and caring connection that this animal manifests — is among the most powerful forces. A dream might indicate that the dreamer's nurturing attitude toward him or herself, the inherent inner creative potential and relationship to others, may need further consideration.

Notes

[1] Macdonald 1987, 124.
[2] Grzimek 1984, 12: 78.
[3] Grzimek 1984, 12: 85-87.

[4] Macdonald 1987, 127.
[5] Hazarika 1994, C4.
[6] Grzimek 1984, 12: 78-79.
[7] Grzimek 1984, 12: 79.
[8] Hazarika 1994, C4.
[9] Cooper 1992, 171.

OTTER
Family: Mustelid.
Size: Overall length is 41-123 centimeters (16-48 inches); tail length is 25-65 centimeters (10-26 inches).
Weight: 5-30 kilograms (11-66 pounds).
Gestation: 60-70 days; up to 12 months with delayed implantation in some species.
Longevity: Up to 12 years in the wild.
Distribution: Worldwide except Australia, New Zealand, and Antarctica.
Habitat: Aquatic, rivers, and seas.

Owl

The uncanny owl — great-headed, saucer-eyed, night-flying predator, with its mysterious call and inscrutable demeanor — has probably been spooking humans since the beginning of history. These remarkable birds have been the target of powerful projections, figuring in ghost stories and mythologies of many races. The order Strigiformes includes over 130 species of nocturnal raptors with sharply curved beaks and large, forward-facing eyes surrounded by distinctively concave facial disks. The largest owls may reach four kilograms (nine pounds); the smallest (the Elf owl) may be less than fifty-nine grams (two ounces).

Owls see accurately in daylight, but their eyes are especially well adapted for hunting in periods of dim light, typically dusk or dawn. Contrary to popular belief, they do not see in the dark, but can hunt in near or total darkness by relying on their remarkable sense of hearing to guide them.[1] The owl's eyes are also nearly immobile in its head, lending its stare a kind of unnerving fixity. To maximize its latitude of vision, the owl can swivel its head up to an astonishing 270 degrees. This ability also allows the owl, with its asymmetrically placed ears, to locate sources of sounds with great accuracy.[2]

Males call to establish territory, but more often to attract females, which respond to their repeated hoots in kind. Mated pairs are not generally gregarious, nor are they nest builders, instead relying on the abandoned nests of other animals on natural declivities in rocks or hollows or in trees (some even use burrows).[3] Well camouflaged by their generally subdued and mottled coloration, owls have fluffy extensions on the barbules of their feathers that muffle the flutter and rustle of their flight, allowing them to pounce on unsuspecting prey in eerie silence.[4] Their prey usually consists of small rodents, but owls will take most kinds of small animals.

The owl has a special connection with death. In ancient Egypt, the hieroglyph for death was the owl.[5] In Native American mythology, it was considered to be a servant of the Great Spirit. The owl is supernaturally powerful in its own right, and its appearance was frequently taken to presage death.[6] As was often the case with spiritually potent animals, the various parts of the owl were considered strong medicine, especially for the treatment of complaints related to the eye.[7]

The owl also plays a very prominent role in the mythologies of many nations. For example, the Athenians were particularly fond of owls, which were sacred to, and an emblem of, Athena, the Greek goddess of war, who in peacetime became the goddess of wisdom. Thus, the owl often symbolizes this attribute.[8] In Germany there are tales of Till Eulenspiegel (Eulen means owls), the legendary and crafty, frequently malicious buffoon whose pranks often have a serious theme.[9] It was believed that the yellow of the owl's eyes was like the sun, alive in the night and the darkness and able to discern the secrets often hidden there.[10]

In Europe, superstitions about owls still have currency. If an owl should alight on the roof of a house, many fear that a family member will soon die. In Rome at the time of Pliny the Elder, the appearance of an owl could signal the imminent destruction of an entire city.[11] Pliny also noted that the owl was considered a foe of Dionysos.[12] In the Old Testament, the owl is considered unclean (Isaiah 34:11, Leviticus 11:17, Deuteronomy 14:16), and Christian writers generally regarded it either as a negative symbol for its connection with darkness or as a positive symbol of Christ because it vanquishes the dark. Being a creature of the night and thought to see in the dark through its eyes' own inner luminance,[13] the owl is often associated with the moon, and therefore with feminine qualities[14] and oracular powers. Everywhere, the owl's low moan in the dark of night provokes startled alarm and seems an omen of evil.

Because the owl is presumed to see in the night, which is a symbol of the human unconscious, it can psychologically represent a kind of vision that actually sees in the unconscious. The owl stands for the capacity to have imaginal sight, to see into another person or into oneself even in the presence of chaotic emotions — thoughts and despairing feelings that would normally drown one's consciousness. Psychologically, if a person is very rational and intensely organized according to rigid structures that deny the lunar emotional imaginal world of the unconscious, then the imaginal sight of the owl not only is unavailable, but also can turn negative. Instead of creative images, there may be paranoid images. The belief that the owl was hateful to Dionysos shows that its particular vision supports collective values and wishes to overcome the chaos of the Dionysian way of seeing, which emerges to overthrow rigidities and existing inflexible structures.

To dream of an owl can indicate a need for a deeper understanding of present cultural values. For example, the owl image can further the capacity to see more deeply into wisdom of these values and to help support their spiritual significance. Dreaming of an owl can compensate for an overly idiosyncratic attitude toward collective life, an attitude that eschews the owl's inherent wisdom. The owl's special capacity for sight during dusk and the motionless eyes can also indicate the dreamer's need to encounter his or her own power of imagination, which calls for integration into the conscious point of view. The image of an owl in a dream would also alert one to the possible connection with death. The dreamer may be in a situation where certain obsolete attitudes must die; if death were a more general issue, the dreamer might be gaining the courage to face it through the symbolism of the owl.

Notes

[1] Holmgren 1988, 61.
[2] Grzimek 1984, 8: 397.
[3] Holmgren 1988, 66.
[4] Grzimek 1984, 8: 392.
[5] Gimbutas 1989, 190.
[6] Holmgren 1988, 41.
[7] De Gubernatis 1968, 247.
[8] Walker 1983, 754.
[9] De Gubernatis 1968, 246.
[10] Andrews 1983, 172-75.
[11] Gimbutas 1989, 190.
[12] Woodman 1980, 103.
[13] Holmgren 1988, 26-27.
[14] Andrews 1993, 172.

OWL

Families: Strigidae and Tytonidae.

Size: The length of the great gray owl is 61-84 centimeters (24-33 inches). The length of the elf owl is only 13-15 centimeters (5-6 inches). The female owl is usually larger than the male.

Weight: Most owls weigh 40-4000 grams (1.4-141 ounces).

Wingspan: Great gray owl is 137-152 centimeters (54-60 inches); elf owl is 38 centimeters (15 inches).

Incubation: Depending on species, incubation period is 15-35 days.

Longevity: 10-19 years in the wild and 35-51 years in captivity.

Distribution: Everywhere except Antarctica.

Habitat: Woodlands and forest; some grasslands, deserts, and tundra.

Parrot

Stereotypical companions to pirates and privateers, these raucous, squawking, often fantastically colored "talking birds" are mainly creatures of the southern hemisphere, known in the north primarily as exotic pets. The name parrot refers loosely to medium- and larger-sized birds (as opposed to the smaller parakeets) of an avian order that includes the cockatoo, the kea, the lory, the budgerigar (a small Australian parrot), and the macaw.

Parrots have opposing pairs of toes on each foot, which gives them an extraordinary ability to grasp and manipulate objects. Their powerful, downward-curved bills are well adapted for cracking and eating seeds and nuts, and they are often used as a "third foot" for clambering about on branches or perches.[1] Human predation has threatened several species, but birds of prey take a significant number as well. Also, eggs and nestlings are vulnerable to arboreal mammals like monkeys. When threatened by predators, flocks of parrots will often fall instantly and completely silent before bursting from cover in a raucously screeching mass — behavior that many predators find daunting.[2]

Parrots, like other birds, do not have a larynx or vocal chords, so they do not have the capacity to "speak." They have a variety of loud dissonant calls, and they learn to control their throat muscles to manipulate air well enough to reproduce tones and sound. Consequently, parrots can be taught to reproduce human speech, depending on their inherent physical capabilities and their environmental motivation.[3] Young parrots may bond strongly with human beings and are capable of jealousy, rage, and willfully destructive behavior.[4]

Most parrots are gregarious, gathering in extended families or small flocks. Their nests are usually in tree hollows, and some species roost together in large nests. They may lay two to eight eggs, and their diet is mainly vegetarian, with occasional small insects.[5] Parrots often mate for life, remaining inseparable and demonstrating and reinforcing their bond with mutual feeding and preening. Many kinds of animals use mutual grooming as a way of cementing social relationships, but for parrots, preening serves a practical purpose as well, keeping their feathers clean and flightworthy.[6] The parrot's dazzling colored plumage can be predominantly green or brown, and while both sexes can have similar coloration, there may be some differentiations.

No doubt because of their mutual, lifelong devotion and the physical attentions they pay one another, parrots have been cherished as symbols of love in many cultures, including ancient India. Many species of parrot are still referred to as "love birds."[7] Wealthy Romans kept parrots as pets, often with lavish trappings, and taught them to speak. The ancient Greek poet and scholar Callimachus saw the bird as a symbol of babbling humans; today, repetition without understanding is still called "parroting."

Early Christian writers strained to make the parrot a symbol of Mary's virginity due to the belief that its feathers were not dampened in the rain. But most symbolists sought meaning in the birds' talent for mimicry.[8] The undiscerning mimicry of the parrot invites comparison to the parroting of dogma, whether religious, political, or social. In that sense, the parrot can represent a kind of mechanistic way of thinking and behaving. In other, more creative forms, the parrot is a symbol of the unconscious that is essentially amoral, that has not been invaded by cultural concepts of good and evil but rather is lacking moral sensibility.[9] In fairy tales, as in many jokes and cartoons, the parrot is often portrayed in a paradoxical and ambiguous way, underscoring its trickster-like nature. On the one hand, it is often a tattler, revealing secrets of its master and sometimes bringing out inner truths or wisdom. Occasionally, this revelation is harmful or destructive and betrays a confidence to an enemy. On the other hand, the parrot often copes with evil, and helps protect Eros from evil powers.

These widely varying interpretations of the parrot image apply to dreams and possibly compensate for the dreamer's tendency to be too rigid, opinionated, ambiguous, and minimally energetic. It would be important to let the parrot image have its trickster-like, mercurial quality, to allow its energy free reign so that its natural spirit can move around the person, taking the individual out of his or her complacency. Thus the parrot image could offer an avenue for change to the dreamer. Some meaning may also be found in the act of "parroting" and "mimicry," and the dreamer might consider whether he or she is listening to the voice of others and society in general rather than his or her own voice.

P

Notes
[1] Perrins and Middleton 1989, 220, 223.
[2] Perrins and Middleton 1989, 226.
[3] http://www.quakerparrots.com/onlineguide/talk.html.
[4] Stevens 1991a, C1.
[5] Perrins and Middleton 1989, 221.
[6] Perrins and Middleton 1989, 225; McFarland 1987, 466.
[7] Stevens 1991a, C1.
[8] Becker 1994, 226.
[9] von Franz 1977, 55-57, 125.

PARROT
Family: Psittacidae.
Size: 9-100 centimeters (3.5-39 inches) in length.
Wingspan: The pygmy parrot has a wingspan of 13-15 centimeters (5-6 inches). The hyacinth macaw has a wingspan of 1.22 meters (4 feet).
Weight: From 65 grams (0.14 lb) to 1.6 kg (3.5 lb).
Incubation: 17-35 days.
Longevity: Parrots have a reputation for extreme longevity. In captivity, some of the larger species live 30-50 years; 80 years has even been reported. The smaller species have much shorter life spans.
Distribution: South and Central America, southern North America, Africa and Madagascar, southern and Southeast Asia, Australasia, and Polynesia.
Habitat: Lowland tropical and subtropical forest and woodland, and occasionally in mountain forest and open grassland.

Peacock

The visually fascinating peafowl is a species of large ground-dwelling birds belonging to the order Galliformes, which includes turkeys, pheasants, grouse, quail, hoatzin, and jacanas. Common peafowl are native to India and Sri Lanka, green peafowl to Southeast Asia and Java; the recently discovered Congo pea-fowl is found only in that African nation. With its iridescent blue and green plumage and its train of four- to five-foot long feathers covering the bases of the wing quills, the male is so visually spectacular that the rather plain brown peahen is often ignored. Both male and female are frequently, if incorrectly, referred to as peacocks. The cock's train feathers, with eye-shaped spots called *ocelli,* are fanned out to dazzling effect in strutting courtship displays.[1]

Because it is ground-dwelling, easily bred, and strikingly beautiful, the peacock has been kept and raised by humans since antiquity, perhaps longer than any other ornamental bird. Peacocks are polygamous, gathering in small flocks, and omnivorous, thriving on seeds, shoots, berries, insects, and small invertebrates. In India, these birds are known as the bane of young cobras, which they eat as well.[2] They are strong runners but, like pheasants, burst into flight only when flushed from cover. They have a loud, whooping call to signal danger.[3] After mating, the peahen will lay a clutch of three to five eggs in a simple nest she has prepared in the underbrush, or occasionally in other opportune sites.[4]

Humans have used the peacock's spectacular plumage for ritual and ornamental purposes for millennia. To some, the "eyes" seemed to suggest mystical sight, wisdom, or watchfulness, and that notion is no doubt behind the Greek myth of Argus, Hera's watchman, who had a hundred eyes. He fell asleep while on duty and was killed, but Hera put his eyes on the tail of the peacock, which was sacred to her.[5] The *Physiologus* records that the peacock

> ... struts about, prides himself on his appearance, displays his feathers, and gazes haughtily about. But when he catches sight of his feet, he lets out an angry shriek: they ill befit his otherwise splendid appearance.

Thus, as early as the second century, the peacock had become a symbol of vainglorious ostentation and pride.[6]

According to Ovid, the bird was sacred to Juno. In Rome, the fan of the peacock's tail was seen as the vault of heaven, with the eyes as stars.[7] Like birds such as the eagle or the flamingo, the peacock has been portrayed as the inspiration for the myth of the phoenix, the bird of resurrection that was consumed in flames and rose from its own ashes. In Egypt, the peacock was associated with the solar god Amon-Ra; with Horus, whose eye was all-seeing; and with Isis, wife of Osiris and mother of Horus.[8]

In Christian hermeneutics, the peacock was considered a symbol of the death and resurrection of Christ, of the soul, and of immortality.[9] Aristotle believed that the flesh of the peacock was incorruptible, that it could not rot; half a millennium later, St. Augustine claimed the truth of this belief.[10] In the elaborate system of alchemical symbols, the tail of the peacock (in Latin, *cauda pavonis*) heralded the end of the alchemical work — the synthesis of all qualities and elements, symbolized by the "philosopher's stone."[11] On the negative side, the peacock is frequently seen as a symbol of vanity.

In its native India, the peacock was associated with Hindra, the thunder god, who became a peacock to escape the demon Ravana.[12] The goddess Sarasvati rode a peacock, and it was one of the many traditional mounts of the

Buddha.[13] Indra was depicted on a peacock throne — a bit of mythology echoed in the twentieth century by the peacock throne of the Shahs of Iran.[14] The peacock was considered a propitious omen in China, a creature with the beauty and dignity to ward off evil spirits and an emblem of the Ming Dynasty.[15]

Because they will occasionally feed on young snakes, peacocks gained a reputation as enemies of serpents that transformed the venom, to which they were believed to be immune, into the iridescence of their plumage.[16] Thus, when a peacock was depicted with a serpent in its mouth, it represented the triumph of light over darkness, good over evil, or positive spiritual energies over more regressive forces of the unconscious. The peacock's fan also mimicked the visual glory of the rising sun, and by extension lent itself to symbolic association with renewal and resurrection.

The appearance of a peacock in a dream could, on the positive side, represent a potentially new state of mind in which the dreamer is capable of feeling an unfolding of inner life. The "eyes" of its feathers might indicate the need for a broader and more watchfully attentive outlook on the dreamer's personal world as well as the world at large. Thus, the peacock's tail is a marvelous symbol of an integration process, as long as the person is not trapped in its negative side of vain pursuits.

Notes
[1] Grzimek 1984, 8: 32.
[2] Ibid.
[3] Perrins and Middleton 1989, 126.
[4] Grzimek 1984, 8: 37.
[5] Andrews 1993, 182.
[6] Biedermann 1994, 258.
[7] Cooper 1992, 179.
[8] Andrews 1993, 182; Cooper 1992, 179.
[9] Andrews 1993, 182.
[10] Becker 1994, 229.
[11] Fabricius 1989, 242; Jung 1975, 16: 480.
[12] Andrews 1993, 182.
[13] Becker 1994, 228.
[14] Biedermann 1994, 258.
[15] Ibid.
[16] Biedermann 1994, 257.

PEACOCK
Family: Phasianidae (The male is called peacock, the female peahen; together they are known as peafowl).
Size: The male Palawan peacock pheasant, endemic to the island of Palawan in the Philippines, averages 51 centimeters (20 inches); the female averages 41 centimeters (16 inches).
Wingspan: The train of tail is 150 centimeters (60 inches).
Weight: At the Woodland Park Zoo in Washington state, the male weighs 594 grams (21 ounces), and the female weighs 503 grams (18 ounces). The wild Palawan peacock pheasants may weigh less.
Incubation: 28 days.
Longevity: Some green peafowl have lived up to 30 years.
Distribution: Southern Asia.
Habitat: Dense jungle on hilly territory near water.

Pelican

With their outsized, scoop-shaped bills and waddling gait, pelicans have a bizarre and distinctly awkward look on land. These large, short-legged, web-footed aquatic birds have a loose pouch of skin below their long lower mandible, giving them a famously distinctive appearance. The upper bill is broad and flat, ending with a small hook, so that the entire apparatus, bill and pouch, functions as an extremely efficient scoop for catching fish, which make up the bird's entire diet. Pelicans' long, broad wings make them strong fliers with exceptional gliding ability; they are also excellent swimmers, possessing subdermal air sacs that give them added buoyancy. When not paired off for mating, nest building, or caring for their young, pelicans gather and fish in flocks and fly in distinctive, diagonal skeins. Nesting may occur in colonies comprised of many pelicans.[2]

Their diet requires that they have access to water, and they are fully capable of traveling hundreds of miles daily to fish. White pelicans skim fish from the surface of the water, often working cooperatively to "drive" them into a small area; brown pelicans dive to catch their food.[3] Both fill the pouch with fish and up to two gallons of water; the latter is expelled by contracting the pouch and trapping the fish, which are then swallowed whole. Parents regurgitate a kind of paste from the crop (gullet), and the young eat directly from their pouches.[4] Full-grown birds, which can weigh up to thirty pounds, have few natural predators.

The pelican figures significantly in Christian and alchemical symbolism, where it represents sacrifice and resurrection. These beliefs, portrayed in allegories and symbols, stem primarily from deep archetypal fantasies stimulated by the bird's natural behavior. At various times, the pelican was thought to offer its own blood to nourish its young when food was scarce, or to sustain itself by drinking its own, inexhaustible supply of blood.[5] An important alchemical retort was called the pelican. In it, the distillate runs back into the vessel, and its recursive shape can be fancied to resemble the curving neck of a pelican pecking at its own breast.[6] Jung says that the pelican could illustrate the process of realization in which new insights emerge, die, go back into the unconscious and return again.[7] Thus, the pelican is a symbol for the human capacity to allow old belief structures that may have been solely devoted to discipline and directed purpose to die, and to nourish new structures and insights that could allow for more fantasy and imagination yet still require a disciplined approach.

Dreaming of this remarkable bird could point to the necessity of embracing a more circular, renewing attitude rather than direct linear problem-solving. The dreamer may tend to grasp an idea — perhaps from a dream, a fantasy, or another person — and then precipitously create something new to solve some problem. If the pelican imagery appeared in a dream, the dreamer may need to consciously let the idea go — in effect, let it dim and germinate until it comes back in a new form. The pelican image could also represent a religious issue for the individual, and it may alert him or her to the age-old belief or experience that new insights come from a process far beyond the scale of ego.

Notes
[1] Grzimek 1984, 7: 163-64.
[2] Perrins and Middleton 1989, 52.
[3] Grzimek 1984, 7: 164.
[4] Grzimek 1984, 7: 165.
[5] Jung 1976, 13: 116.
[6] Fabricius 1989, 210.
[7] Jung 1975, 9ii: 377, note 58.

PELICAN
Family: Pelicanidae.
Size: Length is 170-180 centimeters (5.5-6 feet).
Wingspan: Up to almost 300 centimeters (10 feet).
Weight: 7-14 kilograms (15-30 pounds).
Incubation: Approximately 35 days.
Longevity: 15-25 years in the wild.
Distribution: Most parts of the world.
Habitat: Lakes, rivers, and seacoasts.

Pig

Raised by humans for millennia, the archetype and prime metaphor of greed, indulgence, and socially unacceptable behavior, the domestic pig has been the object of contradictory or ambivalent projections. Loathed as unclean by Islam and Israel alike,[1] it is also seen as a sweet, even beloved figure like Wilbur in E.B. White's children's story *Charlotte's Web* or the talkative hero of the recent movie *Babe,* and as a resource whose every part ("all but the squeal") has economic value. All domestic pigs are descended from subspecies of the European and Asiatic wild pig,[2] or, as some will call it, the wild boar. Technically, the animal is called a pig prior to sexual maturity and swine thereafter. In popular parlance, however, pig is most commonly used.

Pigs are truly omnivorous. They will eat grass, leaves, shoots, sprouts, fallen fruit, seeds, and tubers and roots (using their flexible snouts to dig them up) as well as worms, insect larvae, eggs, birds, snakes, lizards, and small rodents. Pigs are known to go after larger animals that are injured or disabled, and they do not disdain carrion.[3] They have an extraordinary nose for anything edible, even if it is buried deeply in the ground; as a result, they have been trained to hunt truffles, the prized and delicious underground fungi found in France and Italy. When they are on anything more than a minimal diet, a thick layer of fat often forms under the skin.[4]

The pig's eyesight is poor, and it can see only close up.[5] Pigs make a variety of sounds, squeaking and grunting in different ways to maintain contact among themselves, to call their young, to sound alarm or distress and to announce amorous or aggressive intent. They use their snouts to lift and push, to dig and plow through tangled brush. They can be quite aggressive, especially in the rutting season, when males bite their rivals or shove them with their snouts. Sharp canine teeth are used for tearing and slashing and may also be deployed as defensive weapons against predators.[6]

Gregarious by instinct, pigs will live in pairs or small groups, although females go off by themselves to give birth. Sows can have two or even three litters a year, with as many as twenty young in each. In ideal conditions, a sow could, in theory, have seven million descendants in the space of ten years.[7] The pig's fertility, eagerness for food of every sort, and the obvious way that its plump body swells connect it symbolically to every kind of increase. In many cultures, the round body of the sow was connected with pregnancy and, by association, with fertility of seed and field.

Suckling pigs were frequently sacrificed to the goddess Demeter and her daughter Persephone, as well as to other European deities associated with cereal or grain. Pork fat in particular is a fertility symbol; in some places, it is still used in agricultural rituals like the plowing of the first furrow in the spring.[8] In Greek myth, Hades abducted Persephone and carried her down to his underworld home. As the earth opened up, a nearby swineherd and his swine were engulfed in the chasm.[9] To encourage the continued memory of this tragedy, the Greeks sacrificed pigs at Eleusis. At the Thesmophoria, a festival honoring Demeter and Persephone, pigs that had been previously thrown into chasms were recovered and their remains placed on altars and spread as fertilizer in the fields. The abundant, fruitful nature of the pig is clear in the tale of Zeus being suckled by a sow which was as a result considered sacred to him.[10] In contrast, the negative association of the pig is highlighted in the tale of the Odysseus's men being turned into swine by Circe.[11]

In Celtic tradition, the worship of the pig was widespread, and its flesh was regarded as a food of the gods. The great mother figure Kerridwen, the "Old White One," was a sow goddess, as was Phaea, the "Shining One," who represented the moon and fertility. Another Celtic figure, Maccus, was a swine god.[12] In ancient Chinese culture, the pig represented nature, raw and untamed, avaricious and dirty.[13] In the *I Ching,* the Chinese Book of Changes, the pig symbolizes the "Abysmal," a great chasm, a fall, or danger. However, the pig is also regarded as fecund and fertilizing when tamed. Moreover, it was a symbol of strength and a literal measure of wealth. Pigs' jaws were even placed in tombs to indicate the wealth and status of the deceased.[14] In Jewish tradition, the pig is the most unclean of animals. In the parable of the prodigal son, it is an ultimate degradation when he is sent to feed the swine, since any contact with pigs was thought to be defiling. The pig is unclean in Islam as well, and Christian writers associate the pig with Satan as a symbol of gluttony and sensuality.[15]

The contradictory qualities of the pig are especially evident in Egyptian mythology. In its positive aspects, the pig was sacred to the great Egyptian mother goddess Isis. But on the negative side, the black pig was an aspect of the demonic Set, who swallowed the eye of Horus, Isis's son. The pig was thereafter considered unclean for Egyptians, forbidden as daily food.[16] It was consumed as a sacrament just once a year, when pigs were sacrificed to Osiris, god of death and resurrection, to assure his life in the underworld.[17]

The pig can remind us of ourselves in many striking ways. Its internal organs are arranged enough like our own that its corpse was used in the Middle Ages for medical instruction. Its (sometimes) pink and hairless body, jowly, round, and corpulent; its greedy, wallowing ways; even its sexual appetite — all can seem like a grotesque parody of human self-indulgence. There is a suspicion, passed around in jokes and anecdotal cannibal lore, that human flesh tastes most like pork.[18]

Gluttony, which humans project onto the pig, is one of the ways that matter changes and transforms. Flesh becomes food; food becomes excrement; excrement becomes fertilizer; fertilizer becomes food; and food becomes flesh. In this context, one can understand overeating as a deep spiritual problem, one that addresses the most basic mystery — how inanimate matter becomes animate. In facing one's own "piggishness," one can begin to recognize the fundamental power that drives it, the same power that is metaphorically ascribed to a pig goddess or to the sorceress Circe. Avaricious feelings, once they are understood in terms of emotional neediness, can flip over into a positive desire for rebirth and redemption. Awareness of the greedy life force behind the voraciousness of the pig once spurred its use as a sacrifice to the cyclically life-giving deities of agriculture. This same awareness can turn the destructive impulse to overeat into a desire for renewal — one that is respectful of the close nexus between life and death.

Dreaming of a pig might indicate that the dreamer is intended to confront the world of the Great Mother — most likely the aspects of early feelings of need, voraciousness, and insatiable longings. Because the pig is such a powerful symbol of transformation, the dream image may bring attention to a potential change of those desires. Furthermore, the exceptional fertility of the pig might raise questions about the dreamer's relationship to his or her own creativity. If one is not living and acting on this potential, one can instead be frequently involved with all types of "piggish" conduct. The pig is very closely connected to the earth and body. Many people who have not had a good enough relationship to the maternal body or to nature act out all types of socially unacceptable behavior, which then becomes the psychic substitute for healthy, earthy body feelings. Thus, the appearance of a pig in a dream can represent a necessity, and a newly-found capability, to confront these conflicts.

Notes
[1] Cooper 1992, 221.
[2] Grzimek 1976, 507.
[3] Grzimek 1984, 13: 76.
[4] "Pig." *Encyclopedia Britannica*, 1997.
[5] Grzimek 1984, 13: 76-78.
[6] Grzimek 1984, 13: 77-78.
[7] Burton 1981, 591.
[8] Gimbutas 1989, 146.
[9] Johnson 1988, 262.
[10] Cooper 1992, 221.
[11] Walker 1983, 956.
[12] Cooper 1992, 221.
[13] Cooper 1992, 222.
[14] Hai 1995.
[15] Cooper 1992, 221.
[16] Ibid.
[17] Frazer 1979, 24-34.
[18] Hillman 1983, 284-85.

PIG
Family: Suidae.
Size: Length of swine varies according to geographical location, up to about 1 meter (3.3 feet).
Weight: 55-100 kilograms (120-220 pounds).
Gestation: 115 days.
Longevity: 15-25 years.
Distribution: Wild pig originated in Europe, Asia, East Indies, and Africa and was introduced into North and South America, Australia, Tasmania, New Guinea, and New Zealand.
Habitat: Mostly domesticated.

Piranha

With their strong jaws and ferocious teeth, the carnivorous piranha[1] fish of South America are world famous for the furious efficiency with which a frenzied pack, can devour large animals in a short time. We sometimes call a person who preys on others a piranha. Piranha play a significant role in the ecology of South American river basins, eliminating wounded and diseased fish and retarding the spread of infection. They are also of some economic significance locally, since humans eat them, and their teeth are often used as cutting tools, as well as for masks and adornments.[2]

Piranha are gregarious freshwater fish, approximately thirty centimeters (twelve inches) in length and rather innocuous in appearance, except for a mouthful of truly vicious-looking, razor-sharp tricuspids that are perfectly adapted for ripping chunks of flesh off a carcass. They generally feed on other fish (and occasionally on one another), but they will take aquatic rodents. There are rare but widely circulated reports of piranhas devouring large mammals, including humans. However, any kind of purposeful response or self-defense seems to discourage the wild "mobbing" that so captures the popular mind. Most attacks on humans are non-lethal and consist of random bites, which are certainly painful since a piranha is said to take 16.4 cubic centimeters (an entire cubic inch) of flesh in one clean bite.[3] In the case of weakened or unconscious individuals who may have fallen in the water, a kind of dangerous group attacking frenzy may become operative, especially in constricted circumstances when other food is in short supply. The presence of slaughterhouse wastes in river water has also been linked to a greater likelihood of attacks on humans.[4]

In certain marshy areas along the Amazon and Orinoco rivers, where solid ground for conventional burial is at a premium, local tribes place their dead in the water and allow the piranha to strip off the flesh before the skeleton is recovered for ceremonial funeral rites.[5] Outside of these areas, the piranha is known almost exclusively by the sensational accounts, many of them fictitious or exaggerated, of their violent attacks on humans. The image does rouse fear and horror, and that resonance makes it a potent psychological symbol. While an individual piranha is relatively harmless, an onslaught *en masse* is utter devastation and obliteration.

The ecologically balancing, cleansing, and eugenic function of all aggressive predation, including that of the piranha, has a parallel in the psyche. Extreme internal anxieties can clear out what is metaphorically useless, non-functional, diseased, or moribund. Rigid attitudes that once served life can die and be torn apart, leading to considerable anxiety but an ultimate cleansing.

A piranha image, especially a multitude of piranha, appearing in a dream could represent an utter destruction of identity, potentially devastating aggressive impulses turning against the self and literally annihilating it. Consequently, this image could represent a heightened threat of disoriented and confused states of mind, utter destruction of identity, even a psychotic process. However, awareness of the cleansing, renewing nature of the piranha can alert one to the possible mystery of renewal amidst such overwhelming experiences of the unconscious.

Notes

[1] "Piranha." *Encarta 97 Encyclopedia.*
[2] Grzimek 1984, 4: 284, 287.
[3] Banister and Campbell 1988, 73.
[4] Grzimek 1984, 4: 284.
[5] Grzimek 1984, 4: 287.

PIRANHA
Family: Characidae.
Size: 30 centimeters (12 inches) or more in length.
Weight: 5 kilograms (11 pounds) or more depending on size.
Gestation: Scatter eggs among aquatic plants.
Distribution: Africa, South and Central America, and southern North America.
Habitat: Fresh waters.

Porcupine

Looking safe behind its prickly defenses and seemingly unconcerned, the porcupine or "spiny pig" is unprepossessing in appearance, yet no predator that has felt the sting of its quills is likely to attack a second time. Although far less commonly seen than other rodents, it is one of those animals that every child seems to know about. Old World and New World porcupines are similar-looking and occupy similar ecological niches, but they are not closely related, having little in common except their spines.

Old World porcupines are sturdily built; however, because their bodies, especially the upper part of the back, are covered with erectile spines or quills, they tend to look more massive than they really are.[1] Frequently cave dwellers, they find their way by touch, aided by special tactile bristles around the snout and eyes and, to a lesser extent, all over the body. Their search for food is aided by stiff but sensitive hairs, or *vibrissae,* that grow around the nostrils.[2] They are herbivorous and solitary feeders, surviving on the roots, bulbs, fruit, and berries of a variety of plants.[3] They are crepuscular animals, primarily active at twilight, and they tend to keep out of the light during the day.[4]

Only the mating habits of the Old World cape porcupine have been much observed. They engage in various sorts of sexual behavior at any time in the female's sexual cycle, although without intromission. Females reach sexual maturity at about eighteen months old. The estrous cycle takes about twenty-nine days and may occur several times in a year. Actual copulation, accompanied by intromission, is generally initiated by the female and occurs only when she is in heat (every twenty-eight to thirty-six days). The old joke about how porcupines make love (carefully) has some truth to it. The female lays her tail flat against her back, allowing the male to mount her without injury. The young animals are well cared for by the adults. Only one litter is produced each year, most often comprised of just one offspring, and less frequently two. Males and females lick one another when mating as well as at other times (apparently to show affection), and both will lick their young.[5]

New World porcupines average a bit smaller than their Old World cousins. They have large, bulky heads, blunt muzzles, and short, powerful limbs. Some species have long, spineless, prehensile tails. All are quite nearsighted and have keen senses of smell, hearing, and touch. Most produce a wide variety of vocalizations, from moans, grunts, and whines to shrieks, barks, and wails. Strong tree climbers, they are also herbivorous, feeding in summer on roots, stems, leaves, berries, seeds, nuts, and flowers. In the winter, they subsist on conifer needles and on the bark.[6]

The quills of both kinds of porcupines take on a variety of forms. Some are long and needle-like, with tips that are completely rigid; some have rigid shafts with movable tips; others are shorter and bristly at the tip. The points of these bristly quills are so sharp and rigid that one can easily be hurt on contact.[7] A typical porcupine may have thirty thousand quills covering all parts of its body except the face, the underbelly, and the tail. When the animal is disturbed or threatened, these quills can be made to lie flat or stand up.[8]

The porcupine's defenses are strictly passive; the quills are never shot or projected at an enemy, although that notion is ancient and persistent.[9] They are loosely attached, however, and some species will turn backwards, lashing their tails at predators and sometimes even running backwards at them.[10] The quills are not poisonous, but they can be quite painful, and the wounds, if they turn septic, can be serious, even fatal.[11] Nevertheless, wild cats, hyenas, and some large raptors are able to prey upon porcupines successfully.[12]

In Native American lore, which associates particular animals with the cardinal directions, the porcupine represents the South.[13] Perhaps because their spines suggested rays of light, the porcupine represented the sun in some myths and the moon in others.[14] Because it is gentle and non-aggressive unless attacked, the porcupine also symbolizes innocence, faith, and trust;[15] in stories, it is often the companion of the trickster Coyote. In Nigeria, the Hausa people regard porcupines as righteous worldly and otherworldly spirits, with power over men, women and witches.[16]

The salient symbolic characteristic of the porcupine, like the turtle, stems from its defensive armament and the sense of well-protected security that it engenders. But while the turtle's defense is purely passive, the porcupine actually injures its attackers. Whereas the turtle's shell resists attack, the porcupine's very appearance seems to discourage or repel approach. Symbolically, the porcupine would thus represent a sharp personality and a very aggressive kind of passivity.

This kind of symbolism is usually most resonant for humans when fear and vulnerability are protected by dormant anger that is ready to flare up at the first sign of approach, thereby keeping others at an emotional distance. This "porcupine-like" quality can rely on the power of barbed remarks, or it can be silently communicated so that others walk on proverbial eggshells in the vicinity of such a person. This self-protective behavior usually turns out to be alienating or isolating, rendering the individual totally unapproachable. A person who becomes more conscious of his or her "porcupine-like" qualities can gain a greater knowledge of the defensive power of his or her remarks and attitudes, and become aware of how these communicate, even silently. This awareness can lead to an enhanced feeling of safety rather than a rigid, defensive posture.

A person who dreams of a porcupine may consciously need to respect his or her gentle, non-belligerent nature, while realizing that there is a time to protect oneself and a time to fight back. A porcupine can also represent the dreamer's barbed, defensive yet passive nature, which effectively keeps people at a distance.

Notes
[1] Grzimek 1984, 11: 407.
[2] Grzimek 1984, 11: 414.
[3] Grzimek 1984, 11: 407; Macdonald 1987, 704.
[4] Grzimek 1984, 11: 414.
[5] Grzimek 1984, 11: 415; Macdonald 1987, 704.
[6] Macdonald 1987, 686.
[7] Grzimek 1984, 11: 408.
[8] Andrews 1993, 300.
[9] Cooper 1992, 184.
[10] Andrews 1993, 300.
[11] Macdonald 1987, 704.
[12] Grzimek 1984, 11, 411.
[13] Cooper 1992, 184.
[14] Jobes 1962, 2: 1287.
[15] Cooper 1992, 184.
[16] *Funk & Wagnalls Standard Dictionary*, 1972, 881.

PORCUPINE
Family: Hystricidae (Old World).
Size: Head-body length is 37–83 centimeters (14.6–32.7 inches). It has two types of quills: long, flexible quills up to 35 centimeters (13.8 inches) long; and shorter, stout quills, depending on species and geographical location.
Weight: 1.5–27 kilograms (3.3–59.4 pounds), depending on species and geographical location.
Gestation: 90–100 days, according to species and geographical location.
Longevity: Approximately 21 years recorded for the crested porcupines (in captivity).
Distribution: Africa and Asia.
Habitat: Varies from dense forest to semidesert.

PORCUPINE
Family: Erethizontidae (New World).
Size: Head-body length is 30-86 centimeters (12-34 inches); depending on species, quills may be about 7.5 centimeters (3 inches) long.
Weight: 0.900-18 kilograms (2-40 pounds), depending on species.
Gestation: 210 days for North American porcupine.
Longevity: Up to 17 years for North American porcupine.
Distribution: North America (except southeastern United States), southern Mexico, Central America, and northern South America.
Habitat: Forest areas, open grasslands, desert, and canyons.

Puma

Graceful, stealthy, and powerful, the puma, like the jaguar, is a New World cat. Called cougar, mountain lion, catamount, and occasionally panther, it is large — the largest purring cat in the world — but technically it is not classified with the big cats (lions, tigers, leopards, and jaguars). A long-tailed, dark-eyed, lithe-bodied creature, it has a smallish head, black mustache, and pink nose. The puma's fur is unpatterned and generally tawny, but variable in shade from reddish to silvery.[1] Although it lacks the exotic circus appeal of lions and tigers, the puma is a fearsome hunter, capable of killing prey much bigger than itself.[2] Indeed, a single one-hundred pound puma (they rarely, if ever, hunt in groups) can bring down a bull elk weighing more than eight hundred pounds. An unarmed human would be (and has been) easy prey, but these are shy animals, wary of civilization.[3]

Pumas feed by preference on deer and elk[4] but will take whatever prey they can catch, from mice to moose[5] — even other predators like wolves or young bears. They rely on stealth and ambush, killing larger prey with a powerful bite to the neck, which severs the spinal cord.[6] Leftovers are buried for later snacking. An adult puma can effortlessly outrun a bear, and, an excellent climber, it can easily take refuge in trees when threatened by a wolf pack.[7] Humans are its primary scourge. Because they occasionally take sheep or young cattle, pumas have been much reviled, trapped, and hunted by ranchers wanting to protect their livestock. But, like wolves and other predators, they keep the deer population in healthy balance by winnowing out the sick and infirm.[8]

Although they are called mountain lions, pumas can adapt to a wide range of climates and habitats, from the pampas and tropical rain forests of South America to the rocky terrain of the American Southwest.[9] Individual cats may patrol a large exclusive territory, marking it off with scat or scratch marks;[10] others may wander as "transients" until a territory is vacated. Direct challenges do occur, although they are rare. Quintessentially solitary animals, males and females pair up briefly in breeding season, during which couples are inseparable, roaming, sleeping, and hunting together. But once his procreative mission is accomplished, the male loses interest in togetherness, leaving it to the female to raise and educate from one to six cubs for a year or sometimes two before they go off on their own.[11]

In Inca culture, the puma is often confused with the jaguar, and as such is sacred to the Creator god, as well as being a symbol of power.[12] A shaman may also take the form of a puma to access the power of the spirit world.[13] In Native American myths and tales, the puma is often portrayed as a companion to various trickster figures — sometimes as Coyote's elder brother. The Zuni people honor the mountain lion, considering him "Guardian and Master of the Northern World."[14]

Psychologically, the puma or mountain lion could symbolize the nearly supernatural means that a human being can muster to meet his or her needs. Someone dreaming of a puma might see if he or she is becoming too isolated from others and needs to become more involved in the structure of society. The dream might also indicate that the person has more power than consciously recognized, even when up against very large obstacles.

Notes
[1] Grzimek 1984, 12: 328.
[2] Stevens 1994, C1.
[3] Ibid.
[4] Macdonald 1987, 54.
[5] Grzimek 1984, 12: 329.
[6] Stevens 1994, C1.
[7] Grzimek 1984, 12: 330.
[8] Grzimek 1984, 12: 329.

[9] *Funk & Wagnalls Standard Dictionary*, 1972, 753-54.
[10] Grzimek 1984, 12: 329.
[11] Grzimek 1984, 12: 330.
[12] Jobes 1962, 2: 1201.
[13] Cooper 1992, 184.
[14] Cooper 1992, 164.

PUMA
Family: Felidae.
Size: Head–rump length is 105-160 centimeters (41-63 inches), and tail length is 60-85 centimeters (24-33 inches).
Weight: 36-103 kilograms (80-227 pounds).
Gestation: 90-96 days.
Longevity: Over 19 years in captivity.
Distribution: From southern Canada to Patagonia in southern South America.
Habitat: Forest to steppe, including conifer, deciduous and tropical forests, grassland, and desert.

Raccoon

Masked raiders of garbage bins, raccoons are clever, dexterous, and unafraid of humans. They create havoc wherever they stop to forage for food, and they are known for their insatiable inquisitiveness. The curious and hungry "bandit" that upsets the garbage and makes a mess in one's house or on one's property has a symbolic or psychological analogue that turns order on its head, upsets our lives, and creates chaos.

Raccoons are highly adaptable omnivores. As predators, they will eat insects, small mammals, earthworms, crustaceans, snails, mussels, reptiles (especially their eggs), amphibians, fish, and, less often, birds and young muskrats. They never chase living prey but merely take them as they are found. As foragers they will eat wild fruits, berries, grasses, and leaves, while as scavengers they will take just about anything left accessible to their prying hands and persistence. In northern climates, raccoons will gorge in the fall, putting on a layer of fat before spending the period of severe cold in semi-hibernation.[1] Raccoons have well-developed salivary glands, which help them in swallowing food and which generate carbohydrate-splitting enzymes vital to their digestion of certain foods. Domestic raccoons tend to douse aquatic foods (such as crayfish, fish, shrimp, and snails) in water, but they seldom do this to terrestrial foods. No such behavior has been observed in wild raccoons.[2]

Raccoons have keen senses, particularly smell.[3] They are agile and courageous, and can be quite ferocious in self-defense. In addition to being masters of deception, they seem to have excellent judgment about when to fight and when to make themselves scarce.[4] Essentially nocturnal and solitary, raccoons share overlapping territories more or less peaceably, squabbling only when competing face-to-face for food. In such circumstances, heads are lowered, hackles raised, ears laid back and teeth bared, but actual fighting is rare.[5] All of these tendencies may account for their ability to coexist with larger and more effective predators like lynx, foxes, and wolves, and their well-known ability to thrive under the very noses of humans in all but the most intensely populated areas.[6]

R

Raccoons may nest in underground dens, heavy bushes, hollow trees, clefts in the rocks, or even in the rafters or crawl-spaces of houses — generally within a few hundred yards of some form of fresh water.[7] They swim well, and their walk is a distinctive ambling waddle, with head and tail down and back arched. They can also gallop at up to twenty-four kilometers (fifteen miles) per hour over short distances.[8] During the mating season, males tend to wander, sometimes as much as eleven kilometers (seven miles), in a restless search for females. They may mate with several females, but females will copulate with one male only. They remain in heat for three days, ovulating immediately after copulation, and sixty to sixty-five days later they give birth to a litter of from one to seven young.[9]

In Native Americans legends, the raccoon is a trickster figure, although never a creator or transformer like the coyote or other animal tricksters. Nor is the raccoon ever a figure of absurdity or a victim.[10] The chaos that this trickster can bring, mostly as a consequence of foraging and thievery, is the product of a clever and determined entity that will upset anything and everything to get at what it wants. This fierce and reckless energy, which in human beings is usually associated with the shadow (a repressed aspect of the personality), can be either positive or negative, depending on one's conscious attitude and acceptance of change. New and creative possibilities can emerge out of this chaos, or else it can remain an unholy mess. Even as it disorients us, disorder often shows us how to break out of our frozen mindsets — if we will pay attention.

If someone dreamed of a raccoon, and that person was acting in a trickster-like way in his or her conscious life, the raccoon might appear as a self-image — warning about the negative aspects of the trickster, such as deceit, lying for its own sake, and creative disorder that leads only to confusion. However, if the person is too rational and rigid in his or her thinking, obsessively maintaining a status quo, the raccoon can be a marvelous compensatory symbol — demanding change, asking the person to look at those aspects of his or her life that have so far remained unexamined and inflexible. Thus, dreaming of a raccoon suggests that an important aspect of the person, namely the shadow side of the conscious personality, must be acknowledged and integrated into consciousness.

Notes

1 Grzimek 1984, 12, 99.
2 MacClintock 1981, 56-57.
3 Grzimek 1984, 12, 99.
4 Andrews 1993, 306.
5 Grzimek 1984, 12, 100.
6 Pfeffer 1989, 295.
7 Pfeffer 1989, 294.
8 Grzimek 1984, 12, 100.
9 Grzimek 1984, 12, 100-101.
10 *Funk & Wagnalls Standard Dictionary* 1972, 918.

RACCOON
Family: Procyonidae.
Size: Head-body length is 55 centimeters (22 inches); tail length is 25 centimeters (10 inches); females are about one-quarter smaller than males.
Weight: Usually 5–8 kilograms (11–18 pounds), sometimes up to 15 kilograms (33 pounds).
Gestation: 63 days.
Longevity: Not known in wild (over 12 years recorded in captivity).
Distribution: North, Central, and South America.
Habitat: Wooded terrain in the vicinity of ponds, lakes, streams, and swamps; mangrove thickets along subtropical and coastal plains, and on the edges of savannas and semi-arid regions as long as they have access to open water.

Ram

Rams in sexual competition for ewes butt their great horned heads together in a remarkable posture of abandoned and headlong aggression. Rampant, with heads down and hind legs planted, they plunge at one another so fiercely that the hills and valleys echo with the sound of their mighty clash. Thus, the ram has become a verb for smashing heavily into something and a crude symbol of aggressive male energy in general. The ram's horns, especially those of bighorn sheep, which are closest to the spiral motif and the mandala, symbolize creative order and arouse imagination and inspiration.[1] Overall, the ram closely resembles sheep in general physical characteristics.

The ram as a symbol is found in many cultures. The Egyptian god Amon was represented as a ram with curved horns,[2] as was the god of creation, Khnum.[3] For the Yoruba people of western Africa, the ram is identified with the thunder god Shango, and the thunder is thought of as the deafening bleat of the ram.[4] Pre-Roman Celtic images show a serpent with the head of a ram, associating the curl of the horns with the coil of the snake. The ram was thought to have (or share) chthonic qualities and was associated not only with fertilization but also with war and death.[5]

In Greek myth, a ram with a golden fleece carried Phrixus and Helle across the sea to Colchis, the home of Medea and the destination of the Argonauts, a land of fabulous wealth and the domain of sorcery. As a reward, the ram was turned into the constellation Aries.[6] The fleece of the ram was the prize sought by Jason and his fellow Argonauts, and, along with the grail, it remains the prime symbol of all heroic quests. In Greece, the ram was sacred to Zeus as the god of fertility, and specifically as begetter.[7]

In the Old Testament, as Abraham prepares to sacrifice his son Isaac, a ram appears at the last moment as a substitute (Genesis 22:1-14). This is similar to the myth of an older, pre-Yahwistic god (Babylonian and Egyptian) who requires the offering of the firstborn son. This god sacrifices his own impulsive and animal side in the form of the ram, freeing Isaac, Abraham, and himself and his creation from destruction. This ritual is repeated metaphorically at the Jewish High Holidays in the sounding of the ram's horn, or shofar.[8] In Indian myth, the ram is an attribute of Indra[9] and is sacred to Agni, god of Fire.[10] As such, it is connected with the third chakra, Manipura, the kidney.[11] In Islam, the ram is the foremost sacrificial animal, and one of just ten animals admitted to heaven.[12]

Like all animals, the ram can have opposite symbolic aspects. From the positive point of view, the ram generally represents aggression, creativity, and a kinetic energy that pushes its way forward even when tired and exhausted — a manifest strength of action that is displayed when and where it is necessary. From the negative point of view, the ram symbolizes impulsive, attacking behavior, often seen as a negative aspect of masculine energy, which can manifest as a violent burst of unreflective temper and a compulsive "doing" before "thinking." Because of its strong instinctual drives and impetuous behavior, the ram is also cast as an enemy of feminine principles such as reflection, insight, and "being" in distinction to "doing."

In a dream, the ram may represent, in a positive sense, the need for the dreamer to push ahead with some creative task or to be more aggressive or assertive in a situation where he or she might be too passive or reflective. In a negative sense, the ram may also represent the danger of acting out sexually, running amok without any concern for feeling and reflection. The appropriate significance of the dream depends both on the context of the dreamer's conscious life and on the ram's action in the dream.

Notes
[1] Andrews 1993, 307.
[2] *The New Larousse Encyclopedia of Animal Life* (1968), 48.
[3] Becker 1994, 245.
[4] Biedermann 1994, 278.
[5] Cooper 1992, 190.
[6] Biedermann 1994, 278.
[7] Cooper 1992, 189.
[8] Dreifuss 1973, 123.
[9] Becker 1994, 245.
[10] Jobes 1962, 2: 1321.
[11] Leadbeater 1985, 108.
[12] Jobes 1962, 2: 1321.

RAM
Genus: Ovis.
Family: Horned ungulates, with a variety of subfamilies.
Size: The head–rump length of the wild sheep is 110-200 centimeters (44-80 inches); the tail length is 3.5-13 centimeters (1-5 inches); the body height is 65-125 centimeters (26-50 inches).
Weight: 20-230 kilograms (45-505 pounds). The female weighs one-quarter to one-third less than the male.
Gestation: 5 months.
Longevity: Sheep can live as long as 20 years.
Distribution: Australia, New Zealand, China, India, the United States, South Africa, Argentina, and Turkey. Countries that have large areas of grassland are the major producers.
Habitat: Wild bighorn sheep are usually found in uplands, inhabiting alpine meadows, grassy mountain slopes, and foothill country in proximity to rugged rocky cliffs and bluffs.

Rat

Proverbial deserters of ships, carriers of plague, and spoilers of grain and other foodstuffs, rats are much maligned, sometimes unfairly. They occupy nearly every corner of the world in great variety, and the precise number of species is unknown, although approximately 750 genera have been properly identified. Most common are the brown rat, also known as the Norway rat, and various species of the black rat. The black rat, present in Europe as early as the Ice Age, may well have been commensal with humans throughout history.

Although they are unpopular, rats, like cockroaches, are admirably ingenious and perduring survivors — fecund, hardy, and highly adaptable, if not irrepressible. Somewhat uncannily, they are among the most robust survivors in the vicinity of nuclear explosions.[1] Rats have adapted to a number of highly varied habitats, from tropical rain forests to dry bush, from underground burrows to treetops, with many strongly drawn to human habitations. The brown and black rat live in proximity to one another only in human houses; there, the brown rat haunts the damper precincts of the basement, while the black rat typically prefers the attic or the interstitial raceways of walls and ceilings.[2]

The brown rat is sometimes contemptuously known as the "sewer rat," but in its albino form, it is also the classic laboratory rat. Stocky and somewhat sparsely haired, short-tailed and small-eared compared to the black rat,[3] it can survive on the simplest food. Carnivorous by preference, it preys on various invertebrates, small mammals, birds, fish, amphibians, and even reptiles. It will go after young or helpless domestic animals and even human infants, and its bite often carries infection.[4]

Brown rats are great burrowers, and one reason that they are so difficult to keep out of buildings and storage containers is that they can easily gnaw through materials that might well daunt other animals, like wood, plaster, concrete masonry, or even sheet metal. Their sharp incisors grow at the incredible rate of five inches per year, and would be lethal to the animal if they were not ground down by constant gnawing.[5] There is even evidence that they can interpret the sound echoes of their grinding teeth to help them choose paths of least resistance when they are burrowing or gnawing their way into structures.[6] Carnivorous rats also kill with their incisors.

With poor vision,[7] brown rats rely on their highly acute sense of smell to locate prey and mating partners and to distinguish conspecifics from alien species.[8] They can easily be trained to perform any number of tricks or tasks, and they rate highly on intelligence tests that are keyed to their ability to discriminate among smells.[9] Their sense of hearing is also excellent, and they vocalize in ultrasonic frequencies beyond the range of human hearing.[10] Curiosity is the key to rat intelligence. They are naturally inquisitive animals, incessantly exploring their environment.[11]

Largely nocturnal, the black rat, while more or less omnivorous, prefers to eat plant matter, subsisting in the wild on fruit, seeds, and the like. Through its feces and urine, as well as via the fleas with which it is often infested, it has been a carrier of disease for millennia — the classic plague rat of the medieval pandemic. It is responsible for the spoilage of more human goods than any other animal.[12]

Female rats have a brief period of heat (perhaps no more than six hours), during which they will mate multiple times with several males, copulating perhaps as many as five hundred times during a single heat. The male mounts the female and inserts his penis, ejaculates, and immediately leaps backwards, all in less than three seconds. After a gestation period of twenty-two to twenty-four days, rats will give birth to a litter of six to twelve young, all blind, helpless, and hairless.[13] Birth and mortality rates are high, and although it is theoretically possible for a single mated pair to produce eight hundred offspring in a year, in reality it never happens. However, extremely favorable conditions can lead to very large swarms — a form of overpopulation that can spark mass die-offs. A number of animals hunt the brown rat, including the red fox, raptors of one sort or another, and smaller cats, domestic or otherwise.[14] The black rat must fear the mongoose and the ferret, the alligator, the great horned owl, all farm cats, and some breeds of dog.[15]

Social behaviors that have been observed among rats are somewhat contradictory. Cannibalism is fairly frequent, and fights between rivals, especially if they are from different packs, may often be to the death.[16] Yet it is said that injured, blind, or otherwise handicapped rats may be fed and cared for by others all their lives, and there are apparently well-documented cases of rats biting through the tails of brothers to free them from traps.[17] A rat defeated but otherwise totally uninjured in a fight with another may simply crawl off and die. No one really knows why.[18]

Distinctions between mice and rats are drawn casually in the context of myth and folklore, although rats are considered more virulently pestilential, being the larger of the two. In Greek mythology, both were associated with Apollo in his dark aspect, Apollo Smintheus, who was imagined spreading plague with his arrows. In later versions, this same god was depicted as saving humankind from a plague of rats, and rodents were then left at his temple as tribute.[19] In Indian mythology, the rat is associated with the elephant-headed Hindu deity Ganesha, Remover of Obstacles, because it too can overcome many obstacles. Although small and weak, the rat cannot be barred from the granary, gaining access where it will.[20]

Symbolically, a rat can represent problems that gnaw at a person, such as troublesome internal, instinctual, or moral conflicts, rogue energies that are mostly buried deep in the unconscious and rarely seen in conscious light. These unsettling anxieties are detected primarily by their effects, which may include uncontrollable and often undesirable obsessive or compulsive conduct in any sphere of life — eating, sexuality, business, or religion. The image of the rat generally evokes dread and disgust on an inner level because the gnawing, compulsive behavior that it represents degrades the value of conscious life. In psychological terms, the rat destroys and contaminates the good works of the conscious world, creating frustration and a sense of waste or loss.

The rat can represent the destruction of trust, a precious human commodity. In mythology, it is associated with the Devil, as the Great Spoiler; since it lives in the earth, it symbolically shares in the dark, compulsive energies connected with the Terrible Goddess aspect of the Great Goddess. Because of its remarkable instinct for survival and its shrewd adaptability, the rat also has remarkably positive symbolic qualities. Not least of these is the capacity to act in so-called immoral ways when morality is too rigid and life-defeating.[21]

If someone were to dream of a rat, the person would do well to wonder how he or she is being gnawed at on a deep unconscious level. Often the sources of gnawing — worries, doubts, and anxieties — are linked to negative emotions connected to the mother world. Thus, severe, unrecognized fears of abandonment, panic states connected to early traumatic conditions, or a terribly envious environment can contribute to the emergence of the rat in a negative form. The rat is by no means associated only with the maternal world; it is often a symbol of the Devil and can represent frightening and demonic aspects of the male psyche. Anyone dreaming of a rat should look into his or her own nature to discover where a capacity to betray, destroy, or undermine faith resides. Acceptance of such dark sides ultimately strengthens a person, while rejection weakens the individual, making him or her brittle, with an undermined instinctual awareness and a tendency to become obsessive.

In the context of integrating one's "shadow," the word "rat" is often used in a disparaging manner in popular speech. To "smell a rat" denotes that there is danger ahead; "wet as a drowned rat" is often used to describe a person caught in a rain storm; to "rat" on someone is to betray a confidence. And who can forget the James Cagney movies of the 1930s and 1940s where he used the expression "you dirty rat" to represent a traitor?[22]

Notes

[1] Hendrickson 1983, 13.
[2] Grzimek 1984, 11: 356-62.
[3] Ibid.
[4] Pfeffer 1989, 261.
[5] Ritchey 1968, 23-26.
[6] Hendrickson 1983, 14.
[7] Chapman and Feldhammer 1982, 1,078.
[8] Pfeffer 1989, 261.
[9] McFarland 1987, 314.
[10] McFarland 1987, 594.
[11] Hendrickson 1983, 14.
[12] Grzimek 1984, 11: 262.
[13] Barnett 1963, 110; Grzimek 1984, 11: 239.
[14] Pfeffer 1989, 260-61.
[15] Hendrickson 1983, 10-13.
[16] Pfeffer 1989, 261.
[17] Hendrickson 1983, 15.
[18] Attenborough 1990, 210.
[19] Bonnefoy 1992, 139.
[20] Zimmer 1974, 70, 183.
[21] Ritchey 1968, 23-26.
[22] Ammer 1989, 126

RAT
Family: Muridae.
Size: Brown or Norway rat can range in body length from 22-26 centimeters (8.5-10 inches), with a tail length of 18-22 centimeters (7-8.5 inches); black or house rat has a body length from 16-22 centimeters (6.0-8.5 inches) with a tail length of 17-24 centimeters (6.5-9.5 inches).
Weight: Brown or Norway rat weighs 200-400 grams (0.5-1.0 pounds); black or house rat weighs 70-300 grams (0.1-0.5 pounds).
Gestation: 22-24 days.
Longevity: Up to 2 years.
Distribution: Northern and tropical forests, savannas; excluding snow-covered mountain peaks and extreme high Arctic.
Habitat: All terrestrial habitats where food is available.

Rhinoceros

A massive and powerful pachyderm, the rhinoceros looks like a holdover from the age of dinosaurs. Its name, meaning horn nose, refers to the sharp protuberances that jut upward from the snout. African and Sumatran species have two horns in tandem; Indian and Java rhinoceros have a single horn.[1] Rhinoceros, being nearly hairless and endowed with a tough, ample hide that folds into sections, appear to possess plate armor, especially in the Asian varieties.[2]

With poor vision and wide-set eyes, rhinoceros must rely on their excellent hearing and their extraordinary sense of smell. The olfactory apparatus in the rhinoceros's snout is larger in volume than its brain.[3] The horn is composed of densely packed striations of keratin, the stuff of hair as well as horn, and it does at times unravel to look like a growth of hair. It sits on a convex formation of the nasal bone, and if it is torn off by accident, a whole or partial new horn will grow in its place.[4]

Although popularly considered dangerous, the rhinoceros is generally a timid beast, though its size would seem to recommend caution to humans who find themselves near one. It will occasionally rush at an intruder, but the charges are often poorly directed and seem more designed to frighten off trespassers than to engage in battle. The rhinoceros is, however, unpredictable and can be ferocious when injured or trapped. The black rhinoceros is considered the most irritable and aggressive; the white rhinoceros is milder in nature. Fights among males of all species can be quite vicious and bloody.[5]

Rhinoceros sleep both standing up and lying down.[6] Their running gait is a lumbering, modified canter, which enables them to reach a speed of forty-five kilometers (twenty-eight miles) per hour over short distances. Tickbirds and egrets are frequent companions of rhinoceros. While both act as sentinels, tickbirds feed on external parasites on the animal's skin, and egrets on insects that the rhinoceros unearths.[7] All rhinoceros depend on the proximity of water for drinking and wallowing, although they are capable of going four or five days without a drink. Wallowing provides a coating of mud that protects them from biting flies, since their hides, although thick, are sensitive and well supplied with blood vessels just under the outer surface.[8] Young rhinoceros sometimes fall prey to large cats; adults are respectful of elephants but have no enemies other than humans.[9]

All rhinoceros are herbivores. The twin-horned black rhinoceros of Africa has a prehensile upper lip that allows it to browse on twigs, leaves, and shoots; the square-lipped rhinoceros — also a creature of Africa, but more partial to the open savannas — is adapted to a grazing diet consisting primarily of grasses. Heavy brush does not discourage these huge creatures, which weigh nearly four tons and can penetrate the densest thickets by sheer force.[10]

Not much is known about their mating habits in the wild, but Indian rhinoceros have been well observed in zoos. Females come into heat every forty-six to forty-eight days; copulation may go on for an hour, and in that time, the bull may ejaculate anywhere from twenty to fifty times.[11] Most likely, this impressive sexual stamina and capacity, combined with the sheer power of the beast and the obviously phallic shape of the horn, has lead to the belief (still widespread in Asia) that powdered rhinoceros horn is an aphrodisiac. In Africa and China, the horn is also thought to be alexipharmic (an antidote to poisons of all sorts).[12] As a result, for the sake of sexually insecure or anxious humans, these magnificent creatures have been hunted to the point of extinction — often slaughtered and left to rot merely for their horns.

The size and strength of the rhinoceros made it a natural symbol of grandeur and sovereignty in the East as elsewhere, and Asian potentates kept rhinoceros as a kind of living emblem. Buddhists have used the animal to depict the retirement and chastity of the Enlightened One.[13] Romans used them in gladiatorial contests, just for the spectacle of it. The mythos surrounding the one-horned rhinoceros, sometimes called a monoceros, was in the past often confused with myths about the fabulous unicorn.[14] Although the Romans were convinced that the two were not the same, Arab writers frequently described one in terms of the other. The distinction was entirely lost on early Christian writers, who compared Christ with the rhinoceros because they believed that it, like the unicorn, put aside a powerful wrath for gentleness in the hands of a pure virgin.[15]

The outstanding feature of the rhinoceros is clearly its might, although its reputation for being thick-skinned, short-sighted, and ill-tempered contributes to its metaphoric significance. Guided more by smell than sight, a throwback to earlier, more primitive life forms, it is symbolic of powerful, instinctive drives. Any animal so large and strong has its own majesty and will be viewed by humans with awe. Psychologically, the rhinoceros represents a vital life force that often manifests in potent, atavistic forces such as overwhelming sexual and aggressive drives. In the form of a rhinoceros, these drives take on an unpredictable, unstoppable, and extremely dangerous quality. However, the mythology of the rhinoceros suggests that this immense power, with all its potential for ruthless expression, can be tamed by love and concern.

To dream of a rhinoceros would prompt an awareness of these qualities, which can represent a most powerful force — a "god" in a potentially destructive form. But, as Jung once noted, when god appears in the human psyche, the first manifestation one feels is often great discomfort and chaos. Whoever dreams of a rhinoceros, after noting how this image may describe his or her dangerous, single-minded power drive, would do well to ponder the need for deep spiritual renewal.

Notes
[1] Macdonald 1987, 490.
[2] Grzimek 1984, 13: 36.
[3] Macdonald 1987, 490.
[4] Grzimek 1984, 13: 36-41.
[5] Macdonald 1987, 494.
[6] Ibid.
[7] Nowak 1991, 1167.
[8] Macdonald 1987, 492.
[9] Nowak 1991, 1,167.
[10] Macdonald 1987, 490-97.
[11] Grzimek 1984, 13: 46.
[12] Jung 1977, 12: 549.
[13] Cooper 1992, 193-94.
[14] Cooper 1992, 194.
[15] Jung 1977, 11: 408

RHINOCEROS
Family: Rhinocerotidae.
Size: In most species, head–rump length is approximately 200–400 centimeters (75–160 inches); tail length is 60–76 centimeters (20–30 inches); and shoulder height is 100–200 centimeters (40–80 inches).
Weight: 1,000–3,600 kilograms (2,210–7,945 pounds).
Gestation: 15–16 months for most species.
Longevity: 40–45 years for most species.
Distribution: Africa and tropical Asia.
Habitat: Rhinoceros generally live in savannas, shrubby regions, and dense forests in tropical and subtropical regions. The African species usually live in more open areas than do the Asiatic forms.

Rooster/Cock

The rooster is the adult male domestic fowl (such as the chicken), whereas the cock is the adult male wild fowl (such as the pheasant), although in the vernacular the terms are often used interchangeably. The rooster has many of the same characteristics as the chicken. It is distinguished, however, by its bright red comb, gaudy feathers, and of course its crowing at the break of day. Since antiquity the cock has been known nearly universally as an animal of the sun, a symbol of watchfulness, a source of magic,[1] and a paragon of masculine sexual energy.[2] For those steeped in a magical or mythical consciousness, his call dispels the demons of night and his comb is a talisman against nightmares.[3]

In India,[4] as in Celtic, Scandinavian, Greek, and Egyptian traditions, roosters were thought to have miraculous powers over darkness and evil. The rooster is associated with, and often sacrificed to, solar chthonic deities for either appeasement or gain of power.[5] The Chinese word for cock is said to be a homophone of the word "fortunate," and the rooster embodies the yang (male) principles of courage and fidelity, but also aggression and war.[6] In Japanese tradition, the cock calls the sun goddess to rise each morning, and in Hindu legend, a rooster king in the land of Jambudvipa alerts all the cocks in the world to greet the day with their crowing.[7] The solar quality of the cock is also seen in Norse mythology; the cock "Goldcomb" guards Bifrost, the rainbow bridge leading to Asgard, the dwelling place of the gods. Vithafnir, the golden cock, guards against evil at the top of the world tree Yggdrasil; a red cock, Fralar, will rouse the dead heroes of Valhalla for the final battle.[8]

The Romans associated the pugnacious cock with Mars and used it in their auguries. The cock was sacred to Mercury, and its comb was offered to the Lares, household deities originally connected with agriculture.[9] The Greeks (and others) saw in the cock a psychopomp, a guide of souls.[10] To medieval Christians, the cock's connection to the returning dawn made it a symbol of Christ's res-urrection, even as its randiness made it a symbol of lechery. The spires of Christian churches are often surmounted by the figure of a cock, the first part of the church to be touched anew by day's light.[11]

In antiquity the rooster's sexual aggressiveness made him a powerful fertility symbol.[12] As part of the enduring ancient belief in reciprocity — one receives what one gives and gives what one receives — the rooster was often sacrificed as part of harvest rituals. In Europe, even today freshly cut fields are symboli-cally fertilized with the blood of a cock, often one that has been buried up to its neck in the earth, so that the head can be lopped off with a stroke of the scythe.[13] The blood of the rooster also figures significantly in African fetishism; transported to the western hemisphere, it influenced the development of the cults of Voodoo in Haiti and Santeria in Cuba, both of which also make ample ritual use of the cock and his blood.[14] The cock's famous aggressiveness (and the human fascination with it) is nowhere more evident than in the ancient and extraordinarily widespread blood-sport of cockfighting, which was common-place in ancient Persia, Greece, Rome, and other cultures; although often officially suppressed, it is still widespread throughout Latin America and parts of Asia.[15]

The rooster has quite a wide symbolic range. On the one hand, its connec-tion to the sun can represent spiritual development and emerging consciousness, as well as the power to dispel ignorance and illusion. On the other hand, its strutting vainglory, aggressiveness, and sexual irrepressibility can represent a total and destructive indulgence in passions. The widespread motif of sacrifice of the rooster has an important correlate in human psychology. The capacity to refrain from acting on passions in destructive ways can often lead to a revitalizing of inner creativity and a fertile sense of growth.

If someone dreams of a rooster, he or she may be too passive, needing to embrace a more active, aggressive attitude. The dream image might call forth the need to address the dreamer's aggressive sexuality in whatever form it has taken — either overwhelmingly promiscuous or very subdued and repressed and needing to be enhanced and energized in a more conscious way. The dream may also point toward the potential for more vigorous pursuit of spiritual growth.

Notes

[1] Biedermann 1994, 288.
[2] Andrews 1993, 127.
[3] Biedermann 1994, 288.
[4] Ibid.
[5] Cooper 1992, 53-54.
[6] Cooper 1992, 54-55.
[7] Biedermann 1994, 288; Becker 1994, 64.
[8] Biedermann 1994, 288; Cooper 1992, 54.

[9] *Funk & Wagnalls Standard Dictionary*, 1972, 239.
[10] Becker 1994, 64.
[11] Biedermann 1994, 288
[12] Biedermann 1994, 64.
[13] Frazer 1979, 522-23.
[14] Cooper 1992, 54-55.
[15] "Cockfighting." *Encarta 97 Encyclopedia*, 1997.

ROOSTER/COCK

Order: *Galliformes*.
Size: Various breeds show great diversity in size and shape.
Weight: The Brahma cock can weigh up to 5 kilograms (12 pounds).
Incubation: See chicken.
Longevity: 10 years.
Distribution: Worldwide.
Habitat: Terrestrial.

Salamander

Its name (ultimately from the Greek) means "fire-lizard,"[1] but while it is shaped like a diminutive lizard, the salamander is an amphibian, not a reptile, having more in common with frogs than geckos. The term "salamander" is loosely applied to all tailed amphibians, which are classified as urodeles. They are also known, often imprecisely, by dozens of other names, including newts, efts, mudpuppies, and tritons. Most are denizens of the temperate regions.[2]

In the early part of the eighteenth century, a sevety-million-year-old skeleton was discovered in Germany: the fossil remains of a giant salamander, a strictly aquatic animal that is still extant today in China and Japan.[3] Ectothermic (cold-blooded) salamanders[4] represent an intermediate or transitional evolutionary stage from water animals to land animals; the 450 or more species from eight different families undergo varying degrees of metamorphosis — some remaining more or less aquatic, others becoming more or less terrestrial in habit. Some retain their gills, others develop lungs, and still others respire primarily through their skins.[5] Most are oviparous, the female laying up to six hundred or more eggs, and, although mating habits vary considerably, in several species the male guards and protects the fertilized egg sacks.[6] As with some lizards, certain salamanders have "break-away" tails, which detach and allow the salamander to escape when they are molested by predators.

Salamanders feed on small invertebrates: insects, slugs, snails, and worms. They rely on their acute vision to find prey and are better at detecting motion than at discerning or interpreting visual details or shapes. Certain species, like some frogs, can flick their long tongues to capture small prey at surprising distances. Like many fish, salamanders have a row of sensory receptors along the sides of their bodies, called lateral-line organs, which aid in the detection of water motion and locating prey.[7]

Salamanders evince remarkable powers of orientation. Even when blind and deprived of the sense of smell, they are able to find their way to water. A part of the brain called the pineal body, just beneath the bones of the skull, has been shown to be sensitive to light, particularly polarized light; at least some salamanders seem able to navigate by detecting variations in the earth's gravity.[8] A few salamanders also have parotid glands at the back of their heads which produce unpalatable secretions. When attacked, these salamanders will bow their heads, to present the most distasteful part of their bodies. Others rear up and actually lunge at attackers with the glands presented foremost, an effective way of repulsing shrews.[9]

An assumption often found in early literature is that salamanders crawl out of logs thrown onto a fire; this fostered the impression that this rather simple amphibian could survive and indeed thrive in the fiery flames.[10] Aristotle repeated the story that the salamander not only walks through fire but, in so doing, puts it out. The Roman author Pliny endorsed this opinion, adding that it is the most venomous creature in the world and that it "seeks the hottest fire to breed in, but quenches it with the extreme frigidity of its body." The *Physiologus* concurred, although later bestiaries refined the concept, claiming that the salamander lives on continually in the fire and yet is not consumed by it.[11]

The belief that the salamander survives in fire has a number of consequences in terms of its symbolic significance. Primarily, the salamander represents the capacity to withstand the heat of intense emotions, thereby symbolizing the highest level of human development, what the alchemists call their stone or *lapis*[12] and psychologists call the self. Furthermore, since fire is often considered symbolic of consuming emotions, including sexuality and eroticism,[13] the salamander can also represent the transformation of such affects. Fire destroys and cleanses as well as transforms; thus, the salamander is symbolically connected with all three of those processes.

The salamander is thought to be emblematic of chastity and virginity because it survives the flames of passion. In Christianity, these ideas find a symbolic focus in Christ and his mother, who are said to pass through the crucible of mortal life without stain.[14] The salamander's survival in flames is often likened to a baptism of fire;[15] psychologically speaking this is a capacity to hold to one's beliefs and deep orienting center amidst powerful emotional experiences and trials.

Consequently, if someone were to dream of a salamander, it could represent that individual's capacity to deal with intense emotional experiences in ways perhaps far beyond his or her conscious understanding. At the same time, it could represent a personal initiation into the transformative mysteries of passion, as opposed to only its pleasure-giving aspects, excitation acted on with little gain.

Notes

[1] Halliday 1988, 18.
[2] Grzimek 1984, 5: 309.
[3] Grzimek 1984, 5: 283.

[4] Ibid.
[5] "Salamander." *Encarta 97 Encyclopedia*, 1997.
[6] Grzimek 1984, 5: 315.
[7] Halliday 1988, 19, 25.
[8] Halliday 1988, 25.
[9] Halliday 1988, 34.
[10] Halliday 1988, 18.
[11] Curley 1979, 61
[12] Jung 1976, 13: 177.
[13] Fabricius 1989, 76-77.
[14] Charbonneau-Lassay 1991, 177-78.
[15] Jobes 1962, 2: 1390.

SALAMANDER

Family: Salamandridae (includes an assemblage of nine genera that covers many of the newts).

Size: Range from less than 5 centimeters (2 inches) to the Asiatic Giant salamanders which can reach lengths of over 1.5 meters (5 feet).

Weight: Giant salamanders can weigh up to 10.5-63 kilograms (23-140 pounds).

Incubation: The development period of the eggs of the Giant salamander varies. In the wild it can last from 3-8 weeks; development is accelerated by higher temperatures and prolonged by lower temperatures.

Longevity: In captivity, the fire or European salamander can live 20-25 years, and occasionally more than 50 years; very little is known about longevity in nature, but some species do not breed until they are several years old.

Distribution: Temperate regions of northwest Africa, Europe, Asia, and North America.

Habitat: There are aquatic and terrestrial forms, but most are found in or near water, at least in the breeding season.

Salmon

Fat, pink, and tasty, Atlantic and Pacific salmon are staples of the human diet in many cultures, including our own. Born in the shallow estuaries and tributaries of large river systems, the salmon migrate to the sea; the fierce determination of their almost uncanny struggles back again to spawn and die in the places of their birth has deep resonance for the human spirit.

Salmon hatchlings may take anywhere from one to seven years to achieve a length of ten centimeters (four inches). When they do, the salmon begin to migrate slowly downstream, allowing themselves to be taken along with the flow of the river by night, pausing when it is light to feed.[1] When they finally reach the sea, salmon hunt actively by day, using their sharp eyesight to seek out schools of smaller fish. At night, they browse more sluggishly on plankton; carotenoid pigments of tiny planktonic crustaceans give the salmon their pink color.[2]

After several years of ocean dwelling, they reach full size, their bodies take on a significant amount of fat,[3] and they begin to seek out the rivers from which they came. The arduous journey upstream often involves spectacular five-meter (sixteen-foot) leaps up waterfalls and other barriers to reach the very particular stretch of stream or brook where they were hatched. The success of this journey depends on the salmon's extraordinarily well-developed sense of taste, because every stretch of river has a unique mineral and biological flavor.[4] Those that make it lose most of their pink color and up to forty percent of their body weight in the process.[5] They stop feeding shortly after entering fresh water, in most cases retaining just enough energy to beget the next generation.

The female prepares a nest by digging out a depression ten to twenty centimeters (four to eight inches) deep and approximately a meter (three feet) long, while males look on idly, but not without interest. When this work is complete, interested males perform their competitive courtship displays; finally the female will accept one or frequently a series of several males to hover with her for the release of up to thirty thousand eggs and an equivalent amount of sperm into the water just over the spawning pit. In the aftermath, she will carefully cover the spawning pit and may even repeat the whole process slightly farther upstream.[6] After mating, some salmon winter over in their freshwater homes, a very few manage to return to the sea, but most die shortly after spawning — none has been known to make it upstream more than once.[7]

Salmon have many enemies. Eels feed on the roe, and hatchlings are prey to diving birds, perch, pike, and trout. Cormorants, seals, dolphins, sharks, and other large fish, as well as commercial fishermen, prey on adult salmon in the sea. During their perilous journey upstream they fall victim to otters, bears, eagles, and sport fishermen.[8] The damming of rivers in many areas has caused a precipitous decline in the number of salmon able to spawn successfully.

As the buffalo was for Native Americans of the Plains, the salmon remains for the native people of the Pacific Northwest: a vast and dependable source of nourishment that is both physical and spiritual in nature. With its silvery skin and nocturnal habits the sacred salmon reminded ancient people of the moon, and, like the waxing and waning moon, its cyclical journey is sometimes seen as a representation of death and rebirth.[9] Such symbolism is extremely widespread. In Celtic mythology the salmon is a metaphor of wisdom and prescience; Celtic heroes regarded it as an oracle, from which they hoped to receive wisdom from Beyond.[10]

In many cultures the salmon represents deep intuition, a capacity for wisdom and superhuman effort. Since the salmon overcomes incredible hurdles on its way to mating, symbolically it has an erotic feature, characterizing the capacity to overcome obstacles to love.[11] In human beings, these obstacles can manifest as withdrawal, criticism, depression, denial, or inertia, all of which come into any love relationship and tend to degrade positive, heartfelt feelings. The salmon's journey represents the individual's drive toward development, moving against the current of passivity, aligning itself with Eros, and taking the difficult path that leads to higher consciousness rather than to laziness and inactivity.

Therefore, if a person were to dream of a salmon, he or she would become more conscious of the need for a more heroic effort in overcoming inertia in life's tasks. The dreamer may also need to become more aware of responsibilities that are not being performed, especially if he or she is besieged by withdrawal and all manners of apathy as defenses against love.

Notes
[1] Attenborough 1990, 122-23.
[2] Pfeffer 1989, 32.
[3] Grzimek 1984, 4: 215.
[4] Attenborough 1990, 123.
[5] Grzimek 1984, 4: 216.
[6] Ibid.

[7] Pfeffer 1989, 32.
[8] Pfeffer 1989, 32-33.
[9] Cooper 1992, 197.
[10] von Franz 1974, 212-13.
[11] Ibid.

SALMON
Family: Salmonidae.
Size: Maximum length to 1.5 meters (5 feet).
Weight: Atlantic salmon weighs up to 32 kilograms (70 pounds); Pacific salmon weighs up to 45 kilograms (100 pounds).
Incubation: 70-200 days.
Longevity: 6-8 years.
Distribution: Northern temperate and subarctic fresh waters.
Habitat: Oceans and rivers.

Scorpion

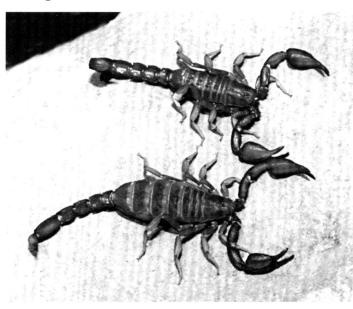

Looking for all the world like miniature, land-locked lobsters, but possessing a lethal sting in their tails, scorpions are the most ancient terrestrial invertebrates, going back four hundred million years to the Silurian epoch. They share the class Arachnida with spiders and mites. Widely distributed in tropical and warm temperate zones, nearly six hundred species[1] are found in habitats ranging from intertidal zones to deep, lightless caverns, from deserts to mountains.[2] Hardy and adaptable, scorpions can survive extremes of temperature that would kill most animals, and some can even survive under water for up to forty-eight hours.[3]

Scorpions generally have flattened body shapes, allowing them to occupy all manner of natural cracks and crevices as well as burrows they may create on their own.[4] Their so-called tails are actually segmented extensions of their abdomens, at the end of which is the telson or stinger,[5] brought into play by whipping it forward over the head. Scorpions have a tough exoskeleton made of a horny white or colorless substance called chitin. It reflects ultraviolet rays with such efficiency that scorpions in a moonlit desert landscape seem to glow in the dark.[6] They are extraordinarily sensitive to light, and are thought to be able to navigate at night by the faint contrasts of starlight and shadows.[7] Their eyes do not resolve images well, and in spite of a variable number of extra eyes along the sides of their bodies,[8] they rely heavily on tactile and chemical sense organs.[9] For example, minute hairs on their pincers are amazingly sensitive to wind direction, providing the scorpion with another means of orientation and navigation.[10]

All scorpions are carnivorous. Extremely effective metabolic processes allow them to hunt and feed infrequently; some are said to be able to live without food for as much as a year. When they do feed, they pre-digest their food externally, dissolving the flesh of their victims with enzymes that they spit up, then sucking up the resulting liquid.[11] Although scorpion stings can be extremely painful, they are only infrequently fatal. Painful swelling and even fever readily pass, except in certain rare instances. For example, the poison from the Sahara scorpion is equal to that of the cobra and can kill a dog in thirty seconds.[12] Scorpion venom is generally comprised of thirty neurotoxins, and remarkably, each of these is designed to fell a different type of prey.[13]

Mating rituals can appear quite violent. Males and females lock pincers and sometimes mouthparts, staggering back and forth in what looks like a cross between a tango and a Sumo wrestling match. The male may sting the female several times in the process, but the female may get even by killing and eating her partner when copulation is done. That may seem extreme, but some scorpions have few scruples about cannibalism, deriving up to twenty-five percent of their nourishment from dining on mates, offspring, and other conspecifics.[14] Scorpions bear their young alive after an extraordinarily long gestation period, often up to eighteen months; despite occasional cannibalistic lapses, the females are attentive and caring mothers, carrying their young on their backs.[15] In theory, they can live for long as twenty years, or even more, but in reality, they suffer heavy predation by owls, snakes, bats, and other animals despite their formidable defenses.[16]

Because of their sometimes lethal sting, scorpions are connected almost everywhere with evil and death. For the ancient Chinese and the Persians,[17] scorpions were the minions of the evil spirit Ahriman. Christians saw in scorpions a symbol of the awful dangers of heresy.[18] Ancient Egyptians associated them particularly with the devil Set, who took the form of a scorpion in order to kill the child Horus. Thoth ultimately cured Horus at the request of Isis, who could herself take the form of a scorpion. The terrible aspect of the great goddess in many cultures has the scorpion for its emblem or symbol.[19]

The scorpion is the eighth sign of the zodiac, connected in astrology and alchemy with the concept of death and resurrection because for many centuries people supposed that when cornered it committed suicide. From this premise, it was surmised that the scorpion must have discovered the secret of ending and renewing its life.[20] As a result, the scorpion has become a symbol of the mysteries of death and rebirth.

On a psychological level, the scorpion represents symbolic death and psychic transformation, so that its appearance in a dream often evokes terror. It is thus useful to recognize its very widespread symbolism and to be aware that it betokens imminent change of existing values, attitudes, beliefs, and behaviors. However, its sting can be a reminder that this kind of change and emotional growth is never accomplished without some pain. The dreamer's consciousness of pain that he or she has inflicted on others and suffered at the hands of others can open his or her awareness to the greater mystery of the scorpion image.

Notes

[1] Grzimek 1984, 1: 413.
[2] "Arachnids, Ecology and Habitats." *Encyclopedia Britannica*, 1997.
[3] "Arachnids, Ecology and Habitats." *Encyclopaedia Britannica*, 1997.
[4] Grzimek 1984, 1: 412.
[5] Angier 1995, 100.
[6] Angier 1995, 99.
[7] "Arachnids, Ecology and Habitats." *Encyclopedia Britannica*, 1997.
[8] Grzimek 1984, 1: 411-12.
[9] "Arachnids, Ecology and Habitats." *Encyclopaedia Britannica*, 1997.
[10] Downer 1989, 20.
[11] Angier 1995, 100.
[12] Grzimek 1994, 1: 412.
[13] Angier 1995, 97-100.
[14] Angier 1995, 98-99.
[15] Grzimek 1984, 1: 412.
[16] Angier 1995, 100.
[17] Angier 1995, 97.
[18] Charbonneau-Lassay 1991, 343.
[19] Cooper 1992, 199.
[20] von Franz 1977, 86-87; Jung 1976, 14: 58, 134 note.

SCORPION
Order: Scorpiones (with a variety of families such as Buthidae,
Scorpionidae, Chactodae, and Vejovidae).
Size: 13–175 millimeters (0.5 to 7 inches).
Weight: Adult scorpions commonly weigh from 0.5–5 grams.
Gestation: Up to 1.5 years.
Longevity: 15–20 years.
Distribution: Deserts and other arid regions, moist or mountain habitats.
Habitat: From intertidal zones (shallow water habitats of mixed mud,
rocks, and gravel) to snow-covered mountains.

Seal

This sleek and streamlined sea mammal falls into two superfamilies: eared seals (sea lions and fur seals) and seals (monk seals, crab-eater seals, hooded seals, and earless seals). Most live in the colder waters of the northern and southern hemispheres. Only monk seals are found in tropical waters, although others, like the northern fur seal, may winter in temperate waters before returning poleward.[1]

Phylogenetically speaking, all of these animals have reverted to a watery habitat and have terrestrial ancestors whose four legs evolved into flippers. Like whales and manatees, they are air breathers, but, unlike those mammals, seals are at least partly adapted to life on land (or on the ice), where they mate, give birth, and suckle their young. They are, nonetheless, awkward on land, half hopping, and half dragging themselves about.[2] Sea lions are an exception and are remarkably agile on land given their bulk, but most seals are vulnerable to predators when ashore.[3] Rookeries are therefore generally quite remote.

Seals have large eyes and excellent vision, especially in low light. Their hearing is also sharp; since some species produce a click-like vocalization when under water, it is tempting to think — although not yet scientifically proven — that they use some form of echolocation to detect prey in particularly dark or murky waters. Their highly sensitive whiskers may also detect vibrations in the water such as those produced by swimming fish. Little is known about their sense of smell.[4]

Pregnant females produce a single pup, which they suckle for a number of months then abandon completely.[5] When pups are weaned, lactation ceases, and the mother comes into heat immediately and mates again. Sea eagles and Arctic foxes prey upon newborn pups, while sharks, killer whales, and polar bears prey on adult seals.[6] Millions of seals of all sorts have been hunted by men for their blubber and for the unusually soft, dense pelts of baby seals. If mother and pup are separated, the mother's distinctive and penetrating call is answered by the pup's own distinctive call. This calling is repeated as the two seek each other in the crowded rookery. When they are reunited, the mother will make an olfactory identity check, just to be sure, before accepting the pup as truly her own and letting it suck her extraordinarily rich milk, which is more than ten times richer in fat and four times richer in protein than cow's milk.[7]

Seals play an important role in the mythologies of Northern people. In the Orkney and Shetland Islands, the Selkies (the name is a variant of sealchie, little seal) are spirits that take the appearance of seals but can also assume human form. Spirit lovers, both beautiful and amorous in their human forms, the Selkies were said to dance in the moonlight. It was believed that if a woman wanting to have children cried seven tears into the water, a Selkie lover would come to grant her wish.[8]

In Celtic myth, fallen angels look like humans on land but like seals or mermaids in the sea. In Germanic myth, the trickster god Loki could take the guise of a seal. Seal skins, so soft, warm, and desirable as fur for human garments, were sometimes imagined to have magical qualities. The Roman Emperor Augustus was said to wear one as protection against lightning.[9] And seal fur was poetically thought to ruffle in sympathy with the tide even after it had been stripped from its original owner.[10]

Seals move between sea and land, more at home perhaps in the former than on the latter. They can be thought of as analogous to unconscious thoughts and feelings that surface in the conscious world of light and air.[11] Since they are descended from land animals, evolutionarily re-adapted to the sea, there is a certain regressive quality to their symbolic importance. The seal's connection between land and sea, as well as its playful nature, makes it a symbolic bridge between consciousness and the unconscious. A healthy interactive relationship between conscious thoughts and feelings and their unconscious counterparts is nurtured by lively interplay between them.[12] The symbolic linking function of the seal is plainly evident in Celtic myth, where the seal is associated with angels. Psychologically, angels connect humans and the gods, that is, consciousness and the archetypal layers of existence.

When a seal appears in a dream, and if the dreamer's conscious life is very ordered, even rigid, the seal could represent the compensatory necessity for a more playful attitude. The seal would indicate the need to build up a relationship between the conscious and unconscious through fantasy and play. One need only watch these animals playing in the water to understand the importance of this image. However, one would also want to keep an eye on the possible regressive meaning of the seal, looking for conscious experiences and attitudes that go back into the sea of the unconscious, taking on less consciously adapted forms.

Notes
[1] Burton 1981, 575.
[2] Grzimek 1984, 12: 395.
[3] Macdonald 1987, 247.
[4] Macdonald 1987, 245.
[5] Macdonald 1987, 247.
[6] Pfeffer 1989, 94.
[7] Trillmich 1987, 42-49.
[8] Andrews 1993, 311-12.
[9] de Vries 1976, 407.
[10] Frazer 1979, 40.
[11] Jung 1975, 8: 131-93, 338.
[12] Jung 1975, 8: 131-93, especially 145.

SEAL
Family: Phocidae.
Size: Head–tail length is from 117 centimeters (50 inches) for the ringed seal to 490 centimeters (193 inches) for the male southern elephant seal.
Weight: From 45 kilograms (100 pounds) for the ringed seal to 2,400 kilograms (5,300 pounds) for the male southern elephant seal.
Gestation: 10-11 months, including 2.5-3.5 months of suspended development (delayed implantation).
Longevity: Up to 56 years.
Distribution: Generally in polar, subpolar, and temperate seas, except for the monk seals of the Mediterranean, Caribbean, and Hawaiian regions.
Habitat: Pack ice, subarctic and arctic waters; offshore rocks and islands.

Shark

Sleek and powerful, streamlined and armed with a mouthful of razor-sharp teeth, sharks are forever marked in the popular imagination as bloodthirsty butchers of the sea. Just a glimpse of a telltale dorsal fin slicing ominously through the water is enough to make the blood of even the most experienced swimmer run cold. Sharks represent an extraordinarily large class of cartilaginous fish, ranging from small and harmless nurse sharks, which feed on plankton,[1] to the huge "man-eating" great white sharks, well known to summer readers and moviegoers. In general, their voracious and bloody reputation is well earned; sharks are top-of-the-food-chain carnivores and very efficient hunters. But they are not vicious, just meat eaters never free of the need to be on the lookout for sustenance. Sharks are very primitive animals, directly descended from ancestors that lived 100 million years ago, and the fossil record shows that creatures not unlike them swam in Paleozoic seas as much as 450 million years ago.[2]

The skeleton of a shark is composed of cartilage, not bone. Its skin is sandpaper rough because it is covered with bony structures called placoid scales, in effect tiny teeth, literally composed of dentine and dental enamel. Their real teeth, which are far from tiny, remain razor sharp in part because they are constantly replaced from a second rank of immature teeth.[3] The jaws of some sharks can exert a closing pressure of 3,000 kilograms per square centimeter (44,000 pounds per square inch). By contrast, humans can exert a closing pressure of only 10 kilograms per square centimeter (150 pounds per square inch).[4]

Sharks have highly sensitive acoustical sensors on the tops of their heads as well as along the lateral line, used for close-up navigational guidance.[5] They are sensitive not only to what we normally call sounds but also to extremely low-frequency vibrations, especially of the sort that might be made by injured or struggling prey animals.[6] Chemical receptors in the mouth and nasal passages and on skin surfaces on and around the snout are exquisitely sensitive to very tiny concentrations of blood, and they may aid the shark in testing the degree of salinity of the water.[7] Also on the snout are organs attuned to electrical current. The functions of these are poorly understood, but they may aid in tracking prey and maintaining balance, and perhaps even in long-range navigation.[8] The shark's eyesight is excellent, and its intelligence is estimated to be quite high.[9] Lacking the swim bladder that keeps other kinds of fish afloat, sharks must constantly move to keep from sinking, as well as to keep a steady flow of water over their gills for respiration.[10] They do not sleep.[11]

Although they are top predators, sharks are hunted by humans for sport, for food, and for the oil in their livers, which is rich in Vitamin D and used for a number of medicinal purposes. Researchers are particularly interested in discovering why sharks seemingly are not vulnerable to cancer.[12] The skin of some sharks is used for bookbinding.[13] A number of sharks, mostly the deep sea-dwelling species, are viviparous, which gives rise to the bizarre phenomenon of *in vivo* cannibalism — unborn sharks seize and eat their siblings inside the mother's body. Not surprisingly, this practice makes for small litters, often just two. In contrast, egg-laying sharks may bear up to eighty offspring at a time.[14]

The infamous great white shark of the film *Jaws* ranges all tropical and subtropical waters, has a length of five to six meters (sixteen to twenty feet) or more, and can weigh up to three tons. It feeds on fish of all kinds as well as dolphins, seals, marine tortoises, and rarely, but notoriously, human swimmers.[15] When normally solitary sharks[16] are attracted by substantial amounts of blood in the water feeding frenzies may occur, involving a level of violence exceeded perhaps only in human warfare.

Obviously an animal as powerful as a shark is likely to appear in many mythologies. In Japanese mythology, the shark is associated with kami, divine spirits, demigods, and other forces of nature, both good and evil.[17] In Polynesia, it was thought that a shark could be used as a sorcerer's familiar or an incarnation of an important person or power — a chief, an ancestral spirit, or even a god. It was called the "Long-blue-cloud-eater" and associated with the Milky Way. Some West African cults hold the shark to be sacred, and if one is accidentally killed, certain rites of atonement need to be performed. A superstition among sailors is that a shark following a ship foretells a death.[18]

When we call someone a shark — a pool shark or a card shark — we generally mean that they are very good at what they do, and that they do it in an unsentimental, predatory way. Indeed, the shark is a paradigm of voracity, and all kinds of sadistic and morbid fantasies and fixations are projected onto it. Symbolically, it represents a deeply aggressive, dark side of the human personality, the opposite of anything warm-blooded, erotic, or empathic. The very cold-blooded ruthlessness that gives the shark its ecologically balancing function — weeding out the sick and the weak[19] — can also give the psychological shark in us a positive function, continually alerting us to what really matters and mobilizing our strength in that pursuit. The "shark in us" can represent a capacity to be assertive and, if need be, destructive to an overly adverse situation. A person's behavior can be dominated and even possessed by a shark-like quality. In this instance, the shark would represent a very dangerous, devastating quality. Often this negative quality functions in a deep, unseen way, just as the shark does in the waters of the ocean. This unseen destructive element might manifest in seemingly innocuous slips of the tongue or in "accidents" that undermine rather than help another person. All of this imagery can be passed off as meaningless, but deeper investigation reveals it to be the remnants of a destructive power that has not been turned to good or constructive use in the human personality.

If a person dreamed of a shark, he or she might need to have a more shark-like, ruthless attitude in a situation where he or she may be blinded by unconsciousness and sentimentality. Alternatively, the dreamer may need to see that the shark-aspect of his or her being is a governing factor in life, in an unfeeling, callous, and sadistic way that has to be acknowledged. Respect and awe for the power of the shark and its dominance in the unconscious would be a suitable response to the image.

Notes

[1] Grzimek 1984, 4: 89.
[2] Coupe 1990, 11.
[3] Grzimek 1984, 4: 86.
[4] Banister and Campbell 1988, 128.
[5] Stevens 1992, C1.
[6] Coupe 1990, 36-37.
[7] Stevens 1992, C1.
[8] Coupe 1990, 36-37.
[9] Cousteau and Richards 1992, 25.
[10] Grzimek 1984, 4: 87.
[11] Sattler 1986, 11.
[12] Sattler 1986, 28.
[13] Grzimek 1984, 4: 89.
[14] Grzimek 1984, 4: 88.
[15] Grzimek 1984, 4: 95.
[16] Cousteau and Richards 1992, 16.
[17] Jobes 1962, 2: 1431.
[18] Cooper 1992, 209.
[19] Cousteau and Richards 1992, 169.

SHARK
Order: Selachii (with 21 families).
Size: Great whites 3.7-4.9 meters long (12-16 feet).
Weight: Up to 3200 kilograms (7000 pounds).
Gestation: The embryo of an oviparous species develops for 4.5 to 15 months before hatching.
Longevity: 20-30 years, it is estimated that some species may live 100-150 years.
Distribution: Temperate coastlines worldwide.
Habitat: Open sea, coastal and inshore water, rivers and connecting lakes, depending on type.

Sheep/Lamb

When we think of sheep, we tend to think of the exceedingly docile, woolly-haired ruminants — fluffy, meek, and mild — that people have been raising for milk, meat, and wool for millennia. These are, however, merely the carefully bred descendants of wild sheep, which have the widest distribution among horned ungulates. Worldwide, there are thirty-seven different varieties comprising two species: wild sheep and bighorn sheep.[1] Male sheep are called rams, females are called ewes, and immature animals up to a year old are classified as lambs.[2]

The mouflon, a European subspecies and the smallest of the wild sheep, is a handsome animal; males with substantial horns are much sought after by hunters looking for trophies. Sheep rely heavily on their vision, which is acute and enhanced by their excellent powers of recognition. Like all ruminants, they also possess a strong sense of smell. Hearing, although presumably adequate, does not play a significant role in their lives.[3] Mouflons reach sexual maturity after eighteen months, although males may not actually copulate for two more years, since competition from older, more dominant males severely limits their opportunity and inhibits their initiative. Fights between the males over breeding rights are settled with loud, forceful head butting, which rarely leads to serious injuries.[4]

North American bighorn sheep live above the timberline and, like mountain goats, are remarkably agile creatures, jumping from ledge to perilous ledge with seeming abandon. Apparently, they need only a two-inch space to get a foothold. The joints of these sheep are specially adapted to help absorb the shocks that result from climbing onto and leaping from their rocky perches. Their hooves are covered with an elastic material that softens impact and gives them a better grip. Sheep are generally herbivores, regurgitating their food and chewing cud, thus enabling their four-sectioned stomachs to properly digest grasses and herbs (particularly the flowers of the latter). In spring and summer, they build up extra layers of fat and a thick, heavy coat, which help them get through the cold winter months.[5]

Among wild sheep, the strong, ample horns of the male curve backward in grand, broad spirals. Females may have short, scimitar-shaped horns or none.[6] Ridges or rings on the horn mark the age of the ram.[7] Wild sheep have hierarchic ranking, for which horn size among rams is significant. Lower-ranking rams, as well as those defeated in battle, behave like females and are treated as such by dominant males, which will mount and even ejaculate on them. In this way, young or weak males are tolerated within the herd, whereas they might otherwise have been run off.[8] Ewes and their lambs must bond within the first six hours of the lamb's birth; lambs taken from their mothers during that time will be abandoned or ignored however, the mother can be manually stimulated to produce a hormone (oxytocin) that apparently causes her to accept a previously rejected lamb.[9]

The domestication of sheep probably began in southwestern Asia as much as nine thousand years ago.[10] Among other qualities, they have been bred for docility, building on their natural flocking instinct, which makes them extremely manageable. Husbandry has resulted in a bewildering variety of breeds, which nevertheless fall into just two categories: woolly sheep, which are kept for meat, milk, and wool; and hairy sheep, which have coarse, bristly hair and are kept only for milk and meat.[11] There are now approximately a billion sheep in the world, mostly in countries with large areas of grassland: Australia, New Zealand, China, India, the United States, South Africa, Argentina, and Turkey. As grazing animals, sheep keep trees and brush from encroaching on grasslands; in areas of the world like Scotland and Ireland, where grazing has been intensive for many centuries, sheep have been responsible for major changes in the physical landscape.[12]

Since sheep must be watched over by a shepherd, it came to symbolize help-lessness and vulnerability to predators.[13] As a result, the sheep became a symbol of human vulnerability, especially with regard to a benevolent and protective god who would look after humankind as shepherds tend their flocks.[14] Because of its guileless simplicity, mildness, and white color, the sheep generally symbol-izes gentleness, innocence, and purity, although symbolically, its meekness and natural impulse to follow the flock also make it a perfect model of an individual given over to the collective will.[15] Colloquially, an outcast or renegade is referred to as "a black sheep"; a "lost sheep" is someone very much out of his or her element; and a "sheepish" person is awkward or embarrassed. Sheep are often contrasted with goats, similar animals whose unruliness has historically caused them to be seen as symbols of evil.

In antiquity, the lamb was the animal most commonly sacrificed; combined with its association with purity, this made it an appropriate symbol for Christ, especially in connection with his sacrificial death.[16] St. John the Baptist refers to Jesus as *agnus Dei,* "the Lamb of God, which taketh away the sin of the world."[17] The lamb was already a Messianic symbol at the time of the original Passover, when its sacrifice betokened submission to God's will. The outer sign of that sacrifice caused the Angel of Death to absolve the Hebrew people from harm as it slew Egypt's first-born male children.[18]

It is the nature of social pressure to ostracize the pariahs, the independent thinkers, the misunderstood ones, the "black sheep," so that the individual feels a compulsion to rejoin the collective. Psychologically, according to Jung, the sacrifice of sheep often represents giving up the comfort and anonymity of following the crowd, doing what others do, or caving in to social pressure. In exchange for this security, the person gains the expanded consciousness of individual growth and development.[19] People must weigh for themselves the advantages of each path.

For many animals, as well as for humans, submission can sometimes power-fully inhibit aggression, and this would appear to be nature's way of avoiding unnecessary carnage. Sometimes, submission can be a fatal mistake, for it can play into the hands of a murderous, if not mad, adversary. Then again, psycho-logically, submission is often the only way to manage or assuage one's own consuming madness or passion. The sheep (lamb) typifies that spirit of surren-der in which one recognizes an overwhelming inner power, and one's smallness in the face of that power. The sacrifice of the innocent lamb also corresponds to giving up identification with childish outlooks or attitudes to become a true adult. If the psychological "sacrifice of the lamb" is refused, as in the sacrifice of identification with naive illusions and viewpoints, the lamb can represent venge-ful or destructive impulses. We find such powerful drives in young rejected parts of the psyche. The wrath of the lamb is depicted in the *Jerusalem Bible* (Revelation 6: 16) and is referred to as "the Great Day of His Anger Coming."

Thus, dreams of a sheep could represent the possibility that the individual is too engaged in a herd-like attitude, mindlessly following some collective idea, or too identified with naïve purity or some illusory idealizations that exclude reality and the darker side of human nature. Then again, for a person who is extremely aggressive in life and individual to an idiosyncratic degree, a sheep could represent the need to become more part of the "herd," to join with others. The lamb and its close connection with sacrifice would also prompt a person to consider whether he or she needs to sacrifice some naïve or childish attitude, and face the consequences of that sacrifice.

Notes
1 Grzimek 1984, 13: 496.
2 "Sheep." *Encyclopedia Britannica*, 1997.
3 Grzimek 1984, 13: 500.
4 Grzimek 1984, 13: 500-501.
5 Andrews 1993, 307-08; "Sheep." *Encyclopedia Britannica*, 1997.
6 Grzimek 1984, 13: 496.
7 Andrews 1993, 308.
8 Grzimek 1984, 13: 514.
9 Angier 1995, 14.
10 Nowak 1991, 1408.
11 "Sheep." *Encyclopedia Britannica*, 1997.
12 Ibid.
13 Biedermann 1994, 304.
14 Cooper 1992, 210.
15 *The Herder Symbol Dictionary* 1986, 114.
16 Becker 1994, 169.
17 Biedermann 1994, 201-02.
18 Jobes 1962, 2: 966.
19 Jung 1976, 1: 89-90.

SHEEP
Genus: Ovis.
Family: Horned ungulates, with a variety of subfamilies.
Size: The head-rump length of the wild sheep is 110-200 centimeters (44-80 inches), the tail length is 3.5-13 centimeters (1-5 inches), and the body height is 65-125 centimeters (26-50 inches).
Weight: 20-230 kilograms (45-505 pounds). The female weighs one-quarter to one-third less than the male.
Gestation: 5 months.
Longevity: Up to 20 years.
Distribution: Australia, New Zealand, China, India, United States, South Africa, Argentina, and Turkey. Countries that have large areas of grassland are the major producers.
Habitat: Wild bighorn sheep are usually found in uplands, inhabiting alpine meadows, grassy mountain slopes, and foothill country in proximity to rugged rocky cliffs and bluffs.

Snake

Beyond question, snakes are the objects of more fears, phobias, and fascination than any other animal in the world, universally mythologized and widely misunderstood. Pervading the legends, folktales, superstitions, and traditions of all cultures, the snake has a remarkable range of meanings. The suborder Serpentes is large, comprising 2,500 species in a vast variety of families.[1] While herpetologists classify snakes into many different categories, the main groups are: water snakes, sea snakes, harmless and ordinary garden-variety snakes, venomous snakes, and constrictors.

Being ectothermic (cold-blooded), snakes are strongly affected by external temperatures. Since cold slows down all of their physical and perceptual processes, climate is a major factor in their geographical distribution, with the heaviest concentration naturally falling in tropical climates. However, they are found in most areas of the world, and the common viper has even been found north of the Arctic Circle.[2] One of the more dangerous and fascinating subfamilies is the viper, which has a pair of long, hollow fangs on the upper jaw that can be folded back in the mouth when not in use for injecting venom into victims. Pit vipers, including copperheads and rattlesnakes, have special heat-sensitive pit organs — facial ridges between each nostril and eye, which help them strike accurately at warm-blooded prey.[3]

With their elongated bodies, snakes have an unusual number of vertebrae and ribs, varying from 180 in vipers to 435 in colubrid snakes and the boids or constrictors.[4] Internal organs conform to the snake's tubular shape, with the stomach in particular stretching to enormous capacity. The snake's scaly skin can exhibit a large range of coloration, from the dull brown of some pythons to the intensely vivid bands of the coral snake. The scales themselves are impregnated with tactile sensory organs.[5] While the skin looks moist and damp, it feels smooth and silky to the touch. Snakes periodically shed their skins, a process that begins as the snake loosens the skin around its mouth by rubbing it against external objects. The animal then literally crawls out of its skin, which remains behind like an inside-out sock. This process restores damage done to the skin in the normal course of crawling about, removes external parasites, and may help maintain the efficacy of the skin's chemical receptors.[6]

With its forked tongue the snake probes for additional tactile sensation, but the tongue is also an important organ of olfaction. Airborne chemicals are carried by the tongue to the Jacobson's organ in the roof of the mouth, where they are interpreted and "smelled."[7] Most snakes have highly developed vision that is especially sensitive to movement, and they are legendary for the reflexive speed with which they can strike at targets in motion. The hypnotic intensity we seem to see in their eyes is nothing more than the absence of eyelids; more accurately, the eyelids are fused together to form a transparent covering.[8] Snakes are quite deaf to all but a few very low-frequency vibrations, so it is likely that the snake charmer's snake is charmed by his motions as he plays rather than by the music of his flute.[9] Rattlesnakes may shake their tails in warning, but they cannot hear the sound that is produced. A new rattle is added each time the snake sheds its skin, although these eventually grow brittle and break off.[10]

The constrictor snakes, such as boas and pythons, kill their prey by compression of their coils.[11] Only the very largest constrictors are capable of suffocating a human being, and they are rare. Only a third of snake species are poisonous enough to be harmful, although understandably they attract the largest share of our fascination, concern, and attention.[12] As a defensive tactic, some snakes, like the African spitting cobra, can spray their venom up to 3 meters (9.8 feet), often at a victim's eyes.[13] Other snakes, such as the diamond-back rattlesnakes and cobras, use poison to kill their prey, striking with lightning speed, biting only long enough to inject their venom, then retreating to wait while the poison does its work. The venom apparently affects the odor of the stricken party, allowing the snake to track it later by smell. That process allows the snake to avoid being injured in a struggle, since the victim is usually dead or dying by the time the snake catches up with it again.[14]

Some snakes' venom, a modified form of saliva, acts as a poison and meat tenderizer combined; it not only kills, but also begins the digestive process even before the victim is completely eaten.[15] Snakes have flexible jaws that allow them to swallow prey larger than themselves. Depending on species, size, sex, season, age, and other variables, snakes' prey range in size from earthworms and ant's eggs to mammals such as pigs and antelopes, which can weigh more than 50 kilograms (110 pounds).[16] Snake venom is generally divided into two categories: neurotoxic venom, which affects the nervous system, and hemotoxic venom, which affects the blood. The poison of cobras acts principally on the nervous system, while that of adders and rattlesnakes mainly affects the blood.[17] Viper venom usually spreads through the lymphatic system, crippling human victims or causing the loss of limbs if untreated. Similarly, the untreated bite of the Indian cobra or the African black mamba (the largest venomous snake in Africa and also of the cobra family) causes muscle paralysis and death by respiratory failure. Stiletto snakes are said to bear a unique and powerful cardiotoxin in their venom. Some snakes carry both types of venom.[18] The venom of many snakes has proven to be medically useful; in addition to the creation of anti-venom, cobra venom has been used as a painkiller, and others have been used to treat epilepsy.[19]

Like other reptiles, male snakes have a pair of barbed copulatory organs called hemipenises, normally retracted; when in use one at a time, they transfer sperm to the cloacal opening of the female and also serve to anchor the male during mating.[20] Sometimes, elaborate courtship behaviors precede copulation, lasting anywhere from a few minutes to a remarkable twenty-five hours in the case of some pit vipers, like western diamond-backed rattlesnakes.[21] Some snakes, like boas and rattlesnakes, are viviparous, bearing their young live, while others, like the cobra, lay eggs.[22]

The snake has been held sacred in many cultures all over the world. People revered the spiraling, coiling energy that extends beyond the boundaries of the animal itself to influence the surrounding world. The dynamism of the serpent is central to its symbolic significance; as with the spider's web, its coiling or spiral shape lends it a hint of metaphysical universality. The representation of the ouroboros, a snake consuming its own tail, is perhaps the most powerful symbol of the cosmic process, the reciprocal continuity of energy and matter, life and death.[23]

Among Native American people, the snake is a symbol of transformation and healing. Snake ceremonies sometimes involved multiple snakebites, the concept being that the venom would mobilize the healing powers of the individual's body and spirit. There is a widespread cultural connection between snakes and healing.[24] The snake was an attribute of Aesculapius, the son of Apollo and the god of medicine. Not coincidentally, the modern symbol of medicine, the caduceus, is a wand with two snakes entwined around it, which was once borne by the Greek god Hermes (Roman Mercury).[25]

In many cultures serpents are emblems of the highest gods or mystical states. The Aztec Quetzalcoatl, one of the major deities of the ancient Mexican pantheon, was depicted as a feathered serpent. There are python worshippers in Africa and cults of the cobra in India.[26] Sovereigns and initiates in ancient Egypt wore a headdress, the Uraeus, in the shape of a cobra, which represented a power of inner sight and control of the universe.[27] Indicative of how the snake can symbolize states of life or death, it was sometimes identified as a variation of the eye of Horus, or as the sacred eye of Ra.[28] But in the same mythology, Apophis, the evil serpent, wages daily war with Ra, the sun god, and is thus the archenemy of consciousness.[29] The dark, death-dealing aspect of the snake is best known as the serpent-seducer in the Book of Genesis of the Old Testament.[30]

The mysterious stealth of the snake's seemingly effortless locomotion, its "invisibility" in tall grass, and its habit of lurking in unexpected corners, nooks, or crevices make the snake's fearsome appearance seem sudden, even uncanny or ghostlike.[31] Its staring glance, with fixed and inexpressive eyes, chills us and seems to epitomize everything inhuman — that which we fear, loathe, and look on with awe.[32] The snake represents human qualities that are very far from consciousness, the lower aspects of the brain and of the spinal cord that can never be consciously experienced.[33] These qualities are known deeply through the body rather than through mental imagery and are felt on a body level as a primary symbol of anxiety. This anxiety is in conflict with the conscious personality's ideals and fears, and it may erupt and literally overpower consciousness at any time.

If a person dreamed of a snake, it would be appropriate to consider that the conscious personality might be too separate and out of harmony with deeper levels of the unconscious. For example, it could indicate that the unconscious is attempting to compensate for an overly intellectual, spiritualized approach of the conscious personality. The snake is associated with the creation of life, fertility, and healing; at the same time, its predatory habits and sometimes venomous bite recall the death-dealing aspects of nature. Sinuous and sensual, its phallic shape makes it a potent symbol of active, penetrating sexual energy. The snake is also associated with the feminine archetype, and its unique ability to engulf victims whole is a symbol of the devouring aspect of the unconscious. Further-more, the snake image could be symbolic of a creative or destructively seductive element that needs to be met. Thus, its appearance in a dream may signify the need of the conscious personality to confront such aspects of his or her being — seduction, creativity, sexuality, fear of being physically devoured. Just as the snake changes its skin, the dreamer may have to encounter such states as part of a fundamental change in his or her life. Then again, the snake could have a very pedestrian meaning, such as to indicate that a person is not to be trusted. Finally, one should note that the snake's appearance in dreams can be an indicator of possible organic illness.[34]

Notes

[1] Grzimek 1984, 6: 353.
[2] Grzimek 1984, 6: 350.
[3] "Vipers." *Encyclopedia Britannica*, 1997.
[4] Grzimek 1984, 6: 346.
[5] Grzimek 1984, 6: 348.
[6] Greene 1997, 27.
[7] "Jacobson's Organ." *Encyclopedia Britannica*, 1997; Grzimek 1984, 6: 349.
[8] Grzimek 1984, 6: 348-49.
[9] Grzimek 1984, 6: 348.
[10] Grzimek 1984, 6: 463-64.
[11] Grzimek 1984, 6: 363.
[12] Grzimek 1984, 6: 349-57.

[13] Grzimek 1984, 6: 357.
[14] Grzimek 1984, 6: 349.
[15] Grzimek 1984, 6: 354.
[16] Greene 1997, 53-61.
[17] Burton 1981, 286.
[18] Greene 1997, 86-87.
[19] Grzimek 1984, 6: 354.
[20] Grzimek 1984, 6: 348.
[21] Greene 1997, 126-27.
[22] Attenborough 1990, 29.
[23] Gimbutas 1989, 121.
[24] Andrews 1993, 360.
[25] Cooper 1992, 204.
[26] "Reptiles — Importance." *Encyclopedia Britannica*, 1997.
[27] Andrews 1993, 361.
[28] Ibid.
[29] Becker 1994, 264
[30] Charbonneau Lassay 1991, 160.
[31] Jung 1975, 9ii: 293-95
[32] "Reptiles — Importance." *Encyclopedia Britannica*, 1997.
[33] Jung 1988, 749
[34] Jung 1984, 251

SNAKE

Suborder: Serpentes (with a large number of families and subfamilies).

Size: Probably the smallest snakes in the world are the blind snakes from New Guinea, which are just 73 millimeters long (3 inches) and as thin as a matchstick. The largest snakes are in the Boidae family, which includes boas, pythons, and anacondas. The anacondas are 7.5-11 meters (25-36 feet). The two largest pythons, the reticulate python and the Indian python, reach a length of up to 10 meters (33 feet). The cobra is 1-3 meters long (3-10 feet).

Weight: Cobras may exceed 3 kilograms (6.5 pounds).

Incubation/Gestation: Some snakes are oviparous, others viviparous. Gestation and incubation periods vary according to species, size, lifestyle, geography, and temperature.

Longevity: There is a relationship between size and life expectancy in snakes. Pythons and boas live the longest of all snakes. An anaconda in the National Zoo (Washington, D.C.) lived 28 years. The boa constrictor can live up to 40 years in captivity, the cottonmouth up to 21 years in captivity, and the garter snake up to 10 years in captivity. The cobra may exceed 30 years.

Distribution: Worldwide.

Habitat: Desert, ocean, and jungles. They are found in, on, and above the ground.

Spider

The spider has a uniquely sinister reputation as a small but potent predator whose venom may injure or kill creatures many thousands of times its size and whose patiently constructed traps mean death to the unwary. Spiders are arachnids, eight-legged arthropods, as are mites and scorpions. These carnivores prey primarily on other arthropods, although the very large, so-called bird-eating spiders will eat lizards and small vertebrates when they can.[1] Spiders may have as many as eight eyes,[2] but for hunting they rely heavily on their exquisite sensitivity to vibrations, often transmitted by the silk strands of webs that they weave, which thus function almost like antennae.[3] Cobwebs are a highly visual, if somewhat overworked, symbol of decay and the inevitable passing of time, exemplified by Miss Havisham's ghostly boudoir in Charles Dickens's *Great Expectations*. Arachnophobia, an irrational or morbid fear of spiders, is a fairly common phenomenon.

Despite the popular impression, not all spiders build webs. Many roam to hunt; others lie in ambush, on flower petals for instance, but do not use a web. Still others may spin lines for various reasons, including escape in threatening situations, but not webs *per se*. The true web spinners hazard their fates and their webs in a single spot and remain there.[4] There are approximately thirty thousand known species of web-building spiders.[5] The spider's silk is exuded as a liquid from spinnerets at the posterior end of the abdomen, and it hardens immediately as the spider pulls on it. The resulting thread can have a greater tensile strength, thickness for thickness, than steel. Other types of spider silk are highly elastic.[6]

Spiders kill by injecting venom into their victims through hollow fangs.[7] The venom may contain toxins affecting nerves, blood, or tissue; in many instances, it is a cocktail meant to affect all three. Most of these toxins, while lethal to the spider's usual victims, are harmless or only mildly irritating to humans. However, some are capable of causing severe local reactions, including gangrene, and the neurotoxins of the black widow and a few other spiders can cause respiratory distress or failure. With the distinctive-looking red hourglass symbol on its abdomen, the black widow is widely distributed over most of the globe and is the spider that children are most commonly taught to fear. The bite of this spider is unpleasant and even dangerous, but most victims recover fully. The name "black widow" is a curiosity; it appears to arise from the fact that immediately after mating, the female kills and eats the substantially smaller male.[8]

Another spider that seems to have captured the popular imagination, largely because its substantial size rattles, is the tarantula. The American tarantula, a large, hairy spider of hot, tropical habitat, has a frightening reputation; in reality, its bite, although painful, is rarely if ever fatal. The European wolf spider, also called tarantula, is completely harmless to humans, although its bite has been wrongly suspected of causing a dancing frenzy called "tarantism."[9]

Reproduction among spiders is quite extraordinary by human standards. The male secretes a drop of sperm from an opening on the ventral surface of its abdomen. He then takes this sperm with one of his pedipalps (the first pair of legs). When the pedipalp is loaded with a sufficient amount of sperm, the male is ready to copulate and to transfer the sperm to the female, which will in many cases (as noted with the black widow spider) reward him for his amorous attentions by having him for dinner.[10] After dinner, and at her leisure, the female will deposit her eggs and the sperm, which she has been storing separately, onto some sort of silk disk that she has spun. Fertilization, therefore, takes place externally, although copulation of sorts has taken place.[11] She will wrap the eggs in more silk, making a kind of egg case. Females generally must produce a large number of eggs, since mortality rates are high for spiders because of predation by birds, reptiles, amphibians, insects, and other spiders.[12]

A widespread tradition among weavers is that to avoid the sin of hubris one must always introduce a flaw into one's weaving; failing to do so is to tempt the wrath of the gods. Ovid tells the classic story of such wrath in the caution-ary tale of the Lydian maiden Arachne, who weaves so flawlessly that Athena becomes jealous and turns her into a spider. In the process, she gave an entire class of arthropods their scientific name.[13]

The spider figures prominently in world mythologies and religions. For exam-ple, in Hindu myth, the spider is associated with Maya, as the spinner of earthly illusion;[14] and in Christianity, the spider is a symbol of Satan, who traps mankind in his web of sin.[15] In Japan, a legend tells of Spider Woman, who lures and traps unwary travelers. Goblin Spider is another demon with shape-shifting powers.[16] Many African cultures have tales of the spider Anansi, a trickster figure — always clever, sometimes playful, and at times malicious.[17] Finally, the spider figures in the mythologies of many Native American cultures. For some, it appears as an

Earth Mother figure. The Navajo believe that spiders taught people how to weave, and Spider Grandmother is a helpful figure in Pueblo folk tales — sometimes a creator, sometimes a keeper of ancient mysteries. Many tribes craft a stylized spider's web of sinew stretched across a wooden hoop. Called a dream-catcher, it separates good dreams from bad and points up the symbolic connection between spiders and the unconscious in general.[18]

Even more than most animals, spiders are ambivalent symbols in the human psyche. Universally fascinating, commonly seen as examples of patience and industry, they are also widely feared as venomous, treacherous, and repulsive. Symbolically, web-spinning connects with feminine principles of creativity, in large part because spinning in human terms is an ancient female activity. "The web of life" is an extended metaphor that connects spiders with fate, often imagined as a woman (or women) who spins out the destinies of mortals and determines when the threads of their lives will be cut off.[19]

The most noticeable feature of spiders is their web, which can be extraordinarily intricate and beautiful. The web's symmetry and interconnectedness is commonly seen as a symbol of wholeness and oneness — a mandala, basically representing the universe in many cultures, and often an attempt by the conscious self to integrate hitherto unconscious material. The radiating strands of its web are sometimes associated with the solar disk, affirming the link of the web to the emergence of consciousness. The spider itself, as the jewel-like center of a mandala-like web, makes a fairly apt symbol of the self, that unconscious organizing power within an individual being. The spider and its web become an equally apt representative image for the invisibly connected dangers that, to one degree or another, people see everywhere, which can engulf them. People who express negative emotions like envy, jealousy, guilt, or anxiety in "invisible" (that is, unacknowledged) ways are casting sticky webs of communication from which it is extremely difficult to separate.

If someone were to dream of a spider, these opposing meanings would have to be taken into account. On the one hand, the spider may signify a fear of entrapment and danger, leading to a life bound up in the condition of feeling controlled by another person's attitude, and of unspoken emotions and attachments that imprison the individual. On the other hand, relating to such unpleasant feelings could reveal the positive aspect of the spider, the road to consciousness and the very center of the psyche. Usually, it is necessary to consider both of these qualities when this dramatic insect appears in a dream. The appearance of the spider image could also alert the dreamer that he or she may be weaving a "web of deceit or intrigue" within certain relationships, or the dreamer may wonder how he or she might be caught up in such a negative web-like situation.

Notes
[1] Grzimek 1984, 1: 417.
[2] Preston-Matham 1984, 21.

[3] O'Toole 1986, 36; Grzimek 1984, 1: 417.
[4] Grzimek 1984, 1: 417.
[5] Preston-Matham 1984, 21.
[6] Preston-Matham 1984, 39.
[7] Preston-Matham 1984, 29.
[8] Gertsch 1979, 228-29.
[9] "Tarantula." *Encyclopedia Britannica*, 1997; Grzimek 1984, 1: 421-22.
[10] Grzimek 1984, 1: 418-19.
[11] Preston-Matham 1984, 81.
[12] O'Toole 1986, 140-41.
[13] Biedermann 1994, 317.
[14] Walker 1983, 957.
[15] Charbonneau-Lassay 1991, 159.
[16] Cooper 1992, 215.
[17] Johnson 1988, 210.
[18] Johnson 1988, 212-13; Andrews 1993, 344.
[19] Neumann 1963, 77.

SPIDER

Order: Araneae (subdivided into a large variety of families).

Size: Body length ranges from 0.7 millimeters (0.03 inches) for the smallest spider species to 9 centimeters (3.5 inches) for the bird-eating species.

Weight: From 1-2 grams (less than 1 ounce) for the average spider; 50-80 grams (2-3 ounces) for larger spiders.

Incubation: 14-30 days for the black widow spider.

Longevity: Most spiders live about 1 year. Some spiders live for 2-5 years, and some species, such as tarantulas, may live up to 25 years in captivity.

Distribution: Worldwide except Antarctica.

Habitat: Wherever there is rich vegetation and plenty of insects, but many species can survive in the desert, on mountaintops, and down mines.

Squid

Squid are generally torpedo-shaped, long-distance swimmers with large posterior fins.[1] Not quite as amorphous as the octopus, the squid is clearly built for swimming speed, not slithering (although the two are closely related cephalopods, as are cuttlefish and nautili). Whereas octopuses have eight "arms," squid have ten — eight "oral" arms and two longer "tentacles." The suckers on the arms are frequently toothed and sometimes equipped with tiny hooks.[2]

Many species have distinct and sometimes surprising characteristics. The Atlantic jeweled squid is about thirteen centimeters (five inches) long; it has a transparent mantle and twenty-two luminescent organs that make it look as if it were covered with glittering jewels. Many species can change skin coloration dramatically, and some have bioluminescent qualities — both adaptations that may help them elude predators and perhaps attract mates as well. Some even flash a light at the end of a tentacle to act as a lure for prey.[3]

The giant squid, dramatically depicted in Jules Verne's novel *Twenty Thousand Leagues Under the Sea*, is a true giant of the depths. Its estimated overall length can be twenty-five meters (eighty-two feet), and it weighs several tons. The eyes of this creature can be forty centimeters (fifteen inches) across, making them the largest in the world.[4] Another species, *Histioteuthis bonellii,* has right and left eyes of significantly different sizes, and the vampire squid has arms linked by a fleshy web that gives it a bat-like (or "Dracula-like") appearance — an effect dramatically enhanced by two huge, shining, deep red eyes.[5] Oceanic or flying squid can propel themselves across the surface of the water.[6]

Squid in deep-sea environments are surprisingly alert, reacting in large schools instantaneously, collectively, and with great precision — as if of one mind.[7] Enemies of squid in general are the bottle-nosed whales (porpoises and dolphins), sharks, rays, cod, and even penguins. Because they migrate in large numbers, either for breeding purposes or in pursuit of migratory prey, some squid are commercially viable for fishermen, and are eaten, used as bait, or processed as fishmeal. Even the colossal giant squid, existing at depths of up to a 1.6 kilometers (1 mile), has its nemesis in the form of deep-diving toothed whales, especially the sperm whale. Any number of plankton-feeders prey on the young, but the various species survive because of the vast number of eggs produced and fertilized.[8] Some species, when attacked, veil their escape behind an inky discharge, which hangs darkly (or, in some cases, luminously) in the water.[9]

The squid can be recognized in Celtic and Cretan ornamental art. Frequently, its tentacles are depicted as a whorl or curl,[10] which associates it symbolically with the web of the spider and other spiral symbols connected with the Great Mother. The squid has many symbolic similarities to the octopus, but, as it can descend into the greatest depths of the sea and exists in huge and monstrous forms, it is, if anything, even more mysterious. At depths very far from conscious awareness, the squid would represent psychic processes that can either create order, as in the symbol of the spider's web, or disorder, like in the deep regressive pull of the unconscious that drags the conscious personality into a state of inertia and weakness.

A person who is feverishly working in an orderly rational way, to the exclusion of anything irrational, might dream of a squid as a chaotic inner structure that is actually dangerous to his rational drive. Conversely, somebody who is less identified with rational processes, and more open to the unconscious and its spontaneous ways, might dream of a squid as representative of a very deep, unconscious form of order. In either case, the image of the squid is powerful and deeply affecting. While compensation for an overly rational approach or a portrayal of inner sources of order may be represented in many ways, the image of the squid brings them home in a particularly forceful and lasting manner.

Notes

[1] Bannister and Campbell 1988, 251.
[2] Grzimek 1984, 3: 208.
[3] Grzimek 1984, 3: 209-10; Broad 1994, C1.
[4] Broad 1994, C1.
[5] Grzimek 1984, 3: 213-14.
[6] Bannister and Campbell 1988, 251.
[7] Grzimek 1984, 3: 208.
[8] Ibid.
[9] Attenborough 1990, 248.
[10] Becker 1994, 279.

SQUID
Class: Cephalopoda.
Size: Giant squid can reach a body length of 6.5 meters (21 feet), with tentacles that measure 10 meters (32 feet).
Weight: Giant squid can weigh up to 3 tons.
Gestation: 30 days, depending on species.
Longevity: Smaller inshore species may have a life span of no more than 1 year or, exceptionally, 2 or 3 years. Nothing is known of the life span of the large oceanic squids, but it is presumed that giants such as Architeuthis attain their bulk only after a period of perhaps 4-5 years.
Distribution: Some of the 375 species of squid are found in North America and Europe, the western and eastern Atlantic, and the eastern Pacific oceans.
Habitat: Throughout warm and cold waters.

Squirrel

"Bright-eyed and bushy tailed," the ubiquitous squirrel is the darting busy-body of park and yard, an alert, industrious rodent with a decidedly cheerful and playful reputation. Its name can be construed as "shadow tail," from the notion that the animal uses its often luxurious caudal appendage to create shade for itself.[1] There are some 267 species of squirrel, with a wide variety of shapes and habits adapted to a broad range of habitats.[2]

As with many rodents, squirrels have incisors that grow continuously and must be worn back with use. Blessed with sharp eyesight and a wide field of vision, they are remarkably agile both at climbing trees and jumping from limb to limb. On most squirrels, the large, bushy tail provides balance when they run or climb and a rudder when they jump. Squirrels also use their tails to communicate a wide range of social signals and to keep warm when they sleep.[3] Some species, like the so-called flying squirrels, have developed loose membranes between their fore and hind limbs, which they stretch out when jumping to make themselves into a kind of para-sail or airfoil.[4]

Squirrels eat mushrooms, fruits and berries, pinecones, nuts and seeds, and even the sap of certain trees; some species may also eat insects or supplement their diets with animal protein.[5] Most species can get enough water from the vegetable matter that they eat (the red squirrel is exceptional in needing to drink). Nuts and seeds are stored away for use in the winter, hidden in holes in the ground, hollows under the roots of trees, and other secure places. While such caches are sometimes lost to other animals, or simply forgotten, red squirrels can smell and relocate pinecones buried a foot or more below the surface.[6]

Sexually mature at one year, some squirrels may have two mating seasons, in spring and in summer. Gestation takes about three to six weeks, and litters average anywhere from three to eight young. In most species, the male leaves after mating, and the female raises the young alone.[7] Some types of squirrels (for example, ground squirrels) have a three-to four-month seasonal hibernation, beginning in October, during which a large amount of weight loss occurs. This weight is regained during the summer and lasts until the next hibernation in October.[8]

Within a particular shared range or territory, squirrels do not exhibit a great deal of social organization, but they do communicate extensively with vocalizations, tail movements, and other postural gestures. They react collectively, not only to their own alarm calls but also to those of the junco bird (small sparrows of the family Fringillidae). Squirrels seem to love moving about and play exuberant games that appear to be mostly about being in motion. They also observe a distinct status hierarchy among both males and females. Animals of lower status are often forced to forage in new territories, frequently including cultivated land, where they are known to strip the bark off valuable trees.[9] Medium-sized predators, especially foxes, martins, and raptors such as owls and hawks, hunt squirrels.[10] Humans hunt them for their pelts, particularly in the North, where their winter fur tends to be longer and softer.

In Germanic mythology, the squirrel called Ratatoskr, sacred to Wotan, lived in the world ash tree Yggdrasil,[11] traveling up and down as a messenger between the eagle above and the dragon below.[12] In the Middle Ages, the squirrel's darting speed may have caused it to be associated with the Devil,[13] which was imagined to be everywhere — behind every tree and bush. In Christianity, perhaps because of its habit of storing up food, the squirrel was viewed as a symbol of greed and avarice.[14] The people of the North considered the squirrel a bringer of rain, water, and snow,[15] and also associated the red squirrel with the devilish and fiery Loki.[16]

In Celtic mythology, Queen Medb, a war goddess, is depicted with a bird and a squirrel perched on her shoulder, symbolizing her connection with the land and sky.[17] Buddhists believed that the squirrel uses its tail to fend off attackers and urged devotees to ward off spiritual attack in like manner. Possibly because of the variety of red and reddish-brown squirrels in various parts of the world, the Mayans and other civilizations sacrificed these animals to their gods, considering the squirrel a fire animal and an attribute of Desana, Master of Animals.[18]

The squirrel is an extraordinarily able climber, constantly scampering up or down trees with consummate agility and ease, shuttling from one realm to another. This relatively unusual way of life lends it a strong symbolic significance as a mediator and transitional link between heaven and earth, as is made explicit in the Germanic myth of Yggdrasil. In most cultures, heaven and earth, as opposites, are paradigms of other polar realities. The earth is commonly associated with the feminine and with instinctual life, and the sky is similarly associated with the masculine and with conscious thought. Thus, symbolically, the squirrel represents a human capacity to link spiritual and instinctual life so that instinctual life becomes spiritualized (less autonomous and less unconscious), and spiritual life becomes increasingly connected to the real ongoing life of the body and reality. Another characteristic of the squirrel is its capacity to "squirrel away" food, thus creating reserves of sustenance. In human life, this tendency can reflect a propensity to hide one's assets. Such an act can be positive when it creates a safe and private space for one's fragile inner life, but its secretiveness can also be negative and alienating.

A dream of a squirrel might cause one to wonder if the dreamer is "squirreling away" thoughts and feelings because bringing them out into the full view of others feels far too risky and makes him or her feel vulnerable. It would also be expedient to contemplate whether the person is someone who does not "squirrel away" enough thoughts and fantasies, but instead merely generates more and more of the same, never allowing anything to germinate. Not showing one's thoughts prematurely is an essential part of the creative process, but not showing them at all may be a warped reaction resulting from excessive fears.

If someone dreamed of a squirrel because of the squirrel's capacity to link above and below, it would be useful to explore the dreamer's connection or lack of connection between mental-spiritual life and bodily-instinctual life. For example, the person might be filled with ideas that he or she is not bringing into reality and/or might be living an overly expansive and dangerous instinctual life, with no real reflection on spiritual values.

Notes
[1] Grzimek 1984, 11: 246.
[2] Macdonald 1987, 612.

[3] Macdonald 1987, 612-14.
[4] "Flying Squirrel." *Encyclopedia Britannica*, 1997.
[5] Ibid.
[6] Andrews 1993, 317.
[7] Macdonald, 1987, 617-18.
[8] McFarland 1987, 253.
[9] Macdonald 1987, 620.
[10] Andrews 1993, 317.
[11] Biedermann 1994, 321.
[12] de Vries 1976, 438.
[13] Becker 1994, 279.
[14] Cooper 1992, 216.
[15] Ibid.
[16] Biedermann 1994, 321.
[17] Green 1992, 192.
[18] Cooper 1992, 216.

SQUIRREL
Family: Sciuridae.
Size: The head-body length of the tiny African pygmy squirrel is 6.6-10 centimeters (2.5-4 inches); it has a tail length of 5-8 centimeters (2-3 inches). The Alpine marmot can have a head-body length of 53-73 centimeters (21-29 inches) and a tail length of 13-16 centimeters (5-7 inches).
Weight: African pygmy squirrel weighs about 10 grams (0.3 ounces). Alpine marmot can weigh 4-8 kilograms (9-17 pounds).
Gestation: 21-40 days depending on species.
Longevity: 8-10 years (up to 16 years in captivity).
Distribution: On every continent other than Australia and Antarctica.
Habitat: From lush tropical rain forests to rocky cliffs or semiarid deserts, from open prairies to town gardens.

Stork

Balanced precariously on its stilt-like legs, the stork is an ungainly bird, yet it is a powerful and graceful flier, noted for the uncanny accuracy of its transcontinental migrations and the fanciful notion that it is the source of newborn human babies. Storks belong to an order of long-necked, long-legged, and long-billed birds called Ciconiformes, which includes herons, ibises, spoonbills, and others. Eighteen species of storks, of which the white stork is probably the most familiar, range from medium-sized to quite large, with a wingspan of nearly seven feet. Known as wading birds, most storks are creatures of the wetlands — swamps, marshes, bogs, and other marshy areas — although white storks are found in grasslands as well.[1]

The migration of storks is unerring, a high-soaring triumph of solar navigation that remains a bit of a mystery even today, and quite consistent. They arrive in Europe from Africa, where they spend the winter months, within a few days of the same date every year. Storks are strong fliers and are always migratory, with some species traveling thousands of miles annually from winter quarters to nest in large flocks of upwards of forty thousand birds.[2] Returning from their migration, most storks recognize their previous partners at a great distance, and repair last year's nest.[3] They circle one another, making a variety of sounds and wing beats. The pair then copulates numerous times, and the female subsequently lays eggs at two-day intervals. Both partners incubate the eggs at regular times.[4]

Storks are not vocally expressive. They lack a fully developed vocal organ, but several species clatter their bills for audible communication; almost all have developed elaborate "dances" as a form of postural signaling. They feed while ambling about, eating worms, insects (especially grasshoppers), fish, lizards, mice, voles, and, of particular symbolic interest, snakes.[5]

The greeting card caricature of the stork carrying a human baby suspended in a diaper-sling from its bill is a familiar image, but the stork is a very ancient representation of new birth, and it has other symbolic connections with the development of the human individual. Storks in fairy tales may sometimes take on human shape and are said to cry human tears if wounded.[6] The natural fecundity of its wetlands habitat suggests the creative waters of the womb, of the Great Mother herself. Because the stork was thought to be particularly dedicated to its young, it was sacred to Juno, Roman goddess of family values.[7] In some myths, the direction of care-giving was reversed, with grateful younger birds feeding and even supporting older birds during their flights.[8]

The postural gesturing and courtship behavior of the stork may have inspired ancient sacred dances, fertility rites, and the ecstatic physicality that linked the corporeal to the spiritual.[9] Inevitably, as a hunter of snakes, the stork is considered a propitious symbol, associated with Christ, who was the bane of all satanic creatures — the serpent foremost among them. In Europe, the stork's punctual return from its migration made it a genuine harbinger of spring, the restoration of life, and, consequently, an apt symbol of Christ's resurrection. The writers of medieval bestiaries made it a symbol of fraternal love and comradely duty.[10]

As with many migratory animals, especially birds, the stork's uncanny ability to navigate accurately seems to suggest divine inspiration or obedience to divine will, which may be interpreted as a symbol of functioning in accord with a deep inner truth that is beyond the rule of the conscious personality.[11] If someone dreamed of a stork, it might reflect the presence of regressive tendencies and outdated attitudes, which require confrontation (as in the stork's famous capacity to hunt snakes and in the familiar anecdote of the stork bringing the baby). Consciously related to and meditated upon, the stork image could release the energy necessary to deal with regression. The stork's maternal quality could at times be central to understanding the dream image. In that case, one might inquire about the dreamer's proper parenting of his or her own small, frail, and childlike aspects. In addition, the unerring migratory and mating capacity of the stork could suggest the dreamer's need to be more focused upon connecting to his or her true home, the inner self.

Notes

[1] Grzimek 1984, 7: 223-24.
[2] Grzimek 1984, 7: 226.
[3] Perrins and Middleton 1989, 75.
[4] Grzimek 1984, 7: 229-30.
[5] Grzimek 1984, 7: 224.
[6] Andrews 1993, 192.
[7] Andrews 1993, 192-93.
[8] Cooper 1992, 217.
[9] Andrews 1993, 193.
[10] Biedermann 1994, 329; Cooper 1992, 218.
[11] von Franz 1974, 47.

STORK
Family: Ciconiidae.
Size: Overall length is 110 centimeters (43 inches).
Wingspan: Can reach over 220 centimeters (86 inches).
Weight: 2.3-4.4 kilograms (5-10 pounds).
Incubation: 32 days.
Longevity: 20-30 years.
Distribution: Tropical Africa and tropical Asia. They particularly nest in Europe, East Asia, north and southern Africa.
Habitat: Wetlands and water margins, fields, and savannas. They prefer warm, continental climates.

Swallow

The swallow is a strong, swift, swooping flier, with a trilling or chirping call and a precise schedule of migration that has made it a celebrated harbinger of spring. With long, pointed wings and a forked tail, this lightly built bird is capable of flying effortlessly, with great stamina and ease.[1] Swallows feed on insects, which they take on the wing, and they must be more or less constantly in flight in order to have enough to eat.

Swallows gather in large flocks and molt in winter quarters, but breed elsewhere. While they do not have a special feeding territory in the usual sense, they will defend their nests. Swallows are monogamous, although indiscretions do occur because the male with the more luxuriant tail is more resistant to parasites, and therefore is more appealing to the female as a stronger and healthier breeder.[2] In the natural course of things, swallows fall prey to falcons, owls, and domesticated cats, among other predators. In flocks, swallows are a feisty lot, capable of dispatching a would-be marauder in an excited mob.[3]

In many cultures, the swallow is connected with fire, sometimes playing a Promethean role in creation myths. Native American legend has it that the swallow stole fire from the sun and carried it on its tail feathers to earth, singeing them in the process, with the result that the swallow's tail became split.[4] In a strikingly similar Latvian myth, after the swallow steals fire, the Devil throws a firebrand at the bird in anger, which gives it its red markings and forked tail. In yet another version, the swallow restores fire to humankind when the Great Flood had extinguished all. The swallow is a fire-bringer in Asian and Celtic myths as well.[5]

As is generally the case with animal symbolism, the swallow can represent opposite qualities. Perhaps because they will harass a predator, swallows are thought by the Chinese to embody the virtues of courage and daring. In its monogamous style of breeding, they see a symbol of fidelity. However, in Japan the swallow can signify unfaithfulness.[6] The swallow was auspicious to the Romans[7] and said to typify purity in Africa;[8] among the Greeks, Plutarch thought it to be a bad omen.[9] In Sumatra, the swallow, as an indicator of spring, is part of a ceremony to raise a curse of infertility. Like a scapegoat, it is released into the wild in the hope that the curse will leave with it. Likewise, in ancient Greece, if a swallow happened to enter the house, oil was poured on it, and then the bird was released in the hope that it would carry away any bad luck.[10]

The swallow's unerring return to its vernal nest, the very spot it had quit at the onset of winter, suggests resurrection. Thus Christian allegorists connect this bird with the parable of the prodigal son, who returns to the bosom of his family (for which they read the Mother Church).[11] The swallow is holy to Islam as well because it returns every year to Mecca.[12] When the famous cliff swallows return on March 19 to the Mission of San Juan Capistrano in California, there is great rejoicing among the devout, the superstitious, and those who merely wonder at nature's cycles and the strange workings of instinct.[13] Because the swallow was once thought to give sight to its young by rubbing celandine (a yellow-flowered Eurasian biennial herb) on their eyes, it is seen by some as an analogue of God's restoration of sight to the dead at the final judgment.[14] In keeping with the opposite qualities that the swallow can represent, one should note that the droppings of the swallow took sight away from Tobias (Tobit 2: 9-11). Others have seen in the swallow's tireless pursuit of insects a model of Satan, who remorselessly pursues Christian souls.[15]

Much has also been made of the bird's rapid, twittering call. The Old Testament Book of Isaiah (38:14) says "like a swallow so did I chatter"; and a tale is told that St. Francis of Assisi's *al fresco* preaching was interrupted by the heedless chattering of swallows, which were silenced when he addressed them as sisters and urged them to listen to the words of God. Writers of the classical period considered their chattering positively frenzied, associating it with epilepsy and the belief that the bird could effect a cure.[16]

Like all birds, the swallow represents the spirit — the creator of inner order — but in a particular way reflected in the bird's behavior. When encountered in a dream, the return of the swallow to its original home, as well as its excessive twittering and chirping, could indicate that the dreamer has lost inner direction and gone astray. The dreamer may need to pay more attention to his or her deepest values, re-orienting and reconnecting to what is vital. Having a connection to sight, the swallow image may alert the dreamer to look more deeply into both his or her inner and outer situations, with the possibility that his or her "outlook" needs more acuity. The association of the swallow with resurrection and fire would underscore an inner psychic potential that is becoming activated and in which a new or rediscovered orientation is possible, perhaps through a creative act.

Notes

[1] Grzimek 1984, 9: 182.
[2] Angier 1995, 6.
[3] Pfeffer 1989, 38.
[4] Andrews 1993, 194.
[5] Armstrong 1958, 179-81; Cooper 1992, 218.
[6] Cooper 1992, 218.
[7] Armstrong 1975, 66.
[8] Becker 1994, 287.
[9] Armstrong 1975, 66.
[10] Frazier 1963, 627.
[11] Charbonneau-Lassay 1991, 219.
[12] Cooper 1992, 219.
[13] Charbonneau-Lassay 1991, 216.
[14] Mohr 1976, 260.
[15] Charbonneau-Lassay 1991, 220-21.
[16] Armstrong 1975, 71-74.

SWALLOW
Family: Hirundinidae.
Size: 10-23 centimeters (4-9 inches) in length.
Weight: 10-55 grams (0.4-1.9 ounces).
Incubation: 13-16 days.
Longevity: 4-9 years depending on species.
Distribution: Worldwide except Arctic, Antarctic, and some remote islands.
Habitat: Open habitats from sea level to high mountains, from small forest clearings to extensive grasslands.

Swan

With its long-necked beauty, pure white color, and gliding, graceful, and stately motion afloat as well as in the air, the swan is a paragon of splendid elegance and impressive dignity. The largest of the waterfowl in the Anatidae family of ducks and geese,[1] swans may weigh up to fifty pounds (twenty-three kilograms); they are powerful fliers, with apparently enough strength in their wings to break a man's arm.[2] In the northern hemisphere, the mute, whooper, whistling, and trumpeter swans are pure white as adults; south of the equator, a black-necked swan is found in Patagonia, and Australia is the home of an all-black swan.[3] The mute swan has a black knob at the base of its orange beak and carries its neck in a distinctive curve, while the whooper, trumpeter, and whistling swans have plain beaks and a carriage that is typically more straight-necked.[4]

Preferring the colder climates of the extreme north and south latitudes, swans nest on shore but are more at home on the water, where most of their food is found.[5] Depending on the type of swan and its habitat, they consume a wide range of plants and aquatic insects, snails, and leaves, stems, roots, and seeds.[6] Pairs mate for life, and the young are tended by both parents, joining in their migratory flights and learning from them routes, landmarks, and the locations of hospitable wetlands along the way. Migrating swans travel at great altitudes in chevron formation.[7]

Swans communicate posturally in a number of ways. Males and females both have a pre-copulatory courtship display. Males will also display in triumph at the defeat of a rival suitor, and their aggressive pose is truly impressive. They fold back the neck in an exaggerated "S," like a cobra poised to strike, elbows akimbo, wing feathers puffed grandly out like sails on some ancient warship.[8]

In Neolithic northern Europe, the swan was the first bird to show up in the symbolic and decorative motifs with which people adorned their tools and utensils, suggesting the worship of a deity and ur-progenitor of the human race.[9] In their iconography, the northern people of prehistory pictured the swan harnessed to a boat or chariot, often pulling the sun itself. In Greek mythology, swans draw Apollo's chariot as well.[10] In the traditions of certain Native American tribes, the swan is a totem of grace, faith, and acceptance of the will of the Great Spirit. In Navajo lore, a great white swan calls up the winds from the four corners of the earth.[11] In many traditions, including the Greek, swans are associated with the power of prophecy. Some swans are mostly silent while in captivity,[12] while others have rather haunting calls, and this may account for the persistent myth that the swan senses its own impending demise and sings a distinctive "death song."[13]

In Greek mythology, Zeus ravishes Leda in the form of a swan, a story which underscores the virile aspects of the bird's symbolic power. Because of its snow-white color, the whitest among birds, the swan seems, like the white dove, irresistibly associated with the idea of purity and therefore with chastity.[14] In northern European mythology, the feminine quality of the swan is dominant, and its beauty was seen as a connection to Virgin Mary.[15] Conversely, the black swan was a symbol of Satan,[16] and even the white swan was at times suspect, because in medieval times it was believed that the bird's flesh was entirely black beneath its white feathers, making it a perfect symbol of hypocrisy.[17]

In many cultures the divine spirit, being perfect, is represented by a hermaphrodite — the two sexes united; it would not have escaped the notice of pre-modern, traditional people that the swan's shape is both phallic and yonic. It is not hard to see in the beautiful swan the embodiment of the divine or creative spirit.[18] According to Pythagoras, all great poets at their deaths took the form of swans, and the connection between poets and swans has continued over the centuries. Homer was called the "Swan of Meander," Virgil the "Mantuan Swan"; the English playwright Ben Jonson called William Shakespeare the "Swan of Avon," and Anna Seward was known as "The Swan of Lichfield."[19] Because of its wings, immaculate whiteness, and the radiance of its extraordinary beauty, the swan often signifies the lifting of depression, despair, or inner darkness.[20]

The motif of metamorphosis — humans bewitched into swans, or magical swans conjured into human form — has a wide currency. In the ballet *Swan Lake,* the evil magician Rothbart turns Odette and her maidens into swans; in the fairy tale *The Six Swans,* the brothers are bewitched. Many fairy/folktales around the world feature a woman who has been changed into the form of a swan; often a hunter finds a swan that is really a beautiful woman. He carries her off, but some catastrophe happens, and she either flies away and disappears forever, or he can redeem her, find her, and bring her back into human form only after a long journey. Psychologically, this is an inner journey in which the hero must redeem his feminine, feeling side and generally his connection to the unconscious, which has been bedevilled by power motives.[21]

With such a rich variety of mythopoetic connections, the swan is bound to be a significant but highly variable figure in dreams. The swan can be an inspirational image, representing a spiritual connection to the dreamer's feminine side, or the swan can represent the feminine in a very bewitched state. This bewitchment can be created by (among other instances) lust, power drives, and early traumatic intrusions into the psyche, reflecting a lack of connection to Eros and to any sense of relatedness. But the swan can also indicate an inner, spiritual self that is, in its pristine chastity, too pure, too lofty — narcissistically self-absorbed, unrelated, and removed from the earth and reality. The goal, as always, is balance — to regain one's earthly connectedness without losing the spiritual quality the swan can represent.

Notes
[1] Perrins and Middleton 1989, 92.
[2] Andrews 1993, 196.
[3] Perrins and Middleton 1989, 90-98.
[4] Grzimek 1984, 7: 279-80.
[5] Ibid.
[6] www.twingroves.district96.k12.il.us/Wetlands/TrumpeterSwan/SwanFood.html.
[7] Grzimek 1984, 7: 279-80.
[8] Perrins and Middleton 1989, 92, 97.
[9] Charbonneau-Lassay 1991, 243.
[10] Becker 1994, 289.
[11] Cooper 1992, 220.
[12] Ammer 1989, 177.
[13] Leonard 1987, 72-73.
[14] Charbonneau-Lassay 1991, 249.
[15] Becker 1994, 289.
[16] Charbonneau-Lassay 1991, 255-56.

[17] Biedermann 1994, 334.
[18] Leonard 1987, 72-73.
[19] Wilmore 1979, 216.
[20] Fabricius 1989, 137.
[21] Leonard 1987, 72-73.

SWAN

Family: Anatidae.

Size: The largest swan, the trumpeter, is about 1.7 meters (5.5 feet) long.

Wingspan: 3-3.4 meters (10-11 feet) for the trumpeter swan.

Weight: The heaviest flying bird, the mute swan, weighs about 33 kilograms (73 pounds).

Incubation: 35-40 days.

Longevity: Up to 20 years.

Distribution: Worldwide except Antarctica.

Habitat: Chiefly coastal and freshwater wetlands.

Tiger

The tiger is the lion of Asia, an enormous, staggeringly beautiful, powerful, and lethal animal — the Eastern king of beasts, at the very top of the food chain. Bold and graphic in appearance, startling in William Blake's memorable phrase "fearful symmetry," the tiger is so perfectly camouflaged in the dark and dappled jungle light that it can evoke apprehensive trembling over lurking, shadowed, sudden death. Tigers vary slightly in their markings from one subspecies to the next, but commonly have a tawny, orange coat and (unique among cats) transverse black stripes.[1] White tigers are occasionally discovered, with white or off-white fur and black-brown stripes. They typically have blue eyes, which can eerily turn yellow when the animal is excited and its pupils dilate.[2]

At home in the jungles of India, the mountains of Tibet, or the taiga of Siberia, tigers require only water, shelter, and an adequate supply of large prey.[3] Like most felids, they are stalking night hunters[4] and nearly always prey on medium-sized animals (such as cattle, lynx, foxes, small jungle cats, rodents, deer, and antelope). They will eat anything from frogs and fish to carrion, if necessary, to satisfy their need for fifteen to twenty pounds of meat a day. Adults are not particularly good climbers, but they are strong swimmers.[5] The heavily built Siberian subspecies, with its longer, fuller coat, includes the largest cats still living in the world. One specimen reportedly measured 290 centimeters (9.5 feet) head to trunk and weighed nearly 270 kilograms (600 pounds).

Usually solitary and territorial,[6] tigers of both sexes mark territories with urine spray enhanced by excretions from special scent glands. Territories of males and females may overlap; in the course of the mating season, males will get together for fighting, which is usually non-fatal. Mated pairs will remain in close proximity for most of the three to ten weeks of the season, during which time the female may be receptive for just three to seven days. On those days, however, the pair may copulate more than fifty times, since the female needs the stimulus of repeated copulation before she will ovulate. Males do not involve themselves with raising cubs; the female, which is considered one of the most dangerous animals in the world when protecting her young, does that. Despite her zealous guardianship, however, only one out of three cubs will survive to maturity.[7]

The first tiger was seen in Rome at the beginning of the Christian era, a gift to the emperor Augustus; consequently, most ancient traditions and myths concerning it are Asian rather than Western in origin.[8] In the East, where people lived and died in proximity to this profoundly impressive beast, its power inspired much awe. Dionysos, god of madness and ecstatic transformation, is strongly associated with the panther in Greek myth, but it seems likely that as his cult spread eastward to India, the tiger gradually took the panther's place iconographically.[9] The overwhelming power and beauty of the tiger make it a prime candidate to represent archetypal powers.

Many gods and heroes are depicted wearing tiger skins, since this is always a symbol of power.[10] In the Hindu tradition, Kali, the goddess of creation and destruction, has a tiger for a mount,[11] and the god Shiva wears a tiger skin when he is depicted in his aspect as the Destroyer.[12] In India, various parts of the tiger (the claws, fangs, and sometimes whiskers) are still prized as ingredients in love philters and as charms against demonic possession.[13] In ancient China, the tiger was the third sign of the zodiac and associated with the active Yang principle, although the albino tiger was compared to the perceptive and chthonic Yin tenet.[14] The tiger's fearsomeness made its image an apt guardian at the entrances to dwellings, and depicting it with wings emphasized the uncanniness of its power. The "God of Wealth" has a tiger for a mount, indicating the power and prestige of wealth in ancient Chinese culture.[15] In Buddhism, the tiger and the dragon are two irresistible forces of the world. The tiger usually represents the power of the terrestrial sphere, while the dragon in this context can represent the heavens. The breath of the tiger is pictured as wind, and the breath of the dragon as water.[16]

From a psychological point of view, the tiger usually represents dangerous, destructive, and deeply negative emotions, such as overwhelming rage and violence. Yet in myths and folktales, one often finds that a child can safely walk among tigers or lions or snakes. Symbolically this image suggests that neither intellect nor power but rather innocence and spontaneity can deal with such emotions.[17] In myths and folktales, one also finds the symbolic image of a person riding a tiger. This image can represent a psychological state in which powerful and dangerous emotions of rage and their destructive capacity have been tamed. Untamed, these emotions can literally tear apart one's consciousness, leaving it scattered, unfocused, overwhelmed by feelings and regressive by nature, making continued adaptation and connection to the world tenuous at best. When such feelings are transformed through adopting a childlike, spontaneous, creative, playful attitude toward them, they can then become great strengths that

T

protect one's deepest values, just as they at times protect the gods and goddesses in mythology. Not only is it necessary to adopt an attitude of spontaneity and naiveté to relate to the divine powers of ecstasy and madness, but one must also be willing to suffer the humiliation and disgrace of one's ego without totally losing one's identity. To feel and respect the overwhelming quality of the intense affects represented by the tiger without being dissolved by them is the path of transforming the tiger-like image from a fierce, destructive force into a positive, protective one.

If an image of a tiger appears in a dream, all of the previous reflections could immediately be brought to bear on its possible meaning. The dreamer must carefully consider how he or she may be a tiger — fierce, ruthless, mad, overly aggressive — and how he or she tears apart life in a destructive way. Then again, if the dreamer were a person who has very little connection to such powerful affects, he or she would be called upon, through the image of the tiger, to try to relate to these darker, powerful chthonic forces within his or her own being. The appearance of the tiger represents the emergence of nothing less than "god" in the psyche, something that can easily overwhelm any structure of consciousness that exists, but equally well can cleanse it and bring about a transformation unimagined by rational, controlled attitudes. This god-like feeling is reflected in Blake's poem:

Tyger Tyger burning bright,
In the forests of the night,
What immortal hand or eye,
Could frame thy fearful symmetry?

Notes

[1] Pfeffer 1989, 332.
[2] Grzimek 1984, 12: 347-48.
[3] Grzimek 1984, 12: 348.
[4] Pfeffer 1989, 332.
[5] Grzimek 1984, 12: 348-350.
[6] Grzimek 1984, 12: 352.
[7] *Tiger.* Time Life Video. WNET 1990, produced by Virginia Alexander and David Heeley.
[8] Biedermann 1994, 344.
[9] Cooper 1992, 227.
[10] Biedermann 1994, 344.
[11] Andrews 1993, 319.
[12] Cooper 1992, 226-27.
[13] Hastings 1910, 530.
[14] Jobes 1962, 2: 1572.
[15] Cooper 1992, 227.
[16] Symmes 1990, 146.
[17] von Franz 1977, 18.

TIGER
Family: Felidae.
Size: The tiger can achieve a body length of up to 3 meters (10 feet).
Weight: Up to 260 kilograms (570 pounds).
Gestation: 103 days.
Longevity: Approximately 15 years (20 in captivity).
Distribution: India, China, and Indonesia.
Habitat: Tropical rain forest, snow-covered coniferous and deciduous forests, mangrove swamps, and drier forest types.

Toad

Looking like a warty-skinned frog, the toad is practically synonymous with loathsomeness. In the vernacular, the word is used in a derogatory manner; to be a "toad" is to be a sycophant, ingratiating toward others to further your own goals. Divided into some three hundred species,[1] toads are similar to their fellow anurans, the frogs, and the names of the two are applied somewhat carelessly in popular speech. Indeed, even experts can disagree, and the classifications have been subjected to a certain amount of tinkering over the years. In the main, however, toads are more comfortable in drier, more terrestrial environments than are frogs. Although there are a number of notably venomous frogs, toads do appear to be the more venomous of the two; even the eggs of the neotropical toad are highly toxic.[2]

Toads are usually not active until dusk, typically hunting in dim light for ants, beetles, and spiders. The visible movements of prey-sized animals trigger predacious behavior. Confronting a potential enemy (raptors, wading birds, crows, snakes, hedgehogs, and the occasional otter), a toad will inflate itself and rise up on tiptoe to maximize its size. This practice may convince a snake, for example, that the toad is too large to swallow. Toads have also been known to drive a snake away by butting heads with it.[3] Since amphibians cannot internally regulate their body temperatures, they have developed patterns of behavior that might seem odd in other animals. For instance, if the outside temperature sinks below about five degrees Celsius (forty degrees Fahrenheit), toads will immediately burrow into the earth, even if they are in the middle of a migration.[4]

The rather common European toad has horizontal pupils and a warty skin that can vary in color from light yellow to black, depending on the mood, humidity, season, and molting activity. Males are smaller and more slender than females. A parotid gland behind each of the eyes secretes a poisonous white fluid, that is irritating to the mucous lining of the eyes, noses, and mouths of potential predators, and which has been found to be intensely toxic if injected into the bloodstream. As a result, toads have few enemies. Males are sexually mature after three to five years, females after four to six years.[5] Another poisonous toad, one of the largest in the world, is the giant toad, native from southern Texas to South America. Considered valuable because it controls pest insects that are destructive to crops, it has been imported to other areas, including Australia, where it has thrived. It feeds on almost anything, including small rodents and birds and many insects, particularly beetles. In favorable climates, the giant toad can breed at any time of year, laying its strands of eggs in water. In a single year, females may lay up to thirty-five thousand eggs, which can hatch into tadpoles in as little as three days. Needless to say, mortality rates are high.[6]

Toads have a remarkable sense of direction.[7] They have an extremely wide field of vision, and their eyes are eighty times more sensitive to light than ours. That competitive advantage is actually enhanced as the temperature drops, because the body heat of warm-blooded animals normally interferes with the clarity of their vision in low light levels; the eyes of the toad, and all so-called cold-blooded animals, are unaffected by this phenomenon.[8] Male true toads have rudimentary ovaries called Bidder's Organs which, if the testicles are removed, actually develop into functioning ovaries, illustrating that, at least among vertebrates, the development of one sexual nature involves the suppression of the other.[9]

In folklore and mythology, the frog is more often a masculine element, whereas the toad is more often feminine. In the West, the toad has long been associated with the Earth Mother, especially in her function of helping with childbirth. In many Catholic countries, people who believe that some part of their body has been cured by the intercession of a particular saint make an *ex voto* offering of a wax image of the healed part — arm, leg, hand, or other body part. But if a woman has been relieved of distress to the uterus or of some complication related to childbirth, she offers instead a wax image of a toad. Until recently, the flesh of the toad was eaten to ameliorate labor pains, its blood was used as an aphrodisiac, and dry toads were hung up as charms.[10]

Whereas the frog was often (although not always) considered a positive symbol, the toad, thought to be poisonous, was far more commonly a negative one, despite its positive attributes for childbirth. Thus, the toad was thought of as a witches' animal, a familiar and a frequently cited ingredient in witches' brews.[11] The toad was thought to have the power to cause madness, as well as the vampiric habit of sucking milk or blood from sleeping humans.[12] In Egypt, the toad was regarded as an animal of death. In the art of the Middle Ages, it was associated with the vices of lust and covetousness,[13] qualities also ascribed to it in Zoroastrianism, where it belongs to the evil spirit Ahriman. There, however, it is also a fertility symbol. In Celtic symbolism, the toad often has the same attributes of evil as the serpent. In Native American lore, it is a symbol of the power of darkness and evil of the Dark Manitou, which can be overcome by the great powers and protective spirits of the Great Manitou,[14] which individuals can learn to use in their own behalf. In Mexican culture, the toad is symbolic of the earth. The magic mushroom that grows in the earth is called a toadstool. Poisons from the mushroom and the toad, used jointly, are psychoactive and were hallucinogens used by the shaman to achieve enlightenment.[15] In European mythology, the toad's head was believed to contain a stone, pearl, or carbuncle that was considered alexipharmic (an antidote against poison or infection). It was called the toad's stone, or bufonite, and was believed to change color when its wearer was poisoned.[16]

The toad plays an important role in the imagery associated with Renaissance alchemy, which is a mine of information about the way psyche transforms.[17] For example, one famous illustration shows an eagle flying through the air, but connected to the earth by a chain linked to a toad, which crawls in the mud.[18] This image is part of the wisdom that one finds in alchemy, in which spiritual life and inspiration must be connected to the earthly reality, while earthly experience must be sublimated upward into spiritual reality. The symbolic attribute of the toad is also linked to its sucking and poisonous quality. In that context, the very primitive drives often attributed to early infant life — of violent attack and devouring needs at the breast — are attributed to the toad and seen in imagery of the toad sucking at the breast. The alchemical wisdom here infers that re-experiencing such drives and impulses has a healing quality.[19]

Precisely because of all its negative connotations — poisonous ones at that — the toad is often depicted as the starting point of spiritual improvement or transformation (as it is in the "Ripley Scrowle," a sixteenth-century depiction of alchemical processes).[20] The implication is that in accepting and gaining compassion for our most venomous selves — the parts of ourselves that poison relationships, undermine health, and enviously destroy — we find a new foundation for our being and a remarkable source of strength. It is not easy to become cognizant of our primitive desires, and doing so while neither rejecting them nor acting them out can push a person to his or her limit of courage. However, suffering such a process is the way one's most poisonous, reprehensible nature becomes inner strength and, as in the case of the toad in alchemy, a source of healing.

Such possible symbolic significance of the toad would have to be taken into account if someone dreamed of a toad. While the more mundane meaning of "being a toad" can represent feelings of inferiority and becoming a sycophant, the deeper meaning can represent the need to confront the obscure and hidden side of one's poisonous nature, such as tendencies toward verbally destructive rage and envy. With the toad symbolism also comes the powerful potential for such drives and impulses to gain a more revitalizing and renewing symbolic quality, as seen in a capacity to stabilize imaginative flight and boundless spiritual potential.

Notes
[1] Whitfield 1984, 478.
[2] Grzimek 1984, 5: 430.
[3] Pfeffer 1989, 97-99.
[4] Grzimek 1984, 5: 360-65.
[5] Grzimek 1984, 5: 419-21.
[6] Whitfield 1984, 478.
[7] Grzimek 1984, 5: 430.
[8] Downer 1989, 61.
[9] Grzimek 1984, 5: 359.
[10] von Franz 1975b, 53-55.
[11] Becker 1994, 302-03.
[12] von Franz 1975b, 53-55.
[13] Becker 1994, 302-03.
[14] Cooper 1992, 228.
[15] Ibid.
[16] de Gubernatis 1968, 2: 384.
[17] Jung 1977, 12: 403, 406.
[18] Fabricius 1989, 55 Figure 85.
[19] Fabricius 1989, 56-58.
[20] Jung 1977, 12: 433 note.

TOAD
Order: Anura.
Size: The common garden toad is 7-13 centimeters (3-5 inches) long, although the larger females may grow to a length of 18 centimeters (7 inches). The giant toad is 10-24 centimeters long (4-9 inches).
Weight: The female Puerto Rican crested toad weighs 90 grams (3.5-5.25 ounces) and the male weighs 50 grams (1.75 ounces). The giant toad can weigh over 1 kilogram (2.5-3 pounds).
Incubation: Eggs can hatch into tadpoles in 3 days.
Longevity: Toads can live for at least 15 years in captivity, and have been observed to breed for at least 5 years in the wild.
Distribution: Over most of the world, except in the far north, Madagascar and Polynesia.
Habitat: Mainly terrestrial, though they breed in water.

Turkey

The turkey is fondly hailed as the dinner "guest" of honor on Thanksgiving Day, the annual holiday feast that celebrates the harvest and other blessings of the past year. To celebrate the success of their arduous transatlantic journey and the establishment of a new colony in Massachusetts in 1620, the English Pilgrim settlers gratefully shared the wild turkey with the Native Americans who greeted and assisted them. This large bird, with a bare head of red and blue wattles and fleshy skin hanging from the throat, has a tail of eighteen feathers that present a dramatic "sunburst" effect when displayed. It was probably first domesticated by the pre-Columbian Indians of Mexico. In 1519 the wild turkey was introduced to Spain and subsequently spread throughout Europe. The English knew the turkey by 1541, and they re-introduced European-bred stocks back into North America in the seventeenth century.[2]

Two basic varieties of wild turkey are native to North America: the common turkey and the oscellated turkey.[3] The common turkey is generally dark with iridescent green and bronze feathers. Males have a naked head, normally bright red but changing to white and blue when the birds are excited. They have wattled chins and a fleshy growth pendant from the forehead called a snood. The oscellated turkey, never domesticated, has a blue head with reddish yellow bumps and a yellow-tipped knob on the crown, as well as long wattles. It has brightly tipped feathers. Both species nest on the ground and forage there by day for vegetable bits, insects, and small animals; at night they roost in trees. Capable of flying for short distances (1 kilometer, 0.6 miles or more if necessary), they nevertheless prefer to walk.[4]

Males (or toms) flock together and remain apart from the females except at mating time in the spring, when a dominant male will stage an elaborate courtship ritual at the old strutting grounds.[5] His wattles swell up and change color; he will puff up his body feathers to appear larger than he really is, fan out his impressive tail, rattle his wings against the ground, and prance about, huffing and rumbling, to attract the notice of sexually mature females. Most of these hens will mate promiscuously at this time, then spend the rest of the year ignoring the toms altogether. On their own, the hens will then hatch and raise their young, many of which are lost to predation by raccoons and possums, snakes, hawks, foxes, coyotes, and even stray dogs.[6]

Turkeys are truly American birds, first domesticated by the Aztecs and Mayans more than five centuries ago. Their numbers have diminished drastically, mostly because of hunting and loss of habitat, although lately they have been making a small comeback.[7] The turkey figures significantly in Native American mythology. Sometimes called the Earth Eagle, it is closely associated with spirituality and the abundance of the Earth Mother. As with the American bison, nearly every part of the turkey was put to use: the flesh for food, feathers for decoration, bones for small implements and whistles. Turkeys appear in Native American creation tales, teaching humans to raise corn and warding off evil spirits; Indian sorcerers were said to be able to shape-change into turkeys in order to roam about other villages.[8] In the language of some tribes, turkey translates as "give-away," and in their lore it embodied a much-respected spirit of self-sacrifice and altruism.[9]

Because of its preeminent size among table-fowl, the turkey is served primarily on festive occasions when many will dine together. As a result, its primary symbolic significance relates to abundance, specifically the bounty of the earth. But because of its strutting displays, the male can also represent vanity, arrogance, pride, and aggressiveness. Its awkward gait and gobbling sound, its stupidity (legendary in the case of domestic birds), may have also contributed to the use of its name as a derisive appellation.

Thus, to dream of a turkey (as with any animal) can have different, sometimes opposing symbolic meanings. On the one hand, this bird symbolizes the bounty of life, and the dream may point out that this bounty is actually present in the dreamer's life, even while the individual might be timid and withdrawn, cut off from any sense of entitlement and nurturing, believing that nothing is really coming to him or her and that he or she is undeserving. Accordingly, the dreamer might consider whether he or she is behaving in a bountiful way, is sufficiently nurturing and caring toward people, or is appreciative of the importance of personal sacrifice and renewal. On the other hand, to dream of a turkey could necessitate an understanding of the colloquial meaning of being a "turkey," that is, acting in some stupid, senseless, awkward, or pointless way in one's life. The turkey's ritual of fanning its magnificent feathers in courtship signifies exhibitionism, especially of a sexual nature, and a turkey image could represent an undeveloped exhibitionistic side of the dreamer's personality that needs to unfold, be admired, and grow into positive ambition. Thus, just as the turkey's richness and generosity gives us a bodily feast at the Thanksgiving festival, it has the same abundance and largesse of meaning when it visits us in our dreams.

Notes
[1] Grzimek 1984, 8: 19.
[2] "Fowl." *Encyclopedia Britannica*, 1997.
[3] Grzimek 1984, 8: 25.
[4] Grzimek 1984, 8: 19, 25, 29.
[5] Grzimek 1984, 8: 25.
[6] Brody 1997, F6.
[7] Andrews 1993, 200.
[8] Andrews 1993, 199-220.
[9] Cooper 1992, 234; Sams and Carson 1988, 161.

TURKEY
Family: Phasianidae.
Subfamily: Meleagrididae.
Size: 90-120 centimeters (3-4 feet).
Weight: 3-9 kilograms (6.5-20 pounds); up to 18 kilograms (40 pounds) in some domesticated forms.
Wingspan: 120-150 centimeters (4-5 feet).
Incubation: 28 days.
Longevity: Up to 12 years.
Distribution: Common turkey from eastern United States to Mexico; oscellated turkey from Yucatan to Guatemala.
Habitat: Both the common and the oscellated turkeys are forest dwellers, but prefer woods with clearings to dense ones.

Turtle/Tortoise

Wondrously self-contained, ponderously slow and proverbially steady, the armored reptiles belonging to the order Chelonia include 230 known species[1] of turtles and tortoises. The name "turtle" is an English corruption of the same root from which "tortoise" comes, but it is now sometimes used to distinguish chelonian species that, if not actually aquatic in habit, are generally found in and around the water, be it ocean, bay, lake, stream, pond, or swamp.[2] In contrast, the name "tortoise" is generally reserved for land-bound species.

Turtles and tortoises have broad, compact trunks that are entirely enclosed in a shell; the bottom part is a flat breastplate or "plastron," and the dome-shaped "carapace" protects the back of the reptile.[3] The plastron and carapace are actually skeletal modifications of the ribs and vertebrae.[4] As a result, the turtle cannot shed or abandon its home.[5] Turtles have a unique arrangement of lung muscles that allows the lungs to be filled when they relax and emptied when they are contracted. The animal can also move air from one part of the lungs to another, allowing them to function as swim bladders do for fish, that is, to shift the center of buoyancy at will.[6]

Chelonian brains are not large, but they are well developed, especially with regard to the sensorium. They have excellent senses of smell and sight, although hearing is questionable. Moveable lids protect the eyes, and retinas are particularly well adapted for seeing in low contrast situations. They are essentially mute, except for certain large tortoise males (the testudonids), which are given to hoarse vocalizations when copulating.[7] Sea turtles exhibit extraordinary capacities for memory and migration, unerringly navigating a thousand miles or more to particular mass nesting sites. At least three species, the green, the leatherback, and the loggerhead turtles, are able to retain their bearings primarily by observing wave motion. Loggerheads are also thought to use the earth's magnetic field to maintain their direction. Nesting cycles are rarely annual, and the specific mechanism by which individual turtles synchronize their migrations remains a mystery.[8]

Courtship can last for several hours and is usually prolonged and strenuous — at least on the part of the male. Copulation itself also seems to be a matter of substantial excitement and exertion by the male, matched by equally substantial indifference on the part of the imperturbable female.[9] All chelonians are oviparous. Neither the eggs (which are generally deposited on land and covered with soil) nor the hatchlings are the objects of any parental concern. The latter must struggle to the surface of the ground, a process often possible only through their combined efforts. In the case of sea turtles, the young must then elude predators and make their way to the water.[10]

Generally omnivorous, chelonians consume insects, plants, fish, amphibians, and even ground-nesting birds and small mammals when they can get them.[11] Lacking teeth, they grasp their food with their sharp beaks, tearing off pieces that they then swallow whole.[12] Like some birds, most chelonians swallow small stones that remain in the stomach and aid them in grinding and digesting food.[13] As many cold-blooded animals, they have a rather slow metabolism and are critically sensitive to seasonal temperature fluctuations; variations beyond specific thresholds usually trigger a period of dormancy,[14] perhaps accounting for their famous longevity.

The cultural interpretations of the turtle/tortoise vary greatly. In ancient Egypt, the tortoise-god Apesh was associated with the powers of darkness and evil. The *Book of the Dead* implies that the turtle is an enemy of Ra, the sun god.[15] The Sumerians considered the turtle sacred to the sea god Ea-Oannes.[16] Christian writers made the mud turtle a symbol of all that is earthbound and unspiritual.[17]

In many parts of the world, including Asia, the domed shell of the turtle was a symbol of the vault of heaven and the flat plastron a symbol of the earth.[18] Slow-moving, steady, and armored as it is — seemingly impervious to attack — the turtle appears a very model of settled, universal order.[19] The Chinese traditionally see the tortoise as a supporter of the world, its four feet being the four corners of the earth. Turtle shells were used in divination and the animal itself was thought to have oracular powers. Called the Black Warrior, the tortoise is a symbol of strength, endurance, and longevity.[20] In Mongolian myths, the central mountain of the universe is carried on the back of a golden turtle.[21]

Like most animals that produce large numbers of offspring, the turtle is associated with fertility, and, probably because of this association, it is sacred to the Greek goddess Aphrodite. Its protruberant head and neck are often interpreted in phallic terms as well. Its longevity makes it a paragon of enduring vitality.[22] To Africans, the tortoise is generally a symbol of wisdom, skill, and power, often depicted as a trickster figure, sometimes benevolent, sometimes vengeful;[23] in Nigeria, it is a symbol of the female sex organs and sexuality.[24] The animistic notion that the qualities of a creature eaten are passed on to those who eat it keeps some African men from eating tortoise, lest they lose their speed at running.[25]

Because it is literally self-contained, the turtle has often been seen as a symbol of focus and meditation.[26] In Hindu tradition, the world rests on the back of an elephant, a male, solar symbol, which in turn stands upon a tortoise, in this case a feminine, lunar symbol. Thus, the two together represent the creative principle. In the *Vedas,* the holy text of Hinduism, the mythological tortoise is identified with Prajapati, the Lord and creator of creatures. This turtle is also the second avatar of Vishnu, one of the principal Hindu deities. In Buddhist tradition, the tortoise was also one of the early incarnations of the Buddha.[27]

Echoing many other myths, the Iroquois of North America believe that they are descended from a turtle that rid itself of its shell, and that the earth sits on the back of the Great Turtle. Other Native American tribes see the turtle as a symbol of endurance and persistence[28] (recalling Aesop's fable in which the tortoise's patience allows it to best the hare in a race). Many tribes have turtle clans, and in many tales, the turtle appears as a trickster figure or cultural hero. Several tribes found significance in the patterns on the turtle's back, which in some species number thirteen. Since that matches the number of lunar cycles in a year, the turtle, as in the Far East, was associated with feminine energies in general.[29]

In many cultures, the earth itself was represented by the turtle/tortoise, so in metaphysical terms it may certainly be seen as symbolizing the very foundation and ground of being. Psychologically, the tortoise represents security, solid grounding, and support. It is seen as slow, steady, and strong, wise with age, protective, and unshakable. This feeling of being supported and protected is a powerfully compelling state which in Judeo-Christian terms is attributed to a connection with a personal god. Some psychological theories see in the turtle a connection with the self, the unity of the personality as a whole; in Eastern religions, the turtle is thought to be the balance of opposing principles, such as heaven and earth. Conversely, the armored turtle can also represent a tendency toward withdrawal, a pulling in of limbs, as it were, to minimize exposure to a world that may feel hostile or threatening. This tendency can be either positive or negative: withdrawal can be either isolating and deadening or it can be vitally self-protective and, in its creative, shielding, active aspect, a form of introversion.

If a turtle image were to appear in a dream, the dreamer might be dealing with deep primary elements in his or her being. It is important to take into consideration the actions of the turtle/tortoise and to determine whether the animal was predominantly in the water (turtle) or on land (tortoise). The former may be more relevant to the dreamer's relation to his or her unconscious, which is usually symbolized by water, while the latter might have more connection to the dreamer's groundedness. While the possible interpretations of withdrawal and hiding need to be taken into account, the turtle/tortoise represents the very fundamental kind of protection and psychological foundation that is central to the development of the nascent self. In actual development, this role of the turtle/tortoise is initially taken by the parents, who strengthen and sustain the child emotionally in its early years, as the very earth and ground. Many people, however, have not experienced that support strongly enough in life, and dreams of a turtle/tortoise can represent the innate capacity of hidden reserves and strengths to emerge at any time and be creatively nurturing for the dreamer.

Notes

[1] Whitfield 1984, 402.
[2] Grzimek 1984, 6: 80.
[3] Andrews 1993, 363.
[4] Whitfield 1984, 402-04.
[5] Andrews 1993, 365.
[6] Grzimek 1984, 6: 78.
[7] Grzimek 1984, 6: 79-80.
[8] "The Secret Behind Feats of Sea Turtle." *The New York Times* (Science Watch) 12 June 1990: C6
[9] Grzimek 1984, 6: 80-81.
[10] Grzimek 1984, 6: 81-83.
[11] Andrews 1993, 365.
[12] Whitfield 1984, 402.
[13] Grzimek 1984, 6: 78.
[14] Andrews 1993, 365.
[15] Budge 1969, 2: 376.
[16] Cooper 1992, 231.
[17] Biedermann 1994, 358.
[18] Andrews 1993, 364.
[19] Biedermann 1994, 358.
[20] Cooper 1992, 229.
[21] Becker 1994, 311.
[22] Jobes 1962, 2: 1590.
[23] Cooper 1992, 229.
[24] Andrews 1993, 364.
[25] Frazier 1979, 574.
[26] Becker 1994, 311.
[27] Cooper 1992, 229.
[28] Waldman 1994, 245.
[29] Cooper 1992, 230.

TURTLE/TORTOISE

Order: Chelonia.

Size: Turtle/tortoise size is expressed as a straight-line distance from the anterior to the posterior edge of the shell. One of the smallest species is the bog turtle, with a length of barely 11 centimeters (4 inches), while some of the giant tortoises of the Galapagos have shells up to 110 centimeters (44 inches) long.

Weight: Giant tortoise weighs 275–320 kilograms (600–700 pounds); green turtle weighs 365–410 kilograms (800–900 pounds).

Incubation: Freshwater tortoise or turtle eggs can take 3 or 4 months. Incubation is dependent entirely upon the warmth of the soil.

Longevity: Only a few turtles live longer than 100 years. The black Seychelles tortoise can have longevity of 152 years; the Galapagos tortoise may have a life span of over 100 years. The snapping turtle's maximum life span is 62 years.

Distribution: Tortoises are found in North America, Europe, Asia, Africa, and Madagascar. Turtles are found worldwide, usually in warm seas.

Habitat: Turtles are mainly aquatic, tortoises mainly terrestrial.

Vulture

The French Legionnaire in the tattered remnants of a uniform has long since abandoned his last empty canteen of water, and now as he staggers across the trackless desert he squints up at the merciless sun and sees the vultures — massive, dark, and repulsive looking. They are circling, circling, and waiting. Thus has popular culture made of this large, carrion-eating bird a clichéd emblem of death.

Large birds with an impressive wingspan[1] and the raptor's hooked beak, most vultures sport a collar of downy or un-barbed feathers that contrast with the nakedness of the neck and head. The naked parts are generally brightly colored and often, in the case of the males, bedecked with fleshy wattles, crests, or warts.[2] Part of the order Falconiformes, which includes raptors such as the falcon, hawk, eagle, and osprey, vultures are divided into physiologically distinct New World and Old World types. Old World vultures rely exclusively on their keen vision to spot food, and have feet ideally adapted for grasping.[3] New World vultures, including the king vulture, the turkey vulture, and the Andean condor, have a keen sense of smell[4] that allows them to hunt in wooded habitats where carrion is less likely to be visible from the air; they have feet better adapted for perching than grasping. New World vultures are nearly voiceless, since they lack a syrinx, the avian equivalent of vocal chords.[5]

Vultures are almost exclusively carrion eaters, and they have evolved a digestive system that allows them to consume amounts and types of bacteria that easily kill other creatures. Although often denigrated as "filthy creatures," scavengers like the vulture serve a crucial function in the natural ecology, removing corpses that are potential sources of infection. Their distinctively naked heads and necks allow them to remain relatively clean in spite of poking their heads into the cavities of rotting carcasses, and vultures are quite fastidious, bathing whenever possible.[6] These birds are persistent and aggressive about claiming food, and some species show a fair amount of intelligent initiative as well. The honey buzzard digs out wasps' nests,[7] and the Egyptian vulture has been

V

known to pick up a rock in its beak to stave in the thick shell of an ostrich egg.[8] Aggressive but rarely injurious behavior among vultures establishes generally respected rights of precedence when feeding, and they will occasionally roost in small groups at night. In Africa, a few species nest in colonies of nearly a thousand, but for the most part, vultures are not particularly social.[9]

In Western society, the vulture provokes a fair amount of disgust; we call those who prey upon the weakness or misfortunes of others vultures, and a culture vulture is someone who voraciously and indiscriminately consumes the offerings of "high culture." Perhaps because the vulture is so closely connected to death, and yet continues to live even amidst the toxins it absorbs, it is naturally associated with life, birth, and power.

Indeed, the vulture has figured prominently in the pantheons and belief systems of many prior cultures. For example, in ancient Egypt, the queen wore a headdress depicting a vulture. The vulture was a symbol of several goddesses, including Nekhebet, who was associated with childbirth,[10] the guardian of Upper Egypt, and especially its head of state. Maat, the Egyptian goddess of truth, is often depicted carrying the feather of a vulture.[11] In Greek mythology Zeus could take the shape of a vulture, and the bird was sacred to Apollo as well. In the *Iliad* (VII, 59) Apollo and Athena, as vultures, perch in a tree and watch the carnage below. Not surprisingly, the vulture was sacred to Mars, the Roman god of war, and to kill one was forbidden.[12] Among the Mayan people, as elsewhere, the vulture was a symbol of death.

The dark side of the Great Mother is sometimes called the "Terrible Mother," and in her guise as bird of the dead, vulture or raven, she is also a goddess of death.[13] The "vulture" or killer aspect of the Goddess is frightening indeed, but the symbols associated with death are also interwoven with those promoting renewal.[14] Just as its carrion-eating ways have widely identified the vulture with death, so its ability to survive the poisons that surround it links the vulture to the possibility of purification and regeneration. A black vulture, Jung tells us, was once used to represent the dark side of the Holy Ghost.[15] Certain African people focused on the transformative aspect of the vulture's conversion of carrion to life energy, imagining it as a kind of avian alchemist, converting dross to gold.[16] To the Pueblo Indians, the vulture played an important part in purification medicine. Its power was invoked to restore harmony that had been broken, or to bring participants in various ceremonies of mediumship and shape-shifting back to themselves, severing connection with the dead, removing charms, and in a sense "resetting" reality.[17]

To dream of a vulture can suggest that some element of our psyche is dying, and that the ability exists to use that death in a creative manner, without being overwhelmed by its toxic qualities, such as depression or resentment. The vulture can thus symbolize the capacity for creative renewal if the dreamer faces this death and allows old, valueless structures and attitudes to die. Consequently, the vulture is a very hopeful symbol, yet many people are terrified of it. When something dies, no matter how worthless and insignificant it has become, they are swallowed by loss and grief. The vulture would represent the human capacity to avoid being consumed these feelings.

Notes
[1] Heintzelman 1979, 12.
[2] Grzimek 1984, 7: 336.
[3] Grzimek 1984, 7: 337.
[4] Grzimek 1984, 7: 347.
[5] "Vultures." *Encyclopedia Britannica CD*, 1997.
[6] Whitfield 1984, 216; Andrews 1993, 204.
[7] Grzimek 1984, 7: 352.
[8] Attenborough 1990, 70.
[9] Perrins and Middleton 1989, 124-25.
[10] Biedermann 1994, 370.
[11] Andrews 1993, 202.
[12] Biedermann 1994, 370.
[13] Neumann 1963, 164.
[14] Gimbutas 1989, 316.
[15] Jung 1976, 2: 299.
[16] Becker 1994, 321.
[17] Andrews 1993, 202.

VULTURE
Family: Cathartidae (New World vultures).
Size: Length 60–120 centimeters (23.5–47 inches). The California condor, one of the largest and heaviest birds in the world, has a length of 114–140 centimeters (45–55 inches).
Wingspan: California condor spans about 290 centimeters (9.5 feet).
Weight: 0.9–14 kilograms (1–31 pounds). California condor can weigh over 11 kilograms (25 pounds).
Incubation: 5–8 weeks depending on species.
Distribution: From southern Canada to the tip of South America.
Habitat: Mainly in open habitats, but also in forests. The habitat of the California condor can also be mountainous.

VULTURE
Family: Aegypiinae (Old World vultures).
Size: European black vulture has a length of up to 103 centimeters (40 inches).
Wingspan: European vulture measures 265-287 centimeters (8.5-9.5 feet).
Weight: 3-14 kilograms (17.5-30 pounds).
Incubation: 5-8 weeks depending on species.
Longevity: Life span of the griffon vulture is 40 years.
Distribution: Europe, Asia, and Africa.
Habitat: High plains and mountainous regions.

Wasp

The swarming, stinging, pinch-waisted wasp, often metaphorically the avenger of slights both intended and accidental, is the unsweetened cousin of its fellow hymenopteran, the bee. The name "wasp" is used for a wide range of what are called aculeate, or sting-bearing hymen-opterans, nearly seventy-five thou-sand species.[1]

These are so varied morphologically and behaviorally that generalizations about them are not easily made. Nevertheless, the members of the superfamily vespoidea, including hornets, are commonly called wasps. They are most easily recognizable by their wings, which are folded longitudinally at rest and so appear thinner than those of bees.

Generally social,[2] although less so than bees, some wasps (of the subfamily Pilistenae) build open combs of a single layer, while others (of the subfamily Vespinae) build their combs in stacked ranks and cover the whole with a paper-like shell. Like bees, social wasps have a caste system, with a large queen sup-ported by infertile female workers[3] and a few good males. Wasps, too, gather nectar from flowers and are therefore also responsible for a significant amount of pollination, but some also pierce the skins of ripening fruit for the sweet juices, causing premature rotting. Although they are largely vegetarian, they do attack sizeable numbers of insects, killing some and merely paralyzing others, but in either case feeding them to their larvae. Paralyzed victims are often placed in proximity to wasp eggs (or vice versa) to ensure a supply of fresh food when the larvae hatch.[4] This predation may be considered helpful in the case of insects that are thought of as pests, but bees and spiders are also among the victims.

The complexity of wasp architecture closely reflects the degree of special-ization developed by a particular species — the two naturally evolving together, even as they do in human society.[5] Like bees, wasps make nests filled with combs comprising a number of hexagonal cells, but where bees build with wax, wasps build with paper, which they make by chewing wood into a pulp. The elaborate

W

hives require not only building skills, but also cooperation in maintaining the temperature within an impressive half-degree of tolerance. Remarkably, heating is accomplished by what amounts to isometric exercises as workers generate heat from extra metabolic activity; they also carry water into the hive and fan it with their wings to cool by evaporation.[6]

Most non-vespinoid wasps lead solitary lives, although some are social to varying degrees. Long-legged spider wasps prey only on spiders. Some are brood parasites of other wasps, sneaking their eggs into alien brood cells. The hatchlings will consume the rightful occupants and, in some instances, continue to be nourished and maintained by the alien workers.[7] The sting of the wasp originally evolved from the structure of the ovipositor, a tube-like extension of the abdomen through which the female deposits her eggs.[8] In some species, distinctive black and bright yellow stripes evolved as a kind of visual warning to birds and other potential predators of the potency of that sting.[9]

The wasp is generally regarded unfavorably, suffering especially in comparison with the bee, which is considered a benevolent creature since it provides people with the sweetness of honey. With nothing similar to offer, the wasp is remembered primarily for its sting, although it rarely stings people other than defensively.[10] This reality did not keep Dante from taking a certain waspish delight in imagining these insects as instruments of purgatorial torment for the morally indifferent.[11] Warriors of tribes in French Guyana purposely endure the stings of wasps to make themselves fiercer in battle.[12] Cupid is the "wasp-headed" son of Venus, because of the sting of his arrows.[13] In the Zoroastrian tradition, wasps are associated with Ahriman, the evil one, and an old Polish saying is that God created bees, while the Devil made wasps.

Not everyone sees wasps in a negative light. Socrates gives them a measure of praise for living in harmonious communities,[14] and a Mongolian people, the Buriats, make the wasp a cultural hero, telling tales of how, as a wasp, a shaman stung the chief god and made him release the soul of the people.[15]

That something as small and innocuous-looking as a wasp can cause such agony makes the sting a shock, a surprise, and therefore a lesson. Not lethal, but still very painful, it can feel like a chastisement, a goad, or a painful reminder that something is amiss in the psyche.

Generally, wasp imagery in dreams represents ideas that have a piercing or tormenting quality, either directed at one's self, like the smarting pain of guilt or shame, or at others, like the verbal aggression of sarcasm (literally "flesh-biting") or unwarranted criticism. The sting of the wasp can also be a painful reminder to step out of a lethargic and complacent state, a wake-up call to help create new attitudes toward qualities that might push the conscious personality beyond its safety net. Impulses represented by the wasp that are "out of character" with one's usual experiences can suggest the operation of a larger power — spiritual or divine when the impulse is sympathetic, infernal or diabolical when it is pathological.

Notes
[1] Grzimek 1984, 2: 421, 435, 436.
[2] Grzimek 1984, 2: 422.
[3] Slater 1987, 118.
[4] "Wasp." *Compton's Interactive Encyclopedia*, 1997.
[5] Slater 1987, 42.
[6] Attenborough 1990, 153.
[7] Slater 1987, 121.
[8] Grzimek 1984, 2: 421.
[9] Slater 1987, 62.
[10] "Wasp." *Compton's Interactive Encyclopedia*, 1997.
[11] de Vries 1976, 493.
[12] Jobes 1962, 2: 1666.
[13] de Vries 1976, 493.
[14] Jobes 1962, 2: 1666.
[15] Cooper 1992, 244.

WASP

Infraorder: Aculeata (with various families).

Size: 0.17–50 millimeters (0.08–2 inches) long.

Weight: Less than one gram.

Incubation: 300 eggs laid per day. Hatching in 4–6 days. Adults emerge 2–3 weeks after pupation.

Longevity: Social wasps: workers (sterile females) have an average lifespan of 12–22 days; queens (fertile females) have an average lifespan of 12 months.

Distribution: On all continents except Antarctica.

Weasel

Lithe and long, small but vicious, weasels belong to the Mustelidae family, which includes the polecat, ferret, mink, marten, otter, and ermine.[1] They are extraordinarily fast and agile. One variety, called the least weasel, enjoys the distinction of being the world's smallest carnivore.[2]

Weasels are ideally adapted for hunting small creatures in tight quarters. They live and hunt in underground tunnels, often dug by the rodents that are their prey, but in any case not of their own making, since they do not dig. These tunnels are used as shelters from the elements and from enemies, which include foxes, wild cats, feral cats, martens, snakes, and raptors such as owls and hawks. In motion, the weasels' flexibility and speed makes them appear almost fluid, and they can dive through openings hardly bigger than their heads. Although they are short of leg, they are long of neck, which allows them to carry off their prey in their mouths without tripping on the carcass; indeed, their habit is to kill and stash away enough food for the day before eating any of it.[3] Not being an accomplished climber or swimmer, the weasel is usually not found around water.[4]

All weasels are solitary, silent stalkers.[5] Requiring a third to half their body weight in food daily, they hunt with restless energy and fierce concentration, looking primarily for small rodents, birds, and lizards; they are also partial to eggs.[6] Weasels are highly adaptable, bold, and tenacious enough to prey successfully on animals larger than themselves. Their usual technique is to bite their victims' neck, severing the spinal cord, or else to hang on until the animal bleeds to death. Indeed, their ferocity is proverbial, and mothers that feel their young threatened have even been known to attack humans.[7]

Weasels have excellent hearing, particularly in the lower registers, and their eyesight is good in both bright and dim light. Like all mustelids, they communicate by scent-marking, advertising the boundaries of their home ranges by secreting a powerfully noisome oil or musk from a pair of glands under the tail.[8] Females avoid males during most of the year, rejecting unwanted suitors with displays of ferocious aggression and accepting amorous advances only when they are in full estrus, a period of two to three days each year. Partners may copulate several times over that period, or the female may mate promiscuously. Pregnant females will appropriate a ready-made nest (forcefully if necessary), collect an adequate cache of food and settle in for the birth.[9] Litters of three to eight are born in April or May.[10] Males take no part in nesting or rearing the young.

In China, the weasel was one of the five animals (along with the snake, fox, hedgehog, and rat) believed to lie in wait on the road and bewitch the unwary who trod upon them. The weasel was sacred in Egypt and said to be worshipped in Grecian Thebes as well.[11] The Roman writer Pliny stated that the weasel eats a bitter-leafed medicinal herb called *rue* to make itself immune to snakebite.[12] In Native American tradition, the weasel symbolizes stealth, energy, and ingenuity; like other underground dwellers, it is believed to hear everything that is said and to know all secrets, seeing beneath the surface of things.[13] Some stories say that Weasel foretold the coming of Europeans and the disasters that would accompany them.[14]

Although small, the weasel has a number of remarkable attributes, as well as an equally remarkable number of projected qualities, some of them clearly fanciful. The *Physiologus* regards it as a dirty animal that has sexual intercourse through its snout and gives birth through its ears.[15] Other sources have it the other way round. Aristotle, Plutarch, and Ovid repeat the false report that the weasel conceives through the ear and gives birth through the mouth.[16] Either way, it seems that what is being addressed is a correspondence between the creative functions of ear and mouth — that is, between hearing and speaking — which may refer to the reciprocal relationship between initiate (hearer) and master (speaker), or simply to the notion of wisdom gained and lost.

Other symbolic qualities of the weasel are astutely based on more accurate observation of the animal's actual nature. The ancients did note the care that mother weasels lavish on their young, frequently moving them to keep them safe from predators. Some saw this movement as inconstancy, but others considered it a symbol of maternal care and vigilance. For its service as a catcher of mice and rats, which were thought of as vices in Christian symbolism,[17] the weasel was at times considered benign. However, it was far more widely seen as aggressive, vicious, destructive, even cruel and cunning, and since all these qualities were ascribed to witches, the weasel came to be thought of as a witch's animal. Living underground, rarely seen in daylight, it catches the projections of dark, negative, and feminine sides of both men and women. Thus, it can symbolize destructive impulses that are petty and vicious, unconscious, and well-hidden — passive-aggressive impulses, envy, and unconscious antipathies of every sort.

To speak of "weaseling" out of a sticky situation not only refers to the weasel's supple agility, but also suggests its slyness, feistiness, and readiness to attack. Where social convention seems to call for honesty, integrity, and openness, the "weasely" person offers lies and bluster, cunning, trickery, or deceit. Bloodily aggressive, even for a predator, it represents vicious qualities, primitive cravings, and human impulses that are gratuitously cruel. The weasel itself is actually none of those things; it is simply preserving its own life as best it can, and so self-preservation is also a part of the weasel's symbolic significance.

If a person were to dream of a weasel, he or she might benefit by considering what it he or she was "weaseling out of." Or it might be appropriate to ask what cunning, aggressiveness, or fierceness might be required in his or her conscious life situation, possibly against some larger foe. The symbolism of the weasel as a "witch's animal" could help alert one to ways that dissociation, self-hypnosis, and unconsciousness, attributed to the witch, may hide such important psychic capacities and aggression from consciousness, turning these forces destructive rather than creative.

Notes

[1] Macdonald 1987, 110.
[2] Pfeffer 1989, 377-78.
[3] King 1989, 18.
[4] Pfeffer 1989, 378.
[5] Andrews 1993, 320.
[6] Pfeffer 1989, 377-78.
[7] Andrews 1993, 320-21.
[8] King 1989, 20-22, 118.
[9] King 1989, 127, 136-37.
[10] Burton 1981, 562.
[11] Cooper 1992, 103, 245.
[12] *Funk & Wagnalls Standard Dictionary*,1972, 1168.
[13] Andrews 1993, 320.
[14] Cooper 1992, 245.
[15] Curley 1979, 50.
[16] Charbonneau-Lassay 1991, 147-48.
[17] Charbonneau-Lassay 1991, 150.

WEASEL

Family: Mustelidae.

Size: Europe's smallest weasel is 16-23 centimeters (6 to 9 inches) long; tail length is 4-7 centimeters (1.5-3 inches). American male least weasel head-body length is 15-20 centimeters (6-8 inches); tail length is 3-4 centimeters (1-1.5 inches).

Weight: European weasel weighs 35-90 grams (1-3 ounces). American male least weasel weighs 30-70 grams (1.5-2.45 ounces).

Gestation: 35-45 days, extended to 337 days by delayed implantation in some species.

Longevity: Less than 1 year in European common weasel, perhaps more in other species.

Distribution: Widespread from the tropics to the Arctic, in the Americas, Eurasia, Africa, and was introduced in New Zealand.

Habitat: From forests to mountains, farmland, semi-desert, steppe, and tundra.

Whale

Approximately fifty to seventy million years ago, well after dinosaurs were extinct and mammals ruled the land, certain pig-sized, warm-blooded quadrupeds began to frequent shallow waters, feeding on the abundant plants and animals there.[1] In the fullness of time, their limbs evolved into fins, and they became what we know as cetaceans, or whales, a category that technically includes dolphins and porpoises. These creatures adapted so completely to their aquatic environment that, unlike seals and other aquatic mammals, they could no longer survive on land.[2] An evolutionary recidivist — returned to the sea that its mammal ancestors once left — the whale is the colossus of the deep, a living Leviathan whose immense size dwarfs all other creatures and boggles the human imagination, giving rise to profound legend and literature as perhaps no other creature has done.

There are two broad categories of whales. Toothed whales, which include sperm whales, feed primarily on squid and cuttlefish, as well as porpoises and dolphins.[3] The largest whale in this family is the killer whale *(Orcinus orca)*, a persistent object of popular fascination, fueled by exaggerated tales of its fierce inclinations and lethal power. Known by their distinctive towering dorsal fins and bold, black and white look, killer whales are formidable predators. With a highly developed social organization, they hunt cooperatively, shrewdly and efficiently. Having no natural enemies, they are fearless as well as curious and almost invariably friendly to humans, in the wild as well as in aquariums and marine theme park complexes.[4]

The second category is the baleen whale, which lacks teeth and instead has sieve-like plates of a flexible substance called "baleen." These plates sift or filter the tiny floating organisms, both plant and animal, called plankton, on which they feed.[5]

For centuries, these whales played a significant role in the economies of many countries and peoples. Whaling became a substantial industry as these giant animals were sought for the oil that was extracted from their blubber and for baleen, which was crucial to the production of ladies' corsets before the age of plastic. Whales are still taken for meat (used in dog food and cattle feed), glue, gelatin, fertilizer, vitamins, ivory, and ambergris for perfume. As a result, many species have been hunted to the point of extinction, including the magnificent blue whale.[6] The largest living creature in the world, the great blue whale weighs more than 13,600 kilograms (30,000 pounds or 15 tons) at maturity, nine times the size of an African elephant[7] and four times the estimated bulk of the largest dinosaurs of bygone ages. This huge size is only supportable because the whale is a sea creature.

Unlike fish, which breathe through gills, the whale is an air breather, forced to come to the surface in order to respire, which is done through a blowhole or nostril on the top of the head. The shape and size of the resulting spout, or "blow," varies distinctively from one species to another; some spouts can be as much as eight meters (twenty-five feet) high.[8] In the process of adapting to an aquatic existence, whales lost most of the fur that their land-dwelling forebears presumably had and developed instead a layer of insulating fat or blubber. As former land animals, they lack the mechanisms of other marine creatures for ridding their bodies of excess salt, and as a result they have developed exceptionally large kidneys. Compared to land animals, they have an unusually large fluctuation in blood pressure when diving and surfacing, which may partly explain their ability to dive as deeply as they do.[9]

Water is a much more efficient transmitter of sound waves than air, and whales take full advantage of this. They generally have excellent hearing and a wide variety of vocalizations, both within and beyond the range of human hearing.[10] The blue whale has an enormous larynx and huge lungs, and it can produce very low notes, giving them an immense intensity. Blasts of 188 decibels have been reported (artillery fire at close proximity has been recorded at 130 decibels). Toothed whales use sounds that they create in their skull cavities for echolocation — a kind of sonar that allows them to locate, recognize, and track their prey.[11]

Whales are migratory and highly social, traveling in herds that are known as pods or gams. They engage in rather extensive courtship prior to copulation, which itself is brief. Often they will swim belly to belly and in some cases breach spectacularly, rising straight into the air together. With the mother often attended by other members of the herd, young are born alive and (most unusually) tail first, then nursed on extraordinarily rich milk for up to a year.[12]

The massive and majestic whale has a dominant place in religious and mythical imagery. In Christian tradition, the jaw of the whale symbolizes the entry to hell.[13] In Norse lore, whales have magical powers and are said to carry witches on their backs. The Ainu people of Japan worship the whale as a mount of their chief sea god.[14]

Psychologically, the vast and limitless sea is the sovereign symbol of the unconscious. An immense, even majestic marine creature, the whale thereby comes to symbolize the awesome primordial power of water, and to be identified with the idea of regeneration. Also, although there is no documented instance of human beings ever being swallowed whole by whales, any animal large enough to do so is bound to inspire awe and fear. As a result, for ages the mythos of the whale has centered on the idea of engulfment. Jonah's ingestion and regurgitation is taken as a parable of death and rebirth, or death and deliverance. The writer of Matthew 12:40 makes it explicit: "For as Jonah was in the belly of the sea monster for three days and three nights, so will the Son of Man be in the heart of the earth for three days and three nights."[15]

The devouring quality projected onto the whale reflects the description of the "Terrible Mother," the voracious and consuming power that threatens the dissolution of the conscious personality and is depicted in many of the world's mythologies.[16] Overcoming this threat of annihilation is the common aim of the heroic quest and of various kinds of initiation rites, in which it is necessary to descend symbolically into the belly of the beast (or into the jaws of hell) before the possibility of new life or rebirth can be realized.[17]

In the wake of such a symbolic death, powers and abilities that have been deadened by disuse and repression can be strengthened or born anew. Where the entrapping, devouring quality of the unconscious, as symbolized by the whale, captures the creative energies of a society, the hero releases them. For example, the heroic, if misguided, figure of the whaler — a tiny speck afloat on the immense sea — faces down the Leviathan of the depths[18] in order to transform its awesome dark power to the rational uses of civilization, oil to light the lamps of reason, as it were, for all of humanity. Observers of the whale, especially Herman Melville in his novel *Moby Dick,* have been fascinated by the anatomical fact that the whale has eyes on widely separated parts of its head. Melville takes this characteristic to represent the spiritually portentous ability to regard opposite qualities simultaneously — a unifying process that is known to be the province of the self, which according to Jung "expresses the unity of the personality as a whole."[19] The conscious personality (ego) of the human being, on the other hand, is only able to regard one and then another state.[20] This remarkable combining quality of the self, projected onto the whale, is something that humans can learn to contact to gain a different kind of "sight." Such sight, different from normal, rational thinking, is the perception of opposites through the power of the imagination. It becomes a stimulus to a unique kind of consciousness, one that can contain opposites rather than identify with one side and repress the other.

Dreams of a whale are clearly very powerful. While representing a potentially devouring experience of the unconscious, the creative, renewing aspect of the symbol would still be effective. Generally, the dreamer would be facing the majesty of the organizing principle of the unconscious, the self. While there are many symbols of the self, when manifested by the whale it has a special grandeur — something so large in scale that the human being can never truly take it into his or her own personality, but which forever lives in him or her as an inspirational reality.

Notes

[1] Minasian, Balcomb III, and Foster 1984, 19.
[2] Grzimek 1984, 11: 457.
[3] Grzimek 1984, 11: 494.
[4] Grzimek 1984, 11: 519-22.
[5] "Baleen Whales." *Encyclopedia Britannica,* 1997.
[6] Grzimek 1984, 11: 469.
[7] "Whales." *Encyclopedia Britannica,* 1997.
[8] Grzimek 1984, 11: 458-59.
[9] Grzimek 1984, 11: 462-67.
[10] Grzimek 1984, 11: 513.
[11] Attenborough 1990, 251.
[12] Grzimek 1984, 11: 468-69.
[13] Biedermannn 1994, 378.
[14] Cooper 1992, 245-46.
[15] Biedermannn 1994, 378.
[16] Jung 1976, 5: 374.
[17] Jung 1977, 6: 444.
[18] Melville 1962, 320.
[19] Jung 1977, 6: 789.
[20] Edinger 1995, 80.

WHALE
Order: *Cetacea.*
Size: The blue whale (Balaenoptera musculus) may reach 21 meters (70 feet) in length.
Weight: The blue whale may weigh 23-13,600 kilograms (50-30,000 pounds); porpoises weigh more than 63 tons (64.4 tonnes).
Gestation: 9-17 months.
Longevity: Some species may live up to 100 years.
Distribution: Whales are found in northern waters.
Habitat: Seas and oceans.

Wolf

Shy of any human presence and crafty enough to avoid it, the wolf is the quintessential predator in the popular mind, red of fang and claw. Its howl, piercing a still, moonlit night in a vast, snowy wilderness, is heart-chilling — the very call of the wild. The largest member of the canine family, with superior tracking ability, the wolf is a formidable hunter, with powerful jaws, great strength, speed, endurance, and cunning to run down almost any prey.[1] For all the dread they inspire, wolves are the immediate ancestors of man's best friend and the first truly domesticated animal, the dog.[2] Wolves are found throughout the northern hemisphere in three more or less distinct species — the gray wolf (also called the timber wolf in North America), the smaller red wolf, and the coyote — although all three can and do interbreed successfully. The gray wolf can vary from nearly solid black to many variegated shades of gray.

An extended family of wolves will live and hunt as a pack with a well-defined hierarchy, a style of life that requires a division of labor and a substantial level of communication.[3] The alpha male and alpha female often mate for life. In general, only dominant males get to breed with receptive females, most often in late winter. Litters average six to eight cubs, and all members of the pack show them care, affection and tolerance.[4] In winter or times of scarcity, smaller packs may combine into groups of as many as thirty. Challenges to hierarchical authority are met aggressively, but submissive gestures generally prevent antagonistic encounters from developing into fatal incidents. In most cases, the loser is not killed but, like older wolves in general, is driven out of the pack to live the rest of its life as a "loner."[5]

The feast-or-famine nature of the wolf's existence as a predator makes it a voracious eater when meat is available.[6] More or less always hungry, a single animal may consume as much as twenty-two pounds of meat in a single day, and then may go four days without feeding again.[7] With great stamina, wolves spend an average of eight to ten hours a day on the move, mostly during the twilight hours.[8] The wolf howls to locate and reassure scattered members of the pack, to warn off rival packs, and sometimes, it may seem to the poetically inclined, in a soulful proclamation of the loneliness of existence.[9] The wolf is a highly intelligent and social animal that uses postures, vocalizations, scent markings, facial expressions, and tail positions to convey subtle nuances of mood and meaning. The wolf's sense of hearing and smell are well developed.[10]

The wolf looms large in every medium of human storytelling: fairy tales, legends, opera, film, literature, nursery rhymes, songs, and even plays. Although few children in the Western world have actually seen a wolf, stories like *Peter and the Wolf, The Wolf in Sheep's Clothing,* and *The Three Little Pigs* have taught them to be frightened of the beast. For centuries the wolf has captured the human imagination in contradictory ways — as a malevolent, ravening killing machine, the essence of what is meant by "bestial," and at the same time as a cunning, intelligent creature whose complicated, hierarchical social structures recall and prefigure our own. Romulus and Remus, the mythical founders of Rome, were suckled by a she-wolf at what some consider to be the very outset of Western civilization, and many enduring legends tell of abandoned children raised feral and nature-wise by wolves. As always, there is an opposite to any symbolic form; the story of *Little Red Riding Hood,* for example, turns upside down the idea of nurturing, as the wolf in grandmother's clothing is easily seen as the devouring aspect of the Great Mother.[11]

The filmmaker Ingmar Bergman reminded us in *The Hour of the Wolf* that this animal is a creature of the twilight times. The wolf's night-howls bespeak an unappeasable hunger and bloody mayhem; its howls at morning evoke an anxious and nameless dread. But they also herald the dawn, the coming of light and, more abstractly, enlightenment and civilization.[12] The many werewolf (literally man/wolf) legends and stories, wherein extreme (and distinctly human) homicidal and sexual atrocities are ascribed to the ascendance of a wolfish nature over an unwilling human one, show how thoroughly wolves are identified in our minds with primal aggressiveness and savagery.[13]

In Greek mythology the wolf is associated with the sun god Apollo, who in turn is psychologically linked to consciousness. The Greek word for wolf is "lykos," which is similar to the Latin word *lux* (light) and the German word *Licht*. Thus, the wolf is deemed an animal of the light, while its activities are mainly nocturnal. The "light of nature" was projected onto the wolf because of its amazing intelligence.[14] Native Americans have traditionally respected the wolf's prowess as a hunter, focusing on its stamina, stealth, bravery and strength.[15] For them, wolves were fellow hunters and worth naming themselves after (such as Fire Wolf, Lone Wolf, and Little Wolf). All over North America, Boy Scouts are taught to strive for the right to wear a wolf badge by emulating those qualities. The timber wolf, unlike the coyote, naturally avoids humans, and earning the trust of a feral wolf has for ages suggested either the possession of supernatural powers, as in Bram Stoker's *Dracula,* or innate nobility and charisma, as in Jack London's *The Call of The Wild.*

Christianity equates the wolf with the Devil, the spoiler of the flocks. It is also an emblem of St. Francis of Assisi, who tamed the wolf Gubbio. The Christian desire to subvert the baser workings of the natural world reaches its logical conclusion when the wolf and the lamb, natural enemies, lie down together to represent the coming of Messianic rule.[16] In the Norse tradition, wolves were ridden across the sky by the warlike Valkyries; in old German mythology, the end of the universe will come when the Fenris wolf gets loose at the end of days. It will devour the sun and the moon, marking the onset of cataclysm.[17]

Irrational fears (no instance of wolves attacking human beings has ever been substantiated) and the vested interests of stockmen (wolves will take sheep or calves when wild prey are unavailable) have caused wolves to be hunted, trapped, and poisoned to the point of extinction in many areas of their former range. Until recently, large bounties were paid for their destruction in many western American states, but the largest ongoing threat to wolves is the intrusion of humans into their natural habitats. Currently, there seems to be a growing feeling, only partly sentimental, that man has gone too far in his reckless destruction of the natural world. Widespread support (particularly among urbanites) now exists for the protection of wolves and their natural ranges, and wolves have recently been successfully reintroduced in Yellowstone Park.

To dream of wolves suggests primal appetites that cannot be denied and energies that are both implacable and ruthless. In psychological terms, these appetites are usually connected with the Great Goddess in her devouring aspect. But the wolf also personifies strength, cunning, intelligence, courage, and curiosity, as well as the transition from darkness to light, from chaos to order, so that the dreamer may need to trust that these qualities are also available to him or her. Consequently, while the wolf image may represent ravenous greed, deep resentment, and dissatisfaction, it can also denote relentless firmness, cooperation, intuitiveness, socialization, and devoted bonding to family.

Notes
[1] Lopez 1978, 102-03.
[2] Grzimek 1984, 12, 209.
[3] Grzimek 1984, 12, 201-02.
[4] Andrews 1993, 325.
[5] Grzimek 1984, 12, 201-02.
[6] Lopez 1978, 53.
[7] Grzimek 1984, 12, 200.
[8] Lopez 1978, 25.
[9] Lopez 1978, 209.
[10] Grzimek 1984, 12, 211; Macdonald 1987, 58.
[11] von Franz 1977, 166-67.
[12] Lopez 1978, 209.
[13] Lopez 1978, 230.
[14] von Franz 1974, 213-15.
[15] Lopez 1978, 102-03.
[16] Cooper 1992, 248-50.
[17] von Franz 1974, 214-15.

WOLF
Family: Canid.
Size: Body length is 1-1.4 meters (3-4.5 feet); tail length is 30-48 centimeters (10-20 inches); shoulder height is 65-90 centimeters (25-35 inches).
Weight: 30-75 kilograms (65-154 pounds).
Gestation: 61-63 days.
Longevity: 8-16 years (in captivity up to 20 years).
Distribution: North America, Europe, Asia, and the Middle East.
Habitat: Forests, taiga, tundra, deserts, plains, and mountain taiga — a moist subarctic forest dominated by conifers (such as spruce and fir) that begins where the tundra ends.

Wolverine

In 1906 the noted naturalist, artist, and writer Ernest Thompson Seton offered a vivid literary depiction of one of the feistiest creatures in the animal kingdom: "Picture a weasel — and most of us can do that, for we have met that little demon of destruction, that small atom of insensate courage, that symbol of slaughter, sleeplessness, and tireless, incredible activity — picture that scrap of demoniac fury, multiply that mite some fifty times, and you have the likeness of a wolverine."[1]

Equipped with a set of vicious claws, heavily muscled and surpassingly strong for its size, the squat and bandy-legged wolverine is a compact paragon of toughness, tenacity, ferocity, and sheer aggression. At approximately twenty-three kilograms (fifty pounds), it is by far the largest of the mustelids, a class which includes weasels, martins, and badgers. It is also called glutton and caracajou, a name of Native American origin.

The wolverine is mainly found in northern regions of both the Old and New Worlds, in taiga and tundra, forests, mountains, and open plains. It ranges over a large territory, which it marks with glandular secretions, feces, and urine. Since its habitual terrain is in the northern latitudes where darkness may prevail for months at a time, it sleeps and rests alternately every three to four hours.[2] A carrion feeder as well as a hunter, it has a strong jaw and chewing muscles, which facilitate the dismembering of carcasses. While mainly terrestrial, it is also able to climb trees and is a good swimmer. Its sense of smell is keen, but its eyesight is poor and its hearing mediocre. The fur is long and thick, generally blackish-brown in color. Arctic inhabitants use it for parkas because it accumulates less frost than other kinds of fur.[3]

The wolverine has an odd, leaping gait and is certainly not a stealthy hunter; in summer, it must often be content with fruits, nuts, and berries in lieu of live prey. In winter, however, it moves more easily through the snow than most animals because the broad soles of its feet act as snowshoes. The snow also tends to muffle the sound of its approach, and the wolverine may then successfully take blue hares, squirrels, mice, and other small animals, typically killing with a neck bite. It is also known to chase much larger prey, like elk and deer, and it will aggressively defend its catch from other predators like foxes, martens, and even lynx and bear. To illustrate its ferociousness, there are many stories of wolverines invading the traps and cabins of hunters to steal their catches, and they can even chase bears away from their kills.[4]

While the wolverine is usually a solitary animal, male and female live together for a short period of time during the breeding season. The female bears two to four young every two years. Implantation can be delayed, and the fertilized egg may float freely in the womb for several months after mating, before embedding in the uterine wall to commence an approximately six-week gestation period. The entire process may take up to nine months.[5]

Inuit and other Native Americans consider the wolverine a link between the earth and the spirit world. In tales of the Montagnais-Naskpi, Cree, Fox, Ojibwa, Menomini, and other tribes, the wolverine is connected with a powerful hero known as Nanabozho, who created the earth. Nanabozho, while considered a supernatural being, is also viewed as a fool, and he is often an object of ridicule because of his folly and greed. In northern British Columbia, a Tahltan legend tells of the people who were cannibals, and thus were changed into wolverines, and still eat carrion.[6] Indeed, in other legends among Native Americans, Lapps, and Mongols, the wolverine was considered impure and the personification of evil.

The wolverine's ferociousness extends well beyond what would appear appropriate to its size; hence, drawing upon its voraciousness and greediness, the wolverine image might symbolize a person's impulse to dare to take more than his or her share. At times in life, this urge is necessary and can represent the total opposite of being limited by propriety or social convention.

The image of a wolverine appearing in a dream of someone who is too inhibited in that way and who may need to act out the dark side of survival could represent a suggestion to take more, to be more aggressive and forceful. Equally, the presence of a wolverine image in dreams could reflect some form of inappropriate aggression or ruthlessness on the part of the dreamer. This may apply to a person who "acts out" these qualities in a life situation and needs to see his or her behavior in the context of an animal whose ferociousness is truly awesome.

Notes

[1] Holbrow, 1976, 62.
[2] Grzimek 1984, 12: 63.
[3] Nowak 1991, 1124-25.
[4] Grzimek 1984, 12: 63.
[5] Nowak 1991, 1125.
[6] Holbrow 1976, 55-61.

WOLVERINE
Family: Mustelidae.
Size: In Alaska, head-body length is up to 83 centimeters (33 inches) and tail length is 20 centimeters (8 inches).
Weight: Up to 25 kilograms (55 pounds); in Alaska males average 15 kilograms (33 pounds), females 10 kilograms (22 pounds).
Gestation: Approximately 9 months.
Longevity: Up to 13 years (18 years in captivity).
Distribution: Circumpolar, in North America and Eurasia.
Habitat: Large forests, forested hills, the taiga of Siberia (a moist subarctic forest dominated by conifers that begins where the tundra ends), and tundra.

Worm

Silent, more or less featureless, and lacking a backbone (or, indeed, a skeleton of any sort), the worm is a kind of minimalist ideal of animated flesh. Like bacteria, it is a mindless and indifferent agent of decay, consuming and excreting anything it encounters. In metaphorical terms, it is often seen as the means by which we return to the earth. The word "worm" is loosely used to denote a number of not necessarily related animals that are spineless, soft-bodied, and elongate in shape.[1] They are generally footless, although some have rudimentary appendages that aid in locomotion. Others, like maggots and caterpillars, are the larval stages of insects. More properly, the name belongs to the phylum of segmented creatures called annelids,[2] some of which (like the tapeworm) are internal parasites, and in particular to the class of Clitellata, which includes the common earthworm.

The earthworm may consist of as many as 150 segments with some internal organs, including the excretory organs, duplicated in each segment. Underground creatures, they are almost totally blind and deaf,[3] although they are said to be sensitive to light and vibration. They literally eat their way through the ground, swallowing earth, digesting whatever is organic and excreting what remains. In this way, they till the soil, stirring, mixing and loosening the earth, making it arable by creating loam.[4]

Sexually mature earthworms have a saddle-shaped thickening around the middle of their bodies, called a clitellum. Being hermaphrodites, they mate in pairs, head to tail, simultaneously giving and getting. During the mating process, cocoons are secreted from the clitella of both worms. As the mating pair slithers by one another, eggs are inserted into these cocoons as they pass over the female pores, and sperm is inserted as they pass over the male pores. The young develop to maturity in the cocoons, which are left behind.[5]

Worms are preyed upon below the ground by moles, ground beetle larvae, and centipedes. However, their greatest peril comes if the ground becomes saturated with water. Then lack of oxygen forces them to the surface, where they are easy prey for birds and vulnerable to desiccation. Agricultural chemicals that penetrate the ground can also pose a threat if they are overused. Although worms are generally objects of revulsion or squeamishness, certain native tribes of South America collect and eat them after a rain.[6] But in the phrase "the conquering worm," we have an apt expression not only of the inevitability of death, but also of the circularity of the food chain — the worm being near the very bottom and human beings at the top.

Being a chthonic creature, the worm lives in the soil and is therefore psychologically and symbolically connected not only with the feminine earth, but also with our soma, our physical bodies, which come from the earth and will return to it (partly through the agency of the earthworm). Like most animals at the lower end of the evolutionary ladder, worms are associated with the primitive, instinctual, and definitively noncognitive parts of the human mind. Indeed, the worm does not have a brain and relies instead on coordination from the sympathetic nervous system, which works with deep bodily sensations and instinctual, lower-brain functioning.[7]

The worm is a lowly creature that we invoke in metaphorical terms to decry spinelessness (cowardice), misery, humiliation, and degradation in humans. Often confused with the maggot, it is to that extent associated with putrefaction, and therefore linked symbolically with dissolution, decay, and death. Thus, the worm can represent an antithesis of consciousness.

In dreams, the worm can also represent a very personal "shadow quality," as in the notion, "But I am a worm; and no man" (Psalms 22:6.) A person behaving without courage is often called a worm. However, the dream symbolism of the worm can also represent the most important aspects of the human being that have been unseen in their beauty and power and relegated by training or the views of others to a very lowly significance. Thus, those aspects of our being that we most undervalue — weaknesses, symptoms, fears, even cowardice, can be shown to hide our deepest values if approached with some objectivity and compassion.

Jung suggests that the worm is so far from human that to dream of being covered with worms may have the positive effect of shocking the dreamer into the awareness that he or she has so withdrawn into the mind as to have departed from his or her humanity, or from human association in general. Jung further notes that the segmented nature of the annelid's body can represent the human tendency to dissociate or compartmentalize life on a very deep level.[8] Dreaming of a worm, then, may show that the conscious personality may be ready to begin to relate to dissociated aspects that are very far from awareness and also from each other.

Notes
[1] *Encyclopedia Americana* 1991, 29, 353.
[2] "Annelid." *Encyclopedia Britannica*, 1997.
[3] Logan 1993, 16.
[4] Grzimek 1984, 1: 378-79.
[5] "Earthworm." *Encyclopedia Britannica*, 1997.
[6] Stevens 1995, C1.
[7] Jung 1984, 233-34.
[8] Ibid.

WORM

Subsection: *Bilateralia* (bilaterally symmetrical animals).

Size: Depending on species. In Europe, length can be 2-30 centimeters (0.04-12 inches); giant earthworm found in the Australian bush can reach a length of up to 3 meters (10 feet) and a diameter of 3 centimeters (1.2 inches). Others vary in size from less than 1 millimeter (0.04 inches) to more than 30 meters (100 feet).

Gestation: Miniature earthworms usually emerge from the cocoon after 2-4 weeks.

Longevity: Small worms live only 1-2 years; others may live as long as 10 years.

Distribution: Worldwide.

Habitat: Marine, freshwater, and terrestrial.

Zebra

Emblematic of the grasslands and open spaces of Africa where it roams free, the zebra reminds us of the horse, to which it is closely related. Unlike the horse, it is a wild creature. Some zebras have been trained to do tricks in circuses and carnivals or to pull wagons, but they have never been successfully domesticated. Of the several types of zebra of the family, the three main ones are the Grevy's zebra, the mountain zebra, and the Burchell's zebra. Grevy's zebra, the largest of the three, is found in sub-desert regions, although it can sometimes migrate over substantial distances in search of forage and water. The mountain zebra, somewhat smaller and with a generally narrower pattern of striping, is found, as its name suggests, on slopes and plateaus of higher elevation. The Burchell's zebra, also smaller than the Grevy's, has broader body stripes, especially on the flanks, although patterns vary geographically. Deviations such as entirely dark coats are possible, as are "reverse" stripes of white on dark background.[1]

Highly sociable, zebras normally live in family groups of five to twenty; during the dry season the groups may merge into herds of many hundreds, often in the company of wildebeest, hartebeest, roan antelope, and sometimes eland or giraffe. When on the move, headed for water holes or sleeping sites, groups are usually led by the highest-ranking mare, followed by other mares in order of their social rank, with the young behind them. The stallions, alert for danger, bring up the rear.[2] Grevy's zebra exhibits more primitive social behavior than other zebras; each stallion ranges a territory up to ten kilometers (six miles) across, within which other males are tolerated but driven away from mares in heat. Transgressing stallions will rarely fight, preferring simply to flee when challenged. If a strange stallion does manage to gain access to a receptive female, both will be driven from the territory. Stallion groups, however, are generally stable, and their members may remain together for several years.[3]

Inquisitive animals, zebras have the speed and endurance of most equines, and although they are regular prey for lions and other big cats, they can often outrun wild dogs and hyenas. They may occasionally browse on leaves and scrub, but they are primarily close grazers, able to get by in areas of skimpy or coarse grasses.[4] They are dependent on daily access to water holes.[5] Zebras generally adapt well to life in zoological gardens, although Burchell's zebras reproduce more readily than mountain zebras and Grevy's zebras in captivity. While they do not mix in the wild, zebras have been crossed with horses and asses, and the resulting offspring are called zebroids.[6]

The zebra, being a strictly African creature, does not appear in the cultures or mythologies of other continents, although Greeks and Romans would surely have been aware of them. They are also surprisingly absent from the Egyptian pantheon. Even though the zebra is undoubtedly significant to tribal cultures within its natural range, other parts of the world remain largely ignorant of its significance.

The most salient feature of the zebra is its black and white stripes. The exact patterns of stripes on individuals are distinctive, if not to our eyes then to other zebras. Infants may use stripe differences to find their mothers, although smell is also important.[7] While individually the zebra is a more or less defenseless prey animal, evidence suggests that the chaotic patterns presented by a large herd confuse potential predators. Along with this possible meaning of the zebra's stripes, the bold contrast evokes the starkness of polar opposites. In the moral and psychological realms, the absence of intermediate "shades of gray" indicates a radically limited range of responses — a rigidly "black and white attitude" toward life, oneself, or others. In the world of the rigid conformist, where the "herd" response is operative, dominant or prevailing opinions tend to be accepted as definitive.

Consequently, to dream of a zebra would tend to call forth a question about the person's rigid attitude. Yet, because of the zebra's vulnerability, it could also represent a defenseless aspect of the individual, one that responds with a herd instinct and a tendency to go along with the collective will as a form of self-protection. More logical ways of thinking are often crowded out by fear and perceived vulnerability as well as by rigid and opinionated responses. Serious reflection on the person's "black and white attitude" toward life would be indicated.

Z

Notes
[1] Grzimek 1984, 12: 542–46; Nowak 1991, 1313-14.
[2] Dorst and Dandelot 1988, 164.
[3] Grzimek 1984, 12: 542–46.
[4] Nowak 1991, 1313.
[5] Dorst and Dandelot 1988, 164.
[6] Grzimek 1984, 12: 547.
[7] Grzimek 1984, 12: 546.

ZEBRA

Family: Equidae.

Size: The Grevy's zebra has a head-body length of 2.5-3.0 meters (8-10 feet), a tail length of 38-60 centimeters (15-24 inches), and a shoulder height of 140-60 centimeters (55-63 inches). The Burchell's zebra has a head-body length of 2.2-2.5 meters (7-8 feet), a tail length of 47-56 centimeters (18-22 inches), and a shoulder height of 110-145 centimeters (43-57 inches).

Weight: Grevy's zebra weighs 352-450 kilograms (777-993 pounds); Burchell's zebra weighs 175-385 kilograms (386-850 pounds).

Gestation: 345-390 days.

Longevity: 10-25 years (35 in captivity).

Distribution: Africa.

Habitat: Mountain grasslands, sub-desert steppe, and arid bushed grassland.

Bibliography

Abs, Michael, ed. 1983. *Physiology and Behavior of the Pigeon*. New York: Academic Press.

Ackerman, Diane. 1995. *The Rarest of the Rare*. New York: Random House.

Aelian, Claudius, born c. 170, Praeneste, Italy, died c. 235. Roman author and teacher of rhetoric. Author of *On the Nature of Animals*.

Aeppli, Ernst. 1943. *Der Traum und seine Deutung*. Zürich: Eugen Rentsch Verlag.

Alderton, David. 1991. *Crocodiles and Alligators of the World*. New York: Facts on File Inc.

Amin, M. D. Willetts, and B. Tetley. 1989. *The Beautiful Animals of Kenya*. Nairobi: Camerapix Publishers International.

Ammer, Christine. 1989. *It's Raining Cats and Dogs and Other Beastly Expressions*. New York: Paragon House.

Andrews, Ted. 1983. *Animal-Speak*. 1983. St. Paul, Minnestoa: Llewellyn Publications.

Angier, Natalie. 1991a. "Can You Like a Roach? You Might Be Surprised." *The New York Times* 12 March: C1, C8.

——. 1991b. "In Recycling Waste the Noble Scarab Is Peerless." *The New York Times* 10 December: C1-C2.

——. 1993. "Animals That Are Peerless Athletes." *The New York Times* 1 June: C1.

——. 1995. *The Beauty of the Beastly*. Boston and New York: Houghton Mifflin Company.

Aristotle, born 384 BC, Stagira, Greece, died 322. Ancient Greek philosopher and scientist. Pioneered the study of zoology, both observational and theoretical.

Armstrong, Edward A. 1958. *The Folklore of Birds*. London: HarperCollins.

——. 1975. *The Life and Lore of the Bird in Nature, Art, Myth and Literature*. New York: Crown Publishers, Inc.

Arnold, C. 1992. *Camels*. New York: Morrow Junior Books.

Attenborough, David. 1990. *The Trials of Life: A Natural History of Animal Behavior*. Boston: Little, Brown and Company.

Baker, Mary L. 1987. *Whales, Dolphins and Porpoises of the World*. New York: Doubleday & Company Inc.

Banister, Keith, and Andrew Campbell, eds. 1988. *The Encyclopedia of Aquatic Life*. New York: Facts on File Inc.

Barnett, S. A. 1963. *A Study in Behavior, Principles of Ethology and Behavioral Physiology, Displayed Mainly in the Rat*. London: Methuen & Co. Ltd.

Batten, Mary. 1993. "When Animals Make Love, They Do It Their Way." *Cosmopolitan* July, 178.

Becker, Udo, ed. 1994. *The Continuum Encyclopedia of Symbols*. New York: Continuum Publishing Company.

Benson, Elizabeth. 1977. *The Maya World.* New York: Thomas Y. Crowell.

Bernal, Ignacio. 1969. *The Olmec World.* Berkeley: University of California Press.

Biedermann, Hans. 1994. *Dictionary of Symbolism, Cultural Icons and the Meanings Behind Them.* Translated by James Hulbert. New York: Penguin Books.

Birkhäuser-Oeri, Sibylle. 1988. *The Mother, Archetypal Image in Fairy Tales.* Toronto, Canada, Inner City Books.

Bonnefoy, Yves. 1991. *Mythologies.* Chicago: University of Chicago Press.

———. 1992. *Roman and European Mythologies.* Chicago: University of Chicago Press.

Bonner, Raymond. 1993. "Crying Wolf over Elephants." *The New York Times Magazine* 7 February: 17.

Boulger, James D., ed. 1969. *Twentieth Century Interpretations of The Rime of the Ancient Mariner.* Englewood Cliffs, New Jersey: Prentice-Hall.

Breland, Osmond P. 1972. *Animal Life and Lore.* New York: Harper and Row.

Broad, William J. 1994. "Squids Emerge as Smart, Elusive Hunters." *The New York Times* 30 August: C1.

———. 1996. "Biologists Closing on Hidden Lair of Giant Squid." *The New York Times* 13 February: C1.

———. 1999. "Evidence Puts Dolphins in a New Light as Killers." *The New York Times* 6 July: C1.

Brody, Jane E. 1990. "In Rats, More to Admire, More to Fear." *The New York Times* 30 July: C1.

———. 1991. "Far From Fearsome, Bats Lose Ground to Ignorance and Greed." *The New York Times* 29 October: C1.

———. 1993. "Picking Up Mammals' Deep Notes." *The New York Times* 9 November: C1.

———. 1997. "Wild Turkeys Return to American Fields." *The New York Times* 25 November: F1, F6.

Brown, Joseph Epes. 1992. *Animals of the Soul, Sacred Animals of the Oglala Sioux.* Rockport, Massachusetts: Element Inc.

Browne, Malcolm W. 1996. "Second Greatest Toolmaker?" *The New York Times* 30 January: C1.

Budge, E.A. Wallis. 1969. *The Gods of the Egyptians.* 2 volumes. Chicago: Open Court Publishing Company.

Burton, Maurice, and Robert Burton. 1975. *Encyclopedia of Insects and Arachnids.* London: Octopus Books Ltd.

Burton, Maurice, ed. 1981. *The New Larousse Encyclopedia of Animal Life.* New York: Bonanza Books.

Campbell, Joseph. 1983. *The Way of the Animal Powers.* Volume 1. San Francisco: Harper & Row.

Castaneda, Carlos. 1990. *The Teachings of Don Juan: A Yaqui Way of Knowledge.* New York: Washington Square Press.

Chapman, Joseph A., and George A. Feldhammer, eds. 1982. *Wild Mammals of North America.* Baltimore: Johns Hopkins University Press.

Charbonneau-Lassay, Louis. 1991. *The Bestiary of Christ.* New York: Parabola Books.

Coleridge, Samuel Taylor. 1989. *Selected Poems.* Manchester: Carcanet Press, Ltd.

Compton's Interactive Encyclopedia. Softkey Multimedia Inc., 1997.

Cooper, J.C. 1992. *Symbolic and Mythological Animals.* London: HarperCollins.

Coupe, Sheena, and Robert Coupe. 1990. *Sharks: Great Creatures of the World.* New York: Facts on File Inc.

Cousteau, Jean-Michel, and Mose Richards. 1992. *Cousteau's Great White Shark.* New York: Harry Abrams Inc.

Croft, David B., editor. *Australian People and Animals in Today's Dreamtime,* 1991, edited by Praeger, New York.

Curley, Michael J., translator, 1979. *Physiologus.* Austin and London: University of Texas Press. (A manuscript written during the second century in or near Alexandria).

Dale-Green, Patricia. 1959. "Apis Mellifica." *Harvest* No. 5: 30B48.

———. 1983. *The Archetypal Cat.* Dallas: Spring Publications Inc.

Decré, Alain. 1993. *The Fight of the Elephants.* Produced by Olivier Brémond.

De Gubernatis, Angelo. 1968. *Zoological Mythology.* 2 volumes. Detroit: Singing Tree Press.

de Vries, Ad. 1976. *Dictionary of Symbols and Imagery.* New York: American Elsevier Publishing Co. Inc.

Delort, Robert. 1992. *The Life and Lore of the Elephant.* New York: Harry N. Abrams Inc.

Dictionnaire des Symboles. 1982. Éditions Robert Laffont S.A. et Éditions Jupiter. Paris.

Dorst, Jean, and Pierre Dandelot. 1988. *A Field Guide to the Larger Mammals of Africa.* London: HarperCollins.

Downer, John. 1989. *Supersense: Perception in the Animal World.* New York: Henry Holt & Co.

Dreifuss, Gustav. 1973. *The Significance of the Shofar in the Rite of the Jewish Holidays.* The Israel Annals of Psychiatry and Related Disciplines, Vol. 11, No. 2.

Drimmer, Frederic, ed. 1954. *The Animal Kingdom.* New York: Greystone Press.

Duellman, William E., and Linda Trueb. 1986. *Biology of Amphibians.* New York: McGraw-Hill.

Edinger, Edward. 1995. *Melville's Moby Dick: A Jungian Commentary.* Toronto: Inner City Books.

Encarta 97 Encyclopedia. Microsoft Corporation, 1997.

Encyclopedia Americana. Danbury: Grolier Inc., 1991.

Encyclopedia Britannica (CD-Rom). Chicago: Encyclopedia Britannica, 1997.

Eranos Yearbook 1982: The Play of Gods and Men. Germany: Insel Verlag, 1983.

Fabricius, Johannes. 1989. *Alchemy, The Medieval Alchemists and Their Royal Art.* London: HarperCollins.

Fenton, M. Brock. 1984. *Just Bats.* Toronto: University of Toronto Press.

Fontana, David. 1993. *The Secret Language of Symbol.* San Francisco: Chronicle Books.

Ford, Barbara. 1980. *Why Does a Turtle Live Longer Than a Dog? A Report on Animal Longevity.* New York: Morrow.

Fountain, Henry. 1999. "How Bees Stay the Course." *The New York Times* 13 July: F5.

Frankel, Ellen, and Betsy Teutsch Platkin. 1992. *The Encyclopedia of Jewish Symbols.* Northvale: J. Aronson.

Frazer, Sir James George. 1979. *The Golden Bough.* New York: Macmillan Publishing Co. Inc.

Funk & Wagnalls Standard Dictionary of Folklore, Mythology, and Legend. Edited by Maria Leach. Toronto: Funk & Wagnalls Publishing Co. Inc., 1972.

Gertsch, Willis J. 1979. *American Spiders.* New York: Von Nostrand, Reinhold Co.

Gamwell, Lynn, and Richard Wells, eds. 1989. *Sigmund Freud and Art: His Personal Collection of Antiquities.* State University of New York, Freud Museum, London.

Gimbutas, Marija. 1982. *The Goddesses and Gods of Old Europe.* London: Thames and Hudson Ltd.

———. 1989. *The Language of the Goddess.* San Francisco: Harper & Row.

Gillespie, Angus K., and Jay Mechling, eds. 1987. *American Wildlife in Symbol and Story.* Knoxville: University of Tennessee Press.

Goodenough, Erwin R. 1956. *Jewish Symbols in the Greco-Roman Period.* Volume 5. New York: Pantheon Books Inc.

Gooders, John, and Trevor Boyer. 1986. *Ducks of North America and the Northern Hemisphere.* New York: Facts on File Inc.

Green, Miranda. 1992. *Animals in Celtic Life and Myth.* London: Routledge.

Greene, Harry W. 1997. *Snakes: The Evolution of Mystery in Nature.* Berkeley: University of California Press.

Grzimek, Bernhard. 1976. *Grzimek's Encyclopedia of Evolution.* New York: Von Nostrand Reinhold Co.

———. 1977. *Grzimek's Encyclopedia of Ethology.* New York: Von Nostrand Reinhold Co.

———. 1984. *Grzimek's Animal Life Encyclopedia.* 13 volumes. New York: Von Nostrand Reinhold Co.

Hai, Willow Weilan. 1995. *Animals of the Chinese Zodiac.* New York: China Institute Gallery.

Halliday, Tim R., and Kraig Adler, eds. 1988. *The Encyclopedia of Reptiles and Amphibians.* New York: Facts on File Inc.

Hannah, Barbara. 1957-58. "The Symbolism of Animals." Notes on lectures given at the C.G. Jung Institute, Zurich, Switzerland, Fall and Spring.

———. 1992. *The Cat, Dog and Horse Lectures.* Edited by Dean L. Frantz. Wilmette, Illinois: Chiron Publications.

Hastings, James. 1910. *Encyclopedia of Religion and Ethics.* Volume 1. New York: Charles Scribner's Sons.

Hazarika, Sanjoy. 1994. "Picky Eaters in Monterey Bay Who Dabble in Petty Theft." *The New York Times* 29 March: C4.

Heinz-Mohr, Gerd. 1976. *Lexicon Der Symbole.* 4th Edition. Cologne: Eugen Diederichs Verlag.

Heinzelman, Donald S. 1979. *Hawks and Owls of North America,* New York: Universe Books.

Hendrickson, Robert. 1983. *More Cunning than Man: A Social History of Rats and Men.* New York: Stein and Day.

The Herder Symbol Dictionary. Wilmette, Illinois: Chiron Publications, 1986.

Hilchey, Tim. 1992. "Skull and Air Sacs Fine-tune Dolphin Sonar." *The New York Times* 10 November: C7.

Hillman, James. 1983. "The Animal Kingdom in the Human Dream." *Eranos Yearbook* 1982, 279-334.

———. 1988. "Going Bugs." *Spring: A Journal of Archetype and Culture* 48: 41-72.

———. 1990. "The Elephant in the Garden of Eden." *Spring: A Journal of Archetype and Culture* 50: 93-115.

———. *Dream Animals.* 1997. San Francisco: Chronicle Books.

Holbrow, W.C. 1976. "The Biology, Mythology, Distribution and Management of the Wolverine (Gulo Gulo L.) in Western Canada." MSc Thesis, University of Manitoba, Winnipeg.

Holmgren, Virginia C. 1988. *Owls in Folklore and Natural History.* Santa Barbara: Capra Press.

Hölldobler, Bert, and Edward O. Wilson. 1990. *The Ants.* Cambridge: Harvard University Press.

Hoyo, Joseph De, Andrew Elliott, and Jordi Sargetal. 1992. *Handbook of the Birds of the World.* Barcelona: Lynx Edicions.

Hulbert, James, ed. 1994. *The Sacred Pipe: Black Elk's Account of the Seven Rites of the Oglala Sioux.* New York: Penguin Books.

Jobes, Gertrude. 1962. *Dictionary of Mythology, Folklore and Symbols.* 2 volumes. New York: Scarecrow Press.

Johnson, Buffie. 1988. *Lady of the Beasts, Ancient Images of the Goddess and Her Sacred Animals.* San Francisco: Harper & Row.

Jung, Carl G. 1972-79. *Collected Works.* Princeton: Princeton University Press.

——. 1976. *The Visions Seminars.* 2 volumes. Zurich: Spring Publications.

——. 1984. *Dream Analysis, Notes of the Seminar Given in 1928-1930.* Edited by William McGuire. Princeton: Princeton University Press.

——. 1988. *Nietzsche's Zarathustra, Notes of the Seminar Given in 1934-1939.* 2 volumes. Edited by James L. Jarrett. Princeton: Princeton University Press.

Kerényi, Karl. 1980. "A Mythological Image of Girlhood." In *Facing the Gods,* edited by James Hillman. Zurich: Spring Publications.

King, Carolyn. 1989. *The Natural History of Weasels and Stoats.* Ithaca: Cornell University Press.

Kluger, Rivkah Schärf. 1991. *The Archetypal Significance of Gilgamesh.* Einsiedeln: Daimon Verlag.

Kruuk, Hans. 1987. "Outermost Otters." *Natural History* July, 35-40.

Lacey, Elizabeth A. 1993. *What's the Difference.* New York: Clarion Books.

Lavine, S. 1979. *Wonders of Camels.* New York: Dodd, Mead, & Company.

Leadbeater, C.W. 1985. *The Chakras.* Wheaton, Illinois: The Theosophical Publishing House.

Leary, Warren E. 1999. "Sunless, Airless and Full of Life." *The New York Times* 6 July: F1.

Leonard, Linda Schierse. 1987. *On the Way to the Wedding.* Boston: Shambhala.

Logan, William Bryant. 1993. "The Lowly Worm Now Exalted." *The New York Times* 26 September: 16.

Lopez, Barry Holstun. 1978. *Of Wolves and Men.* New York: Charles Scribner's Sons.

MacClintock, Dorcas. 1981. *A Natural History of Raccoons.* New York: Charles Scribner's Sons.

Macdonald, David. 1987. *The Encyclopedia of Mammals.* New York: Facts on File Inc.

Masson, Jeffrey Moussaieff. 1999. *The Emperor's Embrace.* New York: Pocket Books.

McFarland, David, ed. 1987. *The Oxford Companion to Animal Behaviour.* Oxford: Oxford University Press.

Melville, Herman. 1962. *Moby Dick.* New York: New American Library.

Minasian, Stanley M., Kenneth C. Balcomb III, and Larry Foster. 1984. *The World's Whales.* New York: Smithsonian Books.

Morgan, Marlo. 1994. *Mutant Message Down Under.* New York: HarperCollins.

Mohr, Gerd Heinz. 1976. *Lexicon Der Symbole.* Düsseldorf and Cologne: Eugen Diederichs Verlag.

Neal, Ernest. 1986. *The Natural History of Badgers.* New York: Facts on File Inc.

Neumann, Erich. 1963. *The Great Mother: An Analysis of the Archetype.* Princeton: Princeton University Press.

The New Larousse Encyclopedia of Mythology. New York: Prometheus Press, 1968.

Nowak, Ronald John. 1991. *Walker's Mammals of the World.* 2 volumes. Baltimore: John Hopkins University Press.

Osborne, Harold. 1968. *South American Mythology.* Feltham: The Hamlyn Publishing Group Ltd.

O'Toole, Christopher, ed. 1984. *The Encyclopedia of Insects.* New York: Facts on File Inc.

Otto, Walter F. 1981. *Dionysus.* Irving, Texas: Spring Publications.

Parrinder, Geoffrey. 1969. *African Mythology.* Feltham: The Hamlyn Publishing Group Ltd.

Perrins, Christopher M., and Alex L.A. Middleton, eds. 1989. *The Encyclopedia of Birds.* New York: Facts on File Inc.

Peterson, Jeanette Favrot. 1992. *Precolumbian Flora and Fauna.* San Diego: Mingei International Museum of World Folk Art.

Pfeffer, Pierre, ed. 1989. *Predators and Predation: A Struggle for Life in the Animal World.* New York: Facts on File Inc.

Pickering, Robert. 1997. *Seeing the White Buffalo.* Boulder, Colorado: Johnson Books.

Pliny, the Elder, Gaius Plinius Secundus, born 23 AD, Novum Comun, Italy, died August 24, 79. Roman savant and author of *Natural History.*

Preston-Matham, Rod, and Ken Preston-Matham. 1984. *Spiders of the World.* New York: Facts on File Inc.

Reichard, Gladys A. 1974. *Navaho Religion: A Study of Symbolism.* Princeton: Princeton University Press.

Reichel-Dolmatoff, Gerardo. 1971. *Amazonian Cosmos: The Sexual and Religious Symbolism of the Tukano Indians.* Chicago: University of Chicago Press.

Ritchey, Melvin S. 1968. "The War on Rats." *The New Yorker* 3 August, 23-26.

Ross, Charles A., ed. 1989. *Crocodiles and Alligators.* New York: Facts on File Inc.

Rue III, Leonard Lee. 1964. *The World of the Beaver.* Edited by John K. Terres. Philadelphia: Living World Books.

Rust, Michael K., John M. Owens, and Donald A. Reierson, eds. 1995. *Understanding and Controlling the German Cockroach.* Oxford: Oxford University Press.

Sams, Jamie, and David Carson. 1988. *Medicine Cards: The Discovery of Power Through the Ways of Animals.* Santa Fe: Bear & Co.

Sattler, Helen Roney. 1986. *Sharks: The Super Fish.* New York: Lothrop, Lee & Shepard Books.

Schwartz-Salant, Nathan. 1982. *Narcissism and Character Transformation.* Toronto: Inner City Books.

"The Secret Behind Feats of Sea Turtle." *The New York Times* (Science Watch) 12 June 1990: C6.

Slater, Peter J.B., ed. 1987. *The Encyclopedia of Animal Behavior.* New York: Facts on File Inc.

"Smart as a Sea Otter." *The New York Times* (Science Watch) 26 September 1989: C6.

Smith, Page, and Charles Daniel. 1975. *The Chicken Book.* Boston: Little Brown and Co.

Spector, W.S., ed. 1956. *Handbook of Biological Data.* Philadelphia: W.B. Saunders Company.

Stevens, William K. 1990. "Monarchs' Migration: A Fragile Journey." *The New York Times* 4 December: C1.

——. 1991a. "Brainy Parrots Dazzle Scientists." *The New York Times* 28 May: C1.

——. 1992. "Terror of Deep Faces Harsher Predator." *The New York Times* 8 December: C1.

——. 1994. "Survival of the Big Cats Brings Conflict With Man." *The New York Times* 2 August: C1.

——. 1995. "It's Natives vs Newcomers Down in the Worm World." *The New York Times* 28 March: C12.

Symmes, Edwin C., Jr. 1990. *Netsuke: Japanese Life and Legend in Miniature.* Rutland, Vermont: Charles E. Tuttle Company.

Trillmich, Fritz. 1987. "Seals Under the Sun." *Natural History Magazine,* October, 42-49.

von Franz, Marie-Louise. 1974. *Shadow and Evil in Fairy Tales.* Zurich: Spring Publications.

——. 1975a. *Creation Myths.* Zurich: Spring Publications.

——. 1975b. *Interpretation of Fairy Tales.* Zurich: Spring Publications.

——. 1976. *Problems of the Feminine in Fairy Tales.* Zurich: Spring Publications.

——. 1977. *Individuation in Fairy Tales.* Zurich: Spring Publications.

——. 1980a. *A Psychological Interpretation of the Golden Ass of Apuleius.* Irving, Texas: Spring Publications.

——. 1980b. *The Psychological Meaning of Redemption Motifs in Fairy Tales.* Toronto: Inner City Books.

——. 1980c. *Alchemy: An Introduction to the Symbolism and the Psychology.* Toronto: Inner City Books.

Waldman, Carl. 1994. *Word Dance: The Language of Native American Culture.*

New York: Facts on File Inc.

Walker, Barbara, G. 1983. *Women's Encyclopedia of Myths and Secrets.* New York: HarperCollins.

Whitfield, Philip, and Edward S. Ayensu, eds. 1984. *Macmillan Illustrated Animal Encyclopedia.* New York: Macmillan Publishing Company.

Wilhelm, Richard, and C.F. Baynes, trans. 1977. *The I Ching.* Foreword by C.G. Jung. Princeton: Princeton University Press.

Wilmore, Sylvia Bruce. 1979. *Swans of the World.* New York: Taplinger Publishing Company.

Woloy, Eleonora M. 1990. *The Symbol of the Dog in the Human Psyche: A Study of the Human-Dog Bond.* Wilmette, Illinois: Chiron Publications.

Woodman, Marion. 1980. *The Owl Was a Baker's Daughter.* Toronto: Inner City Books.

Wootton, Anthony. 1988. *Insects of the World.* New York: Facts on File Inc.

World Book Encyclopedia. Chicago: World Book Inc., 1995.

Yoffe, Emily. 1992. "Silence of the Frogs." *The New York Times* 13 December: 36.

Zimmer, Heinrich. 1974. *Myths and Symbols in Indian Art and Civilizaton.* Princeton: Princeton University Press.

ABOUT THE AUTHOR

Elizabeth Caspari has taught seminars on "Art, Dreams and Creativity" and has produced art works in diverse media. She studied painting at the Art Students League in New York and worked in psychology with Anelia Jaffe, Dr. James Hillman, Dr. Nathan Schwartz-Salant and Dr. Montague Ullman. She was a member of the faculty of the New School for Social Research and gave workshops in animal mask-making at the University of Albuquerque.

Her combined interests in art and Jungian psychology led to her work in art therapy. For the last twenty years, her major professional interest has been the mythology and natural life of animals. This book is the fruit of her years of research and travels to Kenya and Tanzania. She presently lives in New York City.